The Irwin Guide to Stocks, Bonds, Futures, and Options

A Comprehensive Guide to Wall Street's Markets

K. Thomas Liaw, Ph.D.
Ronald L. Moy, Ph.D., CFA

McGraw-Hill

New York   St. Louis   San Francisco   Washington, DC   Auckland   Bogotá   Caracas
Lisbon   London   Madrid   Mexico City   Milan   Montreal   New Delhi
San Juan   Singapore   Sydney   Tokyo   Toronto

Library of Congress Cataloging-in-Publication Data

Liaw, K. Thomas.
The Irwin guide to stocks, bonds, futures, and options / by K. Thomas Liaw, Ronald L. Moy.
p. cm.
Includes bibliographical references.
ISBN 0-07-135947-8
1. Investments. 2. Stocks. 3. Bonds. 4. Futures. 5. Options (Finance) I. Moy, Ronald L., 1958– II. Title.
HG4521 .L637 2000
332.63′2—dc21 0-042389

1 2 3 4 5 6 7 8 9 0 DOW/DOW 0 9 8 7 6 5 4 3 2 1

IBSN 0-07-135947-8

Printed and bound by R.R. Donnelley & Sons Company.

McGraw-Hill books are available at special quantity discounts to use as premiums and sales promotions, or for use in corporate training programs. For more information, please write to the Director of Special Sales, Professional Publishing, McGraw-Hill, Two Penn Plaza, New York, NY 10121-2298. Or contact your local bookstore.

This book printed on recycled, acid-free paper containing a minimum of 50% recycled fiber.

Dedication

To my parents, my wife, Evergreen and our children,
Christine and Kevin.
K.T.L.
To my parents, my wife, Leah and our greatest investments,
Hannah and David.
R.L.M.

Contents

Contents

Preface

The *Irwin Guide to Stocks, Bonds, Futures, and Options* is written for practicing professionals and those who aspire to careers in the field of investments. This book presents the financial products that are available for profitable investments and takes the reader through the process of investing. Our goal is to provide comprehensive coverage of topics and issues that are of major interest to the practicing professional and to the individual investor while omitting topics that are of limited use to them.

This book is targeted at investment practitioners. However, the book is also suitable for college investment courses that emphasize the investment process. The book provides a detailed discussion of the securities that will be part of the investment decision, how they are issued, and the procedures for transacting. For brevity, we have limited our discussion of theoretical pricing models in favor of real-world applications. We have drawn on a number of resources in an effort to produce a book that covers the issues that we believe are most relevant to practicing professionals. The issues we have chosen come from our own experience and from discussions with senior Wall Street executives and practicing professionals.

Chapters 1 through 5 provide the basic tools of analysis, including determining investment objectives, the portfolio management process, and the procedures for underwriting new equity issues. Chapter 6 focuses on the costs of executing transactions and some of the techniques that can be used to minimize costs. Chapter 7 provides a detailed discussion of American depositary receipts, through which American investors can make specific foreign investments without venturing overseas.

Chapters 8 through 11 provide a detailed discussion of the fixed-income market. A complete discussion of how Treasury, corporate, municipal, and asset-backed securities are issued and traded is provided. We also review the market practices and regulations.

Chapters 12 and 13 include a detailed discussion of mutual funds and closed-end funds. A vast majority of investors build a portfolio through the use of investment company products such as mutual funds and closed-end funds. This approach allows investors with limited wealth the opportunity to obtain a diversified, professionally managed portfolio.

Chapters 14 through 16 focus on the uses and applications of derivative securities. As is the case in the rest of the book, we place emphasis on applications that would be of interest to investment practitioners. These chapters provide limited coverage of theoretical pricing models in favor of hedging and portfolio management strategies that would be helpful to the practitioner.

Finally, Chapter 17 concludes the book by examining the construction of benchmarks and how to evaluate the performance of a portfolio. Central to the evaluation are the investment objective and a suitable benchmark.

All in all, it is our sincere commitment to present a book that provides a comprehensive guide to all major investment securities. Most books in this area focus on computational tools used in security analysis but provide only limited information on important technical aspects of these securities. This book fills a void left by most investment books by covering the technical aspects of issuing, trading, clearing, regulations, rules, and taxes.

1

Financial Markets and Investments

The investments business is an exciting and dynamic field. Over the past two decades, the investments business has become more important and more complicated. The types of retirement plans offered by employers have moved from guaranteed payouts during an employee's retirement known as *defined benefit pension plans* to cash-based plans known as *defined contribution plans*. This change has placed increasing importance on an individual's ability to make sound investment decisions. In addition, deregulation and financial innovation have increased the number and types of investment alternatives available to both individuals and institutions.

At the same time, these changes have increased the number of services and responsibilities placed on investment professionals, who must be well versed in a number of areas in order to service clients. A broad-based understanding of investment policy and the types of securities available in the marketplace are essential because of the diverse needs of clients, which will differ significantly from individual to institution. Each circumstance will dictate the need for constructing a different plan in order to meet the client's goals. For example, an individual with limited resources may be unable to fund a sufficiently diverse portfolio of individual stocks. In this case, a well-diversified portfolio can be constructed through the use of mutual funds and perhaps closed-end funds. A wealthier client, on the other hand, will have a greater range of investment options available and may have additional concerns, such as tax considerations and estate planning. This type of individual may wish to include tax-free municipal bonds and various trusts for tax advantages. In addition, this individual may have a great deal of wealth tied up in the stock of one company and may benefit from hedging strategies using derivative securities, such as options, futures, and swaps. An institutional client will provide a different range of circumstances that the investment advisor must consider. Not only will each institution have different needs, but each institution will be governed by different laws and regulations. Pension funds, for example, are governed by the Employee Retirement Income Security Act of 1974 (ERISA). Mutual funds are governed by the Investment Company Act of 1940 and the Investment Advisors Act of 1940. Insurance companies, on the other hand, are regulated predominantly at the state level. Another type of institution, endowment funds, are governed by their corporate charters. Each of these laws and regulations will dictate different needs for each institution.

In some ways, investment professionals should be viewed in much the same way as general practitioners are viewed in the medical community. General practitioners have broad-based training and deal with the basic medical needs of patients. However, when a more complicated medical problem occurs, general practitioners are able to make a preliminary diagnosis and refer patients to an appropriate specialist. In order to service the investment needs of clients, investment professionals must also have similar broad-based training. For example, investment professionals may not be experts in tax law or estate planning but must at least have a basic understanding of the needs and the options available to their clients. When the issue becomes more complicated, investment professionals, like general practitioners, must also recognize the need to refer clients to an expert in these matters. As another example, investment advisors may not be experts in the use of derivative securities for purposes of hedging. Again, they should recognize that a particular client may benefit from such a strategy and should be prepared to work with an expert in the area to produce the best possible advice for the client.

To service the needs of the client, investment professionals must understand the entire investment decision process, which includes:

- Determining the needs of the client.
- Having a sound understanding of the investment vehicles available to the client.
- Recommending an appropriate asset allocation to attain the client's goals.
- Implementing the strategy in an efficient and cost effective manner.
- Re-evaluating the client's situation and adjusting the portfolio accordingly.
- Recognizing the estate planning needs of the client.
- Using tools to hedge the risk a client faces.

In order to service clients' needs, investment professionals must understand how to evaluate the needs and goals of their clients. They also need a sound understanding of the different financial markets and instruments available to their clients and the differences in needs and goals for different types of clients. And, finally, investment professionals need to understand the costs of and procedures used in implementing an investment strategy in order to effectively implement the strategy for clients.

The purpose of this book is to take beginning investment professionals through the major issues necessary to responsibly and effectively serve the needs of their clients.

The Investment Process

The investment process should be an ongoing process that continually monitors the needs of the client and changes in financial markets in order to provide clients with the most suitable portfolio of investments. Clients' needs and circumstances have to be continually monitored for changes that may make some currently held securities unsuitable or may make some previously unsuitable securities appropriate. The process is sometimes illustrated as the feedback loop shown in Figure 1-1.

Individual and institutional investors have different investment needs and objectives. Individuals are generally governed by their own personal objectives, whereas institutions may face various legal constraints. Individuals and institutions also differ in the tax consequences of their investments. Because different types of securities have different tax, risk, and cash flow characteristics, it is necessary to determine the needs of the client before providing any

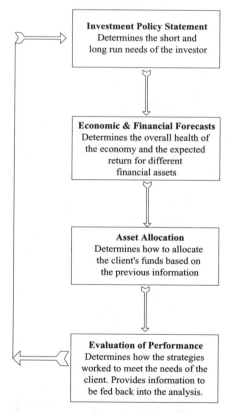

Figure 1-1. Investment management process.

investment recommendation. The soundest method for examining the needs and constraints of different types of clients is to use a systematic approach through an investment policy statement. Once the client's objectives and constraints are determined, an asset allocation recommendation can be put into place to help clients attain their goals.

Overview of Securities Markets

Securities markets play an important role in the economy. They provide a place where corporations and other types of institutions can go to raise capital to finance a multitude of projects. These markets also allow investors an opportunity to participate in the success or failure of a corporation by purchasing the firm's stocks or bonds. By purchasing stock, investors become owners of the corporation. Stock ownership allows the investors (or shareholders) to share in the earnings of the corporation in the same way a part owner of a local restaurant shares in the earnings of that business. Investors who choose to purchase the bond of a company become creditors of the firm in much the same way that a bank becomes a creditor of the person who borrowed money to buy a car. In the case of a bond, bondholders do not share in the earnings of the firm, but simply lend money for a period of time in return for a cash flow of interest payments and the return of the original loan amount. Because stock represents ownership interest, payouts such as dividends are not a legal obligation to the firm. On the other hand, interest payments to bondholders are a legal obligation to the firm. Stock investments, thus, are riskier but potentially more rewarding than investments in bonds. Another important aspect of securities markets is that they provide liquidity to market participants, which allows investors to buy and sell securities at a moment's notice and to receive a fair price.

Recent changes in technology have revolutionized the way securities markets operate. The explosion of the Internet has led to a number of new institutions and services such as online brokers, online road shows, and online securities research. Other advances in technology have allowed buyers and sellers to meet and negotiate prices directly without the use of a broker. Many of these changes have increased the speed of transactions. Understanding these changes in the financial markets is essential for investment professionals.

Historical Returns

Investment professionals will find it useful to be familiar with the historical returns of different asset classes and how these returns can affect the values of clients' portfolios.[1] Many new investors find it difficult to invest in assets such as stocks because of the apparent risks associated with this asset class. A sound understanding of the historical returns will allow investment professionals to educate investors on the merits of equity investing and will enable them to devise a more appropriate investment portfolio for their clients.

Many investors believe that stocks can be extremely risky and therefore exclude this asset class from their portfolios. However, history shows that, over long holding periods, stocks are actually a safer investment than bonds and Treasury bills. Table 1-1 shows the percentage of periods that stocks outperformed bonds and T-bills.

Notice that, in every instance, as the holding period lengthens, the percentage of periods that stocks outperform bonds and T-bills also increases. Based on the data, stocks are less risky over long holding periods.

For another perspective on the risks of stocks, consider the best and worst performance in history for different holding periods. Table 1-2 shows the range of returns.

From Table 1-2, we can see that the range from the best to worst holding period return for stocks narrows considerably as the holding period increases. For a one-year holding period, the range for stocks is −38.6 percent to +66.6 percent. However, for a thirty-year holding period, the range narrows from +2.6 percent to +10.6 percent, a range similar to that of T-bills and bonds. More importantly, when we examine the worst thirty-year holding period, we can see that both T-bills and bonds failed to keep pace with inflation—that is, real returns were negative. This, however, is not the case for stocks, which provide a positive real return for both the worst twenty- and thirty-year hold-

Table 1-1. Holding period comparisons: Percentage of periods when stocks outperform bonds and bills, 1802–1996.

Holding Period	% of Periods Stocks Outperform Bonds	% of Periods Stocks Outperform T-bills
1 Year	60.5	61.5
2 Years	64.9	65.5
5 Years	70.2	73.3
10 Years	79.6	79.6
20 Years	91.5	94.3
30 Years	99.4	97.0

Source: Adapted from Table 2-1, J.J. Siegel, *Stocks for the Long Run.* (New York: McGraw-Hill, 1998), 28.

Table 1-2. Maximum and minimum real holding period returns, 1802–1997.

	Holding Period												
	1 Year		2 Years		5 Years		10 Years		20 Years		30 Years	
	Max (%)	Min (%)	Max (%)	Min (%)	Max (%)	Min (%)	Max (%)	Min (%)	Max (%)	Min (%)	Max (%)	Min (%)
Stocks	+66.6	−38.6	+41.0	−31.6	+26.7	−11.0	+16.9	−4.1	+12.6	+1.0	+10.6	+2.6
Bonds	+35.1	−21.9	+24.7	−15.9	+17.7	−10.1	+12.4	−5.4	+8.8	−3.1	+7.4	−2.0
T-Bills	+23.7	−15.6	+21.6	−15.1	+14.9	−8.2	+11.6	−5.1	+8.3	−3.0	+7.6	−1.8

Source: Adapted from Table 2-1, J.J. Siegel, *Stocks for the Long Run.* (New York: McGraw-Hill, 1998), 27.

Table 1-3. Accumulation values for various asset allocations of a $10,000 investment.

Allocation (%)		Holding Period (Years)		
Stock	Bond	20	30	40
100	0	$75,007	$205,425	$562,607
90	10	$70,263	$189,459	$513,943
80	20	$65,518	$173,492	$465,279
70	30	$60,774	$157,525	$416,615
60	40	$56,029	$141,559	$367,951
50	50	$51,285	$125,592	$319,287
40	60	$46,540	$109,625	$270,623
30	70	$41,796	$ 93,659	$221,960
20	80	$37,051	$ 77,692	$173,296
10	90	$32,307	$ 61,725	$124,632
0	100	$27,562	$ 45,759	$ 75,968

Note: Mean stock return 1926–1997 is 10.6 percent. Mean bond return 1926–1997 is 5.2 percent. Example ignores taxes and costs of investing.

ing periods. Again, given these data, it can be argued that stocks are actually less risky over long time horizons.

A final illustration that can be helpful in explaining to clients the benefits of investing a considerable portion of their assets in stocks is to show them the accumulation values of investing in different asset classes. Table 1-3 shows the accumulation values for a $10,000 investment using historical returns for stocks and bonds.

From Table 1-3, we can see that, based on historical returns, $10,000 invested entirely in stocks grows to $562,607 over a 40-year period, whereas the same investment in bonds grows to only $75,968. These results provide additional evidence that stocks are a better long-term investment than bonds.

International Markets

Over the past two decades, improvements in communications and technology have caused world markets to become highly integrated. No longer can we think of strictly domestic companies or financial institutions. U.S. corporations such as Coca-Cola and Gillette conduct the majority of their business outside the United States. Japanese automakers such as Honda, Toyota, and

Table 1-4. World stock market capitalization, January 1998.

Country	Dollars (billion U.S.)	Percentage
Austria	23.8	0.2
Belgium	78.2	0.6
Denmark	63.3	0.5
Finland	48.0	0.4
France	490.9	3.8
Germany	602.5	4.7
Ireland	24.7	0.2
Italy	262.1	2.0
Netherlands	339.6	2.7
Norway	29.2	0.2
Portugal	36.4	0.3
Spain	170.9	1.3
Sweden	158.3	1.2
Switzerland	483.0	3.8
United Kingdom	1,343.7	10.5
Total Europe	4,154.6	32.4
Australia	174.9	1.4
Hong Kong	143.1	0.3
Japan	1,631.5	12.8
Malaysia	43.4	0.3
New Zealand	17.7	0.1
Singapore	44.6	0.3
Total Pacific	2,055.2	16.0
Canada	299.8	2.4
United States	6,283.6	49.1
Total North America	6,583.4	51.5
Total World	$12,793.2	100.0

Source: Adapted from *Morgan Stanley Capital International Global Investment Monitor,* January 30, 1998, 3.

Nissan all have a significant presence in the United States. The integration of world financial markets can be easily seen by the impact one market can have on other markets around the world. For example, the October 19, 1987, stock market crash in the United States led to similar financial crises in London, Hong Kong, and Tokyo. As another example, the 1997 devaluation of the Thai bhat caused markets around the world to correct, including those in the United States and Russia.

The integration and growth of international financial markets now make them an important consideration in any portfolio construction. Table 1-4 provides an indication of the market capitalization of the world stock markets as of January 1998 for countries with well-developed capital markets.

As shown in Table 1-4, the size of other developed overseas markets is substantial, and investors who exclude these countries from their investment portfolio are excluding more than half of the well-developed capital markets in the world.

Another reason for considering international investments when constructing a portfolio is that overseas markets tend to provide greater diversification benefits to investors than a portfolio that consists of only domestic securities. Investors receive greater diversification benefits when they invest in securities that do not track each other closely.[2] Foreign issues tend to have weaker relationships with U.S. securities and thus improve diversification.

The Use of Derivatives in Investment Management

Over the last two decades, financial institutions have created numerous financial products that can be used to enhance returns and manage risk. These products are sometimes referred to as *derivative securities* because they derive their value from some other asset. The field that creates these new financial products is sometimes referred to as *financial engineering* because new financial products are engineered from other financial products.

A number of derivative securities—such as options and futures contracts—have been around for many years. However over the past two decades, a number of new products have emerged in the marketplace. Some of the new products include asset-backed securities such as mortgage-backed securities, loans backed by credit card receivables, or student loans. Other new products include interest rate and currency swaps, caps, floors, and collars. These products offer investors a multitude of opportunities to enhance returns, manage risk, and transform a series of returns into one with different payoff opportunities. In order for investment professionals to fully assist clients, it is necessary to know about these different products and how they can be employed in the portfolio management process.

Risk Management and Portfolio Rebalancing

Investment professionals must continuously monitor the overall outlook for the economy and any changes in their clients' circumstances. When changes occur, investment professionals must be able to recommend adjustments that will continue clients on their prescribed paths. Adjustment of the portfolio will require weighing the benefits of rebalancing (a better portfolio mix) with the costs of rebalancing (tax consequences and transactions costs). For example, a prolonged bull market can cause a client's asset allocation to become too heavily weighted toward stocks, thus increasing the risk of the portfolio above its desired level. In this case, the investment professional may need to discuss with the client the need to rebalance the portfolio in order to return the portfolio to the desired risk and return composition. When the portfolio to be rebalanced is in a tax-deferred account such as a 401(k) or individual retirement account (IRA), there are no tax consequences to rebalancing. However, when the funds are in a taxable account, the benefits of rebalancing may be overshadowed by the tax liabilities incurred. In this case, the investment advisor may wish to advise the client to adjust contributions to the various funds until the allocation is once again in line with the investment objectives. For example, the client might choose to invest any new contributions entirely into fixed income assets until the stock/bond mix is reached. The investment advisor might also suggest the use of derivative securities such as futures or swaps to adjust the allocation of the portfolio. Through the use of derivatives, it may be possible to adjust the risk of the portfolio without the costs and tax consequences that would occur with the sale of securities.

Scope of This Book

This book takes investment professionals through all of the major areas in investments, including the client relationship, asset allocation, the securities issuing process, stock trading, execution techniques and trading costs, the various investment vehicles that are available, and performance measurement.

The Client Relationship

The most important part of an investment professional's job is to establish sound relationships with clients. In order to properly service clients, investment advisors need to determine the objectives and constraints that each client faces. Only after a client's needs have been established can an investment advisor begin to construct a plan that will meet the client's goals. The objectives and constraints of each client will differ depending on each one's personal circumstances. When the client is an institution such as a pension fund or charitable endowment, the investment manager may be guided by various federal and state laws or by the corporate charter. These objectives and constraints can be formally summarized in an *investment policy statement*. The investment policy statement provides the final destination for the client's journey. Chapter 2 discusses how to prepare the all-important investment policy statement.

Asset Allocation and Portfolio Management

Once an appropriate investment policy statement has been produced, the investment manager can begin to map a route to the client's destination. Asset allocation represents just such a route. Asset allocation deals with how the client's funds are divided among the various asset classes, and it plays the most important role in determining how bumpy and potentially rewarding the client's journey will be. Once the portfolio is created, the investment manager must continue to monitor the portfolio for any possible bumps or detours that will throw the client off course. Chapter 3 provides an overview of portfolio theory and then applies these concepts to the asset allocation decision.

Stock Trading, Stock Selection, and Execution

In many instances, investment managers are responsible for not only creating an investment plan for their clients, but also implementing that plan. In order to successfully implement the plan, investment managers must be aware of the different techniques for evaluating prospective securities and the techniques that can be used to execute orders. Proper execution and the use of different types of orders can reduce both risk and cost and enhance the return received by the client. Clients may also be interested in investing in the stock offering of privately owned companies. Chapter 4 discusses the process used to take private companies public. Chapter 5 discusses procedures for evaluating different types of securities. Chapter 6 discusses some of the costs of execution and different execution techniques.

Types of Investments

Deciding which of the numerous investment vehicles to use depends on the objectives and constraints of the client investor. Different securities have different risks, time horizons, tax implications, and cash flow characteristics. The goal of investment professionals is to match clients' goals to the characteristics of the securities selected for their portfolios.

One distinguishing characteristic of a security is the claim on the firm's assets. Debt instruments such as bonds represent a loan from the bondholder to the corporation. Equity instruments such as stocks represent ownership interest in a firm and thus also represent a residual claim on the firm's assets. Therefore, stockholders participate in the success of the firm, whereas bondholders can only hope to receive the return of their original principal plus interest. This makes stocks potentially more rewarding than bonds as an investment, but also riskier because the cash flows are much less certain. Chapters 7 through 11 discuss the many investment vehicles available to investors.

Once investors decide how to allocate their assets, they can choose how to implement their strategy. They can purchase individual securities to create their portfolio, or they can purchase a pool of investments through mutual funds or closed-end funds. Chapter 12 discusses the mutual funds industry. Chapter 13 discusses closed-end investment companies such as real estate investment trusts and country funds. These types of funds can be used to manage an individual's entire portfolio or can be used as the foundation of a broader investment program.

A third class of securities known as derivative securities because they derive their value from other securities offers investors a number of opportunities in the financial markets. Derivative securities can provide a low-cost method for speculating in the financial markets, managing risk, enhancing return, and managing tax liabilities. Chapter 14 discusses the use of futures contracts, Chapter 15 discusses options, and Chapter 16 discusses swaps and other types of derivative securities.

Benchmarks and Portfolio Performance Evaluation

This book concludes by looking at the different methods that can be used to determine the performance of a portfolio. Comparisons can be made by looking at the performance of the fund relative to some benchmark or on a risk-adjusted basis. Performance evaluation gives both investment managers and clients an opportunity to see how well their investment strategies have performed relative to the goals that were set.

Selected Bibliography

Bogle, J. C. *Common Sense on Mutual Funds: New Imperatives for the Intelligent Investor.* New York: John Wiley, 1999.

Siegel, J. J. *Stocks for the Long Run.* New York: McGraw-Hill, 1998.

Notes

1. An excellent source of returns for different asset class returns is J. J. Siegel, *Stocks for the Long Run.* (New York: McGraw-Hill, 1998.)
2. The relationship between two securities can be measured by the correlation coefficient. A low degree of correlation allows for greater diversification benefit.

2

The Client Relationship

The relationship between investment professionals and clients begins with an understanding of clients' basic needs and constraints. Every client, whether an individual or a corporation, has different objectives and constraints that must be addressed. For example, a person in his seventies may need current investment income to support his retirement, whereas a 45-year-old may have little or no need for current investment income and can therefore seek growth for the portfolio. In addition, each individual has a different psychological makeup that determines how much risk he or she is willing to take.

The one-size-fits-all approach to investing has largely disappeared and has been replaced by efforts to tailor portfolios to the needs of individuals or institutions. This tailoring of investments to meet clients' needs is also required by law and is known as the *suitability requirement*. That is, registered representatives (brokers) are required by law to make investment recommendations that are suitable for their clients. In an attempt to better accommodate their clients' needs, many brokerage houses and mutual fund families now have online questionnaires that allow individuals to determine a portfolio allocation based on their needs, objectives, and constraints.

Investment Policy Statement

This first step investment professionals need to address is determining the needs and constraints of their clients. The use of an investment policy statement (IPS) can be indispensable in helping an individual or institution meet their investment goals. An IPS is analogous to the preliminary interview and medical history that a physician would obtain before beginning any examination or course of treatment for a patient. The policy statement serves a number of useful purposes.[1]

- The IPS provides a paper trail of policies, practices, and procedures for investment decisions that can be a critical defense in litigation and accusations of imprudence.

15

- The IPS ensures continuity of the investment strategy when there is a high turnover of the investment policy board.

- The IPS reassures clients of the investment stewardship of the portfolio.

- The IPS can be valuable in reminding the investment committee or individuals of the investment strategy of the portfolio during turbulent market periods.

- The IPS provides a baseline from which to monitor the performance of the overall portfolio.

In constructing the policy statement, a number of questions should be addressed. Money manager and author, Charles Ellis, believes that answers to the following questions can be beneficial in constructing the investment policy statement:

1. What are the real risks of an adverse financial outcome, especially in the short run?

2. What probable emotional reactions will I have to an adverse financial outcome?

3. How knowledgeable am I about investments and markets?

4. What other capital or income sources do I have? How important is this particular portfolio to my overall financial position?

5. What, if any, legal restrictions may affect my investment needs?

6. What, if any, unanticipated consequences of interim fluctuations in portfolio value might affect my investment policy?

Objectives

The investor's objectives are the starting point for preparing a sound financial plan. The objectives need to clearly outline specific and realistic goals for the investor. Objectives such as making as much money as possible are too broad to allow money managers to produce a sound financial plan. In fact, broad objectives like this may actually lead money managers to invest clients' funds inappropriately. In addition, the objectives laid out in the policy statement need to be realistic. The goal of a recent college graduate to become a millionaire by age thirty may be unrealistic given her $50,000 per year job. However, the goal of saving $1 million and retiring at age fifty may be attainable with a sound financial plan.

The return objectives are only the first part of the analysis. The risk that the client is willing and able to assume also must be taken into consideration. An investor's risk tolerance depends on a number of factors, including the investor's age, current income and expenses, psychological makeup, level of wealth, time horizon, and liquidity needs.

A simple method advocated by the Association for Investment Management Research (AIMR), presents the objectives of an IPS in the following manner.[2]

Return requirements—For individuals, this may include funding a new home, paying for a child's college education, or saving for retirement. For all individuals, the return objective should recognize the devastating impact inflation will have on one's financial well-being, and, therefore, the objective should seek returns that maintain the client's purchasing power.

Risk tolerance—This is perhaps the most difficult to quantify because it is so closely tied to the constraints imposed upon investors (see below) and also can be largely determined by an investor's psychological makeup.

Constraints

The objectives discussed in the previous section are largely determined by the constraints imposed on the investor. Also important in determining how a client's portfolio should be allocated is how soon the client will need use of the money. The investor's liquidity needs should be directly addressed in the policy statement. Several needs may require a portion of the investor's portfolio to remain in highly liquid assets. For example, parents of a college-bound child may require liquid assets to make tuition payments, or a young couple may wish to purchase a house in the next few years.

The second constraint that the investor faces is the investment or time horizon. The general rule is that the time horizon of the assets should match the time horizon of the investor's needs. That is, short-term needs require investment in highly liquid, short-term investment vehicles, whereas long-term investment needs permit investment in long-term assets. For example, a 25-year-old's retirement has a long time horizon and should be invested using long-term, high-return assets such as stocks. A short-term goal of making a down payment on a house in two years should use short-term, highly liquid investments such as money market accounts or bank certificates of deposit.

The third constraint that needs to be considered is taxes. The tax-exempt status of an institution such as an educational endowment allows the money manager to ignore the tax consequences of an investment. In addition, money in an individual's 401(k) or other qualified retirement plan is tax deferred, so, once again, taxes are not an issue in the investment allocation. However, for an individual's taxable accounts, taxes can be an important constraint. Investors who are in high tax brackets may wish to use tax-exempt securities, tax-efficient mutual funds, or stock in companies that pay little or no dividends in order to reduce their tax liability.

The laws and regulations constraining individual investors are minimal, because investors are not bound by government laws and regulations regarding how they invest their funds. The only consideration for individual investors is that they obey the law by not engaging in insider trading or securities fraud. Institutions, on the other hand, are bound by laws, regulations, and corporate charters that may limit how they can invest their funds. Pension funds must comply with the Employee Retirement Income Security Act of 1974 (ERISA). Private endowments are usually limited by their corporate charter, which may place requirements on how much can be spent from the fund and how those funds must be invested. In general, when institutions manage the money of others, they are bound by the *prudent man rule*. This rule determines the reasonableness of an investment by considering whether a "reasonable man" with knowledge of the situation would invest in a like security.

The final consideration in determining an investor's constraints is the presence of any unique preferences or circumstances that the investor may face. For example, a person might wish to have sufficient funds to gift $1 million to a grandchild or a favorite charity. Another individual might have a trust fund that will distribute $100,000 per year when he reaches the age of 25. These special circumstances can play a part in shaping the investment allocation.

Given the constraints listed above, the investment policy statement can be completed by laying out the constraints in the following manner.

Liquidity—liquidity depends on the unexpected need for cash in excess of what can be covered by income. For an individual, liquidity depends on income relative to expenses. If income significantly exceeds expenses, then the individual likely will be able to cover unexpected needs for cash from current income. In this case, liquidity needs would be relatively low. For an institution, liquidity depends on the possibility of unexpected cash out-flows. For example, life insurance companies have relatively predictable cash outflows and therefore have relatively low liquidity needs. Property-liability insurers, on the other hand, have much more unpredictable cash outflows and thus have a need for greater liquidity.

Time horizon—An investor's time horizon is important in asset allocation because individuals and institutions should match the duration of their assets and liabilities.

Taxes—For individuals, taxes can play an important role in defining the appropriate investment strategy. Individuals in high tax brackets may realize higher after-tax returns by investing in tax-free municipal bonds and tax-efficient mutual funds.

Laws and regulations—Individuals generally are required only to obey the law. Institutions, on the other hand, may be governed by federal laws such as ERISA in the case of pension funds or by corporate charters in the case of endowment funds.

Unique preferences and circumstances—Finally, each individual or institution may be guided by some unique circumstances that need to be incorporated into the investment policy statement.

The above objectives and constraints will differ depending on the needs and circumstances of the investor. Preparing clear investment policy statements allows investment managers to best service the needs of their clients. A sound IPS should satisfactorily answer the following questions:[3]

1. Is the policy statement carefully designed to meet the specific needs, risk constraints, and objectives of this particular investor?

2. Is the policy statement written so clearly and explicitly that a competent stranger could manage the portfolio in compliance with the client's needs?

3. Would the client have been able to remain committed to the policies during the capital market experiences of the past fifty to sixty years—particularly of the past ten years?

4. Would the portfolio manager have been able to follow the policy over the same period?

5. Would the policy, if implemented, have achieved the client's objectives?

In addition to the objectives and constraints mentioned above, the IPS should include how money managers are selected and evaluated and provide guidelines on the types and amounts of various securities that are eligible for inclusion in the portfolio. For example, the portfolio might specify that equities should constitute from 50 to 70 percent, with 5 to 10 percent devoted to international funds. Bonds and real estate investment trusts (REITs) might make up the remaining part of the allocation, with 20 to 40 percent devoted to bonds and 5 to 10 percent devoted to REITs. Finally, the IPS should state how often a review of the client's needs and constraints will be completed. In most instances, a client's IPS should be reviewed on an annual basis. If a significant unexpected change in an investor's circumstances occurs, a reevaluation may be necessary before the usual review. Circumstances that warrant reevaluation include the untimely death of the primary wage earner, which might include the distribution of a sizable life insurance policy; a large inheritance; or the possibility of forced early retirement.

Individual Investors

Defining the objectives and constraints of individual investors can be more difficult than doing so for institutional investors. Institutional investors are governed by laws such as ERISA or by charters, as is the case with foundations and endowment funds. Individual investors, on the other hand, have an almost limitless combination of needs and constraints.

Individual investors also differ from institutional investors in how they view risk. Individuals and institutions differ in their perspectives of risk in four ways:[4]

■ Institutions generally view risk as the volatility of returns as measured by the standard deviation or beta. Individuals tend to view risk as the chance of losing money or doing something that feels uncomfortable.

■ Individuals can be categorized by their personality traits, whereas institutions can be categorized by who has a beneficial interest in their portfolio (beneficiaries of the endowment, for example).

■ Individuals can be classified financially by their assets and goals, whereas institutions are a more precise package of assets and liabilities.

■ Individuals must deal with taxes, whereas institutions in many cases are free of taxes as long as they comply with certain regulations.

Individuals generally view three types of investments as risky.[5] First, because of their fear of the unknown, individuals tend to consider unfamiliar instruments to be risky. Second, investors view previous losses in familiar instruments as more risky. Finally, contrary investing tends to be viewed as risky because individuals often find it difficult to go against the prevailing market sentiment. In order to forge a long-lasting relationship with clients, investment professionals must understand not only how an investor views risk, but also the financial products in the marketplace that will be used to construct the client's portfolio. Even when dealing with experienced investors, investment advisors often need to educate clients about the merits of different investment vehicles and strategies.

Many of the objectives and constraints used in forming the IPS can be established by examining the investor's life cycle. This approach breaks the investor's spending and savings patterns into four phases, as shown in Figure 2-1.

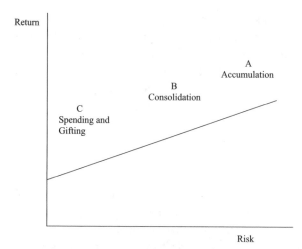

Figure 2-1. Risk/return tradeoff for different life cycle stages.

■ *Accumulation phase*—occurs in the early years of an investor's life. Here the investor's net worth is usually small relative to liabilities. Usually the investor has limited diversification, with the majority of his or her net worth tied up in a home.

■ *Consolidation phase*—occurs in mid to late career stage and is characterized by income that exceeds expenses. Here, the client may have accumulated a significant amount of wealth in a company retirement plan and may be past many of the expenses that younger investors face, such as the purchase of a home or financing a child's education. This investor will be looking to balance the growth and risk of the portfolio.

■ *Spending phase*—occurs when the investor is financially independent, and living expenses are covered by accumulated assets rather than earned income. In this case, the investor does not need to work in order to support his or her lifestyle. This person may have retired or may be considering retirement. If the client chooses to retire, the portfolio needs to be structured to generate sufficient income and growth to meet the client's needs.

■ *Gifting phase*—occurs in the final stage of life when the individual realizes that he or she has more assets than will ever be needed for financial security. In this phase, the client may wish to begin gifting assets in an effort to reduce the size of his or her estate.

Each phase of the investor's life will play an important role in determining an appropriate investment strategy. Each phase of the investor's life may pose numerous objectives and constraints. For example, a 25-year-old may wish to save a sufficient amount of money to meet a long-term goal of retiring at age 55. This individual may also have short-term goals such as saving for the purchase of a house or paying for a wedding. In order to make it easier to prepare the investor's policy statement, two policy statements could be used—one for the long-term retirement portfolio and one for the short-term financial goals. Investors who are in the consolidation, spending, or gifting phases may have goals that can be easily handled with one investment policy statement.

Investor Behavior

In order to serve clients' needs, investment professionals need to understand how investors think and behave. Two approaches for examining investor behavior include classical decision-making theory and behavioral decision research. Classical decision-making theory uses three assumptions to determine the appropriate decisions under risk. First, investors are assumed to look at their investments in a portfolio context. This assumption, known as *asset integration*, implies that investors take a systematic look at all their investments as a whole. Decisions to buy or sell securities are viewed not on an individual basis but rather in terms of how the transaction will affect the entire portfolio. Second, investors are assumed to be *risk averse*, which means that if the expected return is held constant, individuals prefer the prospect with the smaller variance.[6] Finally, decisions are assumed to be based on *rational expectations*, which means that individuals are coherent, accurate, and unbiased forecasters. This assumption requires that investors have the ability to process large amounts of complicated information in order to make investment decisions.

An alternative to classical decision-making theory is behavioral decision research.[7] This approach blends psychology and observations of human behavior to help determine how an individual will behave under uncertainty. Much of the research in this area questions the validity of the classical decision-making assumptions. Researchers have found that individuals' decision making may be hindered by their lack of understanding of the situation. The following examples illustrate the differences between the two approaches.

- *Risk aversion versus loss aversion*—A risk-averse investor or classical decision maker considers the expected value of the outcome relative to the variability. In loss aversion or behavioral decision making, the pain of a loss is greater than the joy of a gain, so investors will always choose the safe alternative unless the risky outcome has a very high expected return.

- *Reference dependence*—In classical decision-making theory, an investor will consider the terminal wealth value; however, in behavioral decision making, an investor's decision also will depend on where they are now, their reference point.

■ *Asset segregation*—In classical theory, investors view assets in a portfolio context. In behavioral decision making, they tend to view each asset individually and will often make mistakes by choosing an incorrect combination of securities.

■ *Mental accounting*—In classical theory, preferences do not depend on how the decision is framed. However, because behavioral researchers have found that individuals tend to place items in specific "mental accounts," the framing of the problem does matter. For example, many individuals tend to have separate mental accounts for entertainment and living expenses. When people are asked whether they will buy a $50 ticket to a show after losing the ticket, they tend to respond differently than when they discover they have lost a $50 bill on the way to the show. In the first case, the person already has spent the "show account" money, whereas in the second case, the person believes the "show account" money has not been spent and the loss comes from some other mental account. In each case, the cost is the same—an additional $50 to attend the show. However, the individual views the situation differently depending on how the situation is posed. From an investing perspective, individuals may have separate mental accounts for vacations, for their child's education, and so forth. Each account must be structured accordingly because of the difficulty many mental accounters have in moving money between accounts. As another example, individuals may have separate mental accounts for the income and principal of their investments. These individuals may have no difficulty spending funds from the income account, but may abhor withdrawing funds from the principal account. Many behavioral researchers believe that mental accounting is used to impose discipline on the investor. For example, parents are less likely to spend their children's college fund when the assets are segregated from other household funds.

■ *Biased expectations*—In classical theory, people make unbiased, rational decisions. However, in real life, researchers have found that people are overconfident in their abilities to predict unknown future events. This is especially obvious when one looks at the number of individuals engaged in day trading.

When preparing investment policy statements, financial advisors need to consider how individuals think and behave. Many individuals will choose portfolios that are too conservative given their circumstances because they misunderstand the risks of different securities and their potential impact on the risk and return of the entire portfolio. An individual investor's IPS will depend on a number of factors, including his or her stage in life. Given the tendency of many individuals to keep mental accounts, it may be beneficial for the investment advisor to prepare more than one IPS for the client. For example, one IPS might be prepared for the client's retirement account and one for the client's taxable account. Let's consider the objectives and constraints for several individual investors who are in different phases of their investment life cycle.

Example 1

For a 25-year-old in the accumulation phase of the investment cycle, it may be best to prepare two investment policy statements—one for the client's retirement plan and one to meet shorter-term goals.

Retirement Plan Investment Policy Statement

Return requirement—Given the young age of the investor, he can seek maximum returns for the investment funds.

Risk tolerance—The youth of this investor allows a high degree of risk to be assumed because of the ability to wait out down periods in the market.

Liquidity—Not a concern because the investor will not be able to withdraw funds until age $59^1/2$.

Time horizon—Very long because of the age of the investor. Thirty or more years until retirement and a life expectancy of twenty or more years after retirement.

Taxes—Not a concern because retirement accounts such as 401(k) accounts and individual retirement accounts (IRAs) are tax deferred and are taxed as ordinary income when withdrawn.

Laws and regulations—No specific laws govern how individuals invest their own money, so this investor needs to be concerned only about obeying the law. Also, this investor should be aware of regulations about the maximum amount that can be contributed to a qualified pension plan and any penalties for early withdrawal of funds.

Unique preferences and circumstances—Might include a sizeable inheritance that could supplement this individual's retirement. Also, goals of retiring early could be incorporated here.

Short-term Investment Policy Statement

Return requirement—Because this investor is in the early stage of his career, he may have little or no savings. In addition, he may have short-term financial obligations such as student loans, plans to purchase a house, etc. that indicate that an average or perhaps even a below-average level of return would be prudent.

Risk tolerance—For the same reasons listed in the return requirement section, this investor should seek average or below-average risks.

Liquidity—This investor's need for liquidity is high. In addition to short-term financial obligations, this client may have limited job security.

Time horizon—This investor has a short to moderate time horizon for current funds.

Taxes—Taxes are a concern for this investor because, unlike the retirement funds, taxes are not deferred.

Laws and regulations—No specific laws govern how individuals invest their own money, so this investor needs to be concerned only about obeying the law.

Unique preferences and circumstances—Might include any inheritance that the client will receive.

Example 2

A 50-year-old married couple in the consolidation phase of the investment cycle. In this case, one investment policy statement will be sufficient to discuss the objectives and constraints of this couple.

Investment Policy Statement

Return requirement—This couple can probably seek average to above-average returns. In this phase, income exceeds expenses, and this couple may have already passed many of the short-term financial obligations of younger investors, such as purchasing a house or providing for a child's education.

Risk tolerance—For the reasons listed above, this couple can assume average to above-average risks.

Liquidity—With a steady income that exceeds expenses, this couple probably has low to moderate liquidity needs.

Time horizon—This couple has two time horizons. The first is the number of years until retirement—say ten years—and the number of years they will live in retirement based on life expectancy—which could be twenty-five years or more. So their time horizon is quite long.

Taxes—The couple may be in a high tax bracket and should consider taxes important in formulating their investment strategy.

Laws and regulations—There are no specific laws regarding how individuals invest their own money, so this couple needs to be concerned only about obeying the law. Also, they should be aware of regulations about the maximum amount that can be contributed to a qualified pension plan and any penalties for early withdraw of funds.

Unique preferences and circumstances—Might include a sizeable inheritance that could supplement their retirement. Also, goals of retiring early, say at age 60, could be incorporated here. This couple might also wish to provide for a large donation to a favorite charity or provide funds to finance a grandchild's education.

Example 3

A 65-year-old married couple who are retired and in the spending and gifting phase of the investment cycle. One investment policy statement will be sufficient to discuss the objectives and constraints of this couple.

Investment Policy Statement

Return requirement—This couple probably should seek below-average to average returns. How much return this couple can seek depends on a number of factors, including other sources of income such as pensions and social security and how much wealth they have accumulated. A couple with only a modest amount of wealth and limited sources of other income will need to seek current income, which will tend to have below-average returns. Couples with greater levels of wealth and/or larger sources of outside income may be able to assume greater levels of risk. In any case, returns should cover their living expenses, adjusted for inflation.

Risk tolerance—For the reasons listed above, this couple can assume below-average to average levels of risk.

Liquidity—This couple's liquidity needs depend on any noninvestment sources of income such as pensions and social security. Couples with large outside sources of income may have moderate liquidity needs, whereas couples who are living on their investment portfolio will likely have a need for greater liquidity.

Time horizon—The time horizon for this couple is still relatively long. Given current life expectancies, one or both of these individuals could live for twenty-five or more years.

Taxes—The couple may be in a high tax bracket and should consider taxes important in formulating their investment strategy.

Laws and regulations—No specific laws govern how individuals invest their own money, so this couple needs to be concerned only about obeying the law.

Unique preferences and circumstances—Might include a sizeable inheritance that could supplement this couple's current income. This couple might also wish to provide for a large donation to a favorite charity or provide funds to finance a grandchild's education.

Tax Considerations

For individuals with taxable accounts, tax strategies can be crucial in maximizing the total after-tax return. Two parts of investors' stock returns are taxed. First, dividends that are distributed to investors are taxed as ordinary income. Second, capital gains, which are the difference between the price at which investors sell their shares and the price paid for those shares, are also taxed. Historically, capital gains have been taxed at a lower rate than dividends. In addition to the lower tax rate, investors can defer the capital gains tax by not selling their shares. Current tax policy also allows for a stepped up cost basis upon the death of the owner, which means that capital gains tax is forgiven.

One key component of the amount of capital gains tax that an investor faces is the rate at which the portfolio is turned over. A stock portfolio that is never sold incurs no capital gains tax, whereas a portfolio with a 100 percent turnover rate will be fully taxed on all capital gains each year. Although capital gains taxes will be incurred when the portfolio is liquidated, the longer an individual can avoid the tax, the greater the ability of the portfolio to grow. Postponing the realization of capital gains allows investors to, in effect, receive an interest-free loan from the government.

An interesting aspect of deferring capital gains by limiting portfolio turnover is that most of the tax damage is done at low levels of portfolio turnover.[8] Why? Consider that the turnover rate is the reciprocal of the holding period. When the turnover rate increases from 1 percent to 25 percent, the holding period falls from 100 years to only four years. However, when the turnover rate increases from 25 percent to 100 percent, the holding period only falls from four years to one year.

One strategy commonly used to reduce an investor's tax liability is to sell securities that have incurred a capital loss to offset any realized capital gains. This can be an effective way to manage an investor's taxes. Investors who plan to sell securities with losses need to be aware of *wash-sale rules,* which prevent individuals from selling a security at a loss and reacquiring a "substantially identical" security within thirty days before or after the loss. The wash-sale rule also applies to the recognition of losses from closing a short-sale position and entering into another short sale of a substantially identical security.

If the wash-sale rule applies, the loss is disallowed, and the basis of the new property is deemed to be the basis of the original property. The holding period of the new security is added to the holding period of the original security.

In addition, the Internal Revenue Service has taken a position of disallowing a loss on the sale of a stock if, within thirty days before or after the sale of the stock, the individual sells an in-the-money put option on the stock, and on the basis of objective factors at the time the put was sold, there is a substantial likelihood that the put will be exercised. The sale of such a put obliges the investor to purchase shares of the stock at the predetermined price, known as the exercise price, which is why the strategy is subject to wash-sale rules.

The difference in tax rates between dividends and capital gains is not the only issue that investors need to consider. Different types of bonds also have different tax consequences. Interest on federal securities such as Treasury bills, notes, and bonds is exempt from state taxes. Municipal bonds, which are issued by state and local governments to finance their operations, are exempt from federal taxes. In addition, if the bondholder is a resident of the state that issues the bonds, then the interest is also exempt from state taxes.

In order to compare taxable and tax-exempt bonds, investors should either convert the taxable return into an after-tax return or, equivalently, convert the tax-exempt rate to an equivalent taxable yield.

$$\text{After-tax return} = \text{Taxable rate} \times (1 - \text{marginal tax rate})$$

$$\text{Equivalent taxable yield} = \frac{\text{Tax - exempt rate}}{(1 - \text{marginal tax rate})}$$

Table 2-1 presents the equivalent taxable yield for different marginal tax rates and different tax-exempt returns. Notice that the higher the tax rate, the greater the taxable equivalent yield. For an investor in the 39.6 percent marginal tax bracket, a 6 percent tax-exempt return is equivalent to a 9.93 percent return on a taxable bond.

A final consideration in the tax planning process is the use of various tax-deferred accounts, each of which offers various advantages. Employer-sponsored retirement savings plans such as 401(k) and 403(b) plans offer

Table 2-1. Equivalent taxable yield for different tax rates.

Tax Rate (%)	Tax-Exempt Rate (%)			
	4	6	8	10
15.0	4.71	7.06	9.41	11.76
28.0	5.56	8.33	11.11	13.89
31.0	5.80	8.70	11.59	14.49
36.0	6.25	9.38	12.50	15.63
39.6	6.62	9.93	13.25	16.56

employees the opportunity to receive a tax deduction for contributions up to a maximum amount. Contributions also benefit because they grow tax deferred. However, when withdrawals are made, both contributions and profits are taxed as ordinary income upon withdrawal.[9]

Traditional IRAs represent another investment vehicle. These IRAs may offer certain individuals the same tax deduction available on 401(k) and 403(b) plans up to a maximum of $2,000 if the individual meets certain requirements. Like 401(k) and 403(b) plans, IRAs offer tax-deferred growth and profits that are taxed as ordinary income upon withdrawal. Whether contributions are taxed depends on whether contributions were made on a before- or after-tax basis.

A relatively new creation, the *Roth IRA* allows investors who do not exceed certain income limits to contribute $2,000 for an individual and $4,000 for a married couple that are not taxed when withdrawn. In addition, certain individuals may benefit from conversion of their traditional IRA to a Roth IRA.

When preparing an asset allocation using these three types of retirement vehicles it is important to consider the universe of investments available in each. Employer-sponsored retirement plans tend to have choices limited to a handful of mutual funds and the company's stock, so this type of account is probably the best place to start when preparing the allocation. Traditional and Roth IRAs offer investors the option to place money in nearly any type of investment, and so offer a much richer range of investment possibilities than employer-sponsored plans. Because accumulations are tax free, many financial advisors believe the Roth IRA is the place for the most aggressive types of investments.

Estate Planning

Closely tied to tax consideration issues is proper estate planning to minimize possible inheritance taxes. Investment advisors will in most instances not be experts in the intricacies of estate planning. Most investment advisors should be viewed as "general practitioners" who have enough knowledge and experience to recognize that the client may need to seek a "specialist." In addition to having sufficient knowledge to recognize that the client may benefit from estate planning, investment advisors should be aware of some of the basics of estate planning in order to educate the client about alternatives.

Estate Planning Basics

The first issue that investment advisors need to be aware of is the limits on an individual's and married couple's wealth that will trigger inheritance taxes. In 1999, the individual exemption was $650,000. This threshold will increase each year and will be $1 million per individual in 2006. Although married couples can bequest an unlimited amount of wealth to the surviving spouse, free of estate taxes, neglecting an estate plan means that only half of the allowable exemption will be used. For example, a married couple with $2 million in assets in 2006 will be able to bequest the entire amount, free of estate taxes, if a proper estate plan is drawn up. However, if the couple neglects estate planning, as much as $1 million would be subject to estate taxes when the surviving spouse passes away.

Investors with substantial wealth can reduce the size of their estates and hence the amount of estate tax that is paid through a number of lifetime gifting programs. Current tax law allows individuals to give $10,000 per year to as many other individuals as they please without incurring gift taxes. For married couples, the threshold is $20,000. Individuals can also make an unlimited payment of tuition or health care payments to a third party free of gift tax as long as the payment is made directly to the third party. For example, a grandparent may wish to pay a grandchild's college tuition directly to the college rather than give a gift to the grandchild.

Wealthier individuals also may choose to reduce the size of their estates by making gifts to charitable organizations. Individuals who have shares of stock that have appreciated significantly will benefit from gifting the stock rather than selling shares and making a cash donation. By gifting the stock, the individual avoids the capital gains tax while still enjoying the benefits of deducting the full value of the donated stock.

A Primer on Trusts

Trusts can be an effective way for an investor to shelter assets from the IRS. Trusts are separate legal entities that are managed by a *trustee*. The trustee can be a spouse, attorney, accountant, or even oneself. Below are some basic trusts that can be used in the estate planning process.[10]

- Revocable living trust—allows people to name a trustee to manage their affairs should they become incapacitated or die. It avoids probate and keeps personal financial details hidden from view. People can name themselves as trustee. Under this type of trust, there are no tax savings over using a will unless other steps are taken.

- Credit shelter trust—also known as a "bypass trust." Allows a couple to take full advantage of the exemption to pass on money tax-free to their heirs. Upon the death of a spouse, money is left to the trust rather than the surviving spouse. The surviving spouse has access to the interest and principal, but these funds will not be included in the surviving spouse's estate.

- Marital trust—usually combined with a credit shelter trust. This trust takes full advantage of the unlimited estate tax deduction for assets passed on to a spouse. Allows money to remain in the family should the surviving spouse remarry.

- Trusts for children—Many parents set up trusts for their minor children. Trusts allow the parents to determine when the money will become available to their children. Trusts can also be used to provide lifelong support for someone unable to care for himself or herself.

- Life insurance trust—By allowing a trust to own a life insurance policy and to be the beneficiary, the value of the life insurance policy is removed from the spouse's estate, a strategy that can create significant tax savings.

- Charitable remainder trust—allows wealthier individuals to gift assets, receive a tax deduction, and still draw an income from the trust.

A complete description of all the technical details of the various types of trusts is beyond the scope of this book and most likely beyond the expertise of most investment advisors. Investment advisors should work with clients to obtain expert estate planning advice.

Institutional Investors

Institutional investors include mutual funds, pension funds, banks, insurance companies, endowments, and foundations. The objectives and constraints of each type of institutional investor differ depending on the laws that govern the institution or the corporate charter in the case of endowment funds. For each type of institutional investor, we provide an outline of the issues that need to be addressed in each part of the investment policy statement.

Mutual Funds

Mutual funds pool together the money from a number of investors and use it to purchase financial assets. Each fund has a specific investment objective, which determines the types of assets the fund purchases. The mutual fund industry is highly regulated. Federal securities laws that govern the industry include the Securities Act of 1933, the Securities Exchange Act of 1934, the Investment Company Act of 1940, and the Investment Advisers Act of 1940.

Illustrating an investment policy statement for a mutual fund is extremely difficult because of the diverse objectives of the different funds.

Return requirement—depends on the objectives of the fund. Some funds seek maximum capital gains, whereas others such as money market funds seek to maintain a constant net asset value while distributing interest income.

Risk tolerance—depends on the objectives of the fund.

Liquidity—Different types of funds have different liquidity needs. However, funds must maintain liquidity sufficient to meet cash redemptions. Funds that have large cash inflows relative to cash outflows have lower liquidity needs.

Time horizon—depends on the objectives of the fund.

Taxes—Mutual funds are tax exempt if they meet certain distributional requirements.

Laws and regulations—governed by the Securities Act of 1933, the Securities Exchange Act of 1934, the Investment Company Act of 1940, and the Investment Advisers Act of 1940.

Pension Funds

Pension funds are set up to help fund the retirement benefits of employees. The two types of pension plans are defined benefit plans and defined contribution plans. A *defined benefit plan* promises to pay employees retirement benefits after retirement. The benefit is usually based on a number of factors, such as the employee's age, salary, and length of service. The firm contributes to the fund on a regular basis. The future benefit represents an uncertain liability to the firm. Whether the plan contains sufficient funds depends on a number of factors, including the size of the firm's contribution, the growth rate of wages, employee turnover, the age of the work force, the life span of employees after retirement, and the return earned on the fund's assets. The investment policy statement for this type of pension is especially critical because the plan's sponsor may hire a number of investment professionals to manage the assets of the fund. Therefore, the fund must be quite exacting in determining what assets are appropriate for the fund and the target allocations before it can determine which investment advisors to hire.

In a *defined contribution plan*, the firm contributes some funds into each employee's account. This amount usually represents some percentage match of an employee's own contribution. In this case, the firm makes no promise of future benefits, and the amount of money in an employee's account depends on the size of the employee's contribution and the performance of the investment vehicles chosen by the employee.

Pension plans are governed by ERISA. There are a number of major provisions of ERISA. First, it establishes funding standards for the minimum contribution that a plan sponsor must make to the pension plan. Second, ERISA establishes the fiduciary duty standards for pension plan trustees, managers, and advisors. Third, ERISA provides for minimum vesting standards. Finally, ERISA created the Pension Benefit Guaranty Corporation (PBGC) to insure vested benefits.

The investment policy statement for a defined benefit pension plan should take into account a number of factors, including the average age of plan participants and how payouts are determined for retirees. Are the benefits dependent on the average salary of an employee, or does the employee receive a flat amount based on years of service? If the average salary is used in the computation, at what rate are salaries expected to increase? The investment policy statement should consider the following:

Return requirements—depend on the rate at which benefits will increase. If benefits to retirees are expected to grow at a rate of 5 percent, then plan assets must generate an appropriate rate of return. This rate also should incorporate sufficient growth to keep pace with inflation. Also, the funded status of the plan will determine the return necessary to meet plan obligations.

Risk tolerance—The amount of risk that a pension plan can assume depends on the average age of employees. A younger work force allows the plan to assume longer-term, riskier assets. Again, the funded status may also play a part in the amount of risk that the plan can assume.

Liquidity—Pension plans usually have low liquidity needs because of the predictability of current and near-term obligations.

Time horizon—Firms that are a going concern will have relatively long time horizons. Even if the age of the average employee is relatively old, retirees are likely to live for two decades or more after retirement.

Taxes—Plan assets are exempt from taxes.

Laws and regulations—Pension plans are governed by ERISA.

Unique preferences and circumstances—could include an increase in the number of retirees due to forced or early retirement.

Insurance Companies

The investment objectives of insurance companies depend on whether they are life or non–life insurers. Life insurance companies tend to have longer-term, more predictable cash outflows than non–life insurers.

Return requirement—Returns should be sufficient to meet actuarial liabilities and should account for changes in the price level (inflation).

Risk tolerance—Insurance is meant to protect the insured from unforeseen losses. Therefore, insurers should assume a low to moderate level of risk in their investment portfolios.

Liquidity—For life insurers, liquidity requirements are relatively low because of the ease of predicting cash outflows. However, for casualty insurers, liquidity needs are greater because of the uncertainty of cash outflows. For example, an earthquake on the west coast or a severe winter in the east that leads to a greater than expected number of auto claims can pose a liquidity problem for casualty insurers. Also, jury awards in liability cases can be highly unpredictable, thus increasing the need for liquidity.

Time horizon—Life insurers have a relatively long time horizon, whereas casualty insurers have a relatively short time horizon.

Taxes—Because insurers are subject to corporate income tax, taxes are an important consideration.

Laws and regulations—Insurers are regulated at the state level. Regulations often include the types of securities an insurer can purchase and the rates they can charge policyholders.

Unique preferences and circumstances—These might include pending legislation on health care reform that would increase costs to the insurer.

Endowment Funds

Endowment funds are set up to receive contributions made to charities or educational institutions. Rather than spend all the contributions that are received, the fund usually invests the money to provide a future income stream to the organization. The endowment's goals typically are defined in its corporate charter. The goal of the fund in most instances is to balance the need for current income with the need to create a growing income stream that maintains the purchasing power of the income stream.

The investment policy statement for an endowment fund depends on a number of factors, including the charter of the endowment, tax laws regarding the minimum distribution of the fund, and the needs of the beneficiary.

Return requirements—These seek to provide an income stream that maintains the fund's purchasing power and that allows for some growth in the assets of the fund.

Risk tolerance—depends on the needs of the beneficiaries. If a certain income distribution is required of the organization, then the endowment may need to be managed for income rather than growth. However, if the income generated from the endowment is used for supplementary purposes, then the fund may be able to take additional risks in order to grow the assets.

Liquidity—usually not a major concern for an endowment.

Time horizon—In principle, endowments have an infinite life and so should be managed with a long time horizon in mind.

Taxes—Endowment fund assets are exempt from taxes.

Laws and regulations—Endowments are governed by their corporate charters.

Banks

In order to fund their investment activities, banks must raise money by paying individuals and institutions for the privilege of using their money. The costs of raising funds are higher for banks than for insurance companies, pension funds, and endowment funds that deal essentially with cost-free funds.

Banks profit from the "spread" between the return earned on their funds and the cost of raising those funds from depositors. In the United States, a dual banking system permits banks to be chartered either federally or at the state level. At the federal level, banks are supervised by the Federal Reserve Board, the Office of the Comptroller of the Currency, and the Federal Deposit Insurance Corporation (FDIC). Historically, bank regulation has taken the following forms:

- Ceilings on the amount of interest that can be paid on deposit accounts.
- Geographical restrictions on branch banking.
- Permissible activities.
- Capital requirements.

Much of the bank legislation following the Great Depression aimed to create a safe banking system by limiting competition. The most recognized piece of legislation during this period is the Glass Steagall Act of 1933, which separated commercial and investment banking activities. However, during the 1970s, rising and more volatile interest rates reduced the flow of funds into the banking industry. In order to help banks and other depository institutions compete, several pieces of legislation were introduced in the early 1980s to address this problem. The Depository Institutions Deregulation and Monetary Control Act of 1980 (DIDMCA) deregulated the banking industry in an effort to allow depository institutions more flexibility in competing with nondepository financial institutions such as mutual funds. The Garn-St. Germain Depository Institutions Act of 1982 continued the deregulation process by giving thrift institutions expanded power in the types of activities they could engage in. In 1987, the Federal Reserve granted banks expanded powers with respect to securities activities as long as such activities contribute only 5 percent to the subsidiary's gross income. This percentage was later raised to 25 percent. These subsidiaries are known as Section 20 subsidiaries because they deal with a reinterpretation of Section 20 of the Glass Steagall Act. In 1999, Congress passed legislation effectively repealing the Glass Steagall Act.

Return requirement—Returns should generate a fair spread over the cost of funds.

Risk tolerance—Banks are meant to provide a safe haven for investors' funds and so should assume a low to moderate level of risk.

Liquidity—depends on the composition of a bank's deposits. A bank with a low percentage of demand deposits may have lower liquidity needs than a bank with a higher percentage of demand deposits.

Time horizon—Banks generally have a short time horizon.

Taxes— important because banks are subject to corporate income tax.

Laws and regulations—Banks are highly regulated by the Federal Reserve, the Office of the Comptroller of the Currency, and the FDIC.

Unique preferences and circumstances—depend on the size of the bank, its locality, the mix of its uncontrollable liabilities, and changes in government regulations.

The Client Relationship and Ethics

The relationship between an investment professional and a client goes beyond many other business relationships because of the fiduciary nature of the relationship. Brokers, for example, are governed by a "suitability" requirement, which means that their investment recommendations must be suitable for the client. The Association for Investment Management and Research (AIMR) provides a code of ethics and standards of professional conduct. Standard IV of the code deals with the relationship between the investment professional and the client. These guidelines (shown in Table 2-2) include investment professionals' responsibility to the profession, employers, clients, and the public. Many of the responsibilities include disclosures of conflicts that may bias the investment professional's objectivity. Accepting the code is a requirement for all AIMR members and chartered financial analyst (CFA) charterholders and candidates.

Table 2-2. Standard IV relationship with and responsibilities to clients and prospects.

A.   Investment Process

A.1   Reasonable Basis and Representation. Members shall:

    a. Exercise diligence and thoroughness in making investment recommendations or in taking investment actions.

    b. Have a reasonable and adequate basis, supported by appropriate research and investigation, for such recommendations or actions.

    c. Make reasonable and diligent efforts to avoid any material misrepresentation in any research report or investment recommendation.

    d. Maintain appropriate records to support the reasonableness of such recommendations or actions.

A.2   Research Reports. Members shall:

    a. Use reasonable judgment regarding the inclusion or exclusion of relevant factors in research reports.

    b. Distinguish between facts and opinions in research reports.

    c. Indicate the basic characteristics of the investment involved when preparing for public distribution a research report that is not directly related to a specific portfolio or client.

A.3   Independence and Objectivity. Members shall use reasonable care and judgment to achieve and maintain independence and objectivity in making investment recommendations or taking investment action.

B.   Interactions with Clients and Prospects

B.1   Fiduciary Duties. In relationships with clients, members shall use particular care in determining applicable fiduciary duty and shall comply with such duty as to those persons and interests to whom the duty is owed. Members must act for the benefit of their clients and place their clients' interests before their own. *continues*

Table 2-2. continued

B.2   Portfolio Investment Recommendations and Actions. Members shall:

   a. Make a reasonable inquiry into a client's financial situation, investment experience, and investment objectives prior to making any investment recommendations and shall update this information as necessary, but no less frequently than annually, to allow the members to adjust their investment recommendations to reflect changed circumstances.

   b. Consider the appropriateness and suitability of investment recommendations or actions for each portfolio or client. In determining appropriateness and suitability, members shall consider applicable relevant factors, including the needs and circumstances of the portfolio or client, the basic characteristics of the investment involved, and the basic characteristics of the total portfolio. Members shall not make a recommendation unless they reasonably determine that the recommendation is suitable to the client's financial situation, investment experience, and investment objectives.

   c. Distinguish between facts and opinions in the presentation of investment recommendations.

   d. Disclose to clients and prospects the basic format and general principles of the investment processes by which securities are selected and portfolios are constructed and shall promptly disclose to clients and prospects any changes that might significantly affect those processes.

B.3   Fair Dealing. Members shall deal fairly and objectively with all clients and prospects when disseminating investment recommendations, disseminating material changes in prior investment recommendations, and taking investment action.

B.4   Priority of Transactions. Transactions for clients and employers shall have priority over transactions in securities or other investments of which a member is the beneficial owner so that such personal transactions do not operate adversely to their clients' or employer's interests. If members make a recommendation regarding the purchase or sale of a security or other investment, they shall give their clients and employer adequate opportunity to act on their recommendations before acting on their own behalf. For purposes of the Code and Standards, a member is a "beneficial owner" if the member has

   a. a direct or indirect pecuniary interest in the securities;

   b. the power to vote or direct the voting of the shares of the securities or investments;

   c. the power to dispose or direct the disposition of the security or investment.

B.5   Preservation of Confidentiality. Members shall preserve the confidentiality of information communicated by clients, prospects, or employers concerning matters within the scope of the client-member, prospect-member, or employer-member relationship unless a member receives information concerning illegal activities on the part of the client, prospect, or employer.

B.6 Prohibition against Misrepresentation. Members shall not make any statements, orally or in writing, that misrepresent

    a. the services that they or their firms are capable of performing;

    b. their qualifications or the qualifications of their firm;

    c. the member's academic or professional credentials.

B.7 Members shall not make or imply, orally or in writing, any assurances or guarantees regarding any investment except to communicate accurate information regarding the terms of the investment instrument and the issuer's obligations under the instrument.

B.8 Disclosure of Conflicts to Clients and Prospects. Members shall disclose to their clients and prospects all matters, including beneficial ownership of securities or other investments, that reasonably could be expected to impair the members' ability to make unbiased and objective recommendations.

B.9 Disclosure of Referral Fees. Members shall disclose to clients and prospects any consideration or benefit received by the member or delivered to others for the recommendation of any services to the client or prospect.

Source: Standards of Practice Handbook 1996 (Charlottesville, Va. AIMR, 1996).

Summary

Establishing the needs and constraints of the client is the most important aspect of an investment advisor's relationship with the client. The needs and constraints for each client are unique and will change over time. Therefore, investment advisors must be prepared to establish long-term relationships with clients in order to help them reach their financial goals.

Selected Bibliography

Ambachtsheer, K. P., J. L. Maginn, and J. Vawter. "Determination of Portfolio Policies: Institutional Investors." In *Managing Investment Portfolios: A Dynamic Process,* eds. J. L. Maginn and D. L. Tuttle. Boston: Warren, Gorham and Lamont, 1990.

Jeffrey, R. H. "Tax Considerations in Investing." In *The Portable MBA in Investment,* ed. Peter L. Bernstein. New York: John Wiley, 1995.

Kaiser, R. W. "Individual Investors." In *Managing Investment Portfolios: A Dynamic Process,* eds. J. L. Maginn and D. L. Tuttle. Boston: Warren, Gorham and Lamont, 1990.

Kritzman, M. "Risk and Utility: Basics." In *Investment Management,* eds. P. L. Bernstein and A. Damodaran. New York: John Wiley, 1998.

Peavy, J. W., and K. F. Sherrerd. *Cases in Portfolio Management.* Charlottes-ville, Va.: Association for Investment Management Research, 1991).

Shefrin, H. *Beyond Greed and Fear: Understanding Behavioral Finance and the Psychology of Investing.* (Boston: Harvard Business School Press, 2000).

Notes

1. See D. B. Trone, W. R. Albright, and P. R. Taylor, *The Management of Investment Decisions.* (Homewood, Ill.: Irwin Professional Publishing, 1996), chap. 5.

2. See Peavy and Sherrerd.

3. See C. D. Ellis, *Investment Policy: How to Win the Loser's Game.* (Home-wood, Ill.: Dow Jones Irwin, 1985), 62.

4. R. W. Kaiser, "Individual Investors." In *Managing Investment Portfolios: A Dynamic Process,* eds. J. L. Maginn and D. L. Tuttle. (Boston: Warren, Gorham and Lamont. 1990.)

5. See Kaiser.

6. Risk aversion is sometimes misunderstood to imply that investors will always choose the safest investment. Risk aversion says that investors need to be rewarded for taking on risk and that, as their level of risk increases, they must receive proportionately greater rewards.

7. Shefrin provides a thorough review of behavioral finance.

8. See Jeffrey.

9. Individuals must begin withdrawing a minimum amount by April 1 of the following year they turn $70^1/2$.

10. For a simple review of the trusts described here, see "Worthy Trusts," *Wall Street Journal,* February 28, 2000, R16.

3

Asset Allocation and Portfolio Management

Once an investment policy statement is developed, it is the investment manager's job to create a portfolio that reflects the objectives and constraints laid out in the policy statement. Asset allocation deals with how the funds in the portfolio will be divided among the various asset classes. Asset allocation is an important component in determining not only the risk and return of the portfolio, but also the composition of those returns. Whether the returns take the form of dividends, interest, or capital gains, they will have both cash flow and tax consequences for the investor.

We begin our discussion by examining the risk and return for a portfolio of assets. First, we must examine the risk and return for the individual securities held in the portfolio and the relationship or correlation between the securities in the portfolio. Once we've gained an understanding of portfolio risk and return, we can begin to apply these tools to help investors formulate a sound investment strategy.

Risk and Return for Individual Securities

Return Calculations

Calculating the return for an asset is the starting point for analyzing the risk and return for a security. The simplest concept of return is the holding period return (HPR), which looks at the income generated by the security and the change in the security's price over the holding period. The holding period return can be computed as

$$\text{HPR} = \frac{E - B + I}{B}$$

where

E = ending price,

B = beginning price, and

I = income.

When we are interested in examining the rate of return over more than one time period, we can use either the *dollar-weighted return* or the *time-weighted return*. The dollar-weighted return or internal rate of return is the interest rate that makes the present value of the cash flows equal to the initial cost of the security.

$$\text{Cost} = \frac{CF_1}{(1+r)} + \frac{CF_2}{(1+r)^2} + \dots + \frac{CF_n}{(1+r)}$$

where

CF_i = cash flow in period i.

Solving for r gives us the dollar-weighted return, which measures the annual rate of return at which cumulative contributions grow. One problem with this method is that cash inflows and outflows are included in the calculation but are largely beyond the control of money managers. This makes the dollar-weighted return inappropriate for evaluating mutual fund managers.

Another measure used to compute return is the *time-weighted rate of return*. This measure does not account for the timing of cash flows and is therefore more appropriate for examining mutual fund returns. The time-weighted return can be computed as

$$TWR = \left[\prod_{i=1}^{n} (1 + HPR_i) \right]^{1/n} - 1$$

where

TWR = time-weighted return,

HPR_i = holding period return for year i, and

n = number of years in the measurement period.

Time-weighted rates of return are sometimes referred to as the *geometric return* or compound return. Geometric returns assume that all income from the security is reinvested and earning the same rate of return.

An alternative to the geometric return is the *arithmetic return*. The arithmetic return is simply the arithmetic average of the holding period returns. This can be computed by summing all holding period returns and dividing by the number of periods. When comparing the arithmetic return with the geometric return, we need to consider the following. First, the geometric mean takes into account the compounding of interest in its rate of return calculations, something that is not accounted for by the arithmetic mean. Second, the arithmetic mean will yield an incorrect return computation when the returns of the asset change from positive to negative. For example, suppose a $100 investment falls in value during year one to $50—a 50 percent decrease—and then rises back to $100 in year two—a 100 percent increase. The value of the investment has not changed, and the average rate of return is zero. However, the arithmetic average will give us an average rate of return of 25 percent over this two-year period (50% + 100%)/2 = 25%. Why does this occur? Simply because there is a change in the value at the beginning of the period. In the first period, the initial value was $100, so a $50 decrease represents a 50 percent change in the value of the asset. However, in the second period, the beginning value is now $50 and a $50 increase represents a 100 percent increase in the value of the asset.

Does this mean that the arithmetic return is inappropriate in financial analysis? No. When calculating an estimate of a future year's returns based on a random distribution of prior years' returns, we should use the arithmetic average.

Risk of an Individual Security

In an uncertain world, we need to be able to quantify the degree of uncertainty of our guesses. Standard financial theory uses the variance or standard deviation of the returns to measure how spread out the values are around the average or mean value. The greater the spread, the more uncertainty exists and, hence, greater risk. The standard deviation, which is sometimes used in place of the variance, is simply the square root of the variance and is used because it is in the same units as the return. The variance can be computed as

$$\text{Var} = \sum_{i=1}^{n} \frac{\left(R_i - \overline{R}\right)^2}{n-1}$$

where

Var = variance of the returns,

R_i = return in year i, and

$\overline{R}$ = mean or average return over the period.

The standard deviation can be computed as

$$\text{Standard deviation} = \sqrt{\text{variance}}$$

One problem with the use of the variance or standard deviation as a measure of risk is that it treats values above the mean the same way it treats values below the mean. In finance, returns above the mean are a good thing and really shouldn't be treated in the measurement of risk. Consider the probability density functions of two investments, A and B.

From Figure 3-1, we can see that the spread of the distribution of security B is greater than that of security A. However, only the shaded area represents risk to the investor. The greater spread in the distribution in the right tail of B represents potential reward for the investor. Several other measures of risk have been proposed as alternatives to the variance. Some analysts look at the possible upper and lower limits of possible returns. For example, XYZ Company has returns that are expected to range from −10 percent to +25 percent. One problem with this method is that it ignores the likelihood of the upper and lower values being reached. In the previous example, if there is only a 1 percent chance of losing 10 percent and a 95 percent chance of earning 25 percent, this asset may not be as risky as the range indicates.

Once the risks and returns for the individual securities are computed, we can find the risk and return for a portfolio of securities. One of the most important concepts of portfolio management is the concept of diversification. At its best, diversification allows an investor to reduce risk without sacrificing return. Diversification is sometimes stated as not putting all your eggs in one basket or spreading the risks of the portfolio over a number of different assets. This concept, although correct in principle, is too simplistic to really understand how diversification reduces risk. An investor can own numerous stocks, but if they are all in the same industry, the investor will see very little diversification benefit. For example, an investor who owns only Dell, Compaq, and Gateway is likely to receive less diversification benefit than if the investment had been spread over companies in different industries. Why? Because these three companies are all in the personal computer industry and their respective successes are determined in large part by the market

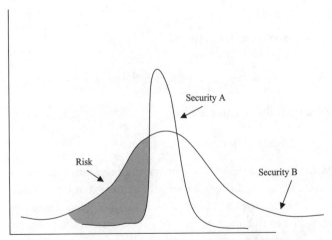

Figure 3-1. Distributions for security A and security B.

demand for personal computers. A dip in demand will affect all three negatively and a rise in demand will benefit all three. Because the price of all three stocks tends to move closely together, there will be only limited benefits of diversifying into all three stocks. Conversely, an investor who buys Dell, Ford, and General Electric will receive greater diversification benefits because only the fortunes of Dell are tied to the personal computer industry. Ford's success is determined by the demand for automobiles, a factor that probably has little effect on Dell and GE. In this case, we can say that movements in these stocks are not closely related.

When a number of securities are combined, the question becomes how to measure the risk and return for the entire portfolio.

Portfolio Risk and Return

Once the expected return and variance for the individual securities have been computed, the issue is how to find the risk and return for a portfolio of securities. The expected return for a portfolio of assets is simply the weighted average of the expected returns of the securities held in the portfolio. The weights used in the calculation are simply the percentages invested in each security.

$$\overline{R}_p = \sum_{i=1}^{n} w_i \times \overline{R}_i$$

where

$\overline{R}_p$ = portfolio expected return,

w_i = the percentage of the portfolio invested in asset i, and

$\overline{R}_i$ = the expected return of asset i.

Given that the expected return for a portfolio is computed as the weighted average of the expected returns of the securities in the portfolio, does this intuition extend to the computation of the variance of the portfolio? Unfortunately, the answer is no. When computing the risk of a portfolio, we need to consider both the risk of the individual assets as measured by the variance as well as the relationship between each pair of assets. This relationship can be measured by looking at the *covariance* or *correlation* between each pair of assets. Why is the relationship between each pair of securities so important? Because two risky assets may in fact have no risk when combined into a portfolio if they move in opposite directions. This negative correlation will reduce or eliminate the risk of the portfolio because losses in one asset will be exactly offset by gains in the other. Even when securities exhibit positive correlations, there will still be benefits from diversification if the relationship between the two securities is not perfect.

To estimate the relationship between two assets, we begin by computing the covariance. The covariance can be computed as

$$\text{Cov}(R_1, R_2) = \frac{\sum_{i=1}^{n}\left[\left(R_{1i} - \overline{R}_1\right)\left(R_{2i} - \overline{R}_2\right)\right]}{n-1}$$

When we examine the covariance between two assets, we are interested in only the sign of the covariance. A positive covariance indicates that the two assets tend to move in the same direction. That is, when security A has a value above its mean, security B will tend to have a value above its mean. Likewise, when security A has a value below its mean, security B will tend to have a value below its mean. In other words, when A is performing above average, usually B is also performing above average. When the covariance is negative, the two assets tend to move in opposite directions. That is, when security A has a value above its mean, security B will tend to have a value below its mean. Likewise, when security A has a value below its mean, security B will tend to have a value above its mean. A covariance that is equal to zero indicates no linear relationship between the two assets.

One problem with the covariance is that it cannot be used to compare the degree of association between different pairs of assets. For example, if the correlation between Stocks A and B is +10 and the correlation between Stocks C and D is +100, we have no way of knowing which pair of assets has a stronger positive relationship. To make an appropriate comparison, we compute a "normalized" covariance, known as the correlation. The correlation will have a value between −1 and +1. A correlation of +1 indicates perfect positive correlation. That is, as stock A goes up, stock B will also go up and always in the same proportion. A correlation of −1 indicates perfect negative correlation. That is, as stock A goes up, stock B will go down and always in the same proportion. The correlation can be computed as follows.

$$\text{Corr}(R_1, R_2) = \frac{\text{Cov}(R_1, R_2)}{\text{Std. Dev. }(R_1) \times \text{Std. Dev. }(R_2)}$$

In the real world, it is rare to find two securities that exhibit either perfect positive or perfect negative correlation. In fact, in most cases, the correlation between pairs of assets will be positive. Even when assets display a positive degree of correlation, there will still be benefits from diversifying into both assets. However, the lower the degree of correlation between two assets, the greater the diversification benefit.

The variance for a portfolio of two securities can be computed as follows

$$Var(R_p) = w_1^2\sigma_1^2 + w_2^2\sigma_2^2 + 2w_1w_2\sigma_{1,2}$$

$$Var(R_p) = w_1^2\sigma_1^2 + w_2^2\sigma_2^2 + 2w_1w_2\rho_{12}\sigma_1\sigma_2$$

where

σ_p^2 = variance of the portfolio,

σ_i^2 = variance of stock i,

$\sigma_{1,2}$ = covariance between stocks 1 and 2, and

$\rho_{1,2}$ = correlation between stocks 1 and 2.

The variance of the portfolio has two parts. The first part, represented by the first two terms following the equal sign, consists of the risks of the individual assets in the portfolio. The second part of the portfolio's variance measures the degree of association between the two assets (covariance or correlation), which measures the diversification benefit. The weaker the association between the two assets, the greater the diversification benefit. Therefore, one of the rules of portfolio management is to seek securities that are not strongly correlated with one another.

Another aspect of diversification deals with the relative importance of the covariance between each pair of assets relative to the variance of each individual security. A portfolio of two stocks has two variance terms and one (different) covariance term. However, as the number of securities in the portfolio increases, the number of different covariance terms will increase at a faster rate than the number of variance terms. For example, a five-stock portfolio will have five variance terms (one for each stock) and ten covariance terms. This makes covariance more important to the risk of the portfolio than the individual risks of each security. A 100-stock portfolio will have 4,950 different covariance terms. The notion of portfolio theory is that you can diversify away the risk of individual securities (variance of each security), but you can't eliminate the covariance risk. This covariance risk is the average covariance between each pair of assets in the portfolio.

Covariance or correlation is pivotal in examining the risk of a portfolio of assets. Let's consider a two-stock case. If stocks A and B are perfectly positively correlated, there will be no benefits from diversification because the two securities move in lock step and therefore behave as one security. You wouldn't expect any diversification benefits from owning two shares of Microsoft rather than one because they are perfectly positively correlated; that is, when the price of one share rises, you know exactly how much the price of the second share will rise. On the other hand, if stock A and stock B are perfectly negatively correlated, the full diversification benefit of owning both securities will be felt. In fact, when the proportions are chosen correctly, it is possible to produce a portfolio of two risky assets that are perfectly negatively correlated that is riskless.[1]

The real world rarely presents the two extreme cases discussed above of perfect positive correlation and perfect negative correlation. Nearly all cases will lie somewhere in between, giving the portfolio some but not total diversification benefits. The graph below illustrates this point.

From Figure 3-2, we can see that when stocks A and B are perfectly positively correlated, there are no benefits from diversification because the risk-return tradeoff is an upward sloping line. When stocks A and B are perfectly negatively correlated, the line bends backward and touches the y-axis, which indicates the possibility of creating a riskless portfolio. Finally, when the correlation is between −1 and +1—for example, zero—the curve bends backward, giving some diversification benefits, but does not touch the y-axis. A backward bending of the curve indicates a greater expected return at a lower level of risk.

Examining the risk-return relationship for different possible portfolios allows elimination of many of the possible combinations because they are *inefficient.* When we speak of *efficient portfolios,* we mean portfolios that

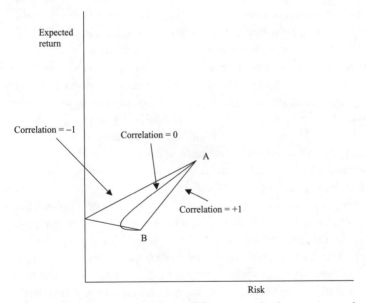

Figure 3-2. The risk-return tradeoff for two stocks that are positively correlated, negatively correlated, and have zero correlation.

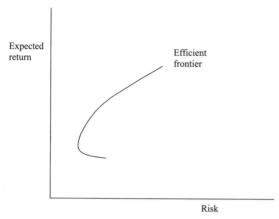

Figure 3-3. The efficient frontier.

either provide the highest expected return for a given level of risk or present the lowest risk for a given level of return.

The efficient portfolios can be graphed in risk return space to create what is known as the *efficient frontier.* Figure 3-3 presents a graph of the efficient frontier.

The efficient frontier tells us what portfolios we should consider when investing, but not which portfolio is optimal. The choice of a best portfolio depends on an investor's risk and return preferences. However, when a risk-less interest rate is introduced that investors can borrow and lend at, the optimal portfolio is the one where a line from the riskless interest rate is just tangent to the efficient frontier. This portfolio has come to be known as the market portfolio because it consists of all risky assets available to the market, held in their market value proportions. The line tangent to the efficient frontier is known as the *capital market line* (CML), which shows the tradeoff between expected return and total risk for a portfolio consisting of money in the riskless asset and risky portfolio M.[2] Figure 3-4 presents a graph of the capital market line.

An interesting insight that can be drawn from the capital market line is that there is only one "best" portfolio. Investors who are more conservative will place a portion of their wealth in the risk-free asset and purchase some of risky portfolio M. More aggressive investors will place 100 percent of their wealth in risky portfolio M or may actually choose to borrow so they can invest additional funds in M. The conclusion of the theoretical model presented here also has a real world implication—simply that the best portfolio will be a broad-based index fund like the Wilshire 5000. Investors can adjust the amount of risk they wish to take by lending some of their funds (pur-

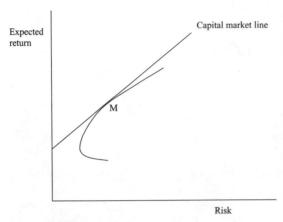

Figure 3-4. The capital market line.

chasing Treasury securities) or borrowing additional funds (purchasing on margin).

The key to successful portfolio management is to combine these theoretical issues of portfolio optimization with an investor's objectives and constraints and current economic forecasts in order to create an appropriate asset allocation for the investor.

Strategic and Tactical Asset Allocation

Asset allocation is arguably the most important decision an investor will make. How an investor's assets are allocated among the various classes of investment vehicles will determine not only the risks the investor faces, but the composition of returns (income versus capital gains), which in turn can affect tax liabilities.

An easy way to view asset allocation is to consider an investor's assets as one large pie. The issue in asset allocation is how the pie should be divided among the different asset classes. As discussed in Chapter 2, establishing the objectives and constraints of the client is the first step in the portfolio management process. Once the investment policy statement has been established, an asset allocation recommendation can be made. The asset allocation decision can be broken into two parts. The long-run decision is determined by the investment policy statement and is referred to as the strategic asset allocation decision. The strategic decision determines the allocation of the policy portfolio. The short-run decision is referred to as tactical asset allocation. Tactical asset allocation refers to deviations from the policy portfolio.

Good asset allocation requires the manager to continually monitor conditions and adjust both the strategic and tactical asset allocation decisions. The strategic and tactical asset allocation decisions can be viewed as a feedback loop.

As shown in Figure 3-5, two sets of inputs affect the asset allocation decision. The boxes on the left-hand side of the figure deal with the capital markets, whereas the boxes on the right-hand side deal with investor preferences. Investor preferences and circumstances can be established by creating an investment policy statement. Once forecasts for security returns and investor preferences are established, the information is fed into M1, an optimizer to determine the correct allocation for the investor. The optimizer can search for the best portfolios given the investor's constraints. The optimizer in essence seeks to generate the previously discussed efficient frontier and finds the opti-

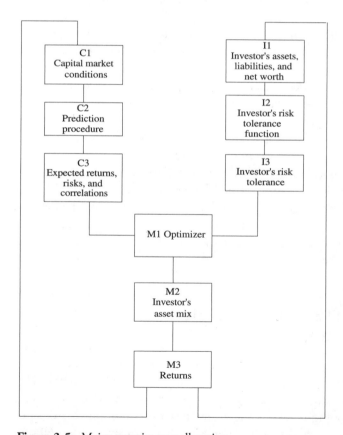

Figure 3-5. Major steps in asset allocation.
Source: W. F. Sharpe, "Asset Allocation," in *Managing Investment Portfolios,* J. L. Maginn and D. L. Tuttle, eds. (Charlottesville, Va.: AIMR), 1990.

mal portfolio given the investor's preferences. Box M3 shows actual returns that are earned by the investor. These returns are used to establish the investor's new financial position I1 and future forecasts of capital market conditions. This information is then fed back into the optimizer in order to determine if any adjustments need to be made to ensure that the investor is holding the optimal portfolio.

The asset allocation decision can be broken into the strategic and tactical decisions. Let's consider how the strategic asset allocation differs from the major steps in the asset allocation decision. Strategic asset allocation uses long-term capital market conditions, and so changes in capital market conditions from period to period are not necessary for predictions. Therefore, box C2, the prediction procedure that links boxes C1 and C3, is omitted. Also, it is assumed that the investor's risk tolerance function given in box I2 does not change even if the investor's risk tolerance does change, so box I2 also is omitted.

Tactical asset allocation is done on a more routine basis, and its goal is to take advantage of perceived inefficiencies in the relative prices of securities. The box C2 prediction procedure is now added to the picture. The prediction procedure is used to make adjustments to the policy portfolio to take advantage of relative mispricings. For example, a portfolio with 50 percent in large-cap stocks and 15 percent in small-cap stocks may choose to adjust this weighting in favor of small-cap stocks if the analyst believes small-cap stocks will outperform large-cap stocks in the short run.

Tactical asset allocation is not without costs. First, the analyst's forecast of future capital market conditions could be wrong. Second, the decision to make changes to the policy portfolio allocation will depend on the benefits and the costs of rebalancing the portfolio. These costs include transaction costs and tax consequences as well as the hidden costs of trading discussed in Chapter 6. However, if the analyst is correct, the investor may benefit from greater returns and perhaps even lower risk.

Dynamic Asset Allocation and Portfolio Insurance

Dynamic asset allocation seeks to adjust the mix of assets in the portfolio in an effort to maximize the return on the portfolio. There are three methods for portfolio asset allocation.[3] In a *buy and hold strategy*, the investor decides on an allocation for the portfolio and maintains that allocation regardless of what happens in the market. For example, an investor may choose a 60 percent stock, 40 percent bond allocation for the portfolio. As stock prices change relative to bond prices, the allocation will move away from the original 60/40 mix. This strategy is sometimes referred to as a *drifting mix strategy*, because the investor does not rebalance the portfolio to return to the designated allocation.

The buy and hold strategy has several advantages. First, because an investor does not choose to buy and sell stocks, transactions costs and possible capital gains tax liability are reduced. Second, by leaving the portfolio intact, he eliminates the mistakes that would be made by buying and selling securities at the wrong times. One disadvantage of the buy and hold strategy is that the investor's portfolio allocation may become overly weighted in stocks if the market is rising or under weighted in stocks if the market is falling. This "do nothing" strategy may cause the investor to move away from the original risk-return objectives.

In a *constant mix strategy*, the investor decides on an allocation for the portfolio and rebalances the portfolio periodically to maintain these proportions. For example, an investor with $100 to invest who places $60 in stocks and $40 in bonds (a 60/40 mix), will sell stocks if stock prices rise and use the proceeds to purchase bonds in order to maintain the 60/40 mix. Likewise, the investor will sell bonds and use the proceeds to purchase stocks if stock prices fall. The constant mix strategy has an investor selling as stock prices rise and buying as stock prices fall.

The advantage of a constant mix strategy is that it imposes a discipline on the investor to sell stocks as the market rises and buy stocks as the market falls. One disadvantage of this strategy is that it can lead to increased transactions costs and tax liabilities in volatile markets.

In a *constant proportion strategy*, the investor determines the amount to invest in stocks based on the following formula,

$$\text{Dollars in stocks} = m(\text{Assets} - \text{Floor})$$

To implement the strategy, the investor sets the multiplier, m, and the floor. Strategies with a multiplier greater than one are referred to as *constant proportion portfolio insurance strategies* (CPPI). In this strategy, as stock prices fall and the value of assets shrinks, the investor will reduce holdings in stocks and increase holdings in bonds. Similarly, as stock prices rise and the value of assets increases, the investor will increase holdings of stocks. Therefore, CPPI has investors buying into a rising market and selling as the market falls.

The purpose of CPPI is to protect the portfolio on the downside by reducing stock exposure as stock prices fall, while still maintaining upside potential by forcing the investor to add to his or her stock position as the market rises. In essence, the CPPI strategy creates a *synthetic call option*—that is, a strategy that has limited downside risk but still retains the opportunity to profit if prices rise.[4]

Which strategy performs the best depends on the direction and volatility of the market.[5] In a flat but oscillating market (one that goes up and down but finishes near its starting point), a constant mix strategy will prevail because it forces investors to sell stocks when they are high and buy them back as stock prices fall. In the absence of taxes and transactions costs, maintaining this mix will increase the number of shares held by the investor. However, this type of market can be devastating to the CPPI strategy because it forces investors to sell stocks when they are low and repurchase them after they have rebounded. The buy and hold strategy will perform somewhere in between the constant mix and CPPI strategies.

In a bull market where reversals are uncommon, the constant mix strategy will have the worst performance because it forces investors to sell stocks as the market is rising, only to see stocks rise further. The CPPI strategy will perform the best in a bull market because it forces the investor to increase the amount of stocks held in the portfolio as the market rises. Once again, the performance of the buy and hold strategy will lie somewhere between the other two strategies.

Finally, if the market continues in a downward spiral, CPPI will perform the best because it forces investors to bail out of stocks as stock prices fall. The constant mix strategy will have the worst performance because it forces investors to buy stocks as prices are falling, only to see the prices fall even further.

Global Asset Allocation

In recent years, investment professionals have begun recommending that investors place some portion of their wealth in international securities. The logic of this recommendation is that additional diversification benefits may be derived from investing abroad since studies have found a relatively low degree of correlation between U.S. and overseas securities. What does this mean? The efficient frontier, discussed previously, will move back to the northwest, which indicates that investors will receive a higher return for a given level of risk than they would by simply investing domestically. Figure 3-6 illustrates the benefits of international diversification and the risk and return tradeoff for different combinations of U.S. and international stocks.

A 100 percent investment in international stocks has a standard deviation of 21.5 percent, whereas a 100 percent investment in U.S. stocks has a standard deviation of 16.2 percent. The interesting point of this figure is that by adding riskier international stocks to a U.S. stock portfolio actually reduces the risk the investor faces. This can be seen by the backward bend in the efficient frontier. Based on the portfolio analysis discussed previously in this

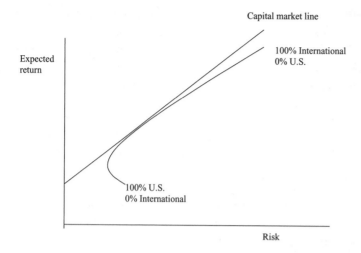

	Risk (%)	Return (%)	International (%)
US	16.2	13.0	0.0
International	21.5	14.7	100.0
Minimum Risk	15.4	13.4	24.9
Efficient Portfolio	15.7	13.7	38.9

Figure 3-6. International diversification
Source: J. J. Siegel, *Stocks for the Long Run.* (New York: McGraw-Hill, 1998), 133.

chapter, the lowest risk portfolio would be a combination of 38.9 percent international stocks and 61.1 percent U.S. stocks.

When investing internationally, investors need to consider several factors:

- Security performance in other countries.
- Possible changes in the exchange rate.
- Should the manager hedge the exchange rate?
- The degree of correlation between the foreign country's securities and U.S. securities.
- The political risks.
- Differing monetary policies, which can impact inflation and interest rates.
- The higher transactions costs that are likely to occur from overseas investing.
- Difficulties in obtaining data.
- Different accounting standards.
- Differing settlement procedures.

When considering investments in foreign countries, it is essential to examine currency exchange rates. An appreciation of the dollar relative to the foreign currency will lead to a lower dollar denominated return because the investor will receive fewer dollars when converting the foreign currency back to dollars. Likewise, a depreciating dollar can enhance dollar returns as an investor receives more dollars when converting the foreign currency back to dollars.

There are several points of view regarding the currency decision. Some financial analysts believe that the expected return to a portfolio of currencies should in the long run be equal to zero, making hedging unnecessary. Others believe that the low degree of correlation between currency returns and foreign market returns makes hedging detrimental because it reduces some of the diversification benefits of holding the foreign currency. Still others argue that, while foreign currency exposure leads to diversification benefits, it also introduces risk into the picture.[6] Money manager and author, Mark Kritzman, argues that the decision depends on the degree of correlation between the foreign asset returns and the exchange rate return. When the correlation is zero, Kritzman maintains that the optimal strategy is to remain unhedged, and when the correlation is 75 percent, then the optimal strategy is to be fully hedged. Kritzman's analysis shows that a high degree of correlation between the foreign asset's returns and the exchange rate produces no diversification benefits from remaining unhedged. Therefore, hedging should be employed. However, when the degree of correlation is relatively low, investors receive greater diversification benefits by remaining unhedged.

How should the market selection and currency decision be treated? When there is no practical forward exchange market, then the two decisions need to be considered jointly. However, when a forward exchange market does exist, the foreign investment decision should be separated into the market decision and the currency decision.[7] The decision to invest in a foreign country is based on the risk premium offered in that country regardless of the country of the investor. Once the market decision has been made, the decision whether to hedge is determined by a simple comparison of the forward return compared to the expected percentage change in exchange rates. If the forward return is greater than the expected change in exchange rates, then it is advantageous to hedge. If the forward return is less than the expected change in exchange rates, then the investor will receive a higher return by remaining unhedged.

Investors will invest in the country that offers the greatest risk premium. The currency decision is then based on hedging into the currency that offers the greatest potential.

Emerging Markets

When considering diversification into international markets, investors usually treat investments in developed nations differently from those in developing or emerging markets. Emerging markets can represent excellent opportunities for investing and can add diversification to an investor's portfolio. One difficulty with investing in emerging markets is that no accepted definition of an emerging market exists. In general, emerging markets are developing countries that offer the kind of growth and change that represent investment opportunities. The World Bank defines a developing country as one with per capita income of less than US$8,626. However, of the 170 economies that fall into this category, only a handful can be considered emerging. For a country to attract the capital of foreign investors, it must be investable. The International Finance Corporation (IFC) includes the stocks of twenty-six countries in its Emerging Markets Data Base (EMDB), of which twenty-five are in its investable index.

Several factors make emerging markets investing attractive. The first is the growth potential offered by industries in these countries. Second, emerging markets tend to exhibit a low degree of correlation with developed nations and thus provide diversification benefits in addition to growth opportunities. Third, emerging market countries tend to exhibit a low degree of correlation with other emerging market countries, so a well-diversified portfolio of emerging markets securities may not be as inherently risky as one would believe.

A number of factors make investments in emerging markets more risky than investments in developed nations. First, because of the immaturity of these types of markets we can expect greater volatility. In addition, many investors tend to incorrectly link all emerging markets together; thus, a crisis in one emerging country can spread quickly to another even when the crisis tends to be a local problem. A third risk with investing in emerging markets deals with liquidity. Many of these markets are not highly liquid, and therefore buying and selling significant numbers of shares can be difficult and costly. Fourth, clearing and settlement procedures may not be well established in these markets. Fifth, there may be political risks involved in these countries. Finally, currency fluctuations can add additional risks to emerging markets investments. As discussed in the previous section, if no practical forward exchange market exists, then the market and currency decisions need to be made jointly.

After-Tax Asset Allocation

Most of the research on using the mean and variance to find optimal port-folios assumes that there are no taxes. For institutional investors, this may be a reasonable assumption, and the solutions to the optimization problem may lead to an appropriate allocation. However, for individual clients, who face federal and state income taxes, reaching the optimal portfolio may not be possible without incurring large taxes. It may seem reasonable to simply adjust the pre-tax portfolios to an after-tax basis in order to find the optimal portfolio; however, this procedure cannot be used. Rebalancing a portfolio to provide the optimal combination of risk and return may require the investor to sell some low cost basis securities, thus kicking off capital gains taxes.

The appropriate procedure is to incorporate taxes into the optimization process, given an investor's needs and constraints. Given an investor's time horizon, it may be beneficial to adjust the portfolio over an extended period of time, thus postponing the realization of much of the capital gains. In cases where the investor is still accumulating assets, a shift in the dollar contributions may allow the investor to move toward the optimal portfolio without incurring large capital gains taxes. When an investor has a short life expectancy, postponing the realization of capital gains until the death of the owner allows for a step up in basis, thus avoiding capital gains altogether.

One important factor that investment advisors need to realize is that, once taxes are factored into the equation, it may be optimal for clients to hold portfolios that are riskier than would be the case in a tax-free environment. Holding the riskier portfolio may be necessary in order to postpone the realization of capital gains. This may not be as great a problem as it appears; taxes actually reduce portfolio risk because the government shares in both the gains and losses of the investor.

Other Considerations

Once a reasonable stock/bond/cash allocation has been determined, the investor needs to consider other factors such as taxes, defined benefit pension plans, and social security.[8] For example, suppose an individual would like to have an allocation of 60 percent stocks and 40 percent bonds. If the investor has $60,000 in a 401(k) retirement plan and $40,000 in a taxable bond account, it would appear that the allocation is correct. However, if the bond account has little or no unrealized capital gains, this investor's allocation actually might be 50 percent bonds and 50 percent stocks once taxes are taken into consideration. A third or more of the value of this investor's 401(k) account might be lost to federal and state taxes, thus taking the after-tax value down to $40,000. In this case, the investor will have a smaller allocation to equities than desired.

Another often-overlooked factor is the impact of a defined benefit pension plan and social security on an investor's allocation. Both behave like bonds because they provide a stream of payments to the recipient. Once again, failing to account for these factors may lead to a misallocation of funds. In this case, investment professionals can assist clients by estimating the after-tax present value of the benefits. Estimates would be based on the life expectancy of the recipient, a reasonable interest rate, and an adjustment for taxes. For example, if a retiree expects to receive from his pension plan $25,000 per year after taxes for twenty years, the factor for determining the present value of this stream of payments at an interest rate of 8 percent is 9.8181. Therefore, the present value of this annuity is approximately $245,000. Accounting for this as a bond may encourage this investor to adjust his 401(k) allocation to hold a higher percentage of stocks. A similar calculation can be done for the expected social security benefit.

Summary

Asset allocation and portfolio management changed significantly during the twentieth century. In the first half of the century, no formal method for asset allocation and portfolio formation existed. Portfolios of this era were most likely a hodgepodge of fixed income investments such as savings and war bonds, with a few stocks added to the mix. In the 1950s, a graduate student, Harry Markowitz changed the course of portfolio management by introducing a formal method for evaluating the risks of asset portfolios. His work led to what is now known as modern finance theory, in which there is one optimal portfolio for all investors. Markowitz's most significant contribution to the portfolio management process is the understanding that portfolio risk is driven more by the correlation between assets in the portfolio and less by the risks of individual assets.

Recently, there has been a movement away from the one-size-fits-all approach to investing. Beginning with the investment policy statement discussed in Chapter 2, investment professionals are realizing that the optimal portfolio depends on the objectives and constraints of their clients.

One significant change that has occurred in the field of portfolio management is the recognition of the importance of diversifying across international markets. The success of the Japanese stock market through the early 1980s as well as the globalization of world financial markets has increased investor awareness of the benefits of global diversification. More recently, investors have begun moving beyond investment in developed countries to emerging markets. Because of their low degree of correlation to the U.S. markets, emerging markets investments can add the proverbial free lunch of added returns and less risk to a well-chosen portfolio.

Taxes remain another important issue that investment advisors should consider in their analyses. Incorporating tax consequences into an investment policy may require that investment professionals to advise clients to diversify over an extended period of time, thus postponing the realization of capital gains. In addition, if a portion of an individual's funds are in tax-deferred accounts such as IRAs or 401(k)s, an adjustment should be made for the after-tax amount of funds in the account in order to determine an appropriate asset allocation.

Selected Bibliography

Arnott, R. "Active Asset Allocation." In *Investment Management,* eds. P. L. Bernstein and A. Damodaran. New York: John Wiley, 1998, 162–182.

Balzer, L. A. "Measuring Investment Risk: A Review." *Journal of Investing* 4:3 (Fall 1995): 5–16.

Barry, C. B., J. W. Peavy, and M. Rodriguez. *Emerging Stock Markets: Risk, Return and Performance.* Charlottesville, Va.: Research Foundation of the Institute for Chartered Financial Analysts.

Brinson, G. P. "Global Management and Asset Allocation." In *Investment Management,* eds. P. L. Bernstein and A. Damodaran. New York: John Wiley, 1998, 117–161.

Jacob, N. L. "After-Tax Asset Allocation." In *Investment Counseling for Private Clients.* Charlottesville, Va.: Association for Investment Management Research, 1999.

Kritzman, M. *The Portable Financial Analyst: What Practitioners Need to Know.* New York: McGraw-Hill, 1995.

Luskin, D. ed. *Portfolio Insurance: A Guide to Dynamic Hedging.* New York: John Wiley, 1988.

Perold, A. F. and W. F. Sharpe. "Dynamic Strategies for Asset Allocation." *Financial Analysts Journal* 44 (January/February 1988): 16–27.

Sharpe, W. F. "Asset Allocation." In *Managing Investment Portfolios: A Dynamic Process,* eds. J. L. Maginn and D. L. Tuttle. Boston: Warren, Gorham and Lamont. 1990.

Singer, B. D. and D. S. Karnosky. "The General Framework for Global Investment Management and Performance Attribution." *Journal of Portfolio Management* 21 (Winter 1995): 84–92.

Steward, C. B. and J. H. Lynch. "International Bond Portfolio Management." In *Managing Fixed Income Portfolios.* New Hope, Penn.: Frank J. Fabozzi Associates, 1997.

Notes

1. For a portfolio consisting of two perfectly negatively correlated securities, the weight in the first security is given as

$$w_1 = \frac{\sigma_2}{\sigma_1 + \sigma_2}$$

2. The equation for the capital market line is

$$\overline{R}_p = R_f + \left[\frac{\overline{R}_m - R_f}{\sigma_m}\right]\sigma_p$$

3. A. F. Perold and W. F. Sharpe, "Dynamic Strategies for Asset Allocation," *Financial Analysts Journal* (January/February 1988): 16–27.

4. This is exactly the profit opportunity of a long position in a call option. A complete discussion of option payoffs can be found in Chapter 15.

5. This analysis assumes that there are no taxes or transactions costs.

6. M. Kritzman, *The Portable Financial Analyst: What Practitioners Need to Know.* (New York: McGraw-Hill, 1995), chap. 21.

7. B. D. Singer and D. S. Karnosky, "The General Framework for Global Investment Management and Performance Attribution." *Journal of Portfolio Management* (Winter 1995): 84–92.

8. J. Clements, "Figuring Asset Mix? Avoid Mix-Ups," *Wall Street Journal,* November 23, 1999, C1.

4

Securities Issuing Process and SEC Registration

Investments in initial public offerings (IPOs) can be extremely rewarding. Many high profile IPOs including Netscape, Ebay, and Martha Stewart Omnimedia, saw the value of their shares soar on the opening day of trading. An understanding of the process of issuing securities can be valuable for investment professionals to assist clients in evaluating the potential risks and rewards from investing in an IPO.

A public security issue is subject to a stringent process. Investment banks purchase the new security and distribute it to investors. The lead manager runs the book. Other houses could participate as members of the underwriting syndicate or the selling group. Investment banks earn billions of dollars each year by underwriting new securities. However, increased competition certainly pressures underwriters for lower fees. Successful investment bankers need to have a strong perception of client capabilities and financial position and a keen awareness of market conditions. This chapter covers the major aspects in underwriting, including the mechanics and process, pricing, underwriter risks and compensation, and aftermarket trading. The chapter also covers expenses associated with an offering and alternative types of offerings.

Market Overview

The new issue market includes initial public offerings and secondary offerings. Major investment banking houses engaged in equities underwriting include Morgan Stanley Dean Witter, Salomon Smith Barney, Merrill Lynch, Goldman Sachs, Credit Suisse First Boston, Lehman Brothers, J. P. Morgan, Bear Stearns, Chase Hambrecht & Quist, Donaldson Lufkin Jenrette, BT Alex Brown, and SBC Warburg Dillon Read. There are also many boutique houses.

In a public offering, the Securities Act of 1933 requires the lead manager to conduct due diligence research. The lead manager must prepare a registration statement to begin the Securities and Exchange Commission (SEC) registration process. This is done in close coordination with the company, accountant, and counsel. Supporting documents such as the underwriting agreement, legal documents, and financial data are made available to the public at SEC offices. The day the investment bank turns in the registration statement with the SEC is the filing date. The amendments to the registration statement, if so required, are submitted to the SEC again. If there are no further changes, registration becomes effective. In addition, if certain conditions are met, the issuer may file for *Shelf Registration* (Rule 415), which allows issuers to register securities they expect to sell within two years; with as little as twenty-four hours notice to the SEC.

Two types of agreements can exist between the issuing company and the underwriter. The first type is the *firm commitment*, in which the investment bank agrees to purchase the entire issue and re-offer to the general public. The second type is known as a *best-efforts agreement*, in which the investment bank agrees to sell the securities but does not guarantee the price.

Other steps also take place during the registration process.[1] The red herring (preliminary prospectus) is printed and distributed. The stock certificates are printed, and the listing exchange and transfer agent are selected. The lead manager forms the underwriting group and promotes the issue in a road show.

After the issue goes public, the lead manager assures sufficient liquidity in the aftermarket by making a market after the underwriting period. A public company is subject to the SEC disclosure requirements, including regular filings of financial data and timely disclosure of material information. The company is also required to send quarterly and annual financial statements to shareholders.

The basic process described above is applicable to both IPOs and secondary offerings. There are, however, some basic differences between IPOs and secondary offerings. First of all, the motivations are often quite different. The purposes of an IPO are to raise capital and to gain future access to the financial markets. A secondary offering, on the other hand, aims at raising capital as a source of ongoing financing. Second, IPOs are typically smaller but more lucrative for underwriters. The stock market responses are more dramatic for IPOs. Share price in an IPO generally surges while a secondary offering remains flat or declines. In addition, the process for a secondary offering is faster because many of the steps are already in place.

The IPO Team

Once the decision to float a new security has been made, the next step is to assemble the IPO team. The team consists of the management and company's legal counsel, the underwriter and its legal counsel, independent accountants, financial consultants and advisors, and in some cases a financial public relations firm.

The quality of the management team is one of the most important factors in a successful offering. A quality management team should be able to foster growth and establish a leadership position in the market, adding credibility to the management's role. A good board of directors comprised of highly regarded business people who can provide objective input is a big plus in an offering.

The selection of an underwriter is important because the investment banker is responsible for setting up the underwriting syndicate to sell the security. Management should begin building an underwriter relationship long before the offering. Usually a company selects one investment bank as the lead underwriter or syndicate manager. The underwriter will typically form a syndicate to underwrite and distribute the issue. When a company selects an underwriter, it considers reputation, experience, distribution, market making capabilities, fees, research support, and after-offering services. The underwriter will perform a preliminary investigation of the company to decide whether to undertake the offering. If satisfied, the investment banker and the company will discuss the type of security to be offered—firm commitment or best efforts underwriting—the range of offering price, and the number of shares to be offered. Then the investment bank issues the letter of intent to formalize the arrangement, which will later lead to the underwriting agreement. Important to note here is that the letter of intent signals the beginning of the quiet period (or silence period), during which the company is subject to SEC guidelines on publication of information outside of the prospectus.

Accountants are a key figure in the process of going public. Much of the financial information contained in the registration statement is obtained from the audited financial statements. SEC regulations require the independent public accountant to certify the financial statements and to examine other information included in the registration statement. The accountants also assist in responding to SEC comments on accounting issues and issue a comfort letter to the underwriters. Comfort letters from accountants expressing assurance on interim financial statements are generally issued to the underwriters on the effective date, followed by an updated letter at the closing date.

A consultant or advisor is sometimes retained on a dedicated basis for a specific task. A knowledgeable consultant can be very helpful in starting a company off on the right foot in the offering process, providing support services, from finding a suitable underwriter to making timely proper filings with the SEC. The best advisors are those who have had extensive experience in the area.

Attorneys are retained to advise on compliance with the securities laws during and after the registration process. In addition, attorneys usually conduct due diligence matters such as reviewing minutes of the board and shareholder meetings, reviewing articles of incorporation, contracts and leases, and the ownership status of major assets. They also coordinate the efforts of other members, resolve any questions arising from SEC comments, and file the necessary amendments. The attorney's competence and experience with the registration process are critical to the timely and effective coordination of the complex process.

Another important member of the IPO team is the financial printer, who is responsible for printing the prospectus and the registration statement according to the SEC format and guidelines. Bankers, attorneys, and accountants are able to recommend financial printers. For example, Manhattan-based Browne & Co. is a leading financial printer.

Sometimes an IPO company might use the services of a financial public relations firm. A PR firm experienced in SEC registrations can often help guide the company through the restrictions of the quiet period and help prepare materials for road shows. A good PR firm can also help in developing a list of analysts and business press editors who follow the industry and provide them with news releases and information about the company.

Finally, a transfer agent should be selected. The transfer agent provides services beyond that of simply transferring stock and recording the transaction. The transfer agent must report to the IRS when dividends are paid and also provide a complete mailing service for sending out reports, proxy statements, and meeting notices to shareholders.

Mechanics and Process

It usually takes at least several months to complete the public offering process. The length of time needed depends on the readiness of the company, the availability of information required in the registration statement, and market conditions. The silence period typically begins once the company reaches a preliminary understanding with the underwriter and ends twenty-five days after the offering becomes effective if the security is listed on an exchange or quoted on NASDAQ. Otherwise it ends ninety days after the effective date. The process includes filing the registration statement, the SEC letter of comments, preparing the amended registration statement, preparing the red herring (preliminary prospectus), conducting road shows, performing due diligence research, negotiating price amendment and signing the underwriting agreement, and closing.

Registration Statement

The SEC registration forms commonly used are Form S-1 and Form SB-2. In general, the same things must be disclosed in SB-2 as in S-1, but SB-2 requires far fewer details.

Form S-1 requires the most extensive disclosure, and hence it will be illustrated here. Major items required in Part I and Part II of Form S-1 are as follows:

Part I

1. Forepart of the Registration Statement and Outside Front Cover Page of Prospectus
2. Inside Front and Outside Back Cover Pages of Prospectus
3. Summary Information, Risk Factors, and Ratio of Earnings to Fixed Charges
4. Use of Proceeds
5. Determination of Offering Price
6. Dilution
7. Selling Security Holders
8. Plan of Distribution
9. Description of Securities To Be Registered
10. Interest of Named Experts and Counsel
11. Information with Respect to the Registrant
12. Disclosure of Commission Position on Indemnification for Securities Act Liabilities

Part II

1. Other Expense of Issuance of Distribution
2. Indemnification of Directors and Officers
3. Recent Sales of Unregistered Securities
4. Exhibits and Financial Statement Schedules
5. Undertakings

Part I is usually distributed as a separate booklet to prospective investors. The prospectus must contain any additional data to make it meaningful and not misleading. Part II contains additional information such as the signatures of company officers, directors, consent of counsel and experts, and the financial schedules called for by Section 12 of Regulation S-X. Part II is made available for public inspection at SEC headquarters in Washington, D.C., or can be accessed online through Electronic Data Gathering, Analysis, and Retrieval (EDGAR).

In general, the registration statement discloses various kinds of important information for investors. Not all items listed above will appear in every registration statement. Some information may be incorporated by reference to another statement filed with the SEC and need not be duplicated in the Form S-1 filing.

The data include information about the company's business, officers, directors, and principal shareholders and their compensation. The company must also disclose the size of the offering, the price range, the intended use of the funds, the audited financial statements, and the risk factors. Additional disclosures include the selling shareholders (if any), underwriting syndicate, type of underwriting, dividend policy, dilution, capitalization, related party transactions, and certain legal opinions. A key portion in Form S-1 filing is the management's discussion that examines the company's financial condition, results of its operations, and the business plan.

Before a filing, companies often hold prefiling conferences with the SEC staff to discuss and ensure adequate disclosure and compliance with relevant regulations. The SEC staff is adept at pinpointing potential problem areas that may arise during the process of assembling information for the registration statement. For example, the SEC staff can advise the company on how to handle a legal or accounting problem or how to deal with questionable regulation compliance in a filing.

Once the registration statement has been filed with the SEC, the waiting period (cooling off) begins. During this period the issue is considered in registration, and there are restrictions on the activities the company or the underwriter may undertake. During the waiting period, the underwriting syndicate begins soliciting indications of interest from potential purchasers, but no actual sales can be made until after the registration statement becomes effective. The effective date is usually the date when the issue is offered to the public for a firm commitment or the date when selling begins for a best-efforts underwriting.

SEC Review and Comments

SEC staff specialists—consisting of an attorney, an accountant, and a financial analyst—review the IPO registration statement. The review group may also include other experts familiar with a particular industry. The staff reviews the documents to determine full and fair disclosure, particularly any misstatements or omissions of material facts that might prevent investors from making a fully informed investment decision. The SEC does not pass judgment on or evaluate the quality of a proposed offering.

After reviewing the registration statement, the SEC typically sends the company's legal counsel a letter of comments concerning deficiencies and suggestions.

Amended Registration Statement

Some common amendments requested by the SEC include a delaying amendment, a substantive amendment, and a price amendment. A delaying amendment is used to request a new effective date if the company has not been able to reply or to make up the deficiencies. Failure to meet these requirements can result in a defective registration or an SEC stop order against the company.

A substantive amendment is typically used to correct the deficiencies in a registration statement. It could be either a reply to the SEC comment or an update of significant interim developments subsequent to the filing. The registration statement must be correct and current when it becomes effective.

A price amendment is commonly used when the price and the size of the offering are not determined until the day of or the day prior to the offering. This amendment supplies the last-minute information.

The Preliminary Prospectus or Red Herring

After the filing, a preliminary prospectus is distributed to brokers and prospective purchasers to gather indications of interest from investors. This is the main document the underwriting syndicate uses to sell the stock. However, as required by the SEC, the cover page must bear the caption "Preliminary Prospectus" in red ink (hence the term red herring) and the following statement:

> Information contained herein is subject to completion or amendment. A registration statement relating to these securities has been filed with the Securities and Exchange Commission but has not become effective. These securities may not be sold nor may offers to buy be accepted prior to the time the registration statement becomes effective.

Under SEC rules, the offering price, underwriting discounts, and other matters dependent on the offering price may be omitted in the preliminary prospectus. Once the effective date arrives, the offering price and the effective date will be added to the prospectus. Then the final prospectus is issued.

Each state has its own securities laws, called blue sky laws. However, as part of efforts to reduce regulatory burdens on issuers, the National Securities

Markets Improvement Act of 1996 exempts listed securities or securities sold to qualified purchasers from state registration requirements but preserves state antifraud authority.

The Road Show

The road show is arranged for potential purchasers to meet with financial analysts and brokers in order to learn more about the company, which hopefully will improve price performance in the aftermarket. The management team explains their market position and how the company will execute its business plan and shows off the quality of the management team. Many analysts consider top management to be among the most important aspects of any company. Investors frequently base their purchasing decision on their perception of a company's management. The road show is also a kind of public opinion trial for the issuer's business plan. By the end of the road show, the lead manager should have a good idea of the investor's interest, which assists in determining the final price and size of the IPO. An effective road show is crucial to the success of the offering.

Due Diligence

Before the registration statement becomes effective, the underwriter will hold a due diligence meeting attended by members of the IPO team. The purpose of this meeting is to list, gather, and authenticate matters such as articles of incorporation, bylaws, patents, completeness and correctness of minutes, and verification of corporate existence.

Due diligence meetings are an important safeguard to reduce the risk of liability associated with filing by ensuring that all material matters have been fully and fairly disclosed in the registration statement. Part of the due diligence activity of legal counsel is to make formal visits to the company's offices and plant sites. Legal counsel typically maintains a due diligence file.

Price Amendment and Underwriting Agreement

The negotiation and final determination of offering size and price are influenced by a number of factors, including financial performance of the company, stock market conditions, prices of comparable companies, market perceptions of the company, and anticipated aftermarket share price. The underwriting agreement is signed when the registration statement is about to become effective. Also at this time the final amendment to the registration statement is filed. The price amendment includes the agreed price, underwriter discount, and the net proceeds to the company. The underwriter will typically request that the offering be declared effective immediately (requesting acceleration) if the staff of the SEC Division of Corporate Finance has no important reservations. The underwriter may then proceed with the sale of the securities if the acceleration is granted.

Closing

The closing date is sometime after the effective date, but the actual date depends on the type of underwriting. The closing meeting includes all key players and is usually held in the conference room of the escrow institution. Various documents as well as the updated comfort letter are exchanged at the closing. The company delivers the registered securities to the underwriter and receives payment for the issue. Closing differs considerably between small offerings on a best efforts basis and larger offerings on firm commitments.

For small, best efforts offerings, the closing takes place after the selling period has been completed—usually 60 to 120 days after the effective date, with an extension allowance of 60 to 90 days by mutual consent. For a firm commitment, closing is usually a week or two after the effective date.

Tombstones

A *tombstone ad* is considered an essential ingredient of the process. More of an announcement than advertisement, a tombstone is a boxed-in ad placed in financial sections of newspapers and magazines that announces the particulars of the new security. It contains the name of the company, the issuing price and size, the lead underwriter, and other members of the underwriting group. A disclaimer also appears at the top:

> This announcement is neither an offer to sell nor a solicitation of an offer to buy any of these securities. The offering is made only by the Prospectus.

Tombstone ads are a good way to introduce the company to the public and pique the public's interest. But tombstones are not as important as effective due diligence meetings and road shows. Management must use all the help it can get from its PR firm and the underwriter in conducting these meetings with a largely critical audience of brokers and analysts who need convincing. The outcomes of these meetings often spell the difference between the success and failure of an offering.

New Issue Valuation and Pricing

The issuer often believes the stock is worth much more than the suggested price. But the underwriter wants to create a demand for the new issue and to sell it quickly, and the best way to do that is to offer the stock at a price attractive enough to encourage prospective purchasers to buy it. In this area, investment bankers need to make the entrepreneur realize that her interests are not in conflict with the investors. When the share does well, she also realizes a huge profit. This is the big difference between being acquired and going public. When a company is acquired, the entrepreneur relinquishes claim to the company's stream of future profits. In a public issue, the entrepreneur retains a big portion of ownership. What has been sold to the public is just a fraction of her potential wealth.

Valuation and pricing are related, but they deal with different issues. Valuation is estimating the value of the company. The underwriter typically conducts a survey of comparable public companies in order to provide a preliminary valuation. The underwriter also looks into the following factors: efficiency, leverage, profit margins, use of proceeds, operating history, operating base, management, and product differentiation. Furthermore, it is important for the underwriter to take into account whether this is a single-product or a multiple-product company. The use of proceeds is a key variable to the underwriter and to the investors. Many underwriters would be deterred or would only engage in best efforts if they perceive that the prime purpose of the issue is for the selling shareholders to bail out.

Pricing refers to setting the offering price. The main concern is how much the market will bear. Most underwriters follow traditions in pricing a new issue. The price should be neither too high nor too low to appeal to potential investors. For example, a price of $5 or less might be considered too risky, and a price of $30 or more might be considered too high unless for a prestigious company. It is common to see an IPO price range between $10 and $30 per share.

One method underwriters often use to set a price is discounting. Underwriters like to price a new security a certain percentage below what they consider a fair value. This creates an incentive for investors to put money into the new issue. This discounting practice is clearly evidenced by observations that a new issue typically trades at a much higher price in the aftermarket.

Timing is also critical. The offering price is adjusted upward when the underwriter has received a higher over-subscription in indications of interest. The offering price needs to be lowered or the issue may be postponed if indications of interest are weak. Certainly the overall market environment in part influences investors' interest.

Underwriting Risk and Compensation

It is customary for the lead underwriter to form a distribution syndicate consisting of the underwriting syndicate and a selling group. Each member in the underwriting syndicate is committed to buying a portion of the new shares, while members of the selling group accept no risk. The lead underwriter's decision to distribute shares outside of its own organization has positive and negative implications. The lead underwriter benefits because each underwriter shares a portion of the underwriting risk. Second, the syndicate manager has the responsibility for ensuring liquidity in the aftermarket. A broad participation by the street provides incentives for other firms to make a market in the security and regularly research it. On the other hand, the lead manager has to make some economic concessions in sharing the underwriting spread. Another risk is that one of the syndicate members might outshine the lead manager and hence gain an edge in competing for future offerings. In general, the selection of an underwriting syndicate and the selling group should be based on a solid distribution of shares and market making ability.

Underwriting Risks

In underwriting, investment bankers "sell" risk services to the issuers by assuming at least part of the floating risk when they underwrite an offering by firm commitment. A firm commitment becomes absolutely firm only on the offering day or the night before, when the underwriting agreement is signed. The signing typically occurs just before the issue becomes effective. By then, all the marketing has been done, the road shows have been conducted, and the underwriter knows the "indication of interests." The risk or uncertainty can occur when the market shifts after a firm commitment on price has been made.

Floating risk is comprised of waiting risk, pricing risk, and marketing risk. During the period after the filing of the registration statement but before it is declared effective by the SEC, changes in market environment often affect the offering price. Such waiting risk is mainly borne by the issuer and has been minimized by the introduction of Rule 415 Shelf Registration. However, the pricing risk and marketing risk are exclusively borne by the underwriters. The pricing risk occurs when the market conditions worsen after the underwriting agreement has been signed. Marketing reduces flotation risk by building a "book of interest" before the effective date and by aftermarket trading. Forming a syndicate in which each member takes only a portion of the total risk also lessens the risk. Institutional sales help bankers place large pieces of new issues.

Compensation to Investment Bankers

The underwriting spread is the difference between the price to the public printed on the prospectus and the price the corporate issuer receives. The amount of the spread is determined through negotiation between the managing underwriter and the corporate issuer. All members of the syndicate are paid out of the spread. The varying amount of risk accepted by the members of the distribution syndicate is reflected in the compensation schedule. The manager's fee is compensation to the managing underwriter for preparing the offering. Participating in a thorough due diligence review and putting the deal together are the primary basis for the compensation.

The underwriting or syndicate allowance covers expenses incurred by the underwriting syndicate, including advertising, legal expenses, and other out-of-pocket expenses. Finally, the selling concession is allocated among all firms based on the amount of securities they accept to sell. Therefore, the syndicate manager receives all three—the manager's fee, the underwriting allowance, and the selling concession. The underwriting dealers receive the underwriting allowance and the selling commission. The selling group is allocated a portion of the total selling concession.

The Price of Going Public

Although there are no hard and fast numbers, the costs of a public offering are substantial. Total costs vary according to the size of the offering and the company's ability to market the offering smoothly and efficiently. For an issue around $150 million, the total costs can be as high as 10 percent. Going public also demands a great deal of time from top management, resulting in internal costs that may be difficult to quantify. Furthermore, there are the costs of underpricing the offering.

Direct Costs

Direct costs include direct expenses plus the underwriting spread. The company pays the direct expenses regardless of whether the offering is completed. The underwriter's commission is contingent on the completion. The first big expense is the gross spread. This is generally negotiable and depends on factors such as the size of the offering, the type of underwriting commitment, and the type of security offered. For many IPOs, the spread averages about 7 percent. Some of the banker's direct expenses are also reimbursed. Additional compensation is in the form of warrants, stock issued to the underwriter before the public offering at a price below the offering, or a right of first refusal for future offerings.

Legal fees are usually the second largest expense. They vary depending on the complexity of the company, the orderliness of its records, and the amount of time necessary to draft and file the registration statement.

Accounting fees are substantial as well. The accountant reviews and verifies the data in the registration statement and issues the comfort letter. These fees do not include audits of the financial statements, which vary depending on the size of the company and the number of years audited.

Printing costs are determined by the length, number of changes made to the registration statement, and the number of photographs. Registration fees, registrar and transfer agent fees, and miscellaneous fees are not insignificant. The SEC registration fee is 0.0295 percent of the dollar amount of the securities being registered (will be gradually reduced to 0.0067 percent by 2007). The National Association of Securities Dealers filing fee is $100 plus 0.01 percent of the maximum dollar amount of the issue. Additionally, there are exchange listing fees.

Underpricing Costs

A public offering is costly in yet another way. Since the offering price is typically less than the aftermarket value, investors who buy the issue get a bargain at the expense of the firm's original shareholders to a certain degree. The original shareholders typically retain a large portion of the company's shares on which they made enormous profits. Furthermore, the public would be eager to subscribe to subsequent offerings.

When a company goes public, it is very difficult for the underwriter to judge how much investors will be willing to pay for the stock. Hence underpricing is a means of soliciting investor interest. Underpricing helps the underwriter because it reduces the risk of underwriting and it garners gratitude from investors who buy the IPO issues. The true cost of underpricing is difficult to judge. If the business is sufficiently competitive, underwriters will probably take all these hidden benefits into account when negotiating the spread.

Hidden and Future Costs

Indirect costs arise during the lengthy process of preparing the first listing of the company, and, although management has considerable control over the amount and extent of some of these hidden costs, they invariably exceed what is anticipated. Some of these hidden costs include transportation costs for consultants, counsel, accountants, and the underwriter; meals and entertainment; postage; and telephone calls, faxes, and messenger deliveries. Thousands of dollars might be spent on promotions required to make the brokerage community and investors aware of the company. Another cost worth mentioning is director's and officer's liability insurance, which is not only difficult to obtain for small companies, but also very expensive. In addition, the one cost that is difficult to put a dollar value on is the management time it takes to complete the offering.

Finally, significant costs and executive time are incurred in preparing and filing reports for the SEC, an expense of being a public company. The SEC requires the company to file periodic reports, including annual Form 10-K, quarterly Form 10-Q, Form 8-K for reporting of significant events, and proxy and information statements.

Summary of Regulations

The SEC requires that a company planning an IPO follow the communications guidelines concerning the quiet period, preliminary prospectus, trading practices rules, offering, and post-offering communications.

Rule 134 of the Securities Act of 1933 sets forth the specific information that can be released to the public during the quiet period. During this period, the prospectus is the most important marketing document for the offering. The investment banks cannot provide any other information to their clients other than what is contained in the red herring. They cannot provide research reports, recommendations, sales literature, or any information from any other firm about the company. Usual ongoing disclosures of factual information are permitted. The SEC also requires that communications proceed at the level that was in effect before the preparations for the offering began. Therefore, it is in the company's interest to establish a fairly high level of public awareness well in advance of the offering.

After the registration statement is filed, the SEC regulations prohibit distribution of any written sales literature about the offering other than the preliminary prospectus and the tombstone ads. Until the quiet period is over, cooperation by the company or its underwriter in the preparation of news stories on the pending offering is not permitted.

The trading practices rules (Regulation M) are aimed at preventing manipulative trading in securities during an offering. The rules govern the activities of underwriters, issuers, selling security holders, and others in connection with offerings of securities. The rules prohibit persons subject to the regulation from bidding, purchasing, or inducing others to bid for or purchase a covered security during the applicable restricted period. A covered security is any security that is the subject of a distribution or any security into which or for which a security that is the subject of a distribution may be converted. For any security with an average daily trading volume (ADTV) of $100,000 or more and having a public float of $25 million or more, the restricted period begins on the latter of (a) the business day prior to the determination of the offering price or (b) the time a person becomes a distribution participant, and it ends when the participation of distribution is completed. For all other securities, the restricted period begins on the latter of five business days prior to pricing or at the time that person becomes a distribution participant, and ends upon completion of such person's participation of distribution. Certain transactions and securities are exempt from the trading restrictions. The exempt transactions cover stabilizing, exercises of securities, basket transactions, transactions among distribution participants, and transactions in Rule 144As. Exempt securities include actively traded securities (ADTV of $1 million and $150 million public float), investment grade nonconvertibles, asset-backed securities, and securities exempted from registration requirements.

Once the registration statement is declared effective, the pricing information is added to the prospectus. The SEC also permits news releases, press conferences, tombstone ads, and one-on-one meetings. However, the quiet period remains in effect for another twenty-five days, unless the security is not listed on an exchange or quoted on NASDAQ, in which case the period is ninety days. The content of these communications must conform to information contained in the prospectus.

After the closing of the offering, the issuer becomes a public company and is subject to the disclosure requirements. The company must file quarterly and annual reports and provide timely disclosure of material information.

Exchange Listing Requirements

The choice of exchange listing is part of the process. The main securities trading markets are the New York Stock Exchange (NYSE), the American Stock Exchange (AMEX), and the National Association of Securities Dealers Automated Quotations (NASDAQ). A brief description of the listing requirements follows. Detailed requirements can be obtained from each exchange.

The listing requirements on the NYSE are extensive. The form for listing is very similar to a full S-1 registration statement. The minimum listing requirements are 2,000 shareholders, one million publicly held shares, market value of public shares of $40 million, and net tangible assets of $40 million.

The AMEX is the second largest exchange. The minimum requirements are at least 800 shareholders; publicly held shares should be at least 300,000 shares, and these shares have a market value of $3 million; income before taxes must be $750,000 annually for the latest fiscal year or two of the last three years; the stockholder's equity is at $4 million or more; and the bid of the stock is at least $3.

The NASDAQ is a computer-based quotation/trading system with terminals in broker/dealer offices all over the country. The minimum listing requirements are 300 shareholders, one million shares of public float valued at $5 million, a bid price of $4, and three market makers.

Aftermarket Trading

Aftermarket trading begins after the new issue has been sold to the original buyers, who purchased the shares at the issuing price. Aftermarket trading is handled differently in a small best-efforts agreement than it is in a larger firm commitment underwriting.

In a large firm commitment issue, the underwriters typically want to stabilize the stock if its price does not perform as anticipated. The underwriter will support the market price of a new issue in order to keep it from falling below the initial offering price when trading of the stock goes into the aftermarket. If the new issue price goes down on the first aftermarket trading, the underwriters could be negatively branded for months. Underwriters want to avoid that. Furthermore, declining new issue price reflects poorly on the judgment of the lead underwriter and the analysts of the selling group.

The SEC requires detailed reports if stabilization is used. The stock purchased for stabilization cannot be resold at a higher price. It must be resold at or below the purchase price. Losses are shared pro rata by the selling syndicate. If the price continues to fall, the underwriters may withdraw support at their discretion without notice. So underwriters will make every attempt to place stock in strong hands among the syndicate members to avoid the necessity for stabilization. Weak members may not enjoy full participation in future offerings or may be eliminated.

On the other hand, a hot new issue will require underwriters to exercise the over-allotment or green shoe option. The name comes from the first company to ever use it, Green Shoe Company. The purpose of over-allotment, like stabilization, is to ensure an orderly aftermarket. It allows underwriters to sell up to 15 percent more of the stock.

When the underwriter anticipates either over-allotment or a possibility of stabilization, the fact must be disclosed on the front cover of prospectus as follows:

> In connection with this offering, the underwriters may over-allot or effect transactions which stabilize or maintain the market price of the common stock of the company at a level above that which might otherwise prevail in the open market. Such stabilizing, if commenced, may be disconnected at any time.

For smaller best-efforts offerings, stabilization is not used. The best that can be hoped for is that the market makers purchase the stock for their own inventory. If the market goes down, it is often because a weak syndicate member is cutting losses rather than an indication of the market reception of the issue. Typically, a minimum/maximum offering is used. The underwriter may get an indication of the range of interest from syndicate members to determine the minimum and maximum of the offering size.

Generally, during the first several weeks or so, a high degree of volatility in the trading price and volume can be anticipated. The issuing company is still subject to the twenty-five-day quiet period during which the company cannot begin any publicity efforts. The company can rely only on the support of the underwriters and the selling group to maintain its stock at a reasonable trading level. Hence, it is important for the company to maintain a strong relationship with brokers during the selling period.

Exempt Offerings

The market environment and the company's ability to accept the responsibilities and pressures of being a public company are among the determining factors of going public or using exempt offerings (private placement). The basic types of exempt offerings are Regulation D offerings, Regulation A offerings, and intrastate offerings.

Regulation D Offerings

Regulation D establishes the parameters of limited offering exemptions, which allow companies in need of capital to sell securities under an exempt offering and avoid the complexity and expense of going public.

Rule 504 allows the sale of securities up to $1 million over a twelve-month period. The number of investors is not limited, and the offering circular is not required. Rule 504 permits an unregistered offering by a nonreporting company without an offering statement if the issuer supplies material information to the purchaser at a reasonable time prior to the sale. Related to Rule 504 is a Small Corporate Offering Registration (SCOR), offering small businesses a low-cost alternative. SCOR allows businesses to raise up to $1 million in equity capital annually for business startup, development, or growth. Companies who wish to take advantage of the SCOR program are required to file Form D and SCOR Form U-7. Form D is filed with the SEC under Rule 504. Form U-7 is filed with states and is uniform for all states. This simplified process reduces a company's legal and accounting fees by up to 75 percent.

Rule 505 allows the sale of securities up to $5 million over a twelve-month period. Except for a maximum of thirty-five nonaccredited investors, all other investors must meet the SEC's definition of accredited investor—a knowledgeable individual or institution that has net worth adequate to make such investments.

Rule 506 permits the sale of an unlimited amount of securities. The requirement is that all nonaccredited investors (maximum of thirty-five) must qualify as sophisticated investors who are capable of evaluating the merit of the investments.

Regulation A Offerings

The second type of exempt offering is under Regulation A, which allows a company to raise capital through a public offering of up to $5 million per year, including no more than $1.5 million in secondary offerings. Unless the offering is less than $100,000, Regulation A requires the use of an offering circular, which contains financial and other information. Notification of the SEC and filing of information are required. Audited financial statements are generally not required. The procedures are similar to a regular registration, but the disclosures are not as extensive. The filings are made to and reviewed by the regional offices of the SEC. A notice of no further comments from a regional office indicates the Regulation A offering is effective.

Intrastate Offerings

The third type of exempt offerings—intrastate offerings—places no limits on the amount of capital to be raised or the number of individuals to whom securities are offered. The qualifications for the company are as follows:

Incorporated in the state of offering.

Maintain the principal offices in the state.

Hold 80 percent of assets in the state.

Derive 80 percent of revenues from sources in the state.

Offer only to investors with principal residence in the state.

Securities purchased via this exemption may not be resold to a nonresident of the state within nine months after the offering.

Summary

This chapter reviews the process in which investment banks underwrite a new security issue. The process begins when the issuer reaches an understanding with the underwriter to move forward with the issuance. The underwriter and the company work together to assemble a team that is charged with the responsibility of the new issue.

The SEC requires a company to file a registration statement for any public security issue. The registration statement must contain detailed information about the company, the management team, purpose of the funds, risk factors, and audited financial statements. Sales personnel of the underwriting syndicate will talk to prospective customers about the new security to get indications of interest to gauge the market demand for the new security. The underwriter and the senior management of the firm will go on road shows to promote the security. Also, the registration statement may require amendments. If the amended registration statement satisfies the SEC requirements, the issue is declared effective. The issue can then be sold to investors. Aftermarket trading starts after the issue has been sold to the original investors.

Selected Bibliography

Cecchetti, S. G. "The Future of Financial Intermediation and Regulation: An Overview." *Current Issues* (Federal Reserve Bank of New York) 5:8 (May 1999).

Kanatas, G., and J. Qi. "Underwriting by Commercial Banks: Incentive Conflicts, Scope Economies, and Project Quality. *Journal of Money, Credit and Banking* 30:1 (February 1998): 119–133.

Krigman, L., W. H. Shaw, and K. L. Womack. "The Persistence of IPO Mispricing and the Predictive Power of Flipping." *Journal of Finance* 54:3 (June 1999): 1015–1044.

Liaw, K. T. *The Business of Investment Banking.* New York: John Wiley, 1999.

Neal, R. S. "Credit Derivatives: New Financial Instruments for Controlling Credit Risk." *Economic Review* (Federal Reserve Bank of Kansas City) (Second Quarter 1996): 15–27.

Sherman, A. E. "Underwriter Certification and the Effect of Shelf Registration on Due Diligence." *Financial Management* 28:1 (Spring 1999): 5–19.

Notes

1. Under the National Securities Markets Improvement Act of 1996, blue sky registration and review are eliminated. The act prohibits states from reviewing or requiring the registration of securities issued by registered investment companies, listed securities, securities sold to qualified purchasers, and securities sold in certain offerings exempt from registration under the Securities Act.

5

Stock Valuation and Stock Selection

Successful stock selection requires that market professionals determine the underlying value of a security. Determining whether a security provides a good value to the market participant can be done in a number of different ways. Some investors look at the underlying fundamentals that drive a firm's earnings. Other analysts look at movements in a stock's price and volume to determine if a trend exists that can be exploited. A third type of analyst focuses on the impact a new type of business will have on society or the economy. These analysts tend to focus on new technologies and how they may impact the "new economy."

Common and Preferred Stock

Common stock is a class of security that represents an equity or ownership interest in a corporation. This interest gives the shareholder the same claim on the earnings of a firm as the owner of a small proprietorship. That is, if the business is successful, the shareholder will benefit either through a dividend paid by the corporation or by an increase in the value of the stock. On the other hand, if the business is not successful, shareholders, just like owners of a small business cannot expect to receive any payout. Another similarity is that shareholders have *voting rights* that allow them to have a say in how the business is run. Voting rights usually include the right to elect the board of directors and to approve mergers and takeovers.

There are several differences between owning common stock and owning a small business. Like owners of a small business, shareholders of a corporation share in the gains of a business; however, a shareholder's liabilities are limited to the amount paid for the shares of the stock. In this case, if the company were to fall into a situation in which its liabilities exceeded its assets, the most the shareholder could lose is the cost of his or her shares. In the case of a proprietorship or partnership, at least one owner is responsible for all debts of the business. For the proprietor of a business, the debts of the business could exceed the amount that was invested in the business.

A second type of equity security is *preferred stock.* The term preferred indicates that this class of security receives preferential treatment in the payment of dividends or in the distribution of the firm's assets in the case of a liquidation over the claims of common shareholders. Preferred stock represents a hybrid between equity and debt. The equity component results from the residual claim on a firm's assets. That is, like common stock, preferred stock will not receive a payout until debt holders and other creditors of the firm are paid. The debt component results from the fixed-income payout that is traditional of most preferred stock. Therefore, unlike common shareholders, preferred shareholders do not participate in the success of the firm. Because of the fixed-income component of preferred stock, it is traditionally classified as a fixed-income security.

One property that is common among preferred issues is the cumulative payment of dividends. Although dividends are not a legal obligation to the firm and need not be paid, cumulative preferred stock must receive any past dividend payments before any payments are made to common shareholders.

In this chapter, "stock" refers to common stock.

Trading Styles

Defining the many investment styles and trading tactics is difficult because of the many dimensions that can be used to define an investor. The most basic approach to defining management style forms two categories: *active management* and *passive management.* Passive managers seek to replicate the returns of some index, like the S&P 500. Active managers seek to add value to a portfolio by selecting securities that will outperform the market or by adjusting the composition of the portfolio based on their forecasts of the overall direction of the market. In general, active managers are classified by the type of analysis they perform. *Fundamental analysis* deals with the analysis of financial statements and/or analysis of economic fundamentals in order to determine the value of a security and its growth prospects. *Technical analysis* is the art of identifying patterns in securities prices and volume. Technical analysts believe that trends can be identified and that these trends will tend to persist. A third investment approach typical of the active management style of investing is *arbitrage* trading. Arbitrage can take several forms, from profiting from price differences between securities in different markets, to betting on the probability that a merger will be completed.

Fundamental Analysis

Analysts who use fundamental analysis might employ a number of approaches. A *top down investment approach* begins with an analysis of the aggregate economy. This information is used to determine which industries will prosper given the general economic outlook. Which companies will be the top performers in the best industries is determined by analyzing the financial statements of these companies in order to determine the overall financial health, growth prospects, and value of a company's security. With a *bottom up approach* the analyst begins at the company level and works up to the aggregate economy to make sure that outlook for the economy will support the company and its industry.

Whether analysts use a top down or bottom up approach, they are usually placed in one of two camps, *value investors* or *growth investors*. Value investors seek out companies that they believe the market has incorrectly undervalued. Growth investors, by contrast, are less concerned about value and more concerned about the growth rate of earnings. Growth investors are looking for companies not only with accelerating earnings growth but whose growth exceeds expectations of other investors. A third type of analyst is a hybrid that looks for growth at a reasonable price (GARP).

All three types of analysts care about both the price of a security and the rate at which earnings will grow. The difference lies in the emphasis they place on each component. Value investors place greater emphasis on the price paid relative to the firm's earnings. That is, they are not looking for firms with superior growth prospects, but rather firms that are inexpensive relative to their current level of earnings. Growth investors, on the other hand, place a great deal of emphasis on the earnings growth relative to the market price. That is, growth investors are willing to pay more for a company that they believe has superior growth prospects that are not already reflected in the stock's price. GARP investors tend to take a more balanced view on the importance of earnings growth and price.

A fourth type of investment style is *sector rotation*. Analysts who follow a sector rotation strategy rotate the portfolio into different industry sectors in order to prosper from perceived mispricings. In addition to shifting between sectors, managers may shift between value and growth stocks or between small- and large-cap stocks.

Finally, there are analysts who attempt to outperform the market through the use of *market timing*—a strategy in which the manager adjusts the stock/ bond mix or the risk of the portfolio based on market forecasts. When the market is expected to rise, the manager increases the portfolio's percentage in stocks or shifts the portfolio into higher risk stocks, which are likely to rise faster than the market. If the market is expected to fall, the manager will reduce the percentage of stocks or decrease the risk of the portfolio. If the analyst is correct, the portfolio will suffer smaller losses. Market timing is generally regarded as the most unreliable method for attempting to beat the market because of the difficulty in predicting the overall movement in the market.

Economic Analysis

Some successful investors, such as Warren Buffett and Peter Lynch, regard economic analysis as fruitless because of the difficulty in forecasting overall movements in the economy and because great companies thrive regardless of the overall movements in the economy. Other investors, such as John Neff, view economic analysis as fundamental to their investment decision making. Some of the economic information that investment analysts use includes:

- Interest rate forecasts—Because interest rates determine the cost of raising funds for firms, they can be important in determining business expansion and profitability. In addition, interest rates determine the return on assets such as bonds, which serve as substitutes for stocks. Therefore, an increase in interest rates makes bonds more attractive relative to stocks.

- Shifts in the yield curve—The yield curve represents a plot of the yield to maturity and the term to maturity for bonds with the same risk characteristics (usually Treasury securities). Shifts in the yield curve often indicate future economic activity. For example, an inverted (downward sloping) yield curve has been a good predictor of recessions.

- GNP or GDP forecasts—Because they represent the income of the aggregate economy, GNP and GDP can be important in determining demand growth for products.

- Leading economic indicators—may provide some indication of the future direction of the economy in the coming months. Building permits for new private housing represent one component of the leading economic indicators.

- Demographic shifts—Changes in the size and age of the population can have profound implications for investing. For example, an aging population may benefit businesses, such as pharmaceutical companies, that cater to an older population.

Industry Analysis

Once an analyst has determined the overall outlook for the economy, analysis usually shifts to the industry. Industry analysis looks at the profitability and future growth prospects of an industry in order to determine which industries will offer the greatest investment opportunities. Professor Michael Porter of the Harvard Business School provides a framework for analyzing the profitability of an industry. Porter's work lists five factors that determine industry competitiveness:

1. Bargaining power of buyers
2. Bargaining power of suppliers
3. Threat of new entrants
4. Threat of substitutes
5. Rivalry among existing competitors

Industries will be more profitable when these factors are in the industry's favor. For example, industries that have products with few substitutes and where entry into the industry is difficult will tend to be more profitable than industries that face less favorable conditions.

Another method for analyzing the future profitability of an industry is to look at the industry life cycle. The industry life cycle model looks at the five phases an industry passes through over its lifetime.

1. Pioneering and development
2. Rapid accelerating growth
3. Mature growth
4. Stabilization and market maturity
5. Deceleration of growth and decline

Industries in the first or second stages of the industry life cycle will tend to see improving profitability, whereas industries in the fourth or fifth stage will tend to see stable or even declining profitability. The industry life cycle model can be difficult to use these days because many firms are in a number of lines of business, all of which may be in different phases of the industry life cycle. For example, Intel Corp. began as a manufacturer of computer memory. However, as the industry matured and the company began to lose business to foreign competition, it moved into the microprocessor industry, which was still in its infancy.

Porter's Generic Competitive Strategies for a Firm

In addition to his work on industry competitiveness, Porter also looks at the generic strategies that a firm can pursue. Firms can choose to be a cost leader or a differentiator or follow a focus strategy. According to Porter, a firm's success depends on how well it pursues its strategy. Firms that try to be all things to all people wind up "stuck in the middle," a position that tends to be least profitable. Firms that follow a cost strategy hope to attain greater profitability by having cost savings in excess of the discount offered to customers. Similarly, firms that follow a differentiation strategy hope to attain greater profitability by charging a price in excess of the added costs of differentiating their product. The final strategy, focus, deals with the breadth of the market that the firm chooses to target using the first two strategies. A firm can try to focus on a narrow segment of the market or target a broader segment of the market.

There are four strategies a firm can pursue. A firm can choose to take a cost leadership role in a very broad market, as Wal Mart has done, or it can choose to take a broad differentiation strategy such as Coca-Cola. A firm can also choose to use cost leadership or differentiation in a fairly narrow market. A good example of a firm that follows a cost focus strategy would be GEICO, the direct marketer of auto insurance. Rather than target all drivers, GEICO focuses only on "good" drivers. An example of a firm that follows a differentiation focus strategy would be Cray, the maker of supercomputers. Both GEICO and Cray have chosen to ignore much of the market and target only a smaller, hopefully more profitable, subset of the market.

Valuation Approaches for Fundamental Analysis

In deciding whether to recommend the purchase of a security, analysts need to determine the value of the asset. Several different methods can be used. Discounted cash flow models look at the present value of future cash flows such as dividends, earnings, or free cash flow to determine the value of a firm's equity. Relative valuation approaches compare the relative value of a security against stocks in the same industry or against the industry average.

Discounted Cash Flow

Discounted cash flow models are based on the principle of present value. Value is found by taking the present value of the future expected cash flows.

$$Value = \sum_{t=1}^{n} \frac{CF_t}{(1+r)^t}$$

The cash flow that is used depends on the asset that is being valued. For stocks, the cash flow will be dividends and a terminal value for the stock. For bonds, the cash flow will be coupons (interest payments) and the maturity value of the bond. The problems of using discounted cash flow methodologies are the determination of an appropriate discount rate and deciding which cash flows should be used and how to forecast these cash flows. In valuing bonds, cash flow estimation is not a problem because the coupon payments and maturity value of the bond are fixed. However, equity valuation is more difficult because the cash flows need to be forecasted and there is no terminal value for a stock. In addition, a number of cash flows can be used in the analysis:

- *Dividends*—represent distributions made by the firm to shareholders. Firms have no legal obligation to pay dividends to shareholders and may retain earnings to fund expansion and other investments the firm may choose to undertake. For example, to date, Microsoft has not paid any dividends to shareholders.

- *Earnings*—represents the income available to owners of the firm after all expenses have been paid. Earnings may be a better measure because of the lack of dividend distribution by many firms.

- *Free cash flow to equity*—represents the residual cash flow leftover after meeting all expenses and providing for any capital expenditures to maintain existing assets and create new assets to fuel future growth.

Once the analyst has determined the appropriate cash flow to use in the valuation model, a discount rate needs to be determined. In general, discount rates are based on three factors:

- general level of interest rates
- expected inflation rate
- uncertainty of the future cash flows.

Estimating the discount rate usually entails adding a risk premium and the expected inflation rate to the riskless rate of interest. The risk premium can be determined using historical data or it can be based on a theoretical model such as the *capital asset pricing model*.[1]

The basic discounted cash flow model assumes that the cash flows from the asset terminate at some given date, making the basic model perfectly suited for valuing fixed-income assets that have a terminal life. However, when valuing the stock of a firm, there is no maturity date and the cash flows (dividends, earnings) from the stock can change over time. Three variations to the basic discounted cash flow model can be used. The three models differ in the assumptions they make about the growth of the cash flow stream.

The constant growth model assumes that the cash flow stream will grow at a constant rate indefinitely. The two-stage growth model assumes that the cash flow will grow at an above-normal growth rate for a short, definable period of time and then slow to its normal growth rate. Finally, the three-stage model is similar to the two-stage model except it assumes that there will be two periods of above-normal growth, one of very high growth and one of high growth. Once these periods have passed, the cash flows will slow to their normal rate of growth.

Which model is used depends on the company and the industry being analyzed. For a mature company with stable growth, the constant-growth model is appropriate. For an established but growing company, the two-stage model may be appropriate. Finally, for a company in its infancy, a three-stage model may be appropriate.

Relative Valuation

The relative valuation approach compares the security with other similar securities. The assumption is that other firms in the industry will have similar valuations. Valuation methods such as the price-to-earnings ratio, price-to-book ratio, or price-to-sales ratio represent relative valuation measures. For example, if the average firm in the industry has a price-to-earnings ratio of 25, then a firm with earnings of $4 per share will have a projected price of $100 per share.

$$Price = Earnings \times \frac{Price}{Earnings}$$

The price-to-earnings ratio is widely used because it measures the cost of $1 of the company's earnings. This measure is widely used by value investors, as they seek out companies that are selling for prices that are low relative to their earnings. When a relative valuation measure such as the price-to-earnings ratio is used, it is important not to use this measure to compare firms in different industries. For example, industries that use a great deal of capital in their manufacturing process, such as the auto industry, have historically had lower price-to-earnings ratios than other industries. Table 5-1 provides a summary of the four major methods for relative valuation.

Alternative Relative Valuation Measures

Three of the four relative valuation measures (price to book value, price to sales, and price to cash flow) allow the analyst to evaluate a firm that is losing money. Analysts also use other relative valuation measures to analyze specific industries. For example, in industries where the number of subscribers plays a crucial part in determining the value of the firm, such as cable television,

Table 5.1. Summary of valuation methods.

Valuation method	Advantages	Disadvantages
Price to earnings—measures how much is paid for every $1 of a company's earnings.	Widely reported. Easy to compute. Allows for comparison between different companies assuming that accounting standards are similar.	Cannot be used when a firm has negative earnings. Most price-to-earnings ratios use historical earnings rather than future earnings. Earnings are influenced by different accounting conventions.
Price to book value—measures how much is paid for every $1 of a company's book value.	Provides a relatively stable value that can be compared to the price of the company. Can be used to compare different companies if accounting standards are similar. Can be used to value firms with negative earnings.	Book values are dependent on accounting conventions, such as different methods of depreciation. If different firms use different account standards, then comparisons may be inappropriate. May not be useful in evaluating service companies that have only a small amount of fixed assets. The book value of equity can become negative if the firm has a significant string of negative earnings reports, which will lead to a negative price-to-book ratio.
Price to sales—measures how much is paid for every $1 of a company's sales.	Can be computed for even the most troubled firm. Is not dependent on the accounting standards used by the company. Tends not to be as volatile as price-to-earnings ratios. Allows examination of the effects of changes in pricing policy and other strategic decisions.	Fails to recognize the cost side of the equation. A firm may have growing sales but falling margins because costs are increasing.
Price to cash flow—measures how much is paid for every $1 of a company's cash flow.	Can be used for firms that have negative earnings but positive cash flows because of sizable depreciation and amortization expenses (non-cash expenses).	Fails to recognize depreciation and amortization as expenses.

91

Table 5-2. Alternative relative valuation methods.

Type of business	Valuation ratio	Comments
Restaurant	Enterprise value to number of restaurants	Measures the value per restaurant in operation.
Hotel	Enterprise value to number of rooms	Measures the value per room.
Cable television/Internet service provider	Enterprise value to number of subscribers	Measures the value per subscriber.
Cellular telephone	Enterprise value to number of persons in coverage area	Measures the value per potential customer.

Internet service providers, and telephone companies, a value can be placed on each subscriber. Table 5-2 presents some of these valuation measures.

These alternative measures may be more useful in determining whether the market has assigned a reasonable valuation to a company than it is for actually valuing a company. For example, on November 1, 1999, America Online had a market capitalization of approximately $148 billion and approximately 19 million subscribers. Therefore, each subscriber is worth ($7,789 = $148 billion/19 million). Is this a reasonable valuation given the $21.95 monthly subscription fee for AOL?

Technical Analysis

Technical analysis is based on the assumption that prices tend to move in trends that persist for certain periods and that these trends can be detected and charted. This approach is a dramatic departure from the *fundamental analysis* or *efficient market hypothesis.* Many academicians equate technical analysis with mysticism. Technicians often criticize fundamentalists and the market efficiency theorists as divorced from the reality of the markets.

Charting is at the heart of technical analysis. Chartists often use *support* or *resistance* to describe whether it is a trading or a trending market. Prices generally move within the support-resistance range (trading range). Traders buy at support and sell at resistance. A move above or below a resistance point is referred to as a breakout. A breakout above a resistance point signals an upward trending market, while a breakout below a support indicates that the market is trending downward. Volume is an essential supporting factor. A new high on heavy volume is considered bullish, while a new high on light trading volume may indicate a temporary move that is not likely to sustain.

There is no single magic formula for identifying trends and trading ranges. Technicians generally combine several methods. When they confirm one another, the signal is considered valid. When they contradict one another, it is better to pass up a trade. This section briefly describes several indicators frequently used by technicians.

Moving Average

Moving average (MA) is one of the oldest and most popular technical indicators. Easy to formulate and less open to interpretation than other methods, the moving average is the arithmetic average price of a security or an index over the past predetermined number of days:

$$MA = \frac{\sum_{t-(N-1)}^{t} P_T}{N}$$

In the above expression, P is the security price or index value, N the chosen time span, and t is the most recent trading date.

As each day passes, the earliest day is dropped and the most recent one is included. Connecting each day's MA produces an MA line. The most important message of a simple MA is the direction of its slope. When it falls, it shows bearish sentiment, during which prices fall below an MA. When it rises, it signals a bull market, during which prices rise above an MA. Hence, a buy signal is given when the security price crosses above the MA and the MA is directed upward. A sell signal is given when the security price crosses below the MA and the MA is trending downward. There are no valid signals when the MA changes direction but the price does not cross over the MA. When price fluctuates in a broad sideways pattern, the MA at times gives false signals, so technicians always use other indicators to confirm the direction of price.

Alternatively, a more complicated scheme involves the use of several MAs. For example, a technician might plot four-week, thirteen-week, and fifty-week MAs on the same graph. A buy signal is generated when the shorter-term four-week and thirteen-week averages cross over the fifty-week MA from below. A sell signal is given when the shorter two averages fall through the fifty-week MA. The two shorter MAs are used to filter false signals.

A weighted MA favors the most recent observations. A frequently used method is described as follows. For simplicity, assume a time span of seven days. Multiply the first price by one, the second price by two, . . . , and the seventh price by seven. Then divide the sum of these multiplications by the sum of the weights. The divisor is $1 + 2 + \ldots + 7 = 28$. With a weighted MA, a buy or sell signal is given when the weighted MA changes direction.

Exponential Moving Average

An *exponential moving average* (EMA) is another form of weighted MA. Technicians believe that EMA is a better trend-following tool because it assigns a greater weight to the latest data and responds faster to changes than a simple MA. The mathematical expression of EMA is:

$$EMA = P_{t+1} \cdot H + EMA_t \cdot (1 - H)$$

> *where*
> $H = 2/(N + 1)$,
> P = security price,
> t = time point, and
> N = the chosen time span.

The first EMA is proxied by a simple MA. Then the line connecting all EMA points obtained from repeating the calculation gives the EMA line. The trading rule is to trade the security from the long side when EMA rises, and trade it from the short side when the EMA falls. When the EMA moves repeatedly from side to side or remains flat, it is a trendless market.

Moving Average Convergence-Divergence (MACD)

Moving average convergence-divergence (MACD) is comprised of two statistics: a difference in short-term and long-term EMAs and the smoothing of this difference. The smoothing is used to generate signals of buys and sells. Hence, the MACD is comprised of three EMAs. The first is the shorter EMA (for example, a twelve-day EMA).[2] The second is a longer EMA (for example, a twenty-six-day EMA). The difference calculated by subtracting the longer EMA from the shorter EMA is the so-called fast MACD line. The final step is to calculate a nine-day EMA of the fast line, which results in the slow signal line. A buy signal is given when the fast MACD line crosses above the slow signal line. A sell signal is given when the fast line crosses below the slow line.

Many MACD systems also use histograms, which some technicians believe offer more insight into the balance of power between bulls and bears. Histograms show not only whether the market is bullish or bearish but also whether it is growing stronger or weaker. An MACD histogram plots the difference between the MACD fast line and the slow signal line. The histogram is positive when the fast line is above the slow line. Hence, when the MACD histogram stops falling and ticks up, it gives a buy signal. When the MACD histogram stops rising and ticks down, it gives a signal to trade on the short side.

Filter Trading Rule

The idea behind a filter rule is to get in on a trend as it is starting and to get out as it begins to reverse. A filter trading technique specifies when a security will be bought or sold. Typically, it specifies that when a security's price moves up by x percent above a previous low, it should be bought and held until its price falls by y percent below a previous high, at which time the trade should be carried out on the short side. The rationale for this rule is that if the security rises x percent from some base, a positive breakout has occurred, and the security price would continue to rise. In contrast, a y percent decline from some peak would be considered a breakout on the downside. The trader would expect a downward trend and would sell any holdings and might even sell short.

The specification of x percent and y percent will determine the frequency of trading. A small percentage specification will result in a large number of transactions. A large percentage specification might miss certain market movements. Studies have found that filter rules may be effective when the filter is small, in the range of 1 to 5 percent.

Relative Strength Index

Relative strength index (RSI) analysis is based on the momentum concept. It measures the strength of a security or an index by monitoring changes in its closing prices. RSI analysis is based on the assumption that higher closes indicate stronger markets, and lower closes indicate weaker markets. The RSI is defined by the following formula:

$$RSI = \frac{AU}{AU + AD} \times 100$$

AU is the average of net up closing changes for a selected number of days. Traders first choose a time span—for example, ten days—then find all days when the security closed higher than the day before and add up the amounts of increases. The *AU* is equal to the sum divided by ten. *AD* is the average net down closing changes for the same number of days. Traders find all days when the security closed lower than the day before and add up the amounts of declines. *AD* is equal to the sum divided by ten. The RSI is obtained by inserting the values of *AU* and *AD* into the formula. As is clear from the formula, the RSI fluctuates between zero and 100. If the ratio is fifty, the ups and downs are equally divided. As the ratio goes above fifty, more closes are ups than downs, indicating an upward trend. Technicians would state that when the RSI passes seventy or eighty the market has reached its top. Conversely, if the RSI falls below twenty or thirty, the market is near its bottom and a reversal is in sight.

Breadth of Market

The *breadth of market* technique measures the strength of advances over declines. The advance/decline (A/D) line shows each day the difference between the number of advancing issues and declining issues, ignoring the unchanged. For example, if 1,234 stocks were traded higher for the day, and 891 stocks declined, the A/D is +343. A cumulative A/D line is created by adding each day's A/D to the previous day's total. The cumulative A/D is then compared with the Dow Jones Industrial Average (DJIA). An uprising cumulative A/D line supported by a higher DJIA signals a strengthening market. Conversely, a declining line coupled with a lower DJIA signals market weakness. Additionally, if a new high in the Dow index is accompanied by a new high in the A/D line, then the rally has broad support. When the DJIA reaches a new high but the cumulative A/D line only goes up to a lower peak than the previous run, it shows that fewer stocks are participating and the bull run may come to an end. Similar analysis applies on a down market.

A variation of the A/D technique is *breadth advance decline* (BAD). Data on NYSE-listed stocks are generally used to construct the BAD. The BAD index is the simple moving average of the ratio of advances over the sum of advances and declines. Technicians believe that when the reading reaches 0.66, significant bull gains can be expected. A ratio of 0.367 or lower signals a bearish market.

For an individual security, there is a technique called *on balance volume* (OBV) that creates a volume line along with a price chart at the bottom. If the stock closed higher, that day's volume is added. If the day closed lower, the volume is subtracted from the starting number. So volume is added on up days and subtracted on down days. Because the OBV often rises or falls before prices, technicians believe that the OBV is a leading indicator of market trend.

Momentum and Rate of Change

Momentum and rate of change (RoC) show when the trend speeds up or slows down. Momentum subtracts a past price from today's price, while RoC divides today's price by a past price. They can be expressed as:

$$Momentum = P_t - P_{t-N} \ , RoC = \frac{P_t}{P_{t-N}}$$

In the expressions above, P_t is today's closing price, and P_{t-N} is the close N days ago. For example, a ten-day momentum equals today's closing price minus the closing price ten trading days ago. A ten-day RoC divides today's price by the closing price ten days ago. The time window is kept short to detect short-term market changes. A long time window is for trend following.

When momentum or RoC rises to a new high, it signals that the prices are likely to rally higher. Conversely, when momentum or RoC falls to a new low, lower prices are expected. When prices rise but momentum or RoC declines, the market is near its top and it's time to take profits or consider shorting. Reverse this approach during downtrends.

Barron's Confidence Index

Barron's confidence index (BCI) is the ratio of Barron's average yield on ten top-grade corporate bonds (y_{top-10}) to the average yield on Dow Jones 40 bonds (y_{DJ}). Specifically, the formula is:

$$BCI = \frac{y_{top-10}}{y_{DJ}}$$

The BCI measures the relative yield ratio between top-quality bonds and a large cross-section of bonds. The BCI is always less than one. Technicians feel that the BCI gives a bullish signal when the index rises above 95 percent and gives a bearish signal when the index falls below 85 percent. The reasoning is that, during periods of prosperity, investors are willing to invest more in lower quality bonds for added yield. This causes a decrease in the average yield for the large cross-section of bonds (relative to the average yield of the top quality bonds), leading to an increase in the BCI value. Conversely, during periods when investors are pessimistic about economic outlook, the BCI falls.

Head and Shoulder

Technicians study price patterns to decide when a trend is likely to continue or reverse. *Head and shoulder* (HS) tops indicate that the market has reached it top. The head is a price peak surrounded by two lower tops (called shoulders). Volume is often higher on the left shoulder than on the head. An uptrend continues as long as each rally keeps on reaching a new high. Rising volume serves as a confirmation. Volume falls when the market is near its top.

The decline from the head to the right shoulder is the beginning of a downtrend. Trading strategies on the existing long position include sell, tighten stop level, or sell some and hold the rest. Another strategy is to short the security and place a protective stop.

In an inverse HS, the head is at the lowest point surrounded by two shoulders. An inverse HS develops when a downtrend is near an end and a reverse is likely. In a downtrend, each new low falls lower than the previous low and each rally fails to reach a higher level. High volume confirms all declines. The decline to head usually comes with low volume. The rally out of the head breaks out of the downtrend and signals a likely bull market. During the right shoulder, there is usually a low volume. An increasing volume associated with each new high confirms that an uptrend has developed.

Mutual Fund Cash Ratio

Mutual funds hold cash for several reasons. One obvious reason is for possible shareholder redemption. Second, the money from new purchases of funds may not have been invested. Third, fund managers might build up their cash position if they have a bearish outlook. Some technicians interpret the mutual fund cash ratio (cash/assets) as a contrarian indicator. They consider mutual funds to be a proxy for the institutional investor group, and mutual funds are generally wrong at market timing. Therefore, a bullish sign is given when the cash ratio rises, and a bearish signal is given when the cash ratio declines.

Additionally, a high cash ratio can be considered a bullish sign because of potential buying power; the funds have to be and will be invested. Alternatively, a low cash ratio means that institutions have bought heavily and are left with little potential buying power.

Short Sales by Specialists

Short sales by exchange specialists are closely watched statistics, because specialist operations consistently generate high returns. Those who want to follow the smart money watch the specialists. Specialists regularly engage in short selling as part of their market-making function, but they will be more aggressive in executing shorts when they feel strongly about the market direction.

The *specialist short sale ratio* is the ratio of short sales by specialists to the total short interest. Technicians view a decline of this ratio below 30 percent as a bullish sign because it means that specialists are attempting to minimize their participation in short selling. In contrast, a reading of 50 percent or higher is a bearish sign.

Short Interest Ratio

Short interest is the total number of shares that have been shorted and not covered. Technicians compute a *short interest ratio* (SIR) as the outstanding short interest divided by the average daily trading volume on the exchange. As an example, short interest of 750 million shares and an average daily trading volume of 500 million shares yield an SIR of 1.50. This means the short interest equals about 1.5 days' trading volume. The SIR can also be computed for an individual stock.

Technicians interpret the SIR contrary to short-sellers. Traders selling short expect stock prices to decline, so an increase in SIR could be a bearish sign. But technicians consider a high SRI bullish because it indicates potential demand for the security by those who have sold short and have not covered the sales. Recent experience suggests that technicians using this technique would be bullish if the SIR approaches three and bearish if it declines toward two.

Put/Call Ratio

The *put/call ratio* is used as a contrarian indicator. Technicians reason that a higher put/call ratio indicates a more pervasive bearish attitude, which to them is a bullish indicator. The ratio is typically less than one because investors tend to be relatively more bullish than bearish and avoid selling shorts or buying puts. A buy signal is given when the ratio approaches 0.70. In contrast, a put/call ratio of 0.40 or lower is considered a bearish sign. A put/call reading of between 0.40 and 0.70 is neutral.

Odd-Lot Theory

The *odd-lot technique* focuses on the trading activities of small investors. Most small investors do not engage in short selling except when they feel especially bearish. Technical analysts interpret heavy short selling by individuals as a signal that the market is close to trough because small investors only get pessimistic after a long decline in prices, just when the market is about to turn around. A buy signal is given when the ratio of odd-lot short sales as a percentage of total odd-lot sales rises above 3 percent. A sell signal is given when the ratio declines to 1 percent or lower.

Another interpretation of the odd-lot behavior is based on a similar belief that small investors are unsophisticated and frequently make mistakes in market reversals. Small investors often do all right but frequently miss key market turns. Specifically, the odd-lot investors are generally in the money as the market is going up. However, as the market continues upward, small investors get greedy and buy strongly just before the market reverses direction. Similarly, small investors are also assumed to be strong sellers right before the market bottoms out.

Investment Advisory Opinions

Technicians practicing the *investment advisory opinions* approach reason that most investment advisory services tend to be trend followers. Technicians develop a trading rule from the ratio of the number of advisory services that are bearish as a percentage of the number of services expressing an opinion. A bearish sentiment index of 60 percent indicates a pervasive bearish attitude by advisory services; contrarians consider this a bullish sign. Conversely, a decline of the bearish sentiment index to below 20 percent indicates a sell signal.

Money Flow

Money flow represents the dollar value of composite uptick trades minus the dollar value of downtick trades. Money flow statistics give us an idea of the flow of funds into a stock. A positive money flow indicates strength, whereas a negative money flow indicates weakness. An up/down ratio can also be established to indicate the value of uptick trades relative to downtick trades. These statistics can be found in the *Wall Street Journal.*

Arbitrage Trading

Arbitrage trading is situated on the proprietary trading desks of Wall Street. The various types of arbitrage are described below. The classical riskless arbitrage opportunities are practically nonexistent in many active markets, which are the results of constant pursuit by arbitrageurs who have low-cost capital, state-of-the-art technology, and an intimate understanding of intraday market-making activities. In developing sectors or markets, however, riskless arbitrage opportunities do occasionally present themselves.

Index Arbitrage

Theoretically, a stock index futures price will differ from the cash price by an amount equal to the cost of carry. Because of transaction costs and other factors, there are boundaries around the theoretical futures price within which there are no arbitrage opportunities. An index arbitrage positions trades in the cash and futures markets when the differences between the theoretical futures price and actual futures price are sufficiently large to generate arbitrage profits. A trader can generate arbitrage profits by selling the futures index if it is expensive and buying the underlying stocks or by buying the futures contract when it is cheap and selling short the underlying stocks. Index arbitrage plays an important role in linking futures prices and cash prices. Program trading is used to execute the buy and sell orders.

Convertible Arbitrage

A convertible arbitrage involves the purchase of convertible bonds or preferred stocks and then hedging that investment by selling short the underlying equity. The resulting position generates income from the accrued interest or preferred dividends and interest earned on the short-sale proceeds. The short sale is intended to protect the investment from adverse stock market movements so that the overall position, if correctly hedged, will be nondirectional. The objective is to correctly position trades that produce certain current income and preserve principal regardless of stock market conditions.

For example, suppose a convertible debenture maturing in one year traded at $1,050 and is convertible into 100 shares of non–dividend paying common, and the common is trading at $10 a share. There is a $50 premium over the conversion value of $1,000. Assume that a bond of similar characteristics without the conversion feature is traded at $920. The $920 is the investment value.

Assume the common stock has an even chance of going to $7.50 or $12.50 over the next year. The conversion value is hence $750 or $1,250 one year later. The convertible arbitrageur could take advantage of this expected relationship by being long one bond at $1,050 and short sixty shares of common at $10. At a price of $7.50, the short position would be in the money for $150 while the bond would be traded at a $130 loss, for a gross profit of $20 per bond. If the price goes up to $12.50, the bond will be converted and result in a gain of $200 while the short position would lose $150. The net profit is $50 per bond. This example illustrates the basics of convertible bond arbitrage. In practice, the convertible bet is more complex, and strategies are constantly changing.

Merger and Acquisition Risk Arbitrage

Risk arbitrage is an integral part of proprietary trading. Arbitrageurs take a position in firms engaged in a merger or a takeover. They are interested in the deal, not in becoming shareholders. In order to commit funds, they must have reasonable belief that the deal will go through. The standard strategy is to go long on the target and short on the acquiring firm. The position is not at the mercy of the market, but is at risk with respect to the consummation of the transaction.

A transaction can involve a cash exchange, an exchange of securities, or a combination of both. First consider the case of a cash offer. Suppose an acquirer is offering to buy the target's stock at a price of $50 per share at a time when it is traded at $40 per share, a 25 percent premium. The target's stock can be expected to rise to about $50. There is always a chance that the acquirer might withdraw or change the offer, and it is likely that the target's stock may rise to, say, $46 rather than $50. An arbitrageur who purchases the target at $46 will realize a profit of $4 per share if the acquisition takes place at $50. The arbitrageur will lose $6 per share if the deal does not go through and the target's share declines back to $40.

When the transaction involves an exchange of securities, the arbitrageur would go long the securities of the target, expecting them to rise in price, and short the securities of the acquiring company, expecting them to decline. There are two risks involved: the acquisition might not be consummated or it will take longer than anticipated. As an example, assume that the stock of an acquirer is trading at $50 per share. The company offers to exchange one share of its stock for one share of the target, which is traded at $40. The transaction is expected to be complete in three months. Suppose that the arbitrageur offers the target stock $46 per share. The target's shareholders can immediately take a $6 profit from the proposed deal by selling now to the arbitrageur. Or these shareholders can wait three months and receive one share of the acquirer's stock. This gives an extra $4 per share profit, but only if the acquisition is completed and only if the shares of the acquirer are still traded at $50 per share.

Suppose the target's shareholder decides to sell to the arbitrageur and take a profit of $6 per share. The arbitrageur will receive a profit of $4 per share if the deal is closed as proposed. The same outcome remains even if the shares of the acquirer are traded at a level lower than $50. For example, if the acquirer's shares are traded at $48 instead of $50, the arbitrageur receives a $2 profit from the short position (acquirer) and another $2 profit from the long position (target). The primary risk is that the deal will not go through and the prices of both companies go back to preannouncement levels.

The level of complexity in risk arbitrage varies depending on the structure of the transaction. To reduce risk, the arbitrageurs must perform comprehensive research to examine the likelihood of the proposed transaction and the structure of the deal.

Evaluating Internet Stocks

The rapid growth of the Internet and the success of Internet-based stocks such as America Online, Amazon.com, eBay, and Yahoo have spurred interest in the future of stocks in this area. Analysis of many of these companies precludes the use of traditional valuation methods because of the lack of positive earnings for many of these firms. Also, the short time span of these businesses makes it extremely difficult to forecast future revenues and earnings.

The analysis of companies in new industries is not new. In the 1980s, personal computer companies represented a new area for analysis, as did companies conducting genetic engineering research. Projections for the future earnings of these companies were just as difficult as they are today for Internet firms.

A variety of techniques can be used to provide comparisons among Internet firms and companies in emerging industries to attempt to determine a fair valuation. Analysts might use one or a combination of these strategies.

- If the analyst can determine some reasonable future cash flows that will be generated by the firm, a present value valuation method can be used. The risk associated with a new company in a new industry can be dealt with by incorporating a higher discount rate into the present value calculations.

- The analyst can look at venture capital markups to determine a reasonable starting point for the analysis.

- The analyst can attempt to determine the number of years it will take the firm to reach a target price-to-earnings ratio. For example, the analyst may determine that a P/E ratio of twenty-five is reasonable for this firm over the long haul. If the firm can attain this within, say, five years or less, the stock would be recommended.

- The analyst might consider the performance level that the firm must sustain in order to justify the current market price. For example, suppose the current selling price of a firm has a ten-year earnings growth rate of 50 percent embedded in the price. The analyst must determine if the 50 percent growth rate is sustainable. A scenario analysis where the analyst determines the value of the stock for different growth rates may provide some insight on the stock's current valuation.

- The analyst might consider the company's cost of acquiring customers. Firms with the lowest cost would be valued the highest.

- The analyst can examine the price to gross profit ratio. The lower the ratio, the more reasonably priced the firm.

- The analyst can examine the growth rate of revenues.

- For Internet stocks, a commonly used approach is looking at the number of people that visit the web site on a regular basis. The logic behind this method is that many Internet companies earn the majority of their money from advertising, and therefore a valuation of Internet stocks is akin to valuing other types of media companies such as television stations or newspapers.

- The analyst can use some of the alternative relative valuation measures previously discussed, such as value per Internet subscriber.

- The analyst might consider how a new firm or technology is likely to change society or the way business is conducted.[3]

- The analyst might consider the market cap of a firm and determine if the fundamentals can justify the valuation. For example, AOL, which regards itself as a media company, especially in light of its proposed merger with Time Warner, has a valuation that is significantly larger than many other established media companies. The question the analyst must ask is "can this valuation be justified?"

- An approach that incorporates scenario analysis and the value of the stock under each scenario and then attempts to determine the probabilities of each scenario occurring can be helpful in putting the stock's current valuation in perspective. For example, if a high probability exists that the best-case scenario will occur and the current value of the stock is below the projection in this scenario, the analyst would recommend purchasing this stock.

An analyst should consider several other factors when evaluating start-up firms. First, successful investment in Internet firms requires analyzing the firm rather than the Internet. Firms that succeed are likely to be the first to establish a dominant position in their industry. For example, in the online auction business, eBay quickly established a dominant position. Even with other Internet powerhouses such as Amazon.com and Yahoo entering the online auction arena, eBay continues to be the preferred site for collectors and antique dealers.

A second consideration is that the expected returns to Internet companies are not likely to be normally distributed, but rather are more likely to have a bimodal distribution. The bimodal distribution results from the fact that Internet companies generally hit it big or go bust, so the analyst's expectation is not likely to be the most likely outcome.

Another issue to consider is the effect of stock options on the value of the stock. Because much of management's compensation will be in the form of stock options, the analyst should consider the possible dilution effects of such options. If options represent a meaningful portion of shareholder equity, then they should be incorporated into the analysis. Investors should also beware that falling stock prices for an Internet firm can have a detrimental effect on the firm's ability to raise capital for acquisitions and growth. Growth through acquisitions is a major component in most Internet companies' business plans. A lower-priced stock lowers the value of the currency for acquisitions (the stock) and thereby reduces expansion plans and impacts current shareholders more because more shares may need to be used in its acquisitions. Finally, an analyst should view investment in Internet companies in the same manner as venture capitalists. In this case, the analyst recognizes that only a handful of firms will succeed, but that the few that do succeed will more than offset the losses from a number of firms. Therefore, investing in a diversified basket of companies may be the best approach for success.

Insider Trading Regulations

As analysts ferret out information about a company, they may obtain information that has not been disseminated to the public. Trading on this type of information may lead to violations of insider trading laws.

There are two types of insider trading. One is legal trading by insiders—corporate officers and directors and beneficial owners of more than 10 percent of registered equity shares. Such insiders must file an initial report on their holdings with the SEC. Thereafter, they must file reports during the month when there are changes in their holdings.

Illegal insider trading is trading on material nonpublic information. State laws play a very limited role in regulating insider trading, mainly through rules against fraud and deceit. Many states have adopted what is known as "special facts doctrine," and some states have expanded the doctrine into the "Kansas rule." Both theories do little to regulate insider trading and apply only where there is an existing shareholder trading with an insider. Also, both rules require privity or face-to-face transactions. Therefore, state law mostly comes into play with stock transactions in closely held companies.

Primarily, Rule 10b-5 of the Exchange Act governs such insider trading. Under Rule 10b-5, "It shall be unlawful for any person, directly or indirectly, by the use of any means or instrumentality of interstate commerce, or of the mails, or of any facility of any national securities exchange, (a) to employ any device, scheme, or artifice to defraud, (b) to make any untrue statement of a material fact or to omit to state a material fact necessary in order to make the statements made, in the light of the circumstances under which they were made, not misleading, or (c) to engage in any act, practice, or course of business which operates or would operate as a fraud or deceit upon any person, in connection with the purchase or sale of any security."

Five elements must be proven to impose criminal or civil liability under Rule 10b-5:

1. Misinformation: The defendant must misrepresent a fact or not disclose a fact.

2. Material and nonpublic: The fact must be material and nonpublic.

3. Knowledge: The defendant must know that he or she made a misrepresentation and intended for the plaintiff to rely on it.

4. Reliance: The plaintiff must rely on the information in the transactions.

5. Causation and injury: The plaintiff must show that his or her trades relied on such information, such misinformation caused losses, and the plaintiff suffered damages.

However, Rule 10b-5 liability cannot be imposed on everyone who trades on the basis of material nonpublic information. For example, a person with no fiduciary responsibility to the shareholders of the company in whose stock he trades does not violate Rule 10b-5 as long as he is not a "tippee" or "misappropriator." Rule 10b-5 liability generally can be imposed on four types of groups:

1. Insiders and constructive insiders: Corporate insiders and constructive insiders (attorneys, investment bankers, and accounts hired by the company) have an abstain-or-disclose duty while in possession of material nonpublic information. It is a violation of regulation if they trade on such information.

2. Tippers: Insiders or constructive insiders may be in violation if they tip the material nonpublic information and someone trades based on such information.

3. Tippees and sub-tippees: A tippee or a tippee of the tippee can be liable for trading on such nonpublic material information.

4. Misappropriators: Under the misappropriation theory, outsiders can be criminally liable if they breach a duty arising from a relationship of trust and confidence and use that information in securities transactions, regardless of whether they owed any fiduciary responsibility to the shareholders of the traded stock.

The misappropriation theory is an important weapon in the SEC's fight against insider trading. In the *United States v. O'Hagan,* an attorney hired by an acquirer was found criminally liable for trading on the target's stocks while in possession of confidential information that his firm's client was planning to launch a tender offer for another company. The attorney would not have been liable without the misappropriation theory. He was neither an insider nor constructive insider of the target company nor a tippee of an insider or constructive insider of the target. He learned of the tender offer from the acquirer, the company to which he was a constructive insider. The misappropriation theory extends Rule 10b-5 to cover this situation. The misappropriation theory also extends liability to the tippers and tippees of the person who misappropriated the information.

In addition, Rule 14e-3 prohibits trading during the course of a tender offer by anyone, other than the bidder, who has material nonpublic information about the offers known to have been obtained from either the bidder or the target. Thus, Rule 14e-3 provides that the misappropriation theory may be used to hold a person liable for securities fraud involving tender offers.

Taxation of Dividends and Capital Gains

Investment professionals should consider the tax consequences of any strategy used to manage clients' assets. For example, technical trading rules, which may require the manager to turn over the portfolio frequently may have detrimental tax consequences for the client.

Another consideration that the investor and the investment professional must consider is the composition of a security's returns. For an individual investor, how the returns are generated can be important in determining the after-tax return. Historically, capital gains have been taxed at a lower rate than interest and dividends. Another advantage of capital gains is that tax liabilities can be postponed by not realizing the capital gains. In addition, current tax laws allow for a stepped-up cost basis upon the death of the owner of a stock, which means that capital gains are entirely forgiven.

The importance of the composition of the total return an investor receives also depends on the type of account the funds are held in. In the case of a tax-deferred retirement account such as a 401(k) plan, the composition of the total return is unimportant because taxes are not due until the funds are withdrawn and all gains are taxed as ordinary income. However, in a taxable account, the composition of the total return can be very important to individuals in high tax brackets.

Summary

An investor can use numerous methods to determine which stocks offer the greatest investment potential. Fundamental analysis uses economic and financial information to determine the long-term prospects of a company. Companies that are highly profitable and have a sound balance sheet offer the greatest investment potential. Technical analysis allows an investor to base decisions on price movements, volume, or the actions of other investors. Each approach offers advantages and shortcomings. Although most analysts fall into one of the two camps, both methods could be combined in the analysis. For example, an analyst that likes a firm's fundamentals could consult various technical indicators to help time the trade or gauge investor sentiment.

Selected Bibliography

Christopherson, J. A., and C. N. Williams. "Equity Style: What It Is and Why It Matters." In *The Handbook of Equity Style Management.* New Hope, Penn.: Frank J. Fabozzi Associates, 1995.

Damodaran, A. *Damodaran on Valuation: Security Analysis for Investing and Corporate Finance.* New York: John Wiley, 1994.

Hooke, J. C. *Security Analysis on Wall Street.* New York: John Wiley, 1998.

Liaw, K. T. *The Business of Investment Banking.* New York: John Wiley, 1999.

Wilson, B. "Valuing Zero-Income Stocks." In *Practical Issues in Equity Analysis.* Charlottesville, Va.: Association for Investment Management and Research, 2000.

Notes

1. The capital asset pricing model prices the return of a risky asset using the nondiversifiable or systematic risk of an asset. This risk is measured by the asset's beta, which is a measure of volatility of the asset relative to some market index like the S&P 500 index.

2. The twelve-day, twenty-six-day, and nine-day EMAs are commonly used in MACD.

3. Sociologist and author Charles W. Smith refers to this as the "transformational idea" in *Success and Survival on Wall Street* (Lanham, Md.: Rowman and Littlefield, 1999).

6

Brokerage Services, Execution Techniques, and Trading Costs

Broker services go beyond the usual research analysis and basic execution of trades for clients. Brokers provide financial planning advice to clients and advice on how to allocate their portfolio among the different asset classes. Many of these issues, such as preparing an investment policy statement and preparing an asset allocation recommendation, were discussed in Chapters 2 and 3.

In addition to the services mentioned above, brokers provide a number of *back office operations* that are important to both individual and institutional clients. Some of the back office services provided by brokers are:

- Safekeeping of securities
- Record keeping and reporting
- Account reconciliation
- Trustee services
- Clearing and settlement
- Loan custody

Although not very glamorous, these services are essential to the financial industry. Some major financial institutions such as the Bank of New York specialize in securities processing and back office operations and sell their services to other financial institutions that prefer to outsource such operations.

Processing Securities

The procedure for processing securities is a major part of the service that a brokerage house offers to its customers.[1] Figure 6-1 presents the steps in processing security transactions.

Sales are only the first step of many that the brokerage house handles. Once an account executive receives an order from a client to buy or sell, the order is

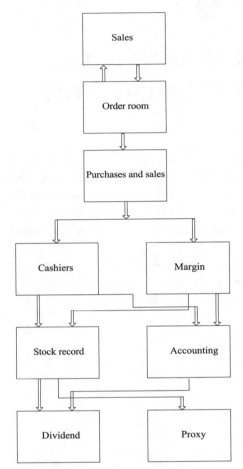

Figure 6-1. Processing securities.

submitted to the order room. Orders can be placed electronically—for example, through the NYSE's Super Dot system, which sends orders directly to the appropriate trading post—or orders can be sent to a floor broker.

After the trade is made, information is sent to the purchase and sales department for recording, figuration, comparison, and booking. This step includes checking that the order is correct. For each buy order, there must be a seller on the other side of the transaction. Orders that do not match are marked DK (don't know) and are sent back to the floor for confirmation.

Once trades are confirmed, the brokerage house is still responsible for monitoring the customer account to ensure that margin requirements are met. The cashiering department needs to handle vaulting and monitor any stock loans. Records also must be kept to ensure that dividends are paid to the appropriate party or that investors who have shorted a security pay the dividend for the borrowed shares. The final job of the brokerage house is to handle proxy votes. Because many securities are held in the "street name" of the broker, individual investors will not receive information regarding proxy votes. The brokerage house must distribute this information to the appropriate stockholders in order to allow them to vote their shares.

Mechanics of the Market

Secondary markets such as the NYSE and NASDAQ provide liquidity to market participants, allowing them to buy and sell stocks at a moment's notice. These markets allow investors to not only buy and sell stocks at the current price, but also put in a number of different types of orders that specify the buy or sell price. Investors also can borrow money to finance their purchases as well as sell stocks they don't own. Many of these functions are handled by individuals or institutions known as specialists.

Specialists Versus Market Makers

In order for a market to function smoothly, an individual or institution needs to facilitate the market transactions by ensuring that a buyer exists for those who wish to sell and a seller exists for those who wish to buy. This facilitator is known as a *market maker*. Market makers exist in both auction markets such as the New York Stock Exchange and in the over-the-counter markets such as NASDAQ. Market makers use their own capital to purchase an inventory of securities. With this inventory of securities, the market maker is in a position to provide liquidity to the market by purchasing from sellers and selling to buyers.

On exchanges such as the NYSE, market makers also serve as *specialists* whose responsibilities differ from the market maker because they are responsible for maintaining a "fair and orderly market." Unlike market makers, who are not required to undertake a transaction, specialists are obligated to buy from sellers when other buyers cannot be found and sell to buyers when there is a shortage of sellers. During periods of market turmoil such as the October 19, 1987, stock market crash or when the specialist's stock is part of a takeover rumor, the specialists may need to hold positions in a security that are detrimental, simply to provide liquidity to the market. These positions can cause the specialist's firm to lose substantial sums of money in very short periods of time. It is essential that the specialist perform this job well because a quarterly rating system used by the NYSE allows customers and floor

brokers to determine the ability of a specialist to create and maintain a continuous liquid market for their stocks, and this rating plays an important role
in determining new stock allocations by the NYSE.

One valuable piece of information specialists have is the *limit-order book,*
which contains limit orders placed by brokers. This information allows specialists to know what traders are thinking. Even though this information may
give specialists an advantage over other market participants, they cannot use
this information to trade ahead of clients, an activity known as *front running.*

Specialists earn their income by providing both the broker and dealer function. In an actively traded stock, specialists have little need to act as dealers
and therefore derive most of their income from the broker function. In stocks
that have low trading volume and high price volatility, specialists will need to
provide more of the functions of a dealer and therefore earn most of their
income from the bid-ask spread. Specialists can deal in more than one stock;
however, each stock will have only one specialist. In general, specialists balance the risks of market making by specializing in some high-volume, low-
risk stocks and some higher risk securities.

One of the keys to being a successful market maker or trader is a keen
awareness of your position. The goal of successful trading is to maintain a balanced position. Traders with excessively large short or long positions subject
themselves to greater risk if the security's price moves in a detrimental direction. In many ways, traders manage their risks the same way sports bookies do.
By setting a line for the game that balances the bets on both teams, bookies
ensure that they will earn a profit, with only limited risk. Likewise, by setting
the bid and ask price appropriately, market makers ensure a balance of buy and
sell orders, thus reducing the price risk that the market maker faces.

Brokers

In continuous auction markets such as the NYSE, it can be extremely costly
for a market participant to find another investor who will take the other half
of a transaction. For example, a buyer may have difficulty locating a seller and
a seller may have difficulty locating a buyer. Therefore, this type of market
allows a broker to serve as a middleman between buyers and sellers. *Commission brokers* are employees of a firm that has membership on the exchange.
These brokers buy and sell for customers of the firm. When an order is placed
with a firm, the firm may contact its commission broker on the floor of the
exchange, who will then go to the appropriate post on the floor and buy or
sell shares as instructed. *Floor brokers* are independent members of an exchange who act as brokers for other members. During busy times, a member
firm may need the services of a floor broker in order to handle all of their

orders. Floor brokers were once referred to as *$2 brokers* because that was what they were paid for each order.

The difference between brokers and market makers is that brokers do not put their own capital at risk by holding an inventory of securities. They simply receive a commission for helping others complete a transaction.

Trading Mechanics

The mechanics of trading begin with the investor's decisions about which type of security to purchase and which type of order to place. The particular security that the investor wishes to purchase determines where the security will be purchased. For example, some securities trade on listed exchanges such as the NYSE and others trade in the over-the-counter market. Stocks and bonds that trade in the over-the-counter market must be purchased from a dealer or market maker in that security. In a dealer market, the dealer holds an inventory of the security and is willing to sell at the *ask* or *offer price* and willing to buy at the *bid price*. The difference between the sell and buy price is referred to as the *bid-asked spread* and represents what the dealer earns. The spread is determined by a number of factors, including the stock's price volatility and trading volume. Because of the reduced price risk to the dealer, more liquid, less volatile stocks will tend to have narrower spreads. In an exchange-listed security, buyers and sellers come together to negotiate price directly in what is referred to as an *auction market*. However, even in auction markets like the NYSE, a market maker—in this case, the specialist—exists to ensure sufficient liquidity of the security. Customers use brokers to perform the difficult job of searching out the other end of the transaction, a task for which they receive a commission.

Order Types

Market and Limit Orders

Once investors decide what to purchase or sell, they must decide what price they are willing to accept. For investors who are willing to accept the current price offered in the marketplace, a *market order* can be used. In a market order, the investor instructs the broker to buy or sell at the best available price in the market. If the investor wishes to buy or sell only at a certain price, a *limit order* that specifies the buy or sell price can be placed with a broker. Once the limit is reached, the order must be filled at the limit price or better. For example, if a buy limit order is placed at $50, the buy must take place at a price of $50 or less. When using a limit order, investors need to specify for how long the order is in effect and how the transaction is to be handled. Investors can specify that the limit order be transacted immediately ("fill or kill"), or the order can be good for part of the day or the full day, or it can be an open-ended order that is good until cancelled.

An investor can use several other types of orders. In a *stop loss order*, the investor directs the sale of a stock if the price drops to a given price. Once the price is reached, the stop loss order becomes a market order, so the investor may receive a lower price than is given in the stop loss order if prices are falling rapidly. For example, if an investor enters a stop loss order to sell at $50, it's possible that the sell price could be much lower than $50 if prices fall rapidly. For short sellers, a *stop buy order* can be used to limit the loss the investor faces if prices rise. Like a stop loss order, a stop buy order becomes a market order when the specified price is reached.

When using stop loss orders or limit orders for protection, investors should be aware of the differences. The transaction price of a limit order must be at the limit price or better. Therefore, in a market where the price of the stock is falling rapidly, the sell limit order may never be executed if the price drops quickly enough through the limit price. On the other hand, if a stop loss order is used, when the appropriate price is reached, the transaction becomes a market order and will be executed at the best available price in the market at that time.

Short Selling

Another type of order that investors can use is to sell a stock that they don't own in the hopes that the stock price will fall. This type of order is referred to as a *short sale*. In a short sale, the investor instructs the broker to sell short, for example 100 shares of Microsoft stock at $100. Because the investor does not own the stock, the broker must borrow the shares from another investor. In order to ensure that short sales do not cause market prices to fall, short sales can only be made on an *uptick trade*, meaning that the last transaction was higher than the previous one. Short sales also can be made when the last trade results in an unchanged price if the previous trade was at a higher price, a trade referred to as a *zero uptick*.

Investors must consider the role dividends play in a short sale. The short seller is responsible for any dividends that the lender of the stock would have received. The final consideration is that short sellers are subject to margin requirements that say the short seller must post the same margin as an investor who purchased the stock. However, the short seller can use any unrestricted securities to satisfy the margin requirement. Unlike the purchase of a security, where there is a limit to how much the investor can lose, there is no limit to the potential loss in a short sale. Obviously, this makes short selling extremely risky.

The maximum profit from the short sale is $100, because the price of the stock cannot fall below zero. There is no limit on how much an investor can

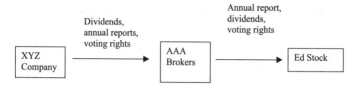

The short sale: Step one.

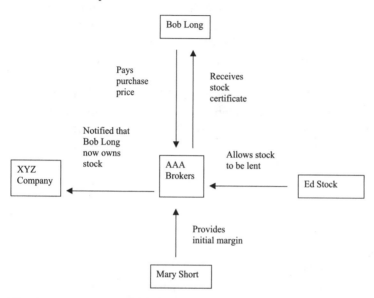

The short sale: Step two.

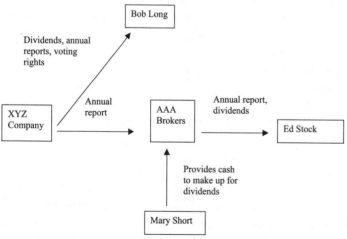

The short sale: Step three.

Figure 6-2. An Illustration of Short Selling.

lose from a short sale because there is no limit on how high the price of the stock can rise.

To illustrate the mechanics of a short sale (Figure 6.2), consider the following example. Prior to the short sale, Ed Stock owns 100 shares of XYZ Company stock that are held for him by AAA Brokerage in street name. Therefore, all relevant correspondences from XYZ Company must be sent to AAA first and then forwarded to Mr. Stock. Mary Short, another customer of AAA Brokerage, informs them that she would like to sell short 100 shares of XYZ Company stock.[2] In order for the short sale to take place, AAA brokers must find someone who is willing to lend their stock. Because Ed Stock has no intention of selling his stock in the short run, he agrees to lend his stock to AAA. AAA takes the stock from Mr. Stock and sells them for Ms. Short to a third party, in this case, Bob Long, who pays the purchase price and receives the stock certificates. AAA informs XYZ Company that Mr. Long is now an owner of its stock. After the short sale is completed, Mr. Long receives any dividends, annual reports, and voting rights directly from XYZ Company. However, Mr. Stock still owns the stock and is entitled to the dividend that is paid by XYZ. This dividend must be paid by Ms. Short, to AAA Brokerage, which forwards the dividends to Mr. Stock.

Margin Transactions

When investors undertake an order, they can pay for the securities in cash or borrow a portion of the cost. Buying on *margin* means that the investor borrowed some of the cost of the security and used the security as collateral for the loan. Not all securities can be purchased on margin. The Federal Reserve Board determines under Regulation T which securities are eligible for margin purchases. In general, all securities listed on national exchanges and over-the-counter securities that have been approved by the Fed are marginable.

Even though the Fed determines which securities can be purchased on margin, a brokerage house may choose not to allow an investor to purchase a marginable security on margin. Although brokerage houses must comply with Regulation T, they often impose stricter borrowing limits on their customers. Buying on margin has the effect of leveraging the purchase—that is, the rate of return (both positive and negative) on the margin transaction will be greater than a cash purchase. For example, current margin requirements are 50 percent, which means that investors can borrow up to 50 percent of the value of the stock. An investor who wishes to purchase $10,000 of stock needs only $5,000 in cash and can borrow the rest. The effect of borrowing $5,000 to purchase $10,000 in stock is that the rate of return on the investor's money will be twice that of a cash purchase. For example, if the stock price rises by 5 percent, then the investor will realize a 10 percent return. If the stock price falls by 5 percent the investor will realize a 10 percent loss. This effect is known as leverage. In this case, the leverage factor is two; that is, returns are twice that of a cash purchase.[3] Table 6-1 shows different returns for different levels of margin.

An important concept that relates to margin is the investor's equity. The margin requirement previously discussed refers to *initial margin,* which is the amount an investor must put up in cash to purchase a security. However, if the price of the security falls in value, the investor's equity will fall and the investor may receive a *margin call,* which will require the customer to place additional funds in his or her account. If the customer elects not to place the necessary funds into the account, the brokerage house can sell some of the security until the margin requirement is met. In order to keep brokerage houses from requiring investors to put additional funds into their accounts every time the stock price falls, investors will not receive a margin call until the price drops sufficiently so that the proportion of equity to the total value of the stock falls to a level referred to as the *maintenance margin.* When an investor's equity falls to the maintenance margin level, the investor receives a margin call and is required to put cash into the account to raise the equity to

Table 6-1. Security returns and margin.

	Cash purchase (100% margin)	Borrow 25% (75% margin)	Borrow 50% (50% margin)
Number of shares at $100	100	100	100
Cost of investment	$10,000	$10,000	$10,000
Less borrowing Equity	0	2,500	5,000
	$10,000	$7,500	$5,000
Return if stock price rises to $120/share			
Value of stock	$12,000	$12,000	$12,000
Less cost	10,000	10,000	10,000
Capital gains	2,000	2,000	2,000
Return on equity	(2,000/10,000) = 20%	(2,000/7,500) = 26.67%	(2,000/5,000) = 40%
Return if stock price falls to $70/share			
Value of stock	$7,000	$7,000	$7,000
Less cost	10,000	10,000	10,000
Capital loss	3,000	3,000	3,000
Return on equity	(−3,000/10,000) = −30%	(−3,000/7,500) = −40%	(−3,000/5,000) = −60%

the initial margin requirement. The amount that the investor must place in the account is referred to as *variation margin.*

Two other cases must be considered when a security is purchased on margin. First, when the price of the security falls, but not sufficiently to require a margin call, the account becomes a *restricted account.* If additional stocks are purchased, the new purchase will require initial margin. Any sales that are made in the account while it is restricted allow the investor to withdraw 50 percent of the proceeds.

The final case occurs when the price of the stock rises. In this case, the increased value leads to excess equity. This "Reg T excess" allows the investor to either withdraw the excess or use the excess to buy additional securities without putting up additional cash.

Trading Rules and Circuit Breakers

The October 19, 1987, stock market crash in which the market fell 508 points or 22.6 percent led government regulators to examine the volatility of securities markets. Although the exact cause of the crash will never be known for certain, the *Brady Report* and other analyses suggest that program trading was at least one of the reasons for the crash.[4] As a result of the crash, the New York Stock Exchange and the Chicago Mercantile Exchange (where S&P 500 Index futures are traded) have implemented trading rules that either restrict or halt trading when certain price limits are reached. The purpose of these circuit breakers is to prevent destabilizing speculation and to allow investors to reexamine valuations in the market. Original circuit breakers used price limits to determine when trading would be halted.

On February 16, 1999, the NYSE, with approval from the SEC, implemented revisions to Rule 80A, which restricts index arbitrage trading. The amendment eliminated the fifty-point collar and allowed the collar to track the DJIA. The new collar is calculated quarterly as 2 percent of the average closing value of the DJIA for the last month of the previous quarter, rounded down to the nearest ten points. The rules are as follows:[5]

- A decline in the DJIA of the predetermined 2 percent value requires all index arbitrage sell orders of the S&P 500 stocks to be stabilizing, or sell plus, for the remainder of the day, unless on the same trading day the DJIA advances to a value within one-half of the 2 percent below its previous day's close.

- An advance in the DJIA of the predetermined 2 percent value requires all index arbitrage buy orders of the S&P 500 stocks to be stabilizing, or buy minus, for the remainder of the day, unless the DJIA retreats to a value within one-half of the 2 percent above its previous day's close.

■ The restrictions are reimposed each time the DJIA advances or declines from the predetermined amount.

Rule 80B imposes trading halts based on 10, 20, and 30 percent decline levels in the DJIA. For example, based on trigger levels for the second quarter of 1999, the following halts will occur:

■ A 1,000-point drop in the DJIA before 2:00 P.M. will halt trading for one hour; will halt trading for 30 minutes if between 2:00 P.M. and 2:30 P.M.; and have no effect if at 2:30 P.M. or later.

■ A 1,950-point drop in the DJIA before 1:00 P.M. will halt trading for two hours; for one hour if between 1:00 P.M. and 2:00 P.M.; and for the remainder of the day if at 2:00 P.M. or later.

■ A 2,950-point drop will halt trading for the remainder of the day regardless of when the decline occurs.

Point levels are set quarterly by using the DJIA closing value of the previous month, rounded to the nearest fifty points. The percentage levels were first implemented in April 1999 and are adjusted quarterly on January 1, April 1, July 1, and October 1.

Trading and Trading Costs

Successful trading requires the abilities to both select securities that will outperform the market and implement these strategies in an effective manner. The difference between paper portfolios and actual portfolio returns has come to be known as the *implementation shortfall*. This shortfall occurs because money managers face hidden costs when implementing their portfolio strategy.

The costs of implementing a portfolio strategy have made execution techniques and trading costs an important part of a firm's competitiveness. Changes in technology have opened up a wide variety of tactics that traders can use to implement trades. The decision of whether to trade is determined by the benefits of trading relative to the costs incurred.

Direct Costs of Trading

Trading securities involves a number of costs. When investors desire to buy or sell a security, they incur one of two direct costs depending on the market where the security is purchased. In an *auction market*, buyers and sellers meet to negotiate a price. In order to reduce the costs of searching for the other end of the transaction, investors use brokers to help complete the transaction. Brokers do not hold an inventory and are simply paid a commission for finding the other end of the transaction. Because brokers do not hold an inventory of the securities, they incur no price risk from adverse changes in the price of the security.

In a *dealer market*, dealers or market makers stand ready to buy or sell securities from their own accounts. Dealers profit from the difference between the selling and buying prices, known as the *bid-ask spread*. The size of this spread is determined by a number of factors, including the volume of trading in the security, the security's price volatility, and the number of other dealers trading the security. The greater the trading volume in a security, the narrower the bid-ask spread should be because dealers will have an easier time managing their inventories. Likewise, lower price volatility should lead to lower inventory risk and hence should narrow the spread.

Hidden Costs

Most people view the costs of trading as simply the commissions charged on a transaction. However, the hidden costs of trading are often much more significant than the commissions paid. These hidden costs are related to the cost of liquidity, and the cost that is paid by the trader is determined by whether the trader is buying liquidity or selling liquidity in the marketplace.

There are four major components to trading costs.[6]

- *Commissions* represent the administrative costs of executing a trade and are incurred on every transaction.

- *Impact cost* represents the cost of buying liquidity and can be measured by the change in price between the time an order is presented to a broker and the time the order is executed. Impact can be thought of as the cost of buying liquidity.

- *Timing cost* represents the costs incurred by not executing the entire order at the same time. Timing can be thought of as the cost of seeking liquidity. Timing costs occur because an order is too large to be presented to the market for a single execution. Smaller orders are parceled out over time, and it may take a number of days to complete the transaction. During this time, the price may move away from the target price.

- *Opportunity cost* represents the cost of not executing the trade. These costs can occur for a number of reasons, including movements in price away from the target range. Opportunity costs are especially hard to measure because the securities that are not purchased are never reflected in the fund's actual performance.

With the exception of commissions, these costs are not directly observable and are difficult to measure. In addition, there is a tradeoff between impact and timing costs. A trader can reduce impact costs on large orders by doling out the trade into smaller trades. However, this technique can increase the timing costs.

Of the different types of costs, only commissions can be measured precisely. Impact, timing, and opportunity costs can only be estimated. Wagner examines 54,000 trades and defines the spread and impact cost as the difference between the price at the time the broker receives the order and the time the order is executed. Wagner also measures the opportunity cost for the shares ordered that were never executed. He finds that these costs depend on market conditions. In liquidity-demanding markets, costs are much higher than in neutral or liquidity-supplying markets.

Because there is a tradeoff between the different types of trading costs, the relative importance of these costs is determined by the type of trader. *Information traders* attempt to profit by trading on information that is not yet known by the market and is therefore not embedded in the price of the security. Time is extremely important to information traders, as they attempt to trade before the market incorporates the information into the security's price. Therefore, impact costs are relatively unimportant to information traders who are trying to acquire a position in the security before the information reaches the market. Information traders will choose to buy the security as long as the costs of executing the trade are less than the expected price movement due to the information. Because information traders may need to seek liquidity in the market, their costs of transacting are generally high relative to other types of investors.

Value traders trade because they believe there is a discrepancy between the trade price and the equilibrium value. Value traders supply liquidity to the marketplace because they generally buy as price is falling and sell when price is rising so they tend to have low hidden transactions costs.

Passive managers, who track some market indices, are somewhere in between information and value traders. Because passive managers buy and sell securities simply to maintain the relationship between their portfolio and the index, they neither supply nor buy liquidity from the market.

In general, information traders have the highest costs of transactions because of the necessity of executing the trade quickly. These costs can reduce the returns to an information strategy. Value investors, on the other hand, tend to buy out-of-favor securities and tend to have lower impact costs for their trades. Finally, the cost of passive management tends to fall somewhere between information investing and value investing.

Execution Techniques

The costs of implementing a real investment portfolio make it crucial to consider execution strategies in the portfolio management process. The implementation shortfall occurs because paper portfolios do not face bid-ask spreads or impact, timing, or opportunity costs. In order to reduce these costs, careful analysis of trading costs must be conducted. The use of a number of different trading methods may be necessary to provide the best possible execution.

Several trading alternatives can be used to improve the opportunity of getting the best execution. Traders can use either a *single-stock approach* or a *portfolio approach*.[7] In the single-stock approach, trading takes place with one stock at a time. In the portfolio approach, a large number of securities are traded simultaneously as one unit.

Single-Stock Trading

Several alternatives can be used in the single-stock approach. The *upstairs block market* can reduce costs relative to other trading alternatives because trades can be executed at or near the bid-offer spread. The upstairs block market gets its name because it takes place upstairs off the floor of the exchange and because these transactions are for large blocks of securities. This market consists of *block houses*, which are investment firms that help institutions locate other institutions that are interested in buying or selling blocks of stocks. This approach has several disadvantages. First, it is not suitable for all transactions. Second, large capitalization securities are generally more appropriate than small capitalization securities. Third, it can be difficult to find the other half of the trade. Finally, the exposure of the order to the marketplace can result in market impact costs.

The use of a *call market* is another method that can be used. Unlike *continuous markets,* in which order flow arrives at different times during the day, leading to inefficient pricing of stocks, in a call market, trading takes place at specified times. The purpose of call markets is to gather all bid and ask prices for a stock and attempt to find the price that will clear the market.

The use of a *dealer market* entails using a broker-dealer to execute the transaction. Immediacy and certainty of execution are advantages of this approach. One disadvantage to this approach is that the dealer market usually has high costs.

Crossing networks are another method that can be used. A crossing network allows institutions to trade a portfolio of stocks rather than individual securities with one another. Crossing networks give buyers and sellers an opportunity to meet and negotiate a price directly, which allows them to trade inside the bid-ask spread. Crossing networks have a number of advantages, including confidentiality, fair pricing, and low commissions. One major disadvantage of crossing networks is their lack of liquidity. Currently, the two largest crossing networks are POSIT and Crossing Network. Crossing Network conducts one session daily, in the early evening, using NYSE closing market prices. POSIT conducts six daily sessions, three in the morning and three in the afternoon. These sessions are based on the prevailing prices at the time of the crosses.

Portfolio Trading

Portfolio transactions entail trading large numbers of securities as a single indivisible unit. *Principal trades* can be divided into two categories: cash only and derivatives related. Two types of derivatives transactions are *basis trades* and *exchange for physicals*. In a basis trade, a broker trades stock index futures in the broker's account during the course of a day and then crosses the client's portfolio into the broker's account at the end of the day at a basis or spread to the average futures price. At completion, the client has the desired cash portfolio and the broker has the offsetting cash position hedged with futures. In an exchange of physicals, the client starts off with futures and exchanges them with a broker for a cash position. Likewise, the client can start off with a cash position and exchange it for futures. One difference between the exchange of physicals and the basis approach is that exchange of physicals transactions must be posted on the relevant futures exchange.

Another method for trading a portfolio of securities is to use a substitution order. For example, suppose you are trying to create a portfolio that tracks the Russell 2000 using 400 stocks. Because a number of stocks will track the Russell 2000 well, it may not be necessary to specify the exact 400 stocks to purchase. A more cost-effective approach to creating the portfolio may be to use a substitution order for a larger set of stocks, say 1,000 stocks. Each day's fills will be fed back into a computer to generate an updated trade list.

Strategies for International Trading

International investing offers a number of opportunities and challenges for investment professionals. Trading across borders allows investors to take advantage of growth opportunities in emerging markets and reduce portfolio risk through international diversification in a way that would not be possible using only domestic investments. This risk reduction results from the low degree of correlation between U.S. and foreign markets.

The opportunities in international investing do not come without costs, however. First, limitations in data in other parts of the world may make it difficult for investors to make fully informed decisions. Second, investments in foreign countries expose the portfolio to a number of different risks, including exchange rate risk and political risk. Also, overseas markets may be less liquid and subject to higher transactions costs.

Beginning the Process

The first step for investment managers is to determine the appropriate allocation to overseas markets. The examination can begin with a look at the historical returns and correlations between each market and the U.S. market. Once investment managers determine how much to allocate to foreign investments, they must decide how to allocate these funds among the different countries. Finally, the allocation decision of how much to invest in each industry and company in each country is made.

Investment managers next need to deal with fluctuations in exchange rates. Foreign exchange rate risk can be left unhedged, can be partially hedged, or can be fully hedged. To hedge foreign exchange rate risk, investment managers have a number of tools available, including futures or forward contracts, options, and swaps.

Trade Analysis

Once the manager has decided which countries and which industries to invest in, a trading strategy must be established. A trading strategy begins by examining the liquidity and volatility for each security. By examining the liquidity in a market, brokers can devise a strategy to control market impact costs.

Morgan Stanley and Company uses a trade liquidity report for each security to identify any problems that may occur in trading a security.[8] The report includes the following information:

- The percentage of principal each name represents within its country
- The quantity the customer has requested to buy or sell
- The price
- The average daily volume (thirty-day moving average)

- The percent the trade represents of average daily volume
- The twenty-day volatility
- The bid and offer
- The percent spread

The above information enables investors to determine which stocks are feasible for the portfolio. Stocks with very low volume may offer great potential to the "paper portfolio"; however, purchasing the requisite amount may be impossible. When problems arise purchasing a desired security, managers need to consider the possibility of substitution.

Transition Trading

One method for implementing a global investment strategy is to handle transactions simultaneously across multiple markets. This method is referred to as transition trading or global program trading. In transition trading, the process is simplified so that the task is reduced to one execution list, one broker, one confirmation, and one settlement network. Another advantage of transition trading is that it allows quick reallocation of assets and effective management of cash flows. For example, different settlement dates in different countries allow a tailoring of the strategy so cash flows match the need for settlement money. One concern about transition trading is that the quick execution may lead to higher market impact costs.

Using Futures

Futures contracts can provide a method for money managers to invest in foreign stocks and offer a number of advantages over the direct purchase of equities. Futures have low transactions costs and can be purchased and sold quickly. They also carry limited currency risk, as only the margin deposit is subject to currency fluctuations.

Full-Service, Discount, and Internet Brokerage

When the New York Stock Exchange was formally established in 1792, members agreed to charge nonmembers a minimum commission schedule. On May 1, 1975, the SEC allowed commissions paid to brokers on all transactions to be fully negotiable. Allowing brokers to lower rates charged to customers led to an entirely new industry, the discount broker. Prior to May

1975, brokers provided full service to customers in the form of security recommendations. The change in government regulations led to a new class of broker, the discount broker, who executed the trade at much lower costs than full-service brokers. This class of broker was designed for individuals who wished to conduct their own research and only needed an outlet for executing the trade.

Changes in the fee structure used by brokers have not deterred brokerage firms from charging fees in excess of the pure costs of transactions. These costs are referred to as *soft dollars* and can be paid when they benefit the client. A 1975 amendment to the Securities Exchange Act provides a safe harbor for investment managers using soft-dollar. arrangements.[9] Soft dollars can be paid to brokerage firms for research services or superior execution. One major concern with the use of soft dollars is that they are sometimes used to court business from an investment management firm. In cases where the investment management firm receives services from the broker that do not benefit the client, a breach of fiduciary duty has occurred.

The 1990s and the proliferation of the Internet brought a new type of discount broker into the picture. Online brokers such as E*trade and Ameritrade allow investors to trade from their home computers for very low commission rates. There are several concerns regarding online trading. First, the question always arises about the quality of the execution. Are traders receiving the best possible price? A concern of government regulators is the rash of day traders who use low-commission online brokers to conduct their transactions. Once, day trading was reserved for market professionals. However, the Internet and online trading has led to a proliferation of online day traders, many of whom have little or no investment knowledge and many of whom have seen their life savings wiped out in a matter of days or weeks. Finally, it is unclear whether online brokerage firms are subject to the same "suitability" requirements that full-service brokers must adhere to—that is, laws that ensure the investments they recommend are suitable for their clients.

The trading of securities online by individual investors appears to be only the beginning of the Internet revolution. Currently, several firms are in the process of offering online trading for corporate finance chiefs. These Internet firms are planning to allow companies to trade more sophisticated financial instruments such as foreign exchange options, interest rate derivatives, and swaps online.[10]

Electronic Exchanges and ECNs

Changes in technology have led to a number of new networks that link buyers and sellers of stocks. *Electronic communications networks* or *ECNs* are computerized trade matching systems that eliminate the need for human traders. These computerized systems attempt to match the best bid and offer prices, while reducing costs and providing anonymity. ECNs generate revenues by charging a fee below that of traditional traders for every successfully matched trade. Some of the better known ECNs include Instinet, POSIT, Island, and Archipelago.

Another model for electronic trading is the Arizona Stock Exchange. Formed in 1990, the Arizona Exchange is an electronic single price auction trading system. The exchange works as a *call auction market*, where buyers and sellers come together at specific times to negotiate price. The scheduled sessions of a call auction market have an advantage over a *continuous auction market* like the New York Stock Exchange, where continuous order flow may keep buyers and sellers from meeting and thus keep them from trading at the best possible price. Holding auctions at designated times means that buyers and sellers can come together at the appropriate time and negotiate the best possible price.

Operating the Trading Desk

The work day for traders begins long before the markets and exchanges open. Traders begin their day by examining the positions they hold and what new buy and sell orders have come from the foreign and branch offices. Examining their position and the incoming buy and sell orders gives traders an idea of what deals need to be made and how to negotiate them. In addition to this information, the traders may attend a morning research meeting in order to gather the latest information from the firm's analysts that may impact price and order flow. Once this information is gathered and examined, traders begin communicating with their customers.

Successful implementation of the trading strategy requires that the portfolio manager communicate the goals of the strategy to the trader. Different portfolio strategies will necessitate different goals of trading. For example, a momentum or information-based manager may be more willing to accept higher market impact costs in order to have the trade executed in a timely manner. On the other hand, a value-based manager may be willing to accept greater timing costs in order to reduce the market impact cost. In either case, if the trading strategy is communicated to the trader, the trader will be in a better position to achieve the goals set out by the portfolio manager.

Organizing and operating a trading desk can be a complicated task. A typical equity trading room may handle trades in equities, convertible bonds, foreign stocks, and options and futures.[11] Trades may be conducted for a number of mutual funds, pension funds, and other funds managed by the firm. Because of differences in time zones, trading will take place around the clock.

After-hours Trading

One recent movement in the financial markets is toward a longer trading day. As world financial markets become more integrated, expanded trading hours recognize that different time zones necessitate trading around the world twenty-four hours a day. Currently, investors can trade equities after the exchanges close on a number of ECNs. At the end of 1999, the NYSE and NASDAQ both had plans to lengthen the trading day.

After-hours trading is not without its problems. First, when the exchanges are closed, the number of buyers and sellers of a security will tend to be small. The low volume generated by the relatively few buyers and sellers may mean that investors will not receive the best possible price for the trade. In addition, the low volume often leads to wider bid-ask spreads. Unlike normal trading hours, when the prices for securities are linked together, the prices on securities trading after hours may differ from ECN to ECN. Therefore, investors are not assured of receiving the best available price on their transaction.

Regulatory Issues

The new technology has not only led to new ways of executing trades, such as through ECNs, but has also opened up a number of inquiries regarding regulation of the exchanges. Currently, a two-tier system regulates the exchanges. First, the SEC is the broad-based regulator of the securities industry. Second, exchanges play an important role in the regulatory process through self-regulation. Exchanges determine the rules of the exchange subject to the SEC.

One major concern resulting from the changes in technology is the possibility for investors to trade securities at various hours and through various exchanges and ECNs. This has led to fragmented markets or *fragmentation,* which often leads to a discrepancy in the price that a security trades at in two different markets. For example, an investor may purchase a security at a price of $25 on one exchange or ECN without realizing that the same security could have been purchased elsewhere for $24. In a series of speeches in late 1999, concern over different trade prices led SEC chairman Arthur Levitt to challenge the exchanges and other trading networks to share price information and to make sure that investors receive the best price for their trades. In early 2000, several major brokerage houses in a confidential white paper submitted to the SEC proposed the adoption of a new market system that includes a single self-regulatory agency and a central display of all stock quotes.

Summary

Brokers offer a number of important services to their clients beyond securities recommendation and basic execution of orders. Although many of these back room operations go unnoticed by investors, they play an important part in the securities industry. One of the most important services offered by brokers is the quality of execution. By carefully communicating with investors and portfolio managers, brokers can tailor an execution strategy to meet the desired goals in the most cost-efficient manner.

Selected Bibliography

Arnott, R. "Trading Costs." In *Investment Management,* eds. P. L. Bernstein and A. Damodaran. New York: John Wiley, 1998, 251–258.

Association for Investment Management Research. *Execution Techniques, True Trading Cost, and the Microstructure of Markets.* Charlottesville, Va.: AIMR, 1993.

Damodaran, A. "The Hidden Cost of Trading." In *Investment Management,* P. L. Bernstein and A. Damodaran. New York: John Wiley, 1998, 259–273.

Leinweber, D. J. "Using Information from Trading in Trading and Portfolio Management." In *Execution Techniques, True Trading Cost, and the Microstructure of Markets,* Association for Investment Management Research. Charlottesville, Va.: AIMR, 1993.

Rose, J. D., and D. C. Cushing. "Making the Best Use of Trading Alternatives." In *Execution Techniques, True Trading Cost, and the Microstructure of Markets,* Association for Investment Management Research. Charlottesville, Va.: AIMR, 1993.

Rubinfeld, A. *The Super Traders: Secrets & Successes of Wall Street's Best & Brightest.* Chicago: Irwin Professional Publishing, 1992.

Treynor, J. L., and W. H. Wagner. "Implementation of Portfolio Building: Execution," In *Managing Investment Portfolios: A Dynamic Process,* eds. J. L. Maginn and D. L. Tuttle. Boston: Warren, Gorham and Lamont. 1990.

Wagner, W. H. "Defining and Measuring Trading Costs." In *Execution Techniques, True Trading Cost, and the Microstructure of Markets,* Association for Investment Management Research. Charlottesville, Va.: AIMR, 1993.

Weiss, D. M. *After the Trade is Made: Processing Securities Transactions.* New York: New York Institute for Finance, 1993.

Notes

1. A complete discussion can be found in D. M. Weiss, *After the Trade Is Made: Processing Securities Transactions.* (New York: New York Institute for Finance, 1993.)

2. For simplicity, we assume that there is only one broker. However, there could be more than one broker involved in the transaction.

3. The leverage factor = 1/percent margin requirement.

4. Program trading is a general term that refers to computer-generated buy and sell orders.

5. See the NYSE glossary on "Circuit Breakers," available at www.nyse.com.

6. W. H. Wagner, "Defining and Measuring Trading Costs," In *Execution Techniques, True Trading Cost, and the Microstructure of Markets,* Association for Investment Management Research. (Charlottesville, Va.: AIMR, 1993.)

7. J. D. Rose and D. C. Cushing, "Making the Best Use of Trading Alternatives." In *Execution Techniques, True Trading Cost, and the Microstructure of Markets,* Association for Investment Management Research. (Charlottesville, Va.: AIMR, 1993.)

8. P. Micioni, "Strategies for International Trading." In *Execution Techniques, True Trading Cost, and the Microstructure of Markets,* Association for Investment Management Research. (Charlottesville, Va.: AIMR, 1993.)

9. Section 28(e) states that an investment manager has not breached a fiduciary duty by paying a price in excess of the best execution price "if such commission was reasonable in relation to the value of the brokerage and research services provided."

10. P. M. Sherer, "Online Trading for Corporate-Finance Chiefs Arrives," *Wall Street Journal,* October 13, 1999, C1, C21.

11. B. C. Browchuk, "Organizing and Operating the Trading Desk—Part I." In *Execution Techniques, True Trading Cost, and the Microstructure of Markets,* Association for Investment Management Research. (Charlottesville, Va.: AIMR, 1993.)

7
American Depositary Receipts

International investing has become an important part of the portfolio management process. Over the past two decades, recognition that international investing can improve the return and risk characteristics of a domestic portfolio has led to tremendous growth in foreign investing. U.S. investment in international securities grew from $17 billion in 1981 to over $1 trillion by 1998 and is projected to reach over $2 trillion by 2003. American depositary receipts (ADRs) present an efficient, cost-effective and liquid method for U.S. investors to make specific foreign investments. The ADR market as a percentage of total U.S. investments in foreign equities doubled from 18 percent in 1991 to 36 percent in 1997, and this upward trend is expected to continue. Foreign companies list their shares in the United States to gain prestige and to raise capital.

Market Overview

An *American depositary receipt* is a negotiable certificate traded in the United States evidencing ownership of shares in a foreign corporation. Each ADR represents a specific number of foreign shares deposited at a local custodian in the issuer's home market. ADRs' flexible structure enables foreign corporations to improve visibility and raise capital in the United States. Structures of ADRs include unsponsored program, sponsored Level-I, Level-II, Level-III, and Rule 144As. ADRs provide U.S. investors an additional venue to acquire and trade non-U.S. securities in U.S. dollars without concern for the differing settlement process and securities custody. ADRs are quoted and pay dividends in U.S. dollars, thus avoiding costly currency conversions. Through ADRs, Americans can achieve benefits of diversification and risk reduction not obtainable in the U.S. domestic markets.

Level-I ADRs are unlisted and trade in the over-the-counter market. A Level-I program cannot be used to raise capital, but is a simple way for a non-U.S. company to increase its recognition among U.S. investors. Level-II and Level-III ADRs are listed programs that trade on one of the exchanges such as the NYSE, AMEX, or NASDAQ. A listed program provides access to the broadest U.S. investor base. The issuer of a listed ADR must comply with applicable SEC registration procedures and individual exchange listing requirements.

Rule 144A ADRs are privately placed depositary receipts. They are traded pursuant to SEC Rule 144A, which improves the liquidity of privately placed securities by allowing qualified institutional buyers (QIBs) to trade these securities with other QIBs without a holding period restriction.[1] This is a popular capital-raising tool for companies from emerging markets and companies entering the U.S. market for the first time. A Rule 144A program can be established side-by-side with a Level-I ADR for the same class of stock. For a global offering, Citibank introduced the first global depositary receipt (GDR) in 1990. A GDR offering generally is available in two or more markets outside the issuer's home country. Most GDRs consist of a U.S. tranche that is offered under Rule 144A and a non-U.S. tranche that is placed outside of the United States in accordance with Regulation S.

In addition to receipts for underlying stock, Sweden's LM Ericsson used American depositary debentures (ADDs) to raise capital in 1993. ADDs are depositary receipts evidencing ownership of debt rather than equity. After the advent of the economic and monetary union in Europe, the euroDR market has been developed. A euroDR represents ownership of shares in a corporation from a country outside of the European economic and monetary union. Furthermore, Singapore depositary receipts (SDRs) represent another step in the globalization of capital markets. SDRs enable non-Singapore companies to establish a presence in Singapore. Similarly, DRs listed in London provide issuers a means of raising capital among international investors.

The number of depositary receipt programs has increased steadily from 836 in 1990 to 1,438 in 1999. The total capital raised in private and public offerings averaged $13.3 billion during the period 1990 through 1999. The total number of sponsored ADRs follows the same trend, from 352 in 1990 to 1,438 in 1999. The number of exchange-listed facilities was 176 in 1990 and 532 in 1999. The dollar value of transactions for exchange-listed ADRs reached over $500 billion in 1997 and $600 billion in 1999. These annual statistics are documented in Table 7-1. Major depositary banks include the Bank of New York, Morgan Guaranty, and Citibank.

Issuance and Cancellation

When establishing a sponsored ADR program, the issuer selects a team of lawyers, accountants, investment bankers, and investor relationships firms. The issuer also chooses a depositary bank to implement and manage the ADR program on an ongoing basis. The issuer works with the depositary

Table 7-1. American depositary receipt programs.

Year	Total number of ADRs	Total number of sponsored ADRs	Total number of exchange-listed ADRs	Annual dollar volume of exchange-listed ADRs (in billions of dollars)
1990	836	352	176	75
1991	886	418	186	94
1992	924	481	215	125
1993	986	574	256	201
1994	1,124	745	317	248
1995	1,209	866	357	276
1996	1,301	992	426	341
1997	1,358	1,066	457	503
1998	1,415	1,138	505	563
1999	1,438	1,175	532	667

Source: Bank of New York.

bank to select a custodian to safekeep the underlying shares in the issuer's home market. The issuer, the depositary bank, and, in most cases, the ADR holders enter into a *deposit agreement* that sets forth the terms of the depositary receipt program. Based on the contract, the depositary bank performs the specified services on behalf of the issuers and investors. Investment bankers are included in the team when new capital is being raised, and not all issuers establish relationships with public relation firms.

The ADRs are created once the underlying shares are deposited with the depositary's custodian in the issuer's home market. The depositary then issues depositary receipts to investors. For example, consider an investor who wishes to purchase new ADRs. To issue new ADRs, the U.S. broker contacts a broker to purchase shares through an exchange in the foreign corporation's local market. Those shares are deposited with a local custodian. The custodian instructs the depositary bank to issue ADRs evidencing ownership of the deposited shares. The depositary bank delivers the ADRs through the Depositary Trust Corporation to the broker who initiated the trade. The broker delivers the ADRs to the customer's account. The ADRs are created.

Once the ADR program is established, the depositary acts as the liaison between the foreign issuer and U.S. investors. Typical services provided by a depositary bank include:

- Account management: provide ongoing support to the issuer and advise on program enhancements.

- Corporate actions processing: pay dividends to registered holders of ADRs, disseminate information to investors about corporate actions, support tax reclamation process, and maintain custodian relationships.

- Broker services: communicate with brokers and ensure smooth and efficient settlement of trades.

- Shareholder services: respond to shareholder inquiries, process IRS tax withholding and reporting, process proxies, and tabulate proxies.

- Information reporting: provide issuers with information about their programs and provide brokers with information about ADR programs.

One important step in establishing an ADR program is determining the ratio of underlying shares to the ADR shares. ADR shares are established as a multiple or a fraction of the underlying shares. Several factors are important in setting the ratio. First, the issuer will want to conform to the price range of industry peers in the United States. Second, each exchange has average price ranges for listed shares. Third, institutional and individual investors also have preference for shares traded in certain ranges. Once the ratio is set, the price of the ADRs should reflect the dollar equivalent price of the shares in the home market. For example, suppose the ratio has been set at two-to-one. Assume the price of the underlying shares in the home market is $15.25, and the ADR is selling for $31.00. The arbitrageur will buy shares and issue ADRs until the arbitrage profits are driven away. In contrast, if the underlying shares are traded at a higher level, the arbitrageur will buy the ADRs, cancel the ADRs, and sell the underlying shares in the foreign local market.

The steps are reversed to cancel the ADR program. To cancel the ADRs, the broker receives ADRs from customers and delivers them to the depositary for cancellation. The depositary instructs the local custodian to release the underlying shares to the local broker who purchased the shares.

Structure of Depositary Receipt Facilities

ADR programs can be grouped into two categories: sponsored and unsponsored. Sponsored facilities include Level-I ADR, Level-II ADR, Level-III ADR, and Rule 144A ADR. Unsponsored programs are not supported by foreign companies. Sponsored facilities are exclusive to one depositary and cannot exist simultaneously with unsponsored ADRs because sponsored and unsponsored ADRs for the same foreign security might trade at different prices, creating confusion. The prices might be different in part because in a sponsored program the issuer reimburses the depositary for its expenses, whereas in an unsponsored facility the ADR holders bear such expenses.

Unsponsored Programs

An *unsponsored ADR* program is not initiated by the foreign issuer. Rather, it is initiated by a bank in response to investor demand. The issuer has no control over the activity of the program because there is generally no deposit agreement between the issuer and the depositary bank.

Registration of the underlying shares is not required, only the ADRs must be registered with the SEC. The depositary and the issuer together submit an application to the SEC under Rule 12g3-2(b) seeking exemption from the full reporting requirements. If granted, the issuer will be notified that it has been included in the list of foreign issuers eligible to claim exemption and assigned a file number.

Upon receipt of SEC approval, the depositary files Form F-6, which is a limited disclosure registration statement. The foreign issuer is not a signatory to the document and generally has no obligation or liability in connection with the registration of the ADRs. The SEC normally grants approval of Form F-6 registration statements within a short period of time. Once approved, the unsponsored ADR program can be traded only in the over-the-counter market. The SEC requires that material public information in the issuer's home country be supplied to the SEC and made available to U.S. investors. The depositary will mail the issuer's annual reports and certain public information to U.S. investors upon request. The SEC does not require this material to be translated into English or adjusted for differences in U.S. generally accepted accounting principles (GAAP) practices.

Unsponsored programs provide two advantages to issuers. They provide an inexpensive and simple way of expanding the investor base in the United States. The SEC compliance and reporting requirements are minimal. Other depositary banks can duplicate an unsponsored program by filing a Form F-6 with the SEC without the consent of the issuer. Also, an unsponsored program can be converted to a sponsored facility. The issuer has to "buy out" the unsponsored ADRs by contacting the depositary bank of the unsponsored program, having it exchange its ADRs for the new sponsored ADRs and paying the cash out fee to the depositary.

Level-I ADRs

A Level-I program is the easiest and least expensive way for a foreign company to gauge interest in its securities and to begin building a presence in the

United States. The issuer is required to obtain a Rule 12g3-2(b) exemption by providing the SEC with English translation or summary information sent to shareholders, made public in the home market or provided to a local exchange. The issuer also has to file a Form F-6 and sign a deposit agreement. The issuer has greater control over a Level-I facility because a deposit agreement is executed between the issuer and one exclusive depositary bank. The agreement defines the responsibilities of the depositary, including requirements for responding to investor inquiries, maintaining stockholder records, and mailing annual reports and other materials to shareholders. Level-I ADRs are not listed on an exchange and are traded in the over-the-counter market. Quotes are available in the pink sheets, and brokers wishing to trade in these securities can contact the listed market makers in the particular security. The main advantages of a Level-I ADR are its low costs and its ability to coexist with a Rule 144A ADR facility (called a *side-by-side program*). The structure allows foreign issuers to combine the benefits of a publicly traded program with the efficiency of a private offering as a capital-raising tool. Also, set up is easy and can take as little as nine weeks. It is relatively inexpensive to upgrade the program to Level-II or Level-III as well.

Level-II ADRs

Level-II and Level-III ADRs are listed on one of the national exchanges. Level-II ADRs must comply with the SEC's full registration and reporting requirements. The issuer must file with SEC a Form F-6 for registering the ADRs and a Form 20-F to meet the reporting requirements (financial statements must be partially reconciled to U.S. GAAP). The compliance allows the issuer to list its ADRs on the NYSE, AMEX, or NASDAQ, each of which has its own reporting and disclosure requirements.

Full registration and listing increase liquidity and marketability and enhance the issuer's name recognition in the United States. The issuer is also able to monitor the ownership of its shares in the United States. Because the foreign issuer must comply with the rigorous SEC requirements, it is well positioned to upgrade and make a public offering in the U.S. market.

On the other hand, the program is more expensive and time-consuming to set up and maintain than a Level-I facility. Another disadvantage is that SEC regulation does not permit a public offering of ADRs under a Level-II program; that is, a foreign company cannot use Level-II to raise capital in the United States.

Level-III ADRs

Foreign companies use sponsored Level-III facilities to raise capital in the United States. ADRs under Level-III are similar to Level-II ADRs. In both programs, the issuer initiates the program, signs a deposit agreement with one depositary bank, lists on one of the U.S. exchanges, and files Form F-6 and Form 20-F with the SEC. The major difference is that a Level-III ADR allows the issuer to make a public offering. For this, the issuer is required to file a Form F-1 (similar to Form S-1 for U.S. companies) to register the equity securities underlying the program. The reporting for Level-III is more onerous than for Level-I or Level-II programs. Financial statements must be fully reconciled to U.S. GAAP. The costs of establishing a Level-III ADR can be substantial and include listing, legal, and accounting fees, investor relations, and road shows. Establishment of a Level-II or Level-III ADR takes fifteen weeks or more, depending on individual program specifics.

In sum, a Level-I facility allows a foreign issuer to enjoy the benefits of a publicly traded security without changing its current reporting process. Companies wanting to list shares on a U.S. exchange use sponsored Level-II programs, and companies wishing to raise capital use Level-III. Each higher level of ADR program reflects additional SEC registration and increases the visibility and attractiveness of the ADR to institutional and individual investors.

Rule 144A ADRs

As an alternative to Level-III, foreign companies can access the U.S. capital markets through *Rule 144A* ADRs to accredited investors, thereby avoiding SEC registration and reporting. The SEC adopted Rule 144A in April 1990, in part to stimulate capital raising in the United States by foreign companies. Restrictions governing the resale of restricted securities are lifted under Rule 144A if the resale is made to QIBs. A QIB is defined as an institution that owns and invests on a discretionary basis at least $100 million in securities of an unaffiliated entity. In the case of registered broker-dealers, the requirement is $10 million.

Through Rule 144A ADRs, foreign companies have access to the U.S. private placement market and may raise capital without conforming to the full burden of SEC registration and disclosure. The costs of issuing Rule 144As are considerably less than the costs of initiating a Level-III ADR. Establishment can take as little as seven weeks. In addition, the NASD established a closed electronic trading system for Rule 144A, called Private Offerings,

Table 7-2. American depositary receipt filing requirements and trading.

Type of ADR	SEC filing	Exchange listing and trading	Raising capital
Unsponsored	**Form F-6** 12g3-2(b)	**Over-the-counter**	**No**
Sponsored:			
Level-I	Form F-6 12g3-2(b)	**Over-the-counter**	No
Level-II	Form F-6 Form 20-F	NYSE, AMEX, NASDAQ	No
Level-III	Form F-6 and Form F-1 Form 20-F	NYSE, AMEX, NASDAQ	Yes
Rule 144A	N/A	Private placement market	Yes

Note: For reporting purposes, Level-II financial statements must be partially reconciled to U.S. GAAP, and Level-III financial reports must be fully reconciled to U.S. GAAP.

Resales and Trading through Automated Linkages (PORTAL). This system is designed to provide a market for privately traded securities. The system is available to both investors and market makers. Essentially, it allows institutions to claim Rule 144As as liquid securities for regulatory purposes.

In sum, the key advantages to issuers are that Rule 144A ADRs do not have to conform to full reporting and registration requirements, and they can be launched on their own or as part of a global offering. There are two disadvantages, however. First, Rule 144As cannot be created for classes of shares already listed on a U.S. exchange. Further, Rule 144As can be traded among only QIBs, so the market certainly is not as liquid as the public equity market. Table 7-2 summarizes the different SEC filing requirements for different ADR programs.

Global Depositary Receipts

Global depositary receipts (GDRs) allow an issuer to raise capital through a global offering in two or more markets at the same time, thus broadening its shareholder base. GDRs can be issued in either the public or private markets in the United States and other countries. Most GDRs include a U.S. tranche and an international tranche placed outside of the United States pursuant to Regulation S, which provides conditions under which securities offered or sold to investors outside the United States are not subject to SEC registration requirements. In 1990, South Korea's Samsung became the first company to issue GDRs.

A U.S. component of a GDR can be structured either as a Level-III ADR or as a private placement under Rule 144A. GDRs placed in Europe are generally listed on the Luxembourg or London exchange or quoted on London's SEAQ International. With the global integration of the major securities markets, the link between the major clearing firms such as Depositary Trust & Clearing Corporation, Euroclear, and Cedel eases settlement and promotes increased liquidity through cross-border trading.

A Note on Trading Foreign Ordinaries

Traditionally, the main methods for Americans to invest in companies in the overseas markets are through international mutual funds or ADRs. *Foreign ordinaries*, stocks in overseas companies that do not trade on U.S. markets, are not easily accessible. Only a handful of options are open to U.S. investors. Merrill Lynch and Charles Schwab provide clients access to foreign ordinaries online or through a broker. Also, Globeshare and Intltrader provide online access to quotes and trading in overseas companies.

Investors who consider going offshore directly need to take into account several important factors. First, investors on foreign exchanges face such hurdles as taxes on trades, foreign exchange risk, and less stringent accounting standards. Another problem is the clock. Market hours in Europe are several hours ahead of the U.S. trading day, and Asian market hours do not overlap with U.S. market hours at all. To minimize such risk in differing trading hours or in thinly traded foreign ordinaries, market makers often widen their bid-ask spreads. They bid less to buy shares and ask more to sell them during off hours.

Advantages of Depositary Receipts

The ADR structure provides several distinct benefits, such as trading simplification, faster dividend payment, risk and cost reduction, investor barrier elimination, and investor communication facilitation. The increased efficiency in the ADR market further benefits brokers and market makers.

Through ADR programs, foreign issuers gain access to the U.S. capital markets at highly competitive costs.

ADRs greatly simplify the trading of foreign equities for issuers, brokers, market makers, and investors. Without ADRs, a single trade of a foreign security involves multiple parties, currency concern, and settlement delays. ADRs standardize the varying securities practices. Securities in ADR forms are easily transferable, and the automated book-entry systems for clearing procedures are well established. ADR holders also have the benefit of a depositary bank collecting dividends, converting the currency, and issuing prompt payment in U.S. dollars or additional ADRs in the case of a stock dividend.

Because ADRs simplify securities processing, settlement risk is reduced. Without ADRs, U.S. investors must find a broker with capabilities in the specific foreign market to execute the trade abroad. Investors buying ADRs save even more because they do not have to pay safekeeping fees to a custodian abroad. ADRs are registered in the United States; therefore records exist here to protect ownership rights. At the same time, ADRs save investors insurance fees necessary to protect securities abroad.

Many institutional investors are restricted from investing in securities that are not traded on a U.S. exchange, so listed ADRs represent a way to add international exposure to a portfolio. Similarly, institutions that invest only in the United States because they have no custodian facilities or arrangements abroad can invest in ADRs. An ADR program also helps investors avoid the regulations of countries that prohibit physical delivery of shares overseas. Another significant advantage ADR holders have over holders of foreign shares is that the price information is more readily available. It is important to note that ADR holders enjoy all the voting rights, as well as the equivalent cash value of non-U.S. subscription right and warrant offerings.

In the ADR market, the Bank of New York publishes an ADR index that tracks the performance of ADRs in the United States. In addition, four regional subindices track ADRs in Europe, Asia, Latin America, and emerging markets. J. P. Morgan also publishes detailed information about the ADR market and company and industry data.

Securities dealers and brokers find ADRs attractive as well. The T+3 settlement cycle, when settlement is three days after the trade day, minimizes losses from fails.[2] The depositaries can also prerelease ADRs to help bridge timing differences in settlement cycles in different nations. In a prerelease, the depositary with the knowledge that the trade of underlying shares has been executed issues an ADR before the underlying shares are physically deposited in an overseas custodian.

For foreign companies, ADRs provide the most effective means of entering the U.S. market, the largest in the world. An ADR program provides a sim-

Table 7-3. Most active American depositary receipt programs by dollar volume in 1999.

Company	Country
Nokia Corporation	Finland
Vodafone Airtouch plc	United Kingdom
BP Amoco plc	United Kingdom
Telebras Holding Company	Brazil
Ericsson Telephone Company	Sweden
Royal Dutch Petroleum Company	Netherlands
Telefonos De Mexico	Mexico
Elan Corporation	Ireland
STMicroelectronics N.V.	Netherlands
Koninklijke Philips Electronics N.V.	Netherlands

Source: Bank of New York. *Depositary Receipts: 1999 Year-End Market Review.*

ple means of diversifying a company's shareholder base. It enhances a foreign company's visibility and name recognition in the United States. It may increase the liquidity and local share price of the issuer as a result of global demand and trading. An ADR program also can be used to help build a stronger financial presence in the United States. ADR ratios are often adjusted to ensure that an ADR trades in a comparable range with those of its peers in the U.S. market. In addition, ADRs provide an easy way for U.S. employees of non-U.S. companies to invest in their companies' employee stock purchase programs. These benefits have motivated foreign companies to launch ADRs in the United States. During 1995 through 1999, the amount of capital raised by ADR offerings per year was $11.7 billion, $19.5 billion, $18.6 billion, $10.2 billion, and 22.0 billion, respectively. Companies from countries such as the United Kingdom, Australia, Japan, Hong Kong, Mexico, Brazil, France, the Netherlands, Germany, Russia, Chile, China, and Taiwan have issued ADRs in the United States. Table 7-3 lists the top ten issuers with the most actively traded ADRs in 1999.

U.S. Securities Regulation on Depositary Receipts

Issuers of ADRs must comply with U.S. securities regulation. For publicly traded ADRs, registration is required. If the ADRs represent new shares, the registration must cover the newly issued shares as well. In addition, Regulation S provides for a safe harbor exemption for securities offered overseas.

Registration of ADRs for Outstanding Shares

The motivations for registration of ADRs for previously issued shares involve either a foreign issuer seeking visibility in the United States through sponsorship of an ADR program or a depositary creating an unsponsored program as a result of perceived demand. The issuer is not engaged in a public offering of its shares. It is the issuance of ADRs that constitutes a public offering requiring registration. In this situation, a Form F-6 is used to register the ADRs under the Securities Act of 1933. The simplified registration procedures are available only where the issuer of the deposited shares has obtained exemption under Rule 12g3-2(a) or (b). The general eligibility requirements are:

■ The ADR holder is entitled to withdraw the deposited securities at any time subject only to the temporary delay caused by closing transfer books.

■ Payment of fees, taxes, and similar charges.

■ The issuer is reporting pursuant to the requirements of Section 13(a) or 15(d) of the Securities Exchange Act of 1934 or the deposited shares are exempt by Rule 12g3-2(b) unless the issuer concurrently files a registration statement on another form for the deposited securities.

Under Rule 12g3-2(a), a foreign issuer is exempt from the 1934 act reporting burden if it does not have a class of equity securities held by at least 300 persons resident in the United States. The exemption under Rule 12g3-2(a) is unlikely to be available if the ADR facility is successful. The issuer then must satisfy the reporting requirements of Section 12(g) or qualify for an exemption provided under Rule 12g3-2(b). Under Rule 12g3-2(b), a foreign issuer is granted exemption if it meets the following requirements:

■ It does not have its ADRs or underlying securities listed on a U.S. exchange or quoted on NASDAQ.

■ It submits to the SEC certain information that was made available to its shareholders or to foreign government authorities in the foreign local market.

■ It provides the SEC the same information during each subsequent fiscal year.

The extent to which the foreign issuer is involved in the registration depends on whether the program is sponsored or unsponsored. Although the terms of deposit are different between these two types of programs, the sponsorship in and of itself does not result in different reporting or registration requirements under U.S. securities laws.

Registration of ADRs for New Shares

When ADRs represent new shares or shares distributed by a statutory underwriter, the ADRs as well as the deposited shares must be registered under the Securities Act of 1933.[3] As discussed above, Form F-6 is available only for the registration of ADRs. The underlying securities must be registered on Form F-1, F-2, or F-3. Each "F" series form requires disclosure of the basic information regarding the issuer that is prescribed by Form 20-F under the 1934 act. The forms differ primarily with respect to the amount of information that a foreign issuer does not have to disclose in full if the issuer has provided or is providing information through Form 20-F and any other 1934 act filings. Unless the foreign issuer has shares registered or is reporting under the 1934 act, Form F-1 must be used.

Form F-1 is the long form registration statement and does not allow information to be incorporated by reference to previous SEC filings. A Form F-1 is available to all foreign issuers who have never filed reports with the SEC or are not qualified or choose not to use Form F-2 or F-3. Form F-1 is typically used for initial public offerings into the U.S. market. To be eligible to use the short forms or the more streamlined Form F-2 or F-3 to register securities, the foreign issuer must already have been filing periodic reports with the SEC. Eligibility also depends on the size of the issuer.

Regulation S

Regulation S provides a safe harbor exemption for securities offered overseas without registration. Regulation S was adopted in 1990 concurrently with Rule 144A. There are two types of Regulation S safe harbors. One is the *issuer safe harbor*, which addresses offers and sales by issuers, their affiliates, and securities professionals involved in the initial offerings of securities. The second is the *resale safe harbor*, which addresses resales by securities professionals such as brokers. Two general conditions must be satisfied to take advantage of the issuer and resale safe harbors: any offer or sale must be made in an offshore transaction and no direct selling efforts may be made in the United States.

Regulation S and Rule 144A are closely related. The SEC has maintained the position that issuers may undertake private placements in the United States (Rule 144A) at the same time they are making an offshore Regulation S offering without violating that regulation's prohibition against U.S. direct selling efforts. Substantial care must nevertheless be taken to avoid spillover of such securities into the U.S. public markets.

In recent years, the SEC has identified abusive practices in offshore Regulation S securities transactions, especially schemes involving the securities of thinly capitalized companies (called *microcaps*). These types of securities are particularly vulnerable to fraud and manipulation because little information about them is available to the public. The SEC in 1998 adopted amendments to Regulation S to prevent further abuses, but also to allow continued reliance on Regulation S in legitimate offshore offerings. The amendments include:

- Equity securities placed offshore by U.S. issuers under Regulation S are classified as restricted securities within the meaning of Rule 144, so resales are restricted.

- The distribution compliance period (restricted period under Regulation S) for these securities is lengthened from forty days to one year.

- Issuers are required to change from Form 8-K reporting to quarterly reporting Form 10-Q.

The SEC indicated that to avoid undue interference with offshore offering practices of foreign issuers, these amendments apply to equity securities of U.S. issuers but not to the equity securities of foreign issuers.

ADRs in Acquisitions and Privatizations

Consolidation and globalization are the trends of the financial services system. Volume of global mergers and acquisitions surged to more than $1 trillion in 1996. By 1998, the volume approached $2 trillion. As part of this trend, foreign companies have used their ADRs as an acquisition currency.

Many acquirers have established ADR programs before the acquisition. An active ADR program provides a liquidity option and transparent pricing for investors. Also, these ADR exchanges are structured in the form of tax-free stock swaps. Thus, a stock swap merger or acquisition results in a pool of new ADR investors. ADR transactions enable foreign acquirers to avoid the burden of taking on additional debt as well, which preserves capital and enhances financial flexibility. The eventual success of the merger may in part depend on an employee stock purchase plan that is conveniently made available by the ADR facilities. Both listed (Level-II and Level-III) and Rule 144A ADRs may be used to fund an acquisition. A listed program could also have the advantage of enabling employee plans that hold company shares to continue without "cashing out" the existing employees.

Another significant contribution of the depositary receipt market is raising funds for privatization programs. The number of privatizations using depositary receipts in their global offerings has steadily increased in recent years.

The EuroDR Market

On January 4, 1999, the financial scene of the eleven first-round participating nations of the European monetary union switched to the euro.[4] The euro's introduction will lead to a dramatic acceleration in cross-border investment. The Paris Bourse, Sicovan SA, and Citibank have joined forces to offer depositary receipts in the new euro, called euroDR. A euroDR is a negotiable certificate evidencing ownership of shares in a corporation from a country outside the European Union (EU). Each euroDR denotes euro depositary shares representing a specific number of underlying shares remaining on deposit in the issuer's home market. The euroDRs are traded in the new euro currency. Table 7-4 lists key features of the euroDRs as compared with GDRs and listed ADRs.

The issuance process of euroDRs in the EU is similar to that of ADRs in the United States. To issue new euroDRs, the European broker must contact a broker in the issuer's home market to purchase shares through the stock exchange in the local market. Those shares are deposited with a local custodian, and then the custodian instructs the depositary bank to issue euroDRs that represent ownership of the shares deposited. The depositary bank issues euroDRs and delivers them through the clearing agency to the broker who initiated the trade. The broker then delivers euroDRs to the customer's account. The euroDR is created.

The cancellation process is the opposite. The investor contacts the European broker and requests sale of the euroDRs. The broker may either sell in

Table 7-4. Global depositary receipts, euroDRs, and listed American depositary receipts.

Type	GDRs	euroDRs	Listed ADRs
Investment vehicle	Private placement	Public listing in EU	Public offering in United States
Investor base	Institutional investors in Europe and U.S. qualified institutional buyers	All investors in EU	All investors in United States
Listing and trading	Traded over-the-counter between institutions	Paris Bourse	U.S. exchanges
Currency	U.S. dollars	euro	U.S. dollars
Visibility	Limited in the EU	Broad exposure in euroland	Broad exposure in United States

the secondary market or cancel the existing program. To cancel the existing euroDR facility, the broker delivers the euroDRs to the depositary bank for cancellation and instructs a broker in the issuer's local market to sell the underlying shares. Investors receive the proceeds of the sale. The euroDR program is canceled.

Summary

ADRs are a cost-effective structure for foreign companies to improve visibility and raise capital in the United States. ADRs provide U.S. investors an additional venue to make specific foreign investments without the problems of differing settlement process and securities custody.

There are several types of ADR programs. An unsponsored ADR facility is not initiated by the foreign issuer and typically does not have a deposit agreement between the issuer and the depositary. It cannot be traded on an exchange, but it is an inexpensive way of expanding the investor base in the United States. For sponsored facilities, there are Level-I, Level-II, Level-III, and Rule 144A ADRs. A Level-I ADR is traded over-the-counter. The main advantage is that it can support a side-by-side program. A Level-II ADR is listed and complies with registration and reporting requirements. A sponsored Level-III facility represents a new issue of securities that raises capital for the foreign issuer. Rule 144A ADRs are an alternative to Level-III for raising capital. Issuers utilize GDRs to raise capital in two or more markets simultaneously.

Issuers of ADRs must comply with U.S. securities laws, including the Securities Act of 1933 and the Securities Exchange Act of 1934. The 1933 act governs registration of new securities issuance while the 1934 act requires registration of broker-dealers and reporting of issuers. For ADR issuers, certain exemption is provided under Regulation S, Rule 144A, and Rule 12g3-2(b).

Selected Bibliography

Bank of New York. *The Complete Depositary Receipt Directory.* New York: Bank of New York, 1999.

Bankers Trust. *Depositary Receipt Handbook.* New York: Bankers Trust, 1997.

Brancato, C. K. *Getting Listed on Wall Street.* Burr Ridge, Ill.: Irwin, 1996.

Coyle, R. J., ed. *The McGraw-Hill Handbook of American Depositary Receipts.* New York: McGraw-Hill, 1995.

Darby, R. "ADRs Shine Again." *Investment Dealers Digest,* August 12, 1996, 12–17.

Hubbard, D. J., and R. K. Larson. "American Depositary Receipts: Investment Alternatives or Quicksand?" *CPA Journal* 65:7 (July 1995), 70–73.

Muscarella, C. J. "Stock Split: Signaling or Liquidity? The Case of ADR Solo-Splits." *Journal of Financial Economics* 42:1 (September 1996), 3–26.

Ogden, J. "Should All Those Foreign Companies Be Listing on the NYSE?" *Global Finance* (July 1996), 54–58.

Securities and Exchange Commission. *Final Rule: Offshore Offers and Sales (Regulation S).* February 1998.

Notes

1. Qualified institutional buyers are institutions that invest at least $100 million in securities of nonaffiliates. For registered broker-dealers, the minimum requirement is $10 million.

2. Fail occurs when the delivery of the security and/or payment of funds are not completed on the settlement date.

3. A statutory underwriter is a person who takes the securities from the foreign issuer with a view toward distribution, causing resale of the securities and possibly the original sale of securities by an issuer, which is in violation of sections 5 and 12(1) of the 1933 act.

4. Only EU countries with sound monetary and fiscal policies are admitted to the monetary union. The Maastricht Treaty requires a low inflation rate, stable exchange rates, comparably low interest rates, and a sustainable level of government debt for participation in the European monetary union.

8

Treasury Securities

The Treasury securities market in the United States is the largest and most liquid fixed-income market in the world. Interest rates on Treasury securities are used as benchmarks in global capital markets. In addition, foreign money often flows to the U.S. Treasury market during times of international crisis, known as the flight to quality. Annual issuance of Treasury securities is about $2 trillion, and daily trading volume averages $200 billion. The steps involved in the issuance of new Treasury securities include the Treasury announcement, auction, and settlement. The time period between the announcement of the auction and new security settlement is the when-issued market. Dealer bidding strategies and when-issued trading are an integral part in the distribution of new Treasury securities.

Market Overview

There are three types of marketable *Treasury securities:* bills, notes, and bonds. *Treasury bills* are short-term securities with a maturity period of thirteen, twenty-six, or fifty-two weeks. These bills are discount instruments; they do not pay coupon interest. Holders of the bills receive the face amount at maturity; the difference between the price paid and the face amount represents the interest received by the bondholder. *Treasury notes* are medium-term securities with a maturity period of two, five, or ten years. *Treasury bonds* are long-term securities with a maturity period of thirty years. Notes and bonds pay coupons every six months; hence, they are also called coupon Treasury securities (or coupon treasuries).

Treasury securities are sold to institutions and individuals through regularly scheduled auctions. Table 8-1 lists the current auction pattern for marketable Treasury securities. The primary dealers, financial institutions that are active in U.S. government securities markets and have established business relationships with the New York Fed, buy most of the treasuries offered at auction. Other market participants such as individuals and institutional investors also bid at auctions regularly. The minimum purchase amount at an auction is $1,000, and any bid in excess of $1,000 must be in multiples of $1,000.

Table 8-1. Current auction pattern for marketable Treasury securities.

Security	Auction schedule
13-week bill	Weekly
26-week bill	Weekly
52-week bill	Every fourth week
2-year note	Monthly
5-year note	February, May, August, November
10-year note	February, May, August, November
30-year bond	February, August, November

Source: Bureau of Public Debt, Department of the Treasury, 1999.

Annual issuance of treasuries increased steadily until 1997. The U.S. Treasury auctioned a record $2.48 trillion in 1996, a 6.6 percent increase from 1995's issuance of $2.33 trillion. From 1990 to 1994, the annual supply was $1.530 trillion, $1.699 trillion, $1.990 trillion, and $2.11 trillion, respectively. Annual issuance declined slightly and remained at about $2 trillion from 1997 to 1999. Most of the funds are used to pay down maturing debt. The government did not raise any new cash at all in 1997, 1998, and 1999. The supply is expected to decrease further as the government runs a surplus. The trading volume averages more than $200 billion a day in recent years. The total amount of marketable treasuries outstanding is about $3.3 trillion.

Coupon Stripping

Coupon stripping strips interest payment from a coupon treasury and treats each component coupon and the principal as a separate security. These strips are frequently referred to in the marketplace as Treasury zeros or Treasury zero coupons. Each coupon strip entitles the owner to a specified amount of cash on a specific date, while the principal strip receives the principal amount at maturity. For example, a ten-year bond with a face value of $1 million and a 6.00 percent coupon rate could be stripped into its principal and 20 semiannual interest payments. The end result is 21 Treasury zeros, each coupon strip receiving $30,000 and the principal strip receiving $1 million. Each of the 21 strips would become a security and each could be traded separately.

Financial institutions and government securities broker-dealers can request that the principal and interest payments of eligible Treasury securities they own be stripped into their separate components by a Federal Reserve Bank.

Generally, Treasury securities with a maturity of five years or longer are eligible to be stripped.

In May 1987, the Treasury allowed the reconstitution of stripped securities. To reconstitute a stripped security, a financial institution or a government securities broker-dealer must obtain the appropriate principal component and all related interest strips for the security. The principal and interest components must be in the appropriate minimum or multiple amounts for the particular security being reconstituted. Once this is done, the institution or broker must forward the components to a Federal Reserve Bank and request that they be reassembled into a fully constituted Treasury security.

Treasury Inflation-Indexed Securities

In 1997, the U.S. government introduced *Treasury inflation-indexed securities* (TIIS). The first auction of TIIS, a ten-year note, was held in January 1997. Since then, the Treasury has also issued TIIS with a maturity of five and thirty years. The coupon rate set at auction remains fixed throughout the term of the security. The principal amount is adjusted for inflation, but the inflation-adjusted principal will not be paid until maturity. The principal amount will not drop below the par at which they were originally issued, even though deflation could cause the principal to decline. The index for measuring the inflation rate is the nonseasonally adjusted U.S. City Average All Items Consumer Price Index for All Urban Consumers (CPI-U).

The introduction of TIIS has increased the types of debt instruments available to investors. Interest is based on a fixed coupon rate applied to the inflation-adjusted principal, so investors are guaranteed a real rate of return above inflation. The real yield is typically lower than the nominal yield. For example, at the close of March 8, 2000, the yield on the thirty-year TIIS was 4.13 percent, while that on the thirty-year fixed-principal bond was 6.16 percent. The yield differential reflects inflation expectation.

A Note on Market Quotations

The *Wall Street Journal* and the business sections of most newspapers publish closing quotes on all treasuries. Data vendors such as Bloomberg, Reuters, and GovPx publish real-time quotes on their proprietary networks and Web sites. For Treasury bills, quotes include the maturity date, the number of days to maturity, bid, asked, change, and asked yield. The bid and asked are quoted in terms of a rate discount. The bid rate is generally lower than the asked rate, because price and interest rate are inversely related. The asked yield is the investment yield or bond equivalent yield based on the asked discount rate quoted.

Quotes on notes and bonds include the coupon rate, maturity, bid price, asked price, change in price, and asked yield. The price quotes are based on the percentage of par value. For example, a bid of 100:04 means the dealer is bidding a price of 100 4/32 (100.125 percent of the par amount), and an asked of 100:06 means the dealer is offering to sell at 100 6/32 (100.1875 percent of par amount). The difference of 2/32 between bid and asked is referred to as the bid-asked spread. Changes are in thirty-seconds. For example, a change of +8 means that the price went up 8/32 over the prior day. The asked yield represents the yield to maturity based on the asked price. Yield to maturity is the rate that discounts all future periodic coupons and principal at maturity to the asked price. A *yield curve* is a plot of the yield to maturity against the term to maturity. A typical yield curve is shown in Figure 8-1. The new issues typically command a higher liquidity and trade at a lower yield. For example, the most recently issued long bond traded at a lower yield than other issues, as reflected in the dip is the long end of the yield curve.

If yields change by the same amount for all terms of bonds, the yield curve is said to have had a parallel shift. But this almost never happens. Under the normal yield curve environment, when the difference between the short-term and long-term yields increases, the yield curve steepens. In contrast, when the yield curve flattens, the difference between short-term and long-term yields decreases. If short-term yields are higher than long-term yields, the yield curve is inverted.

Treasury strips are also quoted in terms of price. Additionally, the type of strip is also indicated. A "ci" indicates a coupon strip, an "np" represents a note principal strip, and a "bp" denotes a bond principal strip. The yield on each of the strips is called a spot rate in the marketplace. A spot rate curve is a graphic plot of spot rate against term to maturity of the strips.

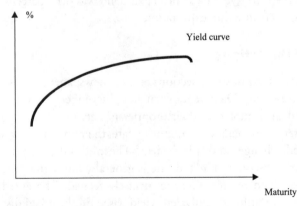

Figure 8-1. The yield curve.

TIIS are also quoted on a price basis. However, the yield is the real yield. It represents the yield investors receive in excess of and above inflation.

Yield to Maturity and Spot Rates

The yield quoted on a Treasury security is called *yield to maturity*—the discount rate that equates the present value of a security's future cash flows to its current market price. However, yield should be used only as a way to quote price, as it is incorrect to apply the same rate to all cash flows that are paid on different dates. For valuation purposes, fixed-income analysts use the spot rate, which is the rate applicable from a value date to the maturity date for a discount instrument that pays a single cash flow at maturity. The Treasury yield curve can be used to estimate the theoretical spot rate curve, which is the graphic depiction of the term structure of interest rates. Based on the theoretical spot rate curve, it is possible to compute the forward rates to gauge the market's expectation of future interest rates.[1]

Yield to Maturity

On March 24, 1999, the Treasury announced the auction results of two-year notes. The coupon rate was 4.875 percent, and the notes were awarded to bidders at a yield of 4.995 percent. The issue was dated March 31, 1999— that is, the coupon interest began to accrue on that date. The price of the security is the present value of all future cash flows. For a face value of $100, the holder of the notes was entitled to receive half of the annual coupon ($2.4375) every six months plus $100 on March 31, 2001. The rate used to discount those coupons and the final principal is half of the annual rate at 2.4975 percent. The price is the present value of all future cash flows and hence is $99.774.

Spot Rates

In the yield to maturity discussion above, every cash flow, regardless of the timing of the receipt, is discounted at the same yield. However, this procedure is incorrect. Each cash flow must be discounted at a rate corresponding to the timing of that particular cash flow. A fixed-income coupon security can be viewed as a package of zero-coupon instruments, with each component having a maturity determined by its coupon date or, in the case of face value, the final redemption date. The value of the bond should equal the total value of all component zero-coupon instruments.

Forward Rates

Suppose that an investor has a one-year investment horizon and is considering two alternatives:

■ Alternative 1: Buy a one-year Treasury bill.
■ Alternative 2: Buy a six-month Treasury bill, and when it matures buy another six-month Treasury bill.

The investor will be indifferent between those two alternatives if both produce the same returns over the one-year investment horizon. The investor has learned that the six-month bills yield 4.00 percent and the one-year bills yield 4.40 percent. But the investor does not know what the rate on six-month bills will be six months from now. The yield on a six-month Treasury bill six months from now is the *forward rate*. Given the observed spot rates, we can determine the forward rate on a six-month Treasury bill that will produce a one-year return equal to the return from purchasing a one-year Treasury bill.

By purchasing the one-year Treasury bill, the investor will receive the face value ($100) at the end of one year. The price the investor pays now is:

$$p = \frac{\$100}{\left(1 + \dfrac{4.40\%}{2}\right)^2} = \$95.74$$

Suppose instead the investor invests $95.74 in a six-month Treasury bill that yields 4.00 percent. After six months, the investor will have $95.74 × (1 + 2.00%) = $97.65. At that point the investor will purchase another six-month Treasury bill. Suppose f is the forward rate on a six-month Treasury bill available in six months when the first six-month Treasury bill matures. The total dollar amount the investor receives at the end of the one-year investment horizon must be $100 if the investor is indifferent between the two investment alternatives; that is,

$$\$95.74 \times (1 + 2.00\%) \times \left(1 + \frac{f}{2}\right) = \$97.65 \times \left(1 + \frac{f}{2}\right) = \$100$$

Solving for the f, the forward rate is 4.80 percent.

The process for deriving the forward rate on a six-month Treasury bill six months from now can be put into a formula:

$$\frac{f}{2} = \frac{\left(1 + \dfrac{y_2}{2}\right)^2}{\left(1 + \dfrac{y_1}{2}\right)} - 1$$

In the expression, y_1 is the six-month spot rate, and y_2 is the one-year spot rate, since every six months are defined as one time period.

Issuing Process and Auction

The U.S. government's debt has grown to more than $5.7 trillion in January 2000. Approximately $3.3 trillion of that debt is in the form of marketable government securities such as Treasury bills, notes, and bonds. The Treasury Department sells these securities at auction. Most treasuries are bought at auction by primary dealers, which are financial institutions active in trading government securities and have established business relationships with the Federal Reserve Bank of New York. Individual investors, typically submitting noncompetitive bids, purchase on a much smaller scale.

The auction process begins with a public announcement by the Treasury that includes the following information:

- Offering amount.

- Description of the offering, including term and type of security, CUSIP number, auction date, issue date, dated date, maturity date, and interest payment dates.

- Strips information—whether the security is eligible for stripping.

- Procedures for submission of bids, maximum bid amount, and payment terms.

Auction Bids

Bids are accepted up to thirty days before the auction and may be submitted electronically via the Treasury Automated Auction Processing System (TAAPS), Treasury Direct, by mail, or in person. Two types of bids can be submitted: competitive and noncompetitive. Small investors and individuals generally submit noncompetitive bids. In a noncompetitive tender, a bidder may not bid for more than $1 million in a bill auction or more than $5 million in a note or bond auction. Primary dealers acting for their accounts or on behalf of clients usually submit large competitive bids. However, a bidder is forbidden from bidding both competitively and noncompetitively for its own account in the same auction. Bids are submitted in terms of discount rate for bills, stated in three decimal places in 0.005 percent increments. The Treasury requires that competitive bids in note and bond auctions be expressed in yields using three decimals in 0.001 percent increments. These bids are accepted until 1:00 P.M. eastern standard time (EST) on the day of the auction. The deadline for noncompetitive tenders is 12:00 noon EST on the auction date.

Competitive bidders are permitted to submit more than one bid, but no bidder may receive more than 35 percent of the total amount of the security being sold. Specifically, under the 35-percent rule, the bidder's net long position in the auction inclusive of futures, forwards, and when-issued markets may not exceed 35 percent of the amount of the security in the auction. When the issue is reopened as a result of scarcity, the net long position will include any position in the outstanding security as well. Once the bidding is completed, the 35-percent rule is lifted.

The bids submitted through TAAPS are consolidated at the Federal Reserve Banks in New York, Chicago, and San Francisco. Immediately after 1:00 P.M. EST, these bids are reviewed and processed in these locations to assure compliance under the Treasury's Uniform Offering Circular. These bids are then sorted and reviewed electronically by the Treasury in Washington, D.C. The Treasury nets out the total amount of noncompetitive tenders and allocates the balance to competitive bidders with bids at or below the high yield (the highest yield accepted at an auction).[2] All competitive bids at higher yields are rejected. The coupon rate is the high yield rounded off to the nearest one-eighth.

An Example of Treasury Auction

The Department of the Treasury employs the *Dutch auction* to sell government securities. Under this system, dealers and financial institutions submit sealed bids, and both competitive and noncompetitive bidders are awarded securities at the price that results from the high yield (or high discount rate, for bills). All tenders at lower yields are accepted in full.

As an example, suppose the Treasury has received $1 billion in noncompetitive tenders in an $11 billion auction for five-year notes. In that case, $10 billion in securities will be awarded to competitive bidders. Suppose there are six competitive bidders, A, B, C, D, E, and F. Table 8-2 lists the yield and amount from each bidder, ranked from the lowest yield to the highest. The highest yield at which the $10 billion of securities can be sold is 4.250 percent. Under the Dutch auction, all accepted bidders (A, B, C, D, and E) will pay a price that reflects a yield of 4.250 percent. In this example, D and E each bid $2 billion at 4.250 percent. After the security is awarded to A, B, and C, the remaining amount is $2 billion. Bidders D and E will each receive $1 billion allocation.

The highest yield accepted at auction (the *high yield*) is also called the *stop yield*. The ratio of the bids received to the amount awarded is known as the

Table 8-2. Yield and quantity of competitive bids.

Bidder	Bid yield (%)	Bid amount (in billions of dollars)
A	4.245	2
B	4.246	3
C	4.248	3
D	4.250	2
E	4.250	2
F	4.252	1

Table 8-3. Main items included in Treasury security auction results of two-year notes (released March 24, 1999).

1. Information on the issue

   Issue date: March 31, 1999

   Dated date: March 31, 1999

   Maturity date: March 31, 2001

   Interest rate: 4 7/8%

2. Yield and price

   High yield: 4.995%

   Median yield: 4.968%

   Low yield: 4.901%

   Price: 99.774% of par

3. Auction allocation (amount in thousands)

   Competitive tender: $31,662,100; accepted: $13,586,030

   Noncompetitive tender: $1,416,952; accepted: $1,416,952

   All public tenders: $33,079,052; accepted: $15,002,952

   Bid-to-cover ratio = $33,079,052/$15,002,982 = 2.20

4. Federal Reserve and foreign official institutions

   Amount submitted by and awarded to Federal Reserve: $3,385,000

   Amount submitted by and awarded to foreign official institutions: $3,200,000

Source: "Public Debt News: Treasury Security Auction Results," Department of the Treasury, March 24, 1999.

bid-to-cover ratio. The higher the ratio, the stronger the auction. Another measure known as the tail of the auction is the difference between the average yield of all accepted bids and the stop yield. Traders use the tail as a measure of success of the auction to form trading strategies after the auction. The interpretation of a tail is more art than science. At times, a short tail signals strength, and hence traders will trade more aggressively. A long tail indicates weakness in market demand, and hence traders will be cautious on the downside. However, at times a long tail has a different implication. In an uncertain market environment, some bidders who need to have the specific security will be extremely aggressive. This will likely lead to a long tail. A short tail means a lack of such aggressiveness. In contrast, when many dealers bid to lose, the implication of the auction tail is very different.

The auction results are released to the public within two hours of the auction, frequently by 1:30 P.M. or 2:00 P.M. EST. The amount of bids received, the total accepted, and the bid-to-cover ratio are made available to the public. In addition, the high, low, median of bids, and the issuing price are made public. For a coupon treasury, the announcement includes a coupon rate as well. Table 8-3 provides an example of the information included in a Treasury announcement of auction results.

When-Issued Trading and Dealer Bidding Strategies

One major feature of the Treasury auction is the *when-issued (WI) trading,* which begins right after the auction announcement and lasts until the issue date. Prior to the scheduled auction, dealers and investors actively participate in the WI market. They may take either a long position or a short position in the security for a future settlement on the issue date. Thus, WI trades are forward contracts with a settlement date equal to the new issue settlement date.

Before the auction, WI trading is in terms of yields. The Treasury announces the coupon after the auction, and then WI trades on a price basis rather than a yield basis. Generally the securities are issued several days after the auction. WI trading ends when the new security settles. Prior to the settlement of the new security, there is no financing cost, nor is there accrued interest. The process of issuance is depicted in Figure 8-2.

WI trading affects the strategy bidders use in the auctions because it affects bidders' positions going into the auction. Bidders who buy a security in the WI market before the auction go into the auction with long positions, and those who have sold go into the auction with short positions. The WI market also serves a price discovery role; trading in this market provides vital infor-

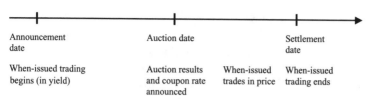

Figure 8-2. Treasury security issuance process.

mation on the strength of demand for the security and on the disparity of bidders' views about the market. Such information is useful in preparing bids. On the other hand, dealers who believe they have very valuable private information such as future interest rates might refrain from WI trading so they can use the information in their bids.

Short Squeezes

All trades in the WI market are settled for delivery and payment on the scheduled issue date. Dealers typically enter the auction with significant short positions, presenting significant risks to the dealers. A dealer who is short and unable to obtain a sufficient quantity of the security at the auction must cover the short position before the issue date by buying in the WI market after the auction. Alternatively, the dealer must borrow the security in the repurchase agreement market on the issue date to make good delivery (repurchase agreement transactions are to be covered in a later section). But in such a reverse, the dealer is still short in the security and is exposed to the possibility of being unable to purchase it at the anticipated price. This is called a *short squeeze.* Looking at it differently, a short squeeze occurs when an auction participant or a group of participants gains control of the stock of a security and withholds the supply from the cash or repurchase agreement markets.

Here is an example of a short squeeze. Salomon Brothers admitted to having controlled 94 percent of the two-year notes auctioned on May 22, 1991, which is in violation of the Treasury regulation that the bidder's long position may not exceed 35 percent of the issue in any single auction.[3] Salomon acquired 44 percent of the notes at the auction, plus the alleged prearranged trades with big investors, which gave Salomon a dominant position in the security.

The two-year notes are generally in high demand because they have the shortest maturity of any coupon Treasury security. Many investors around the world buy them at auction and hold them to maturity. But the price sometimes declines modestly right after the auction, when interest in the note sale fades. Traders and arbitrageurs would short ahead of the auction and cover the short after the price declines. But the price of this particular two-year note jumped sharply after the auction. The two-year notes became so scarce that the collateral-specific repo rates were about 75 to 200 basis points special.

The scandal cost Salomon its top management, and the firm was fined nearly $300 million. The firm lost its credibility in the marketplace and might not have survived had Warren Buffet not provided capital infusion and astute management to restore credibility. More importantly, in response to these problems, the Treasury introduced major changes in the Treasury market, including the right to reopen an issue and the experimentation of Dutch auction in the two-year and five-year notes in 1992. Now all Treasury securities are sold through the Dutch auction technique.

Trading and Clearing

In the Treasury market, trading is mainly over-the-counter, in which dealers, brokers, and other investors make trades by phone. Some dealers have recently provided electronic trading systems. The most active trading is generally in the on-the-run issues.

Treasury bills trade on a basis of discount rate and typically settle the same day.[4] The discount, the difference between the security's purchase price and its face value, is the investor's return. The following formula is used to determine the purchase price for short-term bills:

$$p = FV - d \times \left(\frac{M}{360} \right) \times FV$$

where
    p = the purchase price,
    FV = face value,
    d = discount rate, and
    M = number of days from settlement to maturity.

As an example, suppose a bill with a current maturity of 160 days is quoted at a bid of 4.14 percent and an offer of 4.13 percent. The purchase price per $1 million for the bill is:

$$Purchase\,Price = \$1,000,000 - \$1,000,000 \times 4.13\% \left(\frac{160}{360} \right) = \$981,644.44.$$

Coupon treasuries trade on a price basis. The typical transaction size is $1 million to $100 million for institutions. Trades on coupon treasuries generally settle on the next market day (called $T + 1$, where T is the trade day).

However, cash or corporate settlements (T + 3) can be arranged. The invoice price (also called dirty price) of a coupon security consists of the quoted price (also called the clean price) plus the accrued interest. The accrued interest is calculated on an actual/actual basis.[5] For example, a 5 percent, ten-year note is quoted at a bid of 98:20 and an offer of 98:22. Assume that the number of days between the last coupon date and settlement is 136 days, and the number of days in the coupon period is 183. If an investor purchases $1 million of par amount, the total invoice price is:

$$p = \$1,000,000 \times \left(98 + \frac{22}{32} \right)\% + \$1,000,000 \times \frac{5.00\%}{2} \times \frac{136}{183}$$
$$= \$986,875 + \$18,579.23$$
$$= \$1,005,454.23.$$

The total invoice price reflects the quoted price ($986,875, the first term on the right-hand side of the equation) and accrued interest ($18,579.23, the second term on the right-hand side of equation). The buyer has to pay the offer price plus the accrued interest to the dealer, because whoever has title to the security on the coupon date gets paid the full semiannual coupon. Note that, because the Treasury pays interest every six months, the accrued interest calculation uses half of the annual coupon rate.

Dealer Trading

Each morning dealers distribute to traders and sales personnel information on each issue measures such as price, yield, dollar value of a basis point or *dollar value of an 01* (DV01), and the yield value of a 1/32. The DV01 is the change in the price of a bond resulting from a one-basis-point change in its yield. Frequently, the DV01 is expressed in dollars per million. The yield value of a 1/32 is estimated by calculating the yield to maturity if the bond price changes by 1/32. Then the difference between the initial yield and the new yield is the yield value of 1/32. As an example, a 5 percent, ten-year note trading at par and yielding 5 percent has a value of a basis point (V01) of 0.07798 points or a DV01 of $779.8 per million dollars of par. This is calculated by taking the difference between the price at a yield of 5 percent (par) and the price at a yield of 4.99 percent (100.07798 percent of par).[6] The formula for the yield value of 1/32 is 1/32 × V01, which gives the yield value of 1/32 of 0.401 basis point. In the bills market, the DV01 is 0.01% × FV (M/360). Therefore, the DV01 of a ninety-day bill is $25.

The profits to a dealer are generated from one or a combination of the following sources: (1) the bid-asked spread, which varies from 1/128 to 4/32, depending on liquidity, volatility, and remaining maturity; (2) favorable market movements such as appreciation in the securities long and depreciation in the securities short; and (3) the difference between the interest earned on the securities held in inventory and the financing costs, referred to as carry. A positive carry is a source of profit, meaning interest income is more than interest expense. Conversely, when interest expense is greater than interest income, there is a negative carry.

Dealers trade with each other frequently through government interdealer brokers because of the speed and efficiency these brokers provide. Dealers give bids and offers to brokers, who display the highest bid and lowest offer in a computer network linked to each trading desk. Traders responding to a bid or offer by "hitting" or "taking" pay a commission to the broker. Brokers keep the names of dealers confidential. Major interdealer brokers include Cantor Fitzgerald, Garban, RMJ, Tullett & Tokyo Liberty, and Hilliard Farber. The quotes provided by the brokers represent prices in the interdealer market (also called the inside market). Table 8-4 provides an example of a composite page by Tullet & Tokyo Liberty PLC. The quotations listed represent the best bid and offer at that time. A plus sign after the price quote indicates half of a tick. A number of 2 or 6 after the price quote represents 2/8 or 6/8 of a tick.

In addition to interdealer brokers, GovPX was founded in 1990 by all primary dealers and four interdealer brokers serving the U.S. Treasury market. GovPX provides real-time information on transactions by the primary dealers through five of the six interdealer brokers. Specifically, it publishes the best bid and best offer, size, yields, last trade side (hit/take), and last trade size. GovPX has a distribution network that includes Bloomberg, Reuters, Bridge, Telerate, Fidelity, and MoneyLine.

Electronic Trading Systems

Electronic trading systems have rapidly become essential tools in the government securities markets, changing the way dealers and investors do business. The market is moving from private network or leased-line systems to the Internet because it provides substantial competitive advantages. Internet systems have universal connectivity among all market participants and do not have the costs of expensive private network or leased-line limitations.

Two major types of electronic trading systems in government securities markets are dealer systems and cross-matching systems. Single-dealer systems provide an electronic venue for customers to trade with a specific dealer, while multi-dealer systems consolidate bids and offers from multiple dealers. Cross-matching systems provide real-time or periodic cross-matching sessions. Users can execute

Table 8-4. Tullet & Tokyo Liberty Treasury market composite.

Bills				$6\frac{1}{4}$	8/02	105.24	−272
3 months	3/11	4.40	−385	$5\frac{7}{8}$	9/02	104.19+	−23
6 months	6/10	4.41	−40	$5\frac{3}{4}$	11/02	104.112	−14+
1 year	12/09	4.27	−265	$5\frac{5}{8}$	12/02	104.002	−036
WI3 MO	3/18	4.385	−38	$5\frac{1}{2}$	1/03	103.216	−25
WI6 MO	6/17	4.39	−385	$5\frac{1}{2}$	2/03	103.22+	−256
				$5\frac{1}{2}$	3/03	103.262	−29+
				$5\frac{3}{4}$	4/03	104.286	−00
Short	**Maturities**			$5\frac{1}{2}$	5/03	104.02	−052
$5\frac{3}{8}$	1/00	100.26	−27+	$5\frac{3}{8}$	6/03	103.26	−292
$5\frac{1}{2}$	2/00	101.012	−02+	$5\frac{1}{4}$	8/03	103.10+	−13
$5\frac{1}{2}$	3/00	101.042	−05+	**5 year**		99.19	−21
$5\frac{5}{8}$	4/00	101.12+	−14	$6\frac{1}{4}$	2/07	110.226	−232
$5\frac{1}{2}$	5/00	101.102	−11+	$6\frac{5}{8}$	5/07	113.136	−142
$5\frac{3}{8}$	6/00	101.062	−07+	$6\frac{1}{8}$	8/07	110.036	−04+
$5\frac{3}{8}$	7/00	101.11	−12	$5\frac{1}{2}$	2/08	106.17	−176
$5\frac{1}{8}$	8/00	100.33+	−00+	$5\frac{5}{8}$	5/08	107.112	−12
$4\frac{1}{2}$	9/00	100.00	−01	**10 year**		101.11	−12+
4	10/00	99.046	−06	$6\frac{5}{8}$	2/27	119.22+	−25
2 year		100.122	−13	$6\frac{3}{8}$	8/27	116.162	−19
6	8/00	102.086	−11	$6\frac{1}{8}$	11/27	113.17	−19+
$5\frac{3}{4}$	11/00	102.086	−10	$5\frac{1}{2}$	8/28	106.01+	−042
$5\frac{3}{8}$	2/01	101.252	−266	**30 year**		104.02	−04
$5\frac{5}{8}$	5/01	102.21+	−23+				

Note: Snapshot at 14:27:17 on Monday, December 14, 1998.

Source: Tullet & Tokyo Liberty.

transactions electronically with multiple counterparties on a fully anonymous basis. In addition, the Treasury Department allows customers to purchase Treasury securities through its Treasury Direct Web site service.

Clearing and Settlement

The Treasury offers new securities only in book-entry form. The Treasury began offering new bills exclusively in book-entry form in 1979. In August

1986, the Treasury began marketing all new coupon securities in book-entry form. The book-entry program has largely replaced physical government and agency securities with computer entries at Federal Reserve Banks. All treasuries held in physical form by depository institutions are eligible for conversion to book entry and for transfer by wire.

The government securities are cleared through Fedwire, a system that allows depository institutions to transfer securities and funds for their own accounts and for the accounts of customers directly to one another and to depository institutions throughout the United States.

Every Treasury security issue is represented by an entry on a Federal Reserve Bank's computer. The Fed keeps track of which bank holds what amount of a particular security. At maturity, the Fed transfers funds to the bank. In essence, the Fed acts as a custodian of the Treasury securities for various depositary institutions.

For a trade in government securities, two transactions take place simultaneously when the securities are transferred over the Fedwire. The movement of the security takes place by decreasing the seller clearing bank's book-entry securities account at the Federal Reserve Bank and by increasing the buyer clearing bank's account by the same amount. Funds movement is just opposite to the securities movement described above. The market practice is delivery versus payment (DVP), so funds and securities are transferred at the same time. The Fedwire operating hours for book-entry securities are 8:30 A.M. to 3:15 P.M. EST for transfer origination. The closing time for transfer reversals is 3:30 P.M. The Fed charges a fee for this service.

Repurchase Agreements

Government security dealers borrow huge sums of short-term funds to finance their positions every day, and often they find the least expensive way to do so is in the *repurchase agreement* (repo) market. In a typical repo transaction, a dealer puts up liquid securities as collateral against a cash loan while agreeing to repurchase the same securities at a higher price that reflects the financing costs at a future date. A typical deliverable repo transaction is depicted in Figure 8-3. The start leg is usually settled the same day. The close leg, or the repurchase, is a forward transaction. A repo is in format a securities transaction, but is in essence a collateralized loan to finance the purchase of the underlying security. As such, fixed-income repos have been treated as secured loans for U.S. federal income tax purposes.

Securities market participants enter into repo transactions because they have cash and want a short-term investment or because they have securities

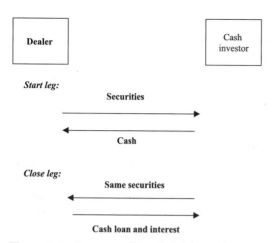

Figure 8-3. Structure of a typical deliverable repo.

and need funding. For example, a dealer purchases and plans to hold over-night $50 million of 6.00 percent, ten-year Treasury notes. The dealer can finance the position with its own funds or by borrowing from a bank. Typi-cally, however, the dealer uses the repo market to obtain financing. Suppose a customer, a municipality, a mutual fund, or an insurance company, has excess funds of $50 million to invest.[7] The overnight repo rate is 5.50 percent. On the start date, the dealer delivers these notes to the customer for cash. In leg two of the repo trade, the dealer buys back the same notes for $50 million plus one day interest of $7,638.89. The result is that the customer has invested $50 million and the dealer has financed the position overnight at an interest rate of 5.50 percent.

The party that sells the securities in exchange for funds is often referred to as the *collateral seller.* The counterparty that takes in the securities and lends out funds is called the *collateral buyer.* In practice, the term "repo" or "reverse repo" is generally described from the dealer's perspective. Thus, the activity whereby a mutual fund lends money to a dealer by way of purchasing the col-lateral and agreeing to resell the same collateral back is usually termed "repo."

Triparty Repo Structure

The expenses associated with deliverable repos and the loss experienced from hold-in-custody repos prompted bond dealers to devise the triparty agree-ment. A custodial bank stands between the repo counterparties and maintains accounts for both parties; hence, the actual delivery of collateral and cash can be reduced to a simple transaction of credit and debit transfers within the same bank. Triparty structure is a very convenient, secure, and recognized option. In a triparty setup, the burdens of obtaining pricing and marking to market become the contractual obligations of the custodian. Typically, broker-dealers pay the fees. The wire charges and fail risk are eliminated as well. The triparty repos are estimated to finance about 75 percent to 80 percent of large U.S. primary dealers' bond inventory.

Another factor that has contributed to the popularity of the triparty formula is the Federal Reserve Board regulations on daylight overdraft that took effect on April 14, 1994. The Fed started charging for *daylight overdrafts*, the amounts overdrawn on Fedwire, on an intraday basis. For the big clearing banks, bond dealers are largely responsible for the overdrafts every morning when they return borrowed cash from the conventional deliverable repo transactions. The overdraft charges give dealers strong incentives to abandon the deliverable format. The triparty agreements, of which most are open, eliminate the need for cash transfers and hence the daylight overdrafts.

Repo Rates

Repo rates in part depend on the collateral used. The higher the credit quality and the easier the security is to clear, the lower the repo rates. Treasury repos trade at lower levels than federal agency repos, which in turn trade at lower levels than mortgage-backed securities. The second factor that determines repo rates is the term of the repo. Most repo transactions have a maturity of three months or less. One-day transactions are called *overnight repos*, longer maturities are called *term repos*. An *open repo* is an overnight repo that rolls over automatically until terminated by either party.

Government securities are the most frequently used collateral. Numerous issues, in particular on-the-run or current issues, are frequently traded at a lower rate in the repo market. The specialness of the given issue is the difference between the general collateral rate and the security-specific repo rate. The special rate may be quoted either as an absolute rate or as a spread below the general collateral rate. For example, if the general collateral rate is 5.50 percent, a special issue trading at 4.00 percent may be quoted as being 150 basis points special.

Other Repo Mechanics

It is common in a repurchase transaction for the collateral seller to have the right to take back that security and simultaneously substitute another collateral of equal value and quality, known as the right of substitution. Also, the market practice is that the coupon interests coming due on the collateralized securities are passed through from the buyer back to the seller of collateral. This is referred to as *coupon pass-through.*

Both parties to a repo transaction are exposed to credit risk, due to changes in the market value of the collateral. The cash lender usually receives a margin, or haircut, in which the mark-to-market value of the collateral is more than the loan as a cushion against a fall in securities value during the term of the repo. In addition, it is helpful to review the counterparty's financial status, its legal and corporate authority to enter into repurchase transactions, and specifics of the transaction.

In general, a collateral buyer's control of the collateral is not crucial. There are two situations, however, in which the control of collateral is crucial to the buyer: reverse to cover shorts and reverse to maturity. In the case of covering a short, the collateral seller lends a specific security to the collateral buyer to cover a previously established short. Hence, the transaction can also be thought of as securities lending. In a reverse to maturity, the dealer reverses in security and sells it to lock in a profit on the trade.

Matched Book Operations

Dealers use repos to finance their inventory and to execute matched book activities. In a *matched book,* the dealer reverses in securities and simultaneously repos out the collateral at a lower rate. The dealer makes a profit on the bid-asked spread, which is in the vicinity of eight to ten basis points and two to five basis points in a tight market. In a perfect matched book, the dealer does not have any interest rate risk.

In practice, dealers tend to regard a wide range of transactions as part of the matched book. The range of repo desk activities includes financing dealer's positions, covering shorts, and acting as intermediary and providing funding to customers.

For dealers, a repo is the cheapest financing alternative. The overnight rate is usually at a spread below the federal funds rate, whereas the dealer loan rate from clearing banks is a spread above the federal funds rate. Financing at the clearing bank is only the last resort. With a matched book, there are other profitable opportunities. For one, a trader might reverse in securities in anticipation of future shorts. The trader could repo out these securities until they are needed to deliver. Another example is a matched book trader who anticipates an issue to go on special in the future and reverses in now while it is still general collateral.

Another responsibility of a repo desk is to reverse in securities traders sold short to make good delivery. In a reverse to cover short, the objective is to have the specific security. This is in contrast to most repos, in which the lender of money demands collateral to limit its credit risk exposure. Finally, repurchase transactions are an important source of funding to customers and hence facilitate sales of securities.

Summary

This chapter describes the Treasury securities. Treasury bills are discount money market instruments. Treasury notes and bonds, also called coupon securities, pay interest every six months. Since January 1997, the Treasury has auctioned inflation-indexed securities with maturity periods of five, ten, and thirty years. In addition, Treasury strips represent an important segment of the marketplace.

Treasury securities are distributed through regularly scheduled auctions. The auction process begins with a public announcement by the Treasury. Market participants submit competitive or noncompetitive bids. The Treasury awards all noncompetitive bids and accepts competitive bidders with a bid at or below the high yield. During the period, right after the announcement and before the issue date, there is a when-issued market for the new security.

Once the security is issued, it is mostly traded over-the-counter. Every day the trading volume averages more than $200 billion. This chapter describes the market convention in quoting bills and coupon treasuries. The transaction value for a coupon security is the sum of the quoted price and accrued interest. Buyers of a coupon treasury pay the offer price plus the accrued interest from the last coupon date to the settlement date.

Government securities dealers borrow huge sums of short-term funds to finance their securities inventory every day, and often they find the least expensive way of doing this is in the repo market. The transfer of ownership in a repo transaction provides the lender of funds better protection, and hence the lender is willing to charge a lower rate.

Selected Bibliography

Bond Market Association. *An Investor's Guide to U.S. Treasury Inflation-Indexed Securities.* New York: Bond Market Association, 1997.

Fabozzi, F. J. *Bond Markets, Analysis and Strategies,* 3d Ed. Upper Saddle River, N.J.: Prentice-Hall, 2000.

Federal Reserve Bank of New York. *Basic Information on Treasury Securities.* New York: FRB, of NY 1999.

Federal Reserve Bank of New York. *Fee Schedule 1999*. New York: FRB, of NY 1999.

Jegadeesh, N. "Treasury Auction Bids and the Salomon Squeeze." *Journal of Finance* 48:4 (September 1993): 1403–1419.

Liaw, T. "Pricing Treasury Coupon Rolls." *Corporate Finance Review* (March/April 1997): 12–16.

Mester, L. "There's More Than One Way To Sell a Security: The Treasury's Auction Experiment." *Business Review,* Federal Reserve Bank of Philadelphia (July–August 1997): 1–10.

Notes

1. A complete discussion on theoretical spot rates can be found in Fabozzi.

2. The Treasury also awards full amounts of the security to Federal Reserve and foreign official bids.

3. After Smith Barney merged with Salomon, the firm was renamed Salomon Smith Barney, a unit of the Citigroup.

4. Settlement means payment for and delivery of a security so the transaction is complete.

5. The accrued interest is calculated based on the actual number of days in the coupon period and the actual number of days in the year.

6. Alternatively, a yield of 5.01 percent can be used. The price would be 99.92209 percent of par.

7. In this example, we ignore the haircut requirements.

9

Corporate Fixed-Income Securities

Corporate fixed-income securities can be an important investment vehicle for investors. Corporate securities come in a range of maturities and have a range of risks. Understanding the market for these securities can be important for creating a fixed-income strategy.

The U.S. bond market, the world's largest, represents more than $14.2 trillion in outstanding debt obligations. Of this $14.2 trillion, government debt accounts for $3.3 trillion, and the corporate debt and money market accounts for $5.1 trillion. The annual volume of corporate debt issuance is trillions of dollars. The market liquidity and efficiency are continuously improved by competition, standardized market practices, and technological innovations. This chapter provides an overview of the corporate debt markets and describes various types of debt instruments. It is important to understand the market conventions and practices and credit ratings in the corporate debt market.

Market Overview

A *bond* is a loan. It reflects a promise by the issuer to repay the amount borrowed at a specific date in the future, plus interest at an agreed-upon rate. The *bond indenture* specifies the rights of the bondholders and the obligations of the issuer. Through the bond markets, corporations that need to borrow money are matched with investors who have funds to lend. In this market, dealers perform a vital role. Dealers buy from issuers and distribute to investors in the primary markets. Once the bonds have been issued, bond dealers bid for bonds that investors wish to sell and offer bonds from their inventory to investors wanting to buy. Distribution of a new bond is referred to as underwriting, while trading with clients is labeled market making.

The bond markets are largely over-the-counter. The means of trading are electronic communications and processing networks through which securities are bought and sold from dealer to dealer, who in turn buy from and sell to investors. Technological advances have shifted portions of the new issue distribution and secondary market trading online.

Bonds are bought by institutions, including mutual funds, pension funds, insurance companies, banks, corporations, state and local governments, and international investors. Millions of individuals also buy and own bonds, either directly or indirectly through mutual funds or pension plans. In general, bond investors are looking for current income, relative safety, and portfolio diversification.

Types of Corporate Fixed-Income Securities

A wide variety of corporate debt securities are available to allow corporations to match certain financing requirements with investor needs. Most debt securities offer investors a schedule of fixed-interest income (coupon) and principal on maturity date. Hence, bonds are also called fixed-income securities. In addition to fixed interest rates, some debt instruments pay a floating-rate interest to bondholders. The maturity date ranges from very short-term, as short as several days, to 30 years to 100 years.

Commercial Paper

Commercial paper is a short-term unsecured promissory note. Financial and nonfinancial firms use it as an alternative to borrowing from banks. Interest rates on commercial paper are often lower than bank lending rates, and the savings, when large enough, provide an advantage over bank credit. Financial companies account for roughly 75 percent of the commercial paper outstanding. For example, at midyear 1999, the outstanding volume was $1.233 trillion, of which $931 billion was from financial companies.

Commercial paper is a cost-effective form of short-term funding, giving corporations visibility in the institutional investor market, thereby facilitating future capital market activities. Commercial paper programs raise floating-rate funds, although derivatives may be used to fix rates for a fixed term. The minimum borrowing amount is typically $50 million, and program sizes can range into the billions.

Commercial paper is usually issued in denominations of $100,000 or more. There are two methods of floating commercial paper. Issuers can sell the paper directly to the buyer or they can sell the paper to a dealer firm, which in turn distributes it to investors. Most of the dealers are large securities firms or subsidiaries of commercial banks. Direct issuers of commercial paper often are financial companies that have frequent and sizable borrowing needs. By some estimates, direct issuers save a dealer fee of 1/8 of a percentage point, or $125,000 for every $100 million issued. Nonfinancial companies or smaller financial companies usually issue dealer-placed commercial paper. For such firms the size and the frequency of the borrowings do not warrant maintenance of a regular sales staff.

Commercial paper maturity ranges from 1 day to 270 days, but most commonly 30 days or less. Because commercial paper maturity does not exceed 270 days, it is exempt from registration with the SEC. Commercial paper rates are quoted on a discount basis. The purchaser pays a discount price and receives the face amount when the paper matures. The return to investors is the difference between the purchase price and the face amount. The maturity, credit quality, market conditions, and investor demand determine the rates.

Commercial paper is a money market instrument; hence, the convention is to assume a 360-day year. For example, the amount of discount for a seven-day paper with $100,000 face value traded at a discount of 5.33 percent can be calculated as follows.

$$d = F \times r \times \frac{M}{360} = \$100,000 \times 0.0533 \times \frac{7}{360} = \$103.64$$

In the above expression, d denotes the dollar amount of discount, r the discount rate, F the face value, and M the maturity. According to the calculation, the paper can be purchased at a discount of $103.64. That is, the purchaser pays $99,896.36 and receives from the issuer $100,000 after 7 days.

Large Time Deposits

Large time deposits are certificates of deposits issued by commercial banks in denominations of $100,000 and up. Most are short-term, even though some have maturities of as long as several years. Big commercial banks frequently rely on large time deposits for liquidity management. This market is very large. At midyear 1999, the outstanding volume was more than $800 billion.

Bankers' Acceptance

A *bankers' acceptance* (BA) is a draft drawn on a bank for approval for future payment. The following example illustrates a BA transaction. Suppose a U.S. importer wants to buy silk from China and pay for it sixty days later. One approach would be for the importer to borrow from its bank. However, short-term rates may be lower in the money markets. If so, and if the importer is not large enough to go into the open market on its own, then it can use the BA route. The importer will have its bank write a letter of credit for the amount of the purchase and send this letter of credit to the Chinese exporter. Upon export of the Chinese silk, the Chinese exporter draws a time draft on the importer's U.S. bank and discounts this draft at its local bank. This allows the Chinese merchant to obtain immediate payment for the silk. The Chinese bank, in turn, sends the time draft to the importer's U.S. bank, which then stamps "accepted" on the draft. The U.S. bank now guarantees payment on the draft and thereby creates an acceptance. The BA is created.

If the Chinese bank does not want cash immediately, the U.S. bank would return the draft to that bank. The Chinese bank could hold it as an investment and present it to the U.S. bank for payment at maturity, sixty days later. If the Chinese bank wants cash immediately, the U.S. bank would pay it and either hold the BA itself or sell it in the open market. Ultimately, the U.S. importer has to provide its bank with sufficient funds to pay off the acceptance at maturity. However, if the importer fails to do so, the U.S. bank is still obligated to honor the payment at maturity.

Medium-Term Notes

A *medium-term note* (MTN) is a corporate debt instrument. The maturity ranges from nine months to thirty years. General Motors Acceptance Corporation (GMAC) was one of the first to issue medium-term notes and continues to be a major supplier in this market with its SmartNotes program.

Medium-term notes have several unique characteristics. First, securities broker-dealers distribute MTNs on a basis of best efforts. In this case, security firms act as brokers helping to place the notes through their vast network of clients. Security firms do not guarantee a price to the issuer. Second, unlike a typical bond issue where bonds are sold in large, discrete offerings, MTNs are sold in relatively smaller amounts on a continuous basis. Third, because the notes offerings are ongoing, they are typically registered with the SEC under Rule 415 (shelf registration), which allows a corporation to issue securities of up to an approved amount over a period of two years. U.S. corporations issued $150 billion in MTNs in 1998, of which financial firms accounted for $128 billion. Table 9-1 lists the amount of annual issuance of MTNs in the United States.

Bonds

Bonds are long-term debt instruments. The issuer is generally required to pay bondholders a fixed amount of interest periodically and to repay the principal value of the bond (also called the redemption value) on the maturity date. So bonds are considered fixed-income securities, though some bonds pay a

Table 9-1. Annual issuance of medium-term notes 1990–1998 (in billions of dollars).

Year	Total issuance	Issuance by financial corporations
1990	46	29
1991	72	45
1992	74	50
1993	86	57
1994	87	70
1995	98	79
1996	93	82
1997	114	98
1998	150	128

Source: Federal Reserve Statistical Release.

floating rate of interest. Bonds have many other characteristics, such as certain protective features, legal status, and the currency they are payable in. Described below are several common types of bonds in the marketplace.

Convertible bonds give the bondholder the right to convert the par amount of the bond for a number of common stocks according to what is known as the conversion ratio. For example, a conversion provision might give the holder the right to convert $1,000 par amount into the issuer's common stock at $50 per share, the conversion price. This conversion ratio is twenty-to-one. The share price substantially affects the value of a convertible. For example, if the shares of the issuer are trading at $40 and the market price of the bond is $1,000, there would be no reason for an investor to convert. A convertible bond with a conversion price far higher than the market price of the stock generally trades at or close to its bond value. On the other hand, when the share price is sufficiently higher than the conversion price, the convertible begins to trade more like equity.

Callable bonds are debt securities that grant the issuers the right to pay off the debt before maturity. Exercising the call provision becomes attractive to the issuer when the yield drops sufficiently. The costs to call include a call premium, administrative expenses, and the expenditures arising from floating a new issue to refund the retired debt. Most call provisions provide for a call premium of one-half of the coupon rate. That means the issuer has the right to pay the bondholders the par amount plus one-half of the annual coupon payment. The call feature is a disadvantage to investors who must give up the higher yielding bonds. Therefore, investors generally demand a higher yield.

Puttable bonds are bonds that contain a put provision, granting investors the right to put the bonds back to the issuer at par. Investors will choose to exercise the right to put back the bonds when yields are rising (prices are falling). Clearly, a puttable bond protects investors from the downside risk in a rising interest rate environment. Therefore, investors are willing to accept a lower yield when purchasing the bonds.

High yield bonds, sometimes referred to as *junk bonds,* get name from the higher yields offered on these securities. Classification of a bond as either junk or investment grade is determined by the credit rating. Credit ratings of BB (by Standard and Poor's) or lower are regarded as noninvestment grade or speculative grade. Before the 1980s, most junk bonds resulted from a decline in credit quality of former investment-grade issues. These issues are known as fallen angels. Michael Milken successfully argued that the risk-adjusted returns for portfolios of junk bonds were quite high. The credit risk of these bonds was more than compensated for by their high yields. Underwriters, notably Drexel-Burnham, soon began to issue new bonds for issuers that were less than investment grade. The new issue junk bonds market provides access to capital markets for less-well-known firms.

A *foreign currency bond* is a bond issued in a currency other than the borrower's national currency. Through foreign currency bond issuance, issuers take advantage of international interest rate differentials. Issuers often use currency swaps to convert the foreign currency into the home currency. Bonds issued by foreign issuers in the United States in U.S. dollars are known as *yankee bonds.* Those issued in British pounds in England are called *bulldogs.* Yen-denominated bonds by non-Japanese issuers are known as *samurai bonds.* Foreign currency bonds have a much different risk and return profile than domestic bonds. Not only are their prices affected by movements in a foreign country's interest rate, they also change in value depending on the foreign exchange rate.

Global bonds are a type of security designed to appeal to investors internationally. In 1989, the World Bank offered the first global bond. Global bonds have several key characteristics:

- The bonds are legally eligible for primary market sale in the world's major bond markets.
- The bonds can be settled and cleared on any one of several systems, and they can flow back and forth between the systems with minimum transaction costs.
- The offering price at launch is validated through an extended period of price discovery dialogue with investors worldwide.
- Selected international syndicates of bond dealers distribute the bonds.

The global bond format has proven to be popular. Many entities with large borrowing needs have used global bonds to raise hundreds of billions of dollars in various currencies.

Asset-backed securities are based on pools of collateral assets. These assets are usually illiquid and private. A securitization occurs to make these assets available for investment to a much broader range of investors. Residential mortgages, for example, provide some insight into the development of the asset-backed securities market. Bank of America issued the first triple-A–rated mortgaged-backed pass-through security in 1977. The originating organization usually keeps the servicing. Large institutional investors participate in this market. Smaller investors have neither the expertise to evaluate the mortgages nor large enough portfolios to properly diversify. The securitization technique has since been applied to other asset types such as credit card receivables, auto loans, mobile homes, and commercial property mortgage loans. In addition, several municipalities such as New York, Jersey City (New Jersey), and New Haven (Connecticut), have moved to securitize tax liens. Other innovative structures include securities backed by future royalties from record sales, receivables from utility bills, tobacco settlements, and junk bonds.

Market Conventions

Bonds generally trade over-the-counter. This section reviews the basics of price quotations, settlement, accrued interest, and yield to maturity.

Dealers and Investors

Bond trading is usually done with bond dealers. Dealers rely on the vast network of telephone and computer links that connect the interested players. Bond dealers make a market for bonds, meaning that they work with traders who specialize in a group of bonds and are prepared to quote a buying price (bid) or selling price (offer). The bid-offer spreads represent one source of profits for dealers. Such market making ensures liquidity for bond investors, thereby allowing them to buy and sell bonds more easily at close to market prices. Dealers also trade via bond brokers.

Major bond investors include financial institutions, pension funds, and mutual funds around the world. These investors and dealers comprise the institutional market in which large blocks of fixed-income securities are traded. A trade of $1 million in the institutional market is a small ticket. Trades involving several hundred million dollars take place regularly. The direct purchase or sale of bonds by individual investors is very limited, and the transaction sizes are much smaller.

Bond Market Basics

In the bond market, the coupon is the percentage interest to be paid on a bond in the course of one year. The interest is commonly paid semiannually, although it can also be payable monthly, quarterly, or annually. For example, if a bond has a face value of $1,000 and a 6 percent coupon, $60 in interest will be paid to the bondholder over one year.

Maturity is the date the bond will be redeemed. For example, if a bond has a maturity date of September 15, 2020, then the investor should expect to be paid off in full at that date. The settlement date is the date payment is made to the seller and the bond is delivered to the buyer. In the United States, the corporate bond market has a practice of settling three business days after the trade date. After the settlement date, the accrued interest belongs to the buyer.

The quoted price is often based on the percentage of par. For example, a bond dealer offering to sell the bond at 102:20 wants to sell at a price equal to 102 percent plus 20/32 of 1 percent of the face value. More specifically, the price offered is 102.625 percent of the face value. For every $1,000 par amount, the price is $1,026.25. Note that 1/32 is called one tick in the bond market. The price quote is always the clean price, the price the buyer pays for principal. The other component of the purchase price, accrued interest, will be discussed later.

The bid price is the price a dealer will pay for the bond. The offer price is the price at which the dealer will sell. The difference between the bid and the offer is the bid-asked spread. For example, if a dealer quotes the bond at a bid of 102:16 and an offer of 102:20, the bid-asked spread is four ticks—or a spread of 4/32 of 1 percent (0.125 percent). Thus, the dollar spread for the dealer is $12.50 per bond (assuming $1,000 par amount).

But an investor purchasing the bond at the asked price will usually have to pay more than $1,026.25. In addition to the quoted price, the buyer has to pay for accrued interest as well. As we know, the bond issuer typically pays coupon every six months. Anyone selling the bond before the coupon date will not receive the coupon from the issuer, because the seller no longer has title to the bond. The buyer, who might have just purchased the bond as little as one day before the coupon date, has title to the bond and will receive the coupon payment. So the buyer has to pay to the seller the portion of the interest that has been accrued since the last payment date, called *accrued interest*, as well as the quoted price for the bond. The *clean price* plus any accrued interest is the so-called *dirty price*, the price the buyer actually pays for a bond. For the bond in the example above, suppose that it has been 122 days since coupon was last paid, and it is 61 days until the next payment. There are 183 days in this coupon period. The accrued interest is equal to:

$$\$1,000 \times 3.00\% \times \frac{122}{183} = \$20.00$$

Therefore, the total purchase price for the bond is \$1,026.25 + \$20.00 = \$1,046.25.

Current yield is the simplest measure of yield on a bond. It is defined as the bond's annual coupon divided by its quoted price. The formula is:

$$current\ yield = \frac{coupon}{price}$$

For example, if the clean price is \$1,026.25 and pays \$60 annual coupon, its current yield is 5.85 percent. Investors do not rely solely on the current yield for their investment decisions. Most investors also look at yield to maturity (discussed next), duration, and convexity (covered in a later section).

Yield to maturity (or yield) is the rate that discounts future cash flows of the bond to the market price. The yield (the discount rate) and the present value are inversely related. As the yield rises, the bond price declines. Conversely, a lower yield implies a higher bond price. From the present value concept, it is clear that a bond selling at par has a yield equal to the coupon rate. If the yield to maturity is greater than the coupon rate, then the bond trades at a discount. If the yield to maturity is lower than the coupon rate then, the bond sells at a premium to its face value. The quoted price of the bond in the previous example is \$1,026.25; hence, the yield is lower than 6.00 percent. As the bond matures, the price will approach par. So an investor buying this bond at a premium will suffer a capital loss. Conversely, if the bond trades at a discount, the investor will be rewarded with a capital gain.

Finally, the term "bond spread" refers to the interest rate differential between two bonds. The spread is the simple subtraction of one bond yield from another, often the yield on Treasury securities with similar maturity.

Private Placements and Shelf Registration

Issuing bonds can be a time-consuming and costly process. The length of time needed depends on the readiness of the company, the availability of information required in the registration statement, and market conditions. The costs include direct expenses, road shows, underwriting spreads, registration fees, listing fees, and management time. Private placements and shelf registration are two important SEC rules that greatly reduce the time and costs associated with floating securities to raise capital. A private placement exempts issuers from registration requirements, and the shelf registration allows certain issuers to file a single registration document to raise up to a certain amount of securities within the subsequent two years.

Private Placements and Rule 144A

Private placements differ structurally from registered public issues because, among other reasons, they are highly negotiated in covenants and pricing and they do not go through the SEC registration process. A private issue can greatly reduce legal and registration expenses compared to a comparable public issue. There are, however, holding period requirements on the securities acquired in a private placement (called *restricted securities*). The requirements are one year for restricted securities when trading limited quantities and two years when trading unlimited amounts.

The holding period restrictions seriously dampen the liquidity of the private market. To enhance liquidity, the SEC adopted Rule 144A to allow the trading of privately placed securities among *qualified institutional buyers* (QIBs) without the holding period restrictions. The liquidity of issues has improved since Rule 144A became effective, and investment banking firms have committed capital and trading personnel to making markets for Rule 144A securities.

The private placement debt market is growing rapidly and accounts for a significant portion of the debt market. The most dramatic growth resulted from Rule 144A deals. The resemblance of Rule 144As to traditional private placements ends with the fact that they are not registered with SEC. Generally, Rule 144A deals are $100 million or more to provide liquidity for resale. Rule 144As look like public offerings but can only be traded among QIBs. These deals are usually underwritten and have two credit ratings.

Most Rule 144A issues carry registration rights, which means that non-investment-grade borrowers can rush out Rule 144A deals quickly to reap the benefits of hitting a strong market and go through the hoops of SEC registration later. Once SEC reporting requirements are satisfied, the securities are upgraded.

Rule 415 Shelf Registration

Rule 415 permits certain issuers to file a single registration document indicating that it intends to sell a certain amount of a certain class of securities at one or more times within the next two years. In essence, securities can be viewed as sitting on a shelf and can be removed and sold to the public quickly.

Once the issuer's nonprice terms are decided, the issue could be placed on the market immediately or overnight. The price risk now shifts to the underwriter and the syndicate. Lead underwriters step up to bid in order to retain the prestige associated with being a lead firm in the syndicate game. In effect, the shortened new-issue process has helped issuers not only reduce risk, but also shift a significant share of the waiting risk from the issuing company to the investment banking firms, not to mention the increased due-diligence risks. The greatest risks are encountered when the inventory of unsold bonds grows due to unfavorable interest rate movements. On top of that, the financing costs move up with the rise in interest rates. The risk-adjusted returns of new underwriting are now less even if the underwriting spreads did not change.

Credit Ratings and Insurance

Credit ratings are an opinion on the ability of a security issue to meet financial commitments on a timely basis. An issue credit rating is a current opinion of the creditworthiness of an obligor with respect to a specific financial obligation, a specific class of financial obligations, or a specific financial program. Credit ratings are not intended to measure other risks in fixed-income investment such as market risk or the risk of loss in market value arising from an increase in interest rate. Additionally, as opinions of credit strength, they are not intended to measure a security's potential for price appreciation.

In the United States, major rating agencies include Standard and Poor's (S&P), Moody's, Fitch IBCA, and Duff & Phelps Credit Rating (DCR). Each of these agencies assigns its ratings based on an in-depth analysis of the issuer's financial condition and management, the characteristics of the debt, and the specific revenue sources securing the bond. Issue credit ratings can be either long-term or short-term. Short-term ratings generally are assigned to obligations considered short-term in the relevant market, having an original maturity of less than 365 days.

Long-Term Credit Ratings

Long-term credit ratings focus on fundamental factors that influence the issuer's long-term ability to meet debt payment. That is, ratings measure the ability of an issuer to generate cash in the future, and they assess the level and predictability of an issuer's future cash generation in relation to its commitments to repay debtholders. In other words, long-term issue credit ratings are based on the likelihood of payment, the nature and provisions of the obligation, and the protection afforded by the obligation in the event of bankruptcy or reorganization.

The issue rating definitions are expressed in terms of default risk. The highest ratings are AAA (S&P, Fitch IBCA, and DCR) and Aaa (Moody's).

Bonds rated in the BBB category or higher are considered *investment-grade*, while securities with ratings in the BB category or below are below investment-grade. Noninvestment grades are considered high yield or junk bonds. Table 9-2 lists long-term issue credit ratings by the four major agencies. It is important to note that the ratings reflect the total expected credit loss over the life of the bonds. They are an assessment of the likelihood that the issue will default and the predicted amount of loss after default occurs.

Moody's publishes an annual bond default study that tracks the actual default and credit loss experience of corporate bond issuers by rating category since 1920. The most recent study shows that the average one-year default rate for Aaa-rated bonds during that period is zero. By contrast, 6.8 percent of bonds rated B defaulted within one year. The study also shows that over ten-year periods, only 0.82 percent of bonds rated Aaa missed payments; the ten-year default rates for bonds rated B is dramatically higher at 43.9 percent.

Short-Term Credit Ratings

Rating agencies use a separate system to rate securities that mature in less than one year, such as commercial paper, bank deposits, or money market funds. The definitions of ratings by the four rating agencies are included in Table 9-3. The highest ratings indicate that the issuer has sufficient access to funds to meet payment on all of its short-term obligations, even under periods of

Table 9-2. Long-term credit ratings.

Credit risk	Standard & Poor's	Moody's	Fitch/IBCA	DCR
Investment grade				
Highest quality	AAA	Aaa	AAA	AAA
High quality	AA	Aa	AA	AA
Upper medium grade	A	A	A	A
Medium grade	BBB	Baa	BBB	BBB
Noninvestment grade				
Somewhat speculative	BB	Ba	BB	BB
Speculative	B	B	B	B
Highly speculative	CCC	Caa	CCC	CCC
Most speculative	CC	Ca	CC	CC
Imminent default	D	C	C	C
Default	D	C	D	D

Table 9-3. Short-term credit ratings.

Credit risk	Standard & Poor's	Moody's	Fitch/IBCA	DCR
Investment grade				
High grade	A-1	Prime-1	F1	D-1
Good grade	A-2	Prime-2	F2	D-2
Satisfactory grade	A-3	Prime-3	F3	D-3
Noninvestment grade				
Speculative	B	Not Prime	B	D-4
High default risk	C		C	
Default	D		D	D-5

market stress. The lower ratings, such as Not Prime by Moody's, represent the opinion that the issuer may not have sufficient access to firm bank lines of credit or other forms of backup funding to meet all of its short-term obligations in periods of market stress. A higher rating implies a higher degree of investor protection.

Bond Insurance

Credit quality can be enhanced by *bond insurance*. Specialized insurance firms serving the fixed-income market guarantee the timely payment of principal and interest on bonds they have insured. In the United States, major bond insurers are MBIA Inc., AMBAC Assurance, Financial Guaranty Insurance Company, and Financial Security Assurance. These bond insurers all have triple-A ratings from several nationally recognized rating agencies. Insured bonds receive the same rating based on the insurer's capital and claim-paying ability. As such, financial insurance has been used to bridge the differences between the needs of issuers and the demands of investors. Issuers of guaranteed securities obtain funds at reduced interest rates, broaden and diversify their sources of funds, and gain access to both domestic and international capital markets. Investors not only obtain triple-A assurance of timely payment but also benefit from extensive credit analysis, due diligence, and post-issuance monitoring by the bond insurers.

Bond insurance provides issuers with an attractive alternative to other sources of financing from banks and governmental and other financial institutions. Insurance allows issuers to reduce their borrowing costs significantly over the life of the debt because all issues insured by the major insurance companies are rated triple-A, which results in a lower interest rate. Issuers realize increased marketability for their transaction since insured securities appeal to a broader range of investors. Issuers also benefit from reduced volatility of prospective costs of funds by virtue of the stable trading spreads on insured triple-A transactions. Financial insurance can provide market access to smaller, less-well-known issuers and expand the marketability for securities issued by larger, better-known entities. Insured transactions can help develop cross-border funding opportunities by attracting investors from outside the issuer's domestic market.

Financial insurance provides investors with guaranteed payment of principal and interest in the event an issuer is unable to meet its financial obligations. The guarantee is unconditional and irrevocable, regardless of whether the underlying rating of the issuer is downgraded. Insured bonds hold their market value even when the issuer's own credit rating is downgraded. The triple-A ratings provide investors in these insured securities with greater price stability and enhanced marketability, both critical to investors during periods of credit volatility.

Valuation of Corporate Bonds

The price of a bond is the present value of all future cash flows from the bond. The future cash flows include the periodic coupons and the par amount at maturity. The discount rate is the yield to maturity. Hence, the value of a bond depends on the size of the coupon payments, the length of time remaining until the bond matures (current maturity), and the yield on the bond.

Bond Valuation Basics

The market prices a bond at the present value of the stream of future cash flows, which is the periodic interest payments plus the redemption value at maturity. The purpose is to determine the price that a bond will command, given the yield to maturity at which the bond is trading. For example, assume that a five-year bond has a coupon rate of 6.00 percent, the interest is paid twice a year, and the bond trades at a yield of 6.20 percent. Every six months investors will receive $30 in interest payment for every bond with a par of $1,000. In addition, investors are paid the par amount when the bond matures. The sum of the component present values is equal to $991.51. This is the value of the bond in the given market environment and is the price a buyer is willing to pay.

Table 9-4 documents the price changes when the yield rises to 6.40 percent or decreases to 6.00 percent. At a yield of 6.20 percent, the price is $991.51.

Table 9-4. Changes in price for a given change in yield.

Term	Cash flow	Present value at 3.1%	Present value at 3.0%	Present value at 3.2%
1	30	29.097963	29.126214	29.069767
2	30	28.223049	28.277877	28.168379
3	30	27.374441	27.45425	27.294941
4	30	26.551349	26.654611	26.448586
5	30	25.753006	25.878264	25.628475
6	30	24.978667	25.124528	24.833794
7	30	24.227611	24.392745	24.063754
8	30	23.499138	23.682277	23.317591
9	30	22.792568	22.992502	22.594565
10	30	22.107244	22.322817	21.893958
10	1000	736.90813	744.09391	729.7986
	Price =	991.51317	1000	983.11241

The price increases by $8.49 to $1,000.00 if yield declines to 6.00 percent. If yield rises to 6.40 percent, price declines by $8.40 from $991.51 to $983.11. The same yield change, in this example 0.20 percent, does not lead to the same change in the price. The reason is that the price and yield relationship is not linear, but rather convex. The issue of convexity will be covered later in the chapter. The change in price will be larger for a decrease in yield than it will be for an equivalent increase in yield.

Bond Valuation in Practice

The bond price valuation in the previous section has been simplified.[1] In reality, bonds trade every business day. Therefore, it is necessary to count the number of days from the last coupon payment date to the settlement date and the number of days from settlement to the next coupon date. One way to calculate the price of the bond is to calculate the value of the bond on the next coupon date and discount that to obtain the present value on settlement date.

Given the availability and power of today's computers and the availability of excellent software programs, the above calculation is impractical. Programs such as Microsoft Excel provide functions to calculate the price of a bond. The function in Excel is:

PRICE("settlement date", "maturity date", coupon rate, yield, redemption value, coupon frequency, day count basis).

The coupon frequency refers to the number of coupon payments in one year. The frequency is one for annual payment, two for semiannual, four for quarterly, and twelve for monthly. The day count basis could be 30/360, actual/365, actual/actual, or other conventions.[2] For example, assume that a bond has a coupon rate of 6.00 percent and a maturity date of October 31, 2015. The bond is quoted at a yield of 5.85 percent, and the trade settles on September 9, 2001. The day count basis is actual/actual. The price is $101.42 per $100 face value:

Price = PRICE("9/9/2001", "10/31/2015", 0.06, 0.0585, 100, 2, 1) = $101.42.

Sometimes, there may be a need to calculate the yield given the price and other specifics of the bond. In Excel, the function to obtain the yield is as follows:

YIELD("settlement date", "maturity date", coupon rate, price, redemption value, coupon frequency, day count basis).

If the price is known but the yield is not, the yield to maturity can be obtained by:

Yield = YIELD("9/9/2001", "10/31/2015", 0.06, 101.42, 100, 2, 1) = 0.0585.

Valuation of Zero-Coupon Bonds

Zero-coupon bonds pay the redemption value on maturity date. There are no periodic coupon payments. The price of such a security is simply the present value of the par amount to be received at maturity. For example, the value of a five-year zero coupon bond traded at a yield of 5.85 percent is equal to $1,000/(1 + 0.0585)^5$, which is $752.57 per $1,000 par amount. In general, the formula is:

$$P = \frac{F}{\left(1 + \dfrac{y}{N}\right)^{N \times M}}$$

where

P = the bond price,

F = the face value,

y = yield to maturity,

N = number of compounding periods in a year, and

M = maturity in years.

Valuation of Perpetual Bonds

A bond that pays regular coupons perpetually commands a price equal to the present value of those future payments. There is no maturity date, so there is no final redemption value. There is, however, an infinite number of coupon payments. The valuation formula is $P = \dfrac{C}{y}$ where C is assumed to be the annual coupon. For example, assume a perpetual bond carries a coupon rate of 6.00 percent and trades at a yield of 5.85 percent. For every $1,000 par value, the market will price it at $1,025.64.

The Settlement Value

The price discussed so far in this section captures a large portion of the value to be settled. On the settlement date, the buyer also has to pay to the seller the accrued interest that has accumulated since the last coupon date until the settlement date of this trade. For example, assume that a bond has a coupon rate of 6.00 percent and a maturity date of October 31, 2015. The bond is quoted at a yield of 5.85 percent or a price of $101.42 per $100 face value. The last coupon was paid 122 days ago, and the next coupon date is 61 days away. The settlement value is more than $101.42 for every $100 redemption value, because the buyer would also have to pay to the seller the accrued interest for 122 days. The total trade value is the sum of the quoted clean price (P) plus the accrued interest (AI). This trade value (V) can be calculated as:

$$V = P + AI = \$101.42 + \$3 \times \left(\frac{132}{183} \right) = \$103.58$$

Hence, a buyer purchasing $100,000 of this bond has to pay $103,580.

Duration and Convexity

An issuer's ability to honor interest and repayment obligations is captured in its credit ratings, which were covered in a previous section. This section focuses on two other types of risks: uncertainty with respect to the level of interest rates and due to the shape of the yield curve. First, an investor purchasing a bond faces reinvestment risk, the risk that the investor will have to reinvest future coupon income at a yield less than the yield to maturity at which the bond was purchased. Second, there is price risk—the risk that the investor might have to sell the bond before maturity at a price lower than anticipated. The yield to maturity earned by the investor may differ from his or her anticipated returns at the time of the purchase. So it is necessary to determine the sensitivity of a bond's price to a small change in yield. Duration and convexity are two measures used for this purpose.

Duration

Macaulay first defined *duration* as the time-weighted average of the discounted future cash flows. Put differently, duration is the weighted average life of a bond, where the weights are based on the present value of the individual cash flows relative to the market price of the bond. For example, the five-year, 6.00 percent bond discussed previously trades at a price of $991.51 per bond. The duration is 4.3899 years, as shown in Table 9-5. Present value calculations are based on yield to maturity at which the bond trades, which in this example we assume to be 6.20 percent. In Table 9-5, the first column represents the semiannual periods. The second column lists the coupon payment every six months and the redemption value of $1,000 when the bond matures after five years (ten semiannual periods). The third column uses a semiannual yield of 3.10 percent to calculate the present value of each cash flow. The total

Table 9-5. Duration example.

Term (t)	Cash Flows	Present value	Present value ÷ Price	t (Present value ÷ Price)
1	30	29.09796	0.029347	0.029347
2	30	28.22305	0.028465	0.056929
3	30	27.37444	0.027609	0.082826
4	30	26.55135	0.026779	0.107114
5	30	25.75301	0.025973	0.129867
6	30	24.97867	0.025192	0.151155
7	30	24.22761	0.024435	0.171045
8	30	23.49914	0.0237	0.189602
9	30	22.79257	0.022988	0.206889
10	30	22.10724	0.022296	0.222965
10	1000	736.9081	0.743216	7.432157
		Price = 991.5132	Sum =	8.779897
			Duration =	4.389948

Note: The five-year bond is trading at a yield to maturity of 6.20 percent. In the first column, t represents semiannual periods. Therefore, the duration of 8.7798 semiannual periods is divided by two to obtain a duration of 4.3899 years.

present value of the cash flows is the price of the bond. In the next column, weights for each period are determined by dividing the present value of each cash flow by the market price. For example, in period four, the present value of the coupon is $26.55135, and this is divided by the price of $991.54 to arrive at 0.026779 in column four. In column five, each period is multiplied by the weights listed in column four. For example, period four is multiplied by 0.026779 to obtain 0.107114 in column five. The procedure is performed for every period, and the values are summed. The final answer is 8.779897 semiannual periods (4.389948 years).

One can use Microsoft Excel to calculate the Macaulay duration. The syntax is:

DURATION("settlement", "maturity", coupon, yield, frequency, basis)

As an example, suppose a bond pays a 6.00 percent coupon, trades at 5.85 percent yield, and matures on October 31, 2015. On September 9, 2001, this bond has a duration of 9.56 years.

Duration and Yield

Duration and yield are inversely related. This inverse relation occurs because higher interest rates cause the cash flows in later time periods to have less weight in the duration calculation. This causes duration to become smaller.[3] For the duration example in Table 9-5, if the yield rises to 6.40 percent, the final answer for duration would decrease to 4.377476 years, as shown in Table 9-6.

Duration and Coupon Rates

Duration and the coupon rate are also inversely related. The higher the coupon rate, the smaller the duration, because higher coupon rate bonds give higher cash flows before maturity and thus tend to weight duration toward earlier years. Conversely, lower coupon rate bonds pay less cash flow before maturity. So duration is weighted closer to maturity. At the extreme, a zero-coupon bond has the same maturity and duration, because there is only one payment, and it is at maturity.

Duration and Price Sensitivity

The popularity of duration as a measure of risk derives from its use in estimating the change in a bond's value arising from a small change in its yield to maturity. Before using duration to proxy the bond price change due to a small

Table 9-6. Duration and yield to maturity.

Term (t)	Cash Flows	Present value	Present value / Price	t (Present value ÷ Price)
1	30	28.98551	0.030244	0.030244
2	30	28.00532	0.029222	0.058443
3	30	27.05828	0.028233	0.0847
4	30	26.14327	0.027279	0.109114
5	30	25.22262	0.026318	0.13159
6	30	24.40502	0.025465	0.152789
7	30	23.57973	0.024604	0.172226
8	30	22.78235	0.023772	0.190174
9	30	22.01193	0.022968	0.206711
10	30	21.26756	0.022191	0.221912
10	1000	708.9188	0.739705	7.39705
	Price =	958.3804	Sum =	8.754953
			Duration =	4.377476

Note: The five-year bond is assumed to yield 7 percent. In the first column, *t* represents semiannual periods. Therefore, the duration of 8.754953 semiannual periods is divided by two to obtain a duration of 4.377476 years.

change in yield, it is common (and more accurate) to derive the *modified duration* (D_{mod}). The formula is:

$$D_{mod} = D_m \frac{1}{(1+y)}$$

Once the modified duration is obtained, we can multiply the modified duration by the change in yield (Δy) to determine the percentage change in the value of a bond (%ΔP):

$$\% \Delta P = -D_{mod} \times \Delta y$$

Modified duration indicates the percentage change in the price of a bond for a given change in yield. As an example, the five-year, 6.00 percent bond that trades at a yield of 6.20 percent has a duration of 4.389948 years. When the yield increases to 6.40 percent, the price will decrease roughly by:

$$\% \Delta P = -4.389948 \times \frac{0.2\%}{(1+6.20\%)} = -0.8267\%$$

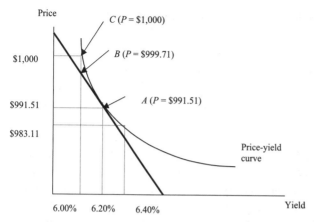

Figure 9-1. Convexity of the price-yield relationship.

Based on the proxy, the bond price will decrease from $991.51 by 0.8267 percent to $983.31. This is very close to the actual price of $983.11 when the yield rises to 6.40 percent. The proxy overestimates the price by $0.20 per bond. On the other hand, the price will increase from $991.51 by 0.8267 percent to $999.71 when yield declines from 6.20 percent to 6.00 percent (from point A to point B in Figure 9-1). The discrepancy between the estimated and actual change in the bond price is due to the convexity of the price-yield relationship, as shown in Figure 9-1.

As noted, the previous percentage price change calculation is inaccurate because it fails to account for the curvature or convexity of the price-yield relationship. Because of the shape of the price-yield curve, for a given change in yield, the gain in price for a drop in yield will be greater than the fall in price due to an equal rise in yield. Mathematically, the duration is the first derivative of price with respect to yield, and convexity is the second derivative.

Summary

The chapter provides a comprehensive overview of the corporate fixed-income securities. The importance of understanding market conventions such as settlement, maturity, redemption value, clean price, accrued interest, current yield, yield to maturity, and coupon date cannot be overemphasized. For example, the settlement date is the date that money is paid to the seller and securities are delivered to the buyer. A seller failing to deliver on the settlement date provides free financing to the buyer and will not receive the accrued interest. The calculation of accrued interest is based on day count conventions. The capital market assumes a 365-day year. The assumption is

360 days a year in the money market, where commercial paper and bankers' acceptances are traded.

Default risk is an important element in the corporate sector. Market participants rely on credit ratings to gauge the credit quality of a security. The four major rating agencies are Moody's, Standard & Poor's, Fitch IBCA, and DCR. Corporate issuers without sound financial status often purchase financial insurance to raise the rating.

Valuation of bonds depends on maturity, coupon rate, and yield to maturity. Standard textbooks assume discrete time periods, such as five or seven years. This approach is oversimplified. In reality, bonds trade every day. The valuation of a fixed-income security is determined not only by the quoted price but also by the accrued interest, which requires counting the days in the coupon period and the number of days since last coupon date to the settlement date. Furthermore, duration and convexity are used to examine price volatility and approximation accuracy when yield changes by a small amount.

Selected Bibliography

Campbell, C. J. "Private Security Placements and Resales to the Public Under SEC Rule 144." *Corporate Finance Review* 2:1 (July/August 1997): 11-16.

Fabozzi, F. J. *Bond Markets, Analysis and Strategies.* Upper Saddle River, N.J.: Prentice-Hall, 2000.

Liaw, K. T. *The Business of Investment Banking.* New York: John Wiley, 1999.

Stigum, M., and F. L. Robinson. *Money Market and Bond Calculations.* Chicago: Irwin Professional Publishing, 1996.

Tuckman, B. *Fixed Income Securities: Tools for Today's Markets.* New York: John Wiley, 1996.

Notes

1. As discussed in the previous chapter, the theoretically correct approach is to use the spot rates for valuation purposes. But the yield to maturity is widely used to quote prices.

2. The numerator represents the number of days in a month, and the denominator denotes the number of days in a year. Therefore, 30/360 assumes a 30-day month and a 360-day year. The day count basis of actual/actual means the accrued interest calculation takes the actual number of days in the month and in the year.

3. Another way to view duration is as the slope of a line tangent to the price-yield curve. As yield rises, the slope becomes flatter, which means that duration will be lower.

10

Municipal Securities

Municipal securities (munis) can be a very useful financial vehicle for individuals in high marginal tax brackets. Understanding the market for munis can be important in developing an appropriate investment strategy using municipal bonds. States, cities, counties, and other government entities issue municipal securities to raise money to fund projects for the public good. Most municipal bonds offer interest income that is exempt from federal taxes and may also be exempt from state taxes. Even though the interest earned on a municipal bond is exempt from taxation, an investor in municipal securities can recognize capital gains that are subject to taxes when the bond is sold. A separate market for municipal securities that are federally taxable offers a state and local tax exemption on interest paid to residents of the state of issuance. Many municipal securities are purchased and held until maturity. The secondary market trading is therefore not very active. As with other types of securities, technology has impacted this market significantly. Online auction for new issues and Internet trading of outstanding securities in the secondary market has gained popularity in recent years.

Market Overview

Municipal bonds are fixed-income securities issued by states, cities, counties, and other government entities to raise money to fund projects. These public capital projects include bridges, highways, mass transit systems, sewage treatment plants, courthouses, and electric generating plants. They also finance certain types of private projects that serve important public purposes, such as low-income housing, private hospitals and colleges, and industrial facilities. Approximately 50,000 state and local governments and agencies of government issue municipal securities. The federal government grants tax-favored status to municipal securities, so those services can be financed at lower interest rates. Investors, especially those subject to a high marginal income tax rate, can participate in the financing of public services and benefit from the tax-favored treatment of interest income such bonds receive.

The market for municipal securities is more than $1.5 trillion. There are about 1.5 million municipal issues outstanding. Annual issuance passed the

$100 billion mark in 1982, with $124 billion issued that year. The annual volume has continued on an upward path. The supply in 1993 surged to a record $340 billion. Since 1993, the volume of annual issuance has leveled off and is currently in the $200–300 billion range (except 1998, when the total municipal issuance was $321 billion). A vast majority of the funds raised have a maturity of more than 13 months.

Types of Municipal Securities

General obligation bonds (GOs) are backed by the full faith and credit of the issuer for scheduled payments of principal and interest. Most GOs also have the added security that municipalities can raise property taxes to assure payment. These bonds are regarded as very safe and are voter approved. Furthermore, sometimes additional fees, grants, and special charges secure certain GOs. These GOs are known as double-barreled.

Revenue bonds are municipal securities whose payments are secured by revenues derived from certain revenue-producing agencies or projects. Examples include water and sewage treatment facilities, hospitals, schools, and airports. Special authorities created for the purpose issue many of these bonds. The agency or authority often has the ability to levy charges and fees for its services. Usually, the yield is higher than that of a general obligation bond because taxes are more secure than revenues.

In addition to the two general types, a variety of municipal securities has been issued. Limited and special tax bonds are revenue bonds payable from a pledge of the proceeds against a specific tax. This tax could be a gasoline tax, a special assessment, or an ad valorem tax levied at a fixed price. Unlike GOs and their ability to raise taxes, with these bonds, the issue is limited to the specific source of the revenue to pay the bonds.

Industrial revenue bonds are issued to help develop industrial or commercial property for the benefit of private users. The agency raises funds by issuing municipal bonds. The money raised from this type of bond issue is used to pay for the construction of the new facilities, which are then leased to the corporate guarantor. Hence, the safety of an industrial revenue bond depends on the creditworthiness of the corporate guarantor.

Housing bonds are secured by mortgage payments on single-family homes. Added protection comes from federal subsidies for low-income families, Federal Housing Authority insurance, Veteran Authority guarantees, and private mortgage insurance.

Moral obligation bonds are revenue bonds that, in addition to their primary source of security, possess a structure whereby, in the event of a revenue shortfall, the state would make up the difference. There is no legal obligation for the state to honor such a payment, but the market perception is that failure to honor the moral pledge would have negative consequences for the state's own creditworthiness.

Municipal notes are short-term debt instruments issued by state and local authorities. Their maturities run from about sixty days to one year. They are usually available in denominations of about $25,000. Municipalities use this type of financing as an interim step in anticipation of future revenues. Tax anticipation notes are issued by municipalities in anticipation of future tax revenues. The security of the issue depends on the security and amount of the tax revenues the municipality intends to receive. Usually, these funds are used to finance current obligations. *Bond anticipation notes* (BANs) are issued when funds are anticipated from a bond issue. To avoid poor market conditions, an issuer might delay a bond issue, or the issuer might want to combine several projects into one larger issue. During this process, they issue the BANs. *Revenue anticipation notes* are issued in anticipation of revenue coming in from the state or federal government.

Major Investors

The major owners of tax-exempt municipal securities are households, mutual funds, money market funds, property-liability insurance companies, and commercial banks. In recent years, households and mutual funds have become the largest investors in the municipal market. Table 10-1 lists municipal securities ownership from 1990 to 1999. Though households' direct ownership declined from 48.3 percent in 1990 to 32.6 percent in 1999, trends in the holdings of municipal securities by mutual funds, money market funds, and unit investment trusts are on an upward path. These three types of investment funds held 20.1 percent of municipal securities in 1990. By 1999, their holdings accounted for 33.7 percent. Insurance companies' holdings increased from 10.0 percent to 13.8 percent during this time period. Other types of municipal investors held a stable percentage of ownership over the same time period.

New Issues

Two principal methods are used to float a new municipal bond issue: a *competitive bond sale* and a *negotiated bond sale*. Each method has its own advantages and disadvantages. A competitive bidding involves solicitation of bids from various underwriters. It is a public auction in which bonds are sold to the highest bidder—that is, the bid that produces the lowest financing costs

Table 10-1. Municipal securities ownership 1990–1999.

	Total amount outstanding (in billions of dollars)	Households (%)	Mutual funds (%)	Money market funds (%)	Closed-end funds (%)	Bank personal trust (%)	Banks (%)	Insurance companies (%)	Others (%)
1990	$1,184	48.5	9.5	7.1	1.2	6.8	9.9	11.6	5.4
1991	1,272	48.3	11.0	7.1	2.0	7.1	8.1	10.0	6.5
1992	1,302	44.9	12.9	7.4	3.0	7.4	7.5	10.3	6.6
1993	1,378	40.1	15.3	7.7	3.8	7.9	7.2	10.6	7.5
1994	1,342	37.4	15.4	8.5	4.0	8.5	7.3	11.5	7.5
1995	1,294	35.4	16.3	9.9	4.6	8.4	7.2	12.4	5.8
1996	1,296	33.6	16.5	11.1	4.8	8.0	7.3	13.5	5.2
1997	1,368	31.2	16.1	12.2	4.4	7.7	7.1	14.2	7.1
1998	1,464	31.3	16.6	13.2	4.2	7.2	7.2	14.4	6.0
1999	1,510	32.6	16.6	13.0	4.1	7.1	7.1	13.8	5.7

Source: The Bond Market Association.

for the municipality. A financial advisor is generally hired to advise and handle the bond sale. The financial advisor's responsibilities may include preparing the preliminary official statement and the final official statement, recommending the structure of the issue, proposing a sale date, and evaluating the submitted bids. An *official statement* for a municipal bond issue is a document that gives in detail the terms of the proposed issue of securities, financial information, and operating data. Such a document for a stock or corporate bond issue is called a *prospectus*. MunisOnline—a source for real time municipal bond sale information—publishes official statements and notices of sales on the Internet.

After the financial advisor designs the bond issue and the municipality approves it, notice of the bond sale is announced publicly. The notice of sales provides information on telephone bids, facsimile bids, minimum bids, whether the security is book-entry, and other relevant material. The notice also specifies the date and time for submission of sealed bids. Underwriters or syndicates of underwriters review the specifications of the proposed bond issue and, if interested, submit sealed bids to the financial advisor.

Following submission of the bids, the municipality will evaluate each of the proposals. The financial advisor will analyze and compare the various bids. If the structures of the bond issue and coupon or discount interest rates are established in advance, the bid evaluation is relatively simple because the highest bid represents the lowest cost option. Where interest rates are not established in advance, issuers need to use the net interest cost or true interest cost method to determine the lowest cost bid.

In contrast, the negotiated deal differs significantly from the competitive bidding approach. In a negotiated sale, the first step is the selection of the underwriter or underwriting syndicate. In some cases, the underwriter is selected without solicitation and comparison of competitive proposals. This occurs when an underwriter has handled prior bond issues for the issuer. In other cases, the municipal issuer requests proposals from several underwriters. The municipality then makes its selection after evaluation of the proposals. In such a negotiated deal, the underwriter handles most of the activities associated with the bond issue on behalf of the municipality. Usually the issuer does not use the services of an independent financial advisor in a negotiated deal. The interest costs and other terms of the bond issue are negotiated between the issuer and the underwriter. These costs and terms include the interest rates, the underwriter's fees and charges, the original issue discount, and the issue date.

The main advantage of the competitive sale is the perceived fairness and openness of the process. There is no perception of political influence. The bidding process is accomplished by confidential, sealed bids, so the issuer does not know in advance which underwriting firm will be selected. An additional level of impartiality is added by the use of an independent financial advisor who handles the bid's opening and evaluation process. There are disadvantages to the competitive sale, however. For example, financial advisors usually advise an issuer to use a negotiated strategy if the bond issue is unusually large or complex. The competitive bidding method may be inferior for a municipality if the bonds are likely to receive low ratings or only a few underwriters are expected to submit bids.

Certain disadvantages of the competitive sale are thus advantages of the negotiated strategy. A major advantage of the negotiated bond sale is that an underwriter can better time entry into the financial markets. This flexibility can produce lower financing costs for an issuer. Another advantage is the level of assistance provided by the underwriter, who typically handles most of the administrative and technical aspects of the bond issue. The negotiated strategy also affords an underwriter the opportunity to presell the bond issue. This can be a significant advantage, particularly for more complex bond issues or for issues with low credit ratings, because these issues take more time to sell. However, the most significant disadvantage of the negotiated bond sale strategy is that the coupon rates on the bonds and the underwriter's fees are negotiated privately, not by competitive bidding. In addition, the selection of an underwriter may be based on political or personal relationships rather than merit.

According to a Bond Market Association (formerly Public Securities Association)) study, there is no clear empirical evidence as to whether competitive bidding or negotiated deals brings in more money or lower yield for municipalities. Another study that examines the overall financing costs of competitive and negotiated bonds sold by Pennsylvania school districts in 1993 concludes that the bond marketing strategy (whether competitive bidding or negotiated sale) is not a statistically significant factor in the determination of overall financing costs.

Disclosure to Purchasers

Historically, municipal securities have been relatively free from federal regulation. But beginning July 3, 1995, SEC Rule 15c2-12 requires issuers to:

- Prepare official statements meeting the content requirements of the rule.
- File certain financial information and operating data with national and state repositories each year.
- Disclose any material events on a timely basis.

The final official statement sets forth information about the terms of the issue, financial information, operating data, and annual updating and event disclosure. The rule also requires underwriters to review a preliminary official statement deemed final by the issuer. It is expected that both the contents of the disclosure and the timely dissemination of the preliminary official statement will improve.

The rule addresses an additional perceived problem relating to lack of reliable information in the secondary market. The rule now requires issuers to provide continuing disclosure throughout the life of each of their bond issues. In addition to the obvious investor benefits, continuing disclosure is beneficial to municipal issuers as well. To the extent that continuing disclosure enhances the liquidity of a security in the secondary market, investors may accept a lower yield at issuance that saves issuers interest costs. Reliable continuing disclosure could avoid potential issuer liability as a result of incomplete publicly available information.

To accomplish continuing disclosure, the issuer's financial information must be filed with each *Nationally Recognized Municipal Securities Information Repository* (NRMSIR). The four NRMSIRs are Bloomberg Municipal Repositories, DPC Data, J. J. Kenny Repository, and Thomson NRMSIR. There are also state information repositories.

The third requirement listed above is for material event disclosure. The concept of materiality refers to an event or fact that is material if it is likely that it has significance in the deliberations of a reasonable investor. The event disclosure must be filed with each NRMSIR or the *Municipal Securities Rulemaking Board* (MSRB) and with the appropriate state information repository in a timely manner.

The three requirements of SEC Rule 15c2-12 apply only to issues of $1 million or more. Issues of less than that amount need not comply with any of the provisions of the rule. The rule also contains three general exemptions provided that the securities are in minimum denominations of $100,000 or more:

- A private placement exemption for securities sold to no more than thirty-five sophisticated investors who purchase for investment, not distribution.

- An exemption for certain securities which the holder has a right to tender at a price of at least par at least as frequently as every nine months.

- An exemption for securities with maturity of nine months or less.

Municipal Securities Rulemaking Board

The MSRB was established in 1975 by Congress to develop rules regulating securities firms and banks involved in underwriting, trading, and selling municipal securities. The MSRB sets standards for all municipal securities dealers. Like the New York Stock Exchange or the National Association of Securities Dealers, the MSRB is a self-regulatory organization that is subject to oversight by the Securities and Exchange Commission.

Online Auctions

Traditionally, municipal issuers go to banks or securities dealers to sell their debt. The issuer picks one firm to negotiate for the entire bond issue or there is a competitive sale among brokerage firms. The underwriter then marks up the price and reoffers them to institutional and individual clients. Such traditional approaches cost issuers gross commissions that averaged $5 per bond. In addition, the traditional method does not allow bidders to see their status relative to other bids and improve their own. The typical competitive bid process allows only one bid per bidder. It does not allow maturity-by-maturity bids. And it is done often by fax transmission.

The new online auction/bidding systems allow dealers and investors to bid directly on new issues. For example, MuniAuction is an Internet-based electronic auction for new municipal bond issues conducted in real time. The issuer offers bonds for sale on the MuniAuction. Registered bidders can select from a variety of auctions and review the notice of sale and preliminary official statement online before entering the auction of choice. They visit the site at the scheduled auction time and submit bids to purchase all of the bonds or selected maturities. Underwriters have the opportunity to view either their status relative to other bidders or the best bid and repeatedly improve their own bid. The issuer can watch the auction in progress from its MuniAuction Web page. It can see winning bids as they are submitted, as well as winning bidders. MuniAuction also computes the true interest associated with the winning bids.

Form of Issuance

A growing number of municipal bonds today are issued in book-entry form, similar to the way U.S. government securities are issued. Ownership is recorded through data entry at a central clearinghouse. An investor's confirmation of purchase from a bank or brokerage firm provides the written record of the transaction. Book-entry bonds offer a number of protections and conveniences to bondholders, including protection from loss or theft, automatic payment of interest, notification of calls, and ease of transfer.

Municipal Bond Insurance

More than half of all new-issue municipal securities come to market with bond insurance. The well-publicized fiscal problems of major municipalities—such as New York's default in the mid 1970s, the Washington Public Power Supply System default in 1984, and the Orange County bankruptcy in 1994—have increased the demand for municipal bond insurance. The percent of new-issue long-term municipals insured is on an upward trend, increasing from 27 percent in 1990 to 57 percent in 1997. Insurance makes municipal bonds more attractive as an investment because municipal bond insurers guarantee scheduled interest and principal payments. The guarantee covers 100 percent of interest and principal for the full term of the issue. This level of assurance increases the marketability of the protected bonds and helps them retain their value.

Benefits to Investors

For investors, there are three main benefits of municipal bond insurance. First, each insured municipal is triple-A rated. Second, the insurance guarantees that investors will receive principal and interest payments without delay. If the issuer of the bond defaults, the insurance company makes funds available for scheduled payment on the next business day following notification. Third, for new municipal bond issues, the insurance coverage is good for the life of the bond.

Benefits to Issuers

Most municipal bond issuers can benefit from insurance as long as their own credit is of investment-grade quality or higher.[1] The difference between what the issuer would have to offer as yield on bonds carrying its own rating and what the market will accept as yield on triple-A insured bonds represents gross interest cost savings. The gross savings minus the premium paid to the bond insurer are the net savings. While issuers with triple-B and single-A ratings would seem to have the most to gain, double-A and triple-A issuers also find insurance cost-effective. The Association of Financial Guaranty Insurors estimates that, since the inception of municipal bond insurance in 1971, municipalities had saved approximately $25 billion in borrowing costs through bond insurance by 1998. In 1998 alone, they saved about $3.7 billion using insurance on $160 billion of municipal bonds.

For a smaller municipal issuer, buying insurance may be simpler and less expensive than applying for a credit rating from the major rating agencies.

Insurance can also increase the marketability of an issue. Small or infrequent issuers are unknown to most municipal investors, and bond insurance may improve the market's acceptance of their securities.

Municipal bond insurance is available for both negotiated and competitive-bid transactions. In the competitive market, insurance may be obtained at the bidder's option or through direct purchase. Under the *bidder's option method*, the syndicate making the winning bid selects the insurer and pays for the insurance. Under the *direct purchase method*, the issuer and its financial advisor select the insurer, and the premium is paid from the bond proceeds. The premium is based on the insurer's evaluation of the credit, the complexity of the transaction, and market competition. In addition, premiums are affected by the cost of capital that insurance companies must assign to each transaction in order to properly manage their resources and maintain their triple-A rating.

Municipal bond insurance is available in the secondary market as well. Municipal bond insurers provide insurance to traders, dealers, and institutional investors to improve the quality and marketability of the municipal securities.

An Example

Historically, downgrades of unsecured municipal bonds have exceeded upgrades. In contrast, insured bonds maintain their triple-A ratings and liquidity regardless of the financial difficulties of the issuer. For example, the price and liquidity of uninsured bonds associated with Orange County (California) were negatively affected after the county filed for bankruptcy in December 1994. The insured bonds retained the rating and held their market value much better than their uninsured counterparts. The county's Transportation Authority Sales Tax Revenue 6-percent 2/15/08 bonds, both insured and uninsured, were traded at $99.44 per $100 par value on October 31, 1994, before bankruptcy filing. On December 16 of the same year, after the bankruptcy filing, the uninsured bond was traded at $77.09 per $100 par value. The insured bond was traded at $92.12 per $100 par value.[2]

Municipal Insurers

Municipal bonds are mostly insured by monoline insurers. The four largest municipal insurers are MBIA, AMBAC, Financial Security Assurance, and Financial Guaranty Insurance Company. All of these insurers carry ratings of Aaa by Moody's, AAA by Standard and Poor's, and AAA by Fitch ICBA. Bonds insured by these organizations receive the same triple-A rating.

Financial insurance companies must meet the requirements of insurance regulators in every state where they do business. They are also subject to intense scrutiny from the rating agencies that evaluate and assign a rating to every transaction they insure. To test the adequacy of the companies' capital resources, the rating agencies apply a computer-simulated stress test that measures their ability to pay claims at a level comparable to those experienced during the Great Depression.

For insurers, the most important measure of financial strength is the margin of safety. The margin of safety takes into account the full range of the insurer's claims-paying resources as well as the quality and diversification of risk in the insurer's portfolio. To calculate the margin of safety, a computer simulation is run to demonstrate how the bond insurer would fare in a prolonged economic depression.

Secondary Market

Even though municipal bonds are publicly traded, municipalities are not required to prepare the equivalent of an 8-K or 10-K. Over the past several years, there have been many efforts to improve the quality and extent of information available regarding municipal securities. On November 10, 1994, the SEC adopted amendments to Rule 15c2-12. The rule effectively imposes a new requirement that municipal issuers provide a continuous flow of information to bondholders and the securities markets. The rule also requires material event disclosure to be filed with each NRMSIR or the MSRB and to the appropriate state information repository on a timely manner.

Secondary Trading

The municipal market has historically traded over-the-counter, with market participants executing transactions by telephone. There are more than 50,000 different issuers and 1.5 million different issues, each of which has its own structural characteristics. It is not an ideal market for electronic trading systems. But the market has changed in recent years, as technology has increasingly allowed dealers and clients to interact through electronic media. This has, in turn, led to the creation of more sophisticated systems that allow for instantaneous electronic transactions. The popularity of these systems is expected to grow substantially over the next decade.

One of the greatest factors contributing to the increased use of electronic trading systems has been the phenomenal growth of the Internet. The low cost of Internet access allows even the smallest individual investors access to tools and information sources that were, until recently, the private domain of institutional investors.

In secondary market trading on municipal bonds, an odd lot is $25,000 or less in par value for retail. For institutions, anything less than $250,000 is considered an odd lot. Dealer spreads vary depending on factors such as liquidity, volatility, and market conditions. The retail spreads range from a quarter of a point for large blocks to several points for odd-lot sales of an inactive issue. For institutional investors, the spreads are no more than half of a point.

Tax Advantages

Tax-exempt municipal securities are among the most popular types of investments for high-tax-bracket investors. Under federal income tax law, interest income from municipal securities is free from federal income taxes.[3] Therefore, municipal securities often trade at yields lower than that for Treasury securities of comparable maturities.[4] Table 10-2 lists a sample of municipal yields as of the close on November 5, 1999. The yields of AAA municipal bonds as a percent of Treasuries increase from 71.06 percent for one-year maturity to 96.03 percent when maturity increases to thirty years. Put differently, the yields of AAA municipals and of Treasuries converge as maturity extends. To better understand the reason behind such a convergence, we calculate the equivalent taxable yield for AAA municipals (column five of Table

Table 10-2. Municipal yields (as of the close on November 5, 1999).

(1) Maturity	(2) AAA Municipal yield (%)	(3) AAA as a percent of Treasuries	(4) Treasuries (%)	(5) Equivalent taxable yield of AAA (%)	(6) Quality spreads (5)–(4) (%)
1 year	3.83	71.06	5.39	6.34	0.95
2 years	4.12	72.28	5.70	6.82	1.12
5 years	4.51	77.23	5.84	7.47	1.63
7 years	4.71	78.11	6.03	7.80	1.77
10 years	4.94	83.73	5.90	8.18	2.28
30 years	5.80	96.03	6.04	9.60	3.56

Note: The calculation of equivalent taxable Yield assumes a marginal tax rate of 39.6 percent.

Source: Yields are obtained from J. J. Kenny Drake.

10-2). Then the yield differentials between AAA municipals and Treasuries are calculated. The yield differentials are the result of differences in quality of the securities; hence, they are called *quality spreads.* Treasury securities are perceived as free of default risk, but municipals possess a certain degree of risk, even with the added insurance guaranty. Because investors' concern over the credit risk is more serious in the long run, municipals must offer a higher yield spread to compensate for such risk.

Equivalent Taxable Yield

As previously discussed, interest income from municipal securities is exempt from federal taxation. One of the best ways to appreciate the tax-favored advantage of a municipal security is to compare it to a comparable taxable investment, by converting tax-exempt yield into equivalent taxable yield. The *equivalent taxable yield* is calculated as follows:

$$\text{Equivalent taxable yield } = \frac{tax\ exempt\ yield}{1 - marginal\ tax\ rate}$$

For example, assume an investor is in the 36 percent federal tax bracket. Assume the investor has $100,000 to invest and is considering two investment alternatives: a tax-exempt municipal bond yielding 5.00 percent and a taxable corporate bond yielding 7.50 percent. Which investment is more advantageous? There are several ways the investor can compare these two alternatives. The first way is to use the formula listed above to obtain the equivalent taxable yield for the municipal bond:

$$\text{Equivalent taxable yield } = \frac{5.00\%}{(1 - 0.36)} = 7.8125\%$$

Obviously, the municipal bond provides a better return.

A second approach is to convert the yield on taxable corporate bond into an after-tax yield and then compare it with the municipal bond yield. The formula is:

$$\text{After-tax yield} = (\text{taxable yield}) \times (1 - \text{ marginal tax rate})$$

A 7.50 percent taxable yield can be converted to an after-tax yield:

$$\text{After-tax yield} = 7.50\% \times (1 - 0.36) = 4.80\%$$

Hence, the municipal bond provides a higher after-tax return to investors.

Alternatively, a $100,000 investment in the municipal bond will earn the investor $5,000 a year and pay no federal income tax. The taxable bond investment will produce $7,500 in interest income, but the investor has to pay federal tax at the 36 percent rate. Therefore, the after-tax income is only $4,800. The investment in the municipal bond returns the investor $200 more.

The benefits from investing in the tax-favored municipal securities are quite significant if the investor's taxable income is high and is subject to a high marginal tax bracket. Table 10-3 lists tax-exempt/taxable yield equivalents. As shown in the table, a 5 percent tax-exempt yield is equivalent to a taxable yield of 5.88 percent if the investor is in the 15 percent tax bracket. The equivalent taxable yield is 8.28 percent if the investor is subject to a marginal tax rate of 39.6 percent.

So far we have shown the effects of federal taxation on investment returns. Municipal bonds are free from federal tax on the accrued interest and also free from state and local taxes if they are issued in the state of residence. Such exemptions from state as well as federal income taxes are regarded as double exemption. For example, a resident of New York who buys a municipal bond issued by the state of New York will not pay New York state or local taxes on the investment. However, the same resident of New York who buys a munic-

Table 10-3. Tax-exempt/taxable yield equivalents.

Tax Bracket	15%	28%	31%	36%	39.6%
Tax-Exempt Yield (%)	Equivalent taxable yield (%)				
3.0	3.53	4.17	4.35	4.69	4.97
3.5	4.12	4.86	5.07	5.47	5.79
4.0	4.71	5.56	5.80	6.25	6.62
4.5	5.29	6.25	6.52	7.03	7.45
5.0	5.88	6.94	7.25	7.81	8.28
5.5	6.47	7.64	7.79	8.59	9.11
6.0	7.06	8.33	8.70	9.37	9.93
6.5	7.65	9.03	9.42	10.16	10.76
7.0	8.24	9.72	10.14	10.94	11.59
7.5	8.82	10.42	10.87	11.72	12.42
8.0	9.41	11.11	11.59	12.50	13.25
8.5	10.00	11.81	12.32	13.28	14.07
9.0	10.59	12.50	13.04	14.06	14.90
9.5	11.18	13.19	13.77	14.83	15.73
10.0	11.76	13.89	14.49	15.63	16.56

ipal bond issued by a city in Connecticut must pay state and local tax on the accrued interest. The tax rate varies from state to state. Therefore, the additional benefit investors receive from tax-favored municipal bond investments depends upon the individual state. For high tax rate states like New York, the additional tax benefits are significant. For Alaska and Nevada, where there is no state income tax, the benefit of federal tax exemption represents the entire benefit received by the investor.

More on Taxation of Municipal Bonds

Even though the interest earned on a municipal bond is exempt from taxation, a bondholder can recognize gain or loss that is subject to federal income tax on the sale of such a bond. The amount of gain or loss is equal to the difference between the sale price of the bond and the purchase price (or tax basis). There are two types of capital gains: long-term and short-term. A long-term gain applies if a bond is held for more than twelve months before it is sold, while a short-term gain is the result of holding a bond for twelve months or less. When a bond is sold before maturity, an investor may also recognize a capital loss if the sale proceeds are less than the bondholder's tax basis (costs). In such a case, capital losses are first applied against capital gains of the same type to reduce the gains. Thus, a long-term capital loss will first reduce long-term capital gains, and a short-term capital loss will first reduce short-term capital gains. Under current tax law, any capital losses remaining after offsetting all available capital gains can then be used to reduce ordinary income by up to $3,000 per year. Any losses exceeding that amount may be carried forward to reduce capital gains or ordinary income in future years.

If a tax-exempt bond is originally issued at a discount, the difference between the issue price and the par amount is considered the *original issue discount* (OID). For example, if a ten-year bond with a $1,000 face amount and a stated coupon rate of 5.00 percent payable semiannually is issued for $925.61, the bond is treated for federal tax purposes as having $74.39 of original issue discount. Because this is a tax-exempt bond, the OID is tax-free. However, the OID may increase the investor's tax basis in the bond for the purpose of calculating gains or losses if the investor trades the bond before maturity. The IRS provides that the investor's basis will increase over time based on a constant yield to maturity (CYT) method. The constant yield to maturity on the bond is the yield to maturity that equates the price at issue to the present value of all future cash flows from the bond. For the bond cited above, the constant yield to maturity is 6.00 percent. This 6.00 percent yield will enter into the accretion of the investor's basis. A sale price of higher than the accreted basis will produce a capital gain, which is taxable. If a tax-exempt bond is purchased at a premium, whether at original issue or in the secondary market, the bond premium is amortized over the remaining term until maturity using the same constant yield to maturity method.

When the municipal issuer redeems the bond prior to its maturity date at a fixed price, the bondholder should treat it as a sale of the bond. Thus, the bondholder may recognize a capital gain or loss on such a sale. In some instances, if the purchase of the bond is financed by borrowed money, the interest expense is tax deductible. However, a taxpayer may not deduct from federal income tax interest on indebtedness incurred to purchase municipal bonds.

Taxable Municipal Securities

Taxable municipal bonds exist when the federal government does not subsidize the financing of certain activities that do not provide a significant benefit to the general public. Investor-led housing, local sports facilities, and borrowing to replenish a municipality's underfunded pension plan are just a few types of bond issues that are federally taxable. Taxable municipal securities offer yields more comparable to those of other taxable securities.

Risks

Investors face several types of risks when investing in municipal securities. One primary risk in the municipal bond market, as in other fixed-income markets, is the issuer's inability to meet its financial obligations, called *default risk* or credit risk. The second risk is the *market risk*, reflecting the fact that the market price of a municipal security changes as market conditions change. In addition, the *call risk* refers to the possibility that some bond issues allow the issuer to retire all or a portion of the bond before maturity.

Default Risk

Municipal debt is generally regarded as low risk. According to Fitch IBCA's study, general obligation bonds, tax-backed, water/sewer, transportation, and public higher education bonds are among the least risky. The cumulative default rates (percentages of bonds that eventually default) for these bonds range from 0.01 to 0.40 percent. The cumulative default rates in health care, electronic utilities, and multifamily sectors range from 1 to 4 percent. The most risky municipal sector is industrial development bonds, with cumulative default rates close to 15 percent.

Table 10-4. Municipal bond ratings.

Credit risk	Standard and Poor's	Moody's	Fitch IBCA
Prime	AAA	Aaa	AAA
Excellent	AA	Aa	AA
Upper medium	A	A	A
Lower medium	BBB	Baa	BBB
Speculative	BB	Ba	BB
Very speculative	B, CCC, CC	B, Caa	B, CCC, CC, C
Default	D	CA, A	DDD, DD, D

Credit ratings can be used as an indicator of default probability. Rating agencies, such as Standard and Poor's, Moody's, and Fitch ICBA, grade municipal bonds. Municipal bonds that are rated BBB or higher (by Standard and Poor's and Fitch ICBA) or Baa or higher (by Moody's) are considered investment grade. Bonds below these ratings are considered noninvestment grade or junk bonds. Table 10-4 lists bond ratings by these rating agencies. Fitch IBCA estimates that 80 to 85 percent of the municipal market is rated investment grade or insured. Fitch IBCA's estimated default rates for investment grades averaged from 0.31 to 0.33 percent. In contrast, the default rates are substantially higher for municipal bonds rated below investment grade, estimated at 3.05 to 4.06 percent.

For nonrated municipal bonds, a Bond Market Association study that examined defaults during 1986 to 1991 showed that the nonrated municipal securities represented 23.5 percent of the total number of issues. In terms of dollar volume, the nonrated issues accounted for 8 percent. The default rate averaged 1.1 percent, and the default rate by dollar volume of issuance was 2 percent for the studied period.

Market Risk

The coupon rate for a fixed-rate municipal security does not change during the life of the bond. The market price changes as market conditions change, and it may be more or less than the original purchase price. Municipal bond prices fluctuate in response to changing interest rates. Prices increase when interest rates decline, and prices decline when interest rates rise. When interest rates fall, new issues come to market with lower yields than older securities, making the older securities more valuable. When interest rates rise, new issues provide investors with higher yields than older securities, making the older ones less valuable.

Call Risk

Some municipal bond issues allow the issuers to call all or a portion of the bonds at par or at a premium before the scheduled maturity date. Dealers often quote yield to call and yield to maturity when yield to call is lower. Municipal bonds are likely to be called when they are trading at a price above the initial price—that is, interest rates have declined. Calling the bond and floating another issue saves the municipality interest costs, because the new issue will carry a lower coupon rate in the lower interest rate environment.

Recent Developments

Municipal securities have two unique characteristics: Interest income from municipal securities is generally exempt from federal taxes, and financial insurance is common. The market has grown to a size of $1.5 trillion. In recent years, the abuses of yield burning and pay-to-play have received intense government scrutiny. To prevent future abuses, the MSRB has adopted new rules, and the Bond Market Association has taken steps to improve the transparency of the municipal bond market.

Yield Burning

Advance refunding is a financing structure under which new municipal bonds are issued to pay off an outstanding bond issue prior to its call date or maturity date. Generally, the proceeds of the new issue are temporarily invested in special government securities. The interest and principal payments on those invested securities are then used to pay off the old municipal issue. During this waiting period, federal law restricts the interest that can be earned on the escrow account to be no more than the interest paid on the new issue to prevent the municipality from engaging in a tax arbitrage.

Since tax-exempt municipal rates are lower than most other yields, financial institutions managing the escrow account must make sure that the escrow account earns a below-market rate. To keep the earnings low, the Treasury issues special low-interest securities called *state and local government series* (SLGS). SLGS securities are offered for sale in book-entry form and are nonmarketable. The interest rate earned on time deposit securities is five basis points below the estimated Treasury borrowing rate of comparable maturity. The SLGS demand deposit security is a one-day certificate of indebtedness. The principal and daily accrued-interest are automatically rolled over each day until redemption is requested. The interest rate on SLGS demand deposit securities is based on an adjustment of the average yield in the most recent auction of the thirteen-week Treasury bills.

Unfortunately, in many cases broker-dealers used this as an opportunity to overcharge the municipalities for open market Treasuries used in the escrow accounts created in conjunction with the advance refunding. Where the yield on the Treasury securities was greater than the yield on the newly issued bond, the escrow provider would slap excessive markups on securities used to complete municipal bond deals. Since bond prices and yields move in opposite directions, when underwriters mark up the bonds, they "burn down" the yield, thus violating federal tax rules. This is referred to as *yield burning*, which is the subject of intense government investigation in recent years. The IRS has informed local governments across the country that their tax-exempt municipal bonds may be declared taxable if yield burning occurred on their watch.

Pay to Play

The practice of cozying up to government officials to win bond contracts is called *pay to play*. In 1994, the MSRB passed a rule that barred securities firms and restricted many of their employees from making campaign contributions to issuer public officials who select underwriters to sell municipal securities.

But in recent years many Wall Street firms have hired consultants and have used their contacts and knowledge of state and local politics to help them win municipal bond deals. The MSRB hence asked the SEC to approve a new rule requiring Wall Street firms to disclose each quarter how much their municipal bond consultants are contributing to public officials.

New MSRB Rules

The MSRB has adopted new rules, Rule G-37 and Rule G-38, to address the problems associated with political contributions and prohibitions on municipal securities business. Rule G-37 prohibits any broker-dealer from engaging in municipal securities business with an issuer within two years after any contribution to an official of such issuer. Under Rule G-37, each broker-dealer is required to send to the MSRB information on contributions to officials of issuers by the last day of the month following the end of each calendar quarter. In addition, Rule G-38 requires disclosure of all consultants hired by the broker-dealer during each calendar quarter. Such reports should include the consultant's name, company, role, and compensation arrangement. Furthermore, the reports should indicate the dollar amount of payments made to each consultant during each calendar quarter if any such payments are related to the consultant's efforts on behalf of the broker-dealer that resulted in particular municipal securities business.

The Bond Market Association Initiatives

The Bond Market Association has initiated steps to improve the transparency of the municipal bond market. The association publishes daily trading volume on its Web site and cooperates with Bloomberg L.P. to publish municipal bond yields. It also publishes a benchmark for particular categories of municipal bonds. The yields are a composite of round lot prices based on bonds that have coupons that reflect current market conditions.

Summary

The municipal securities market consists of short-term notes and long-term bonds. More than four-fifths of the annual municipal issuance is long-term financing. This $1.5 trillion market is highly fragmented because there are more than 1.5 million different issues outstanding. Unlike the $3.3 trillion Treasury market—where there are about 200-plus issues outstanding, and daily trading volume averages $200 billion—most municipal bonds are purchased and held until maturity.

One important characteristic of municipal securities is the tax-favored treatment on their interest income. This tax-free benefit on interest income lowers the interest rate a municipality has to pay to raise capital to fund projects of public good. Frequently, a municipality needs to float a new issue to pay off the maturing debt. But because of the subsidy on tax-free interest income, federal law restricts the interest that can be earned on the escrow account to be no more than the interest paid on the new issue. To accommodate this restriction, the Treasury issues state and local government series securities. However, some financial institutions managing the escrow account illegally "burn down" the yields in the escrow account. The SEC and the MSRB have taken steps to prevent "yield burning" and pay to play practices.

The SEC adopted amendments to Rule 15c2-12 in 1994 to require disclosure of material information in the official statement for new bond issues. After the security has been issued, the SEC also requires municipal issuers to make timely disclosure of material information. Such requirements for municipal securities are now in line with those for corporate securities. In addition, the MSRB requires the firm selling a customer a new municipal security to deliver to the customer a copy of the official statement.

Selected Bibliography

Bond Market Association. *An Examination of Non-Rated Municipal Defaults: 1986–1991.* New York: Bond Market Association (previously the Public Securities Association), 1993.

Bond Market Association. *An Investors' Guide to Municipal Bonds.* New York: Bond Market Association, 1999.

Bond Market Association. *eCommerce in the U.S. Fixed Income Markets.* New York: Bond Market Association, 1999.

Leonard, P. A. "An Empirical Analysis of Competitive and Negotiated Offerings of Municipal Bonds." *Municipal Finance Journal* (Spring 1996): 37–67.

Mysak, J., and M. R. Bloomberg. *Handbook for Muni Bond Issuers.* New York: Bloomberg Press, 1998.

Pauelz, A. V. "Municipal Bond Issue Structuring." In *Handbook of Debt Management,* ed. G. J. Miller. New York: Marcel Dekker, 1996, 401–431.

Stevens, L., and R. P. Wood. "Comparative Financing Costs for Competitive and Negotiated Pennsylvania School District Bonds." *Journal of Public Budgeting, Accounting & Financial Management* (Winter 1998).

Notes

1. Insurers generally do not accept credits rated noninvestment grade.
2. This example is used in MBIA's marketing brochures, based on data obtained from J. J. Kenny.
3. Any profit realized from the purchase or sale is not exempt from tax. Only the accrued interest is tax exempt.
4. Interest income from Treasury securities is exempt from state and local taxation.

11

Asset-Backed Securities

Asset-backed securities offer investors yet another important investment alternative. This relatively new market continues to grow and expand into different types of securities. The growth in the market for asset-based financing to trillions of dollars has been fueled by the benefits that securitization brings to both issuers and investors. Securitization can provide financial institutions with added liquidity and regulatory capital relief and provide businesses with access to cost-effective funding. For investors, asset-securitized instruments provide a broad selection of fixed-income alternatives with higher credit ratings and fewer downgrades than corporate bonds, and higher yields than Treasury securities. Securitization began with mortgage pass-throughs in the 1970s, and the technique has since been applied to other asset types, such as credit card receivables, auto loans, sports financing, tax liens, tobacco settlements, commercial loans, and junk bonds. This chapter describes the structure and basic elements of securitization. Essential to the success of the asset-backed market are the various forms of credit enhancement that upgrade the credit of the securitized instruments to a level higher than the credit of the underlying collateral.

Market Overview

Asset securitization pools together relatively homogeneous assets and packages them for sale, with added credit enhancement, in the form of securities. Propelling the growth of this multi-trillion-dollar market are the advantages that securitization of mortgage and nonmortgage financial assets brings to issuers and investors. For issuers, securitization provides more efficient funding for operations and greater flexibility for balance sheet management. For investors, asset-backed securities present opportunities to participate in asset classes otherwise unavailable.

Market Development

The first mortgage-backed pass-through security was issued by Bank of America in 1977. Since then, banks and thrifts have used securitization to transform themselves from mortgage lenders to mortgage originators. For nonmortgage assets, initial growth has come from the development of sectors such as automobile loans, credit card receivables, and home equity loans.

As investors became increasingly comfortable with newer asset classes and innovative structures, the securitization of commercial assets emerged. Motivated by regulatory capital relief and efficient balance sheet management, issuance of securities backed by high-yield bonds, known as *collateralized loan obligations*, and by commercial loans, called *collateralized bond obligations*, are at record levels. More recently, a number of Wall Street firms have pitched the so-called tobacco bonds to cities and states that are promised a chunk of the tobacco settlement money. Such tobacco settlement bonds are backed by the annual payments from the tobacco companies through the year 2025 and possibly beyond.

Collateral

The underlying collateral can take the forms of existing or future income-producing assets. In an asset-backed securitization, an existing pool of assets is sold by the originator to the *special purpose vehicle* (SPV), thus removing the assets from the balance sheet of the originator. Investors who purchase the securities do not assume the originator performance risk. In contrast, in a future cash flow securitization, the originator sells the assets to the SPV before the assets have come into existence. The proceeds from the issuance of the securities by the SPV are used to make a prepayment to the originator. Investors, hence, assume the originator performance risk, because the payments will be made only if the originator continues in business and creates the assets.

Structure and Basic Elements

A typical securitization process begins with the originator transferring its assets or receivables to a trust called a special purpose vehicle. The SPV acts as an intermediary between the originator and the investors of the newly created securities by acquiring the assets or receivables from the originator and by issuing securities backed by these assets. These assets are held for the beneficial interest of the asset-backed security holders in an SPV that is separate from the company sponsoring the securitization. Frequently, the creditworthiness of the assets is enhanced through various techniques so that the credit of the securities backed by the collateral is elevated to investment grade. The basics of a securitized transaction are depicted in Figure 11-1.

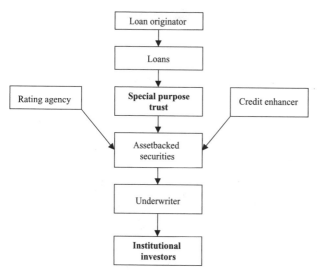

Figure 11-1. Basic asset-based securities transaction structure.

Originator

The originators make the loans and create the assets that will become the underlying collateral. The entities that originate these assets include banks, finance companies, credit card issuers, and securities firms. The originator generally transfers assets to the pool through a true sale. The creditworthiness of the originator is a concern, though an originator's bankruptcy impacts an asset-backed security in ways not directly related to credit. It is the quality of service for the collateral that might be compromised if the originator defaults.

Servicer

Servicing includes the collection of payments and other steps necessary to ensure that the debtors meet their obligations and the rights of investors are protected. Many securitization programs retain the originator as the servicer due to the economic inefficiencies of appointing a substitute servicer and the desire of the originator to maintain good relationships with its customers. This is important for certain asset types that might involve extensive administrative responsibilities or require timely servicing in order to produce cash flows. However, most programs provide for the appointment of an independent backup servicer if certain events occur. In order to minimize the detrimental impact on the true sale analysis due to the originator's retention of control over the assets, the originator's role must be clearly limited to that of a collection agent for the trust, and the originator must be paid a reasonable servicing fee.

Special Purpose Vehicle

The remoteness of the possibility of bankruptcy for the SPV is one primary factor that mitigates the risk of a securitization transaction. Generally, a securitization transaction is structured to achieve a true sale when the originator transfers the assets to the SPV. Also, the business activities of the SPV are restricted to those associated with the securitization through constraints in the transaction documents. These documents prohibit the SPV from incurring additional debt or otherwise transferring or encumbering assets.

Credit Enhancement

Securitization could employ several levels of *credit enhancement* to mitigate the potential loss arising from the credit risk of the underlying assets. Internal credit enhancements often include overcollateralization, excess spread, or a reserve account. External credit enhancements may be in the form of a bank letter of credit, a surety bond, or a financial guarantee from a bond insurance company. Major bond insurers are MBIA, AMBAC, Financial Guaranty Insurance, and Financial Security Assurance. The party providing this enhancement must be an entity with a rating at least as high as the desired transaction rating.

Rating

Credit ratings provide investors with an indication of credit risk and the likelihood that they will be repaid on time and in full. In analyzing a securitization program, rating agencies analyze the legal and structural protections provided to investors. In future cash flow transactions, the agencies will also review the generation and business risks applicable to the origination.

Mortgage-Backed Securities

The *mortgage-backed security* (MBS) market enables mortgage lenders to access a larger reservoir of capital and make financing available at lower costs. Mortgage securitization began with simple *mortgage pass-throughs* in which the monthly mortgage payments, net of servicing and insurance fees, are passed along to investors. Hence, the pass-through investors continue to receive payments as long as the mortgages, a vast majority of which are thirty-year, are outstanding. One issue that arises with mortgage pass-throughs involves homeowners' option of prepaying the outstanding balance. MBS investors were faced with the uncertainty about the amount and the timing of the cash flows, which caused growth to slow. To deal with this problem, Wall Street later devised collateralized mortgage obligations (CMOs) to better suit investor objectives and to rejuvenate the MBS market.

There were several other favorable developments as well. The Tax Reform Act of 1986 further allowed mortgage security pools to elect the tax status of a real estate mortgage investment conduit (REMIC). Since 1986, most CMOs have been issued in REMIC form. Since the generic CMOs were introduced, several derivative mortgage products have been developed. As noted in Table 11-1, the total outstanding volume of agency MBS crossed the $1 trillion threshold in 1990 and increased to more than $2 trillion by the end of 1998. The average daily trading volume increased from $12.8 billion in 1991 to more than $70 billion in 1999.

Mortgage Pass-throughs

The most basic mortgage securities are known as pass-throughs, representing a direct ownership interest in a pool of mortgage loans. Most pass-through MBSs are issued and/or guaranteed by the Government National Mortgage

Table 11-1. Outstanding agency mortgage-backed securities (in billions of dollars).

Year	GNMA	FNMA	FHLMC	Total
1990	403.6	299.8	321.0	1,024.4
1991	425.3	372.0	363.2	1,160.5
1992	419.5	445.0	409.2	1,273.7
1993	414.1	495.5	440.1	1,349.7
1994	450.9	530.3	460.7	1,441.9
1995	472.3	583.0	515.1	1,570.4
1996	506.2	650.7	554.3	1,711.2
1997	536.9	709.6	579.4	1,825.8
1998	537.4	834.5	646.5	2,018.4
1999	582.0	960.9	749.1	2,292.0

Note: Data are obtained from the Bond Market Association. Data for 1999 are as of September 30, 1999.

Association (Ginnie Mae), the Federal Home Loan Mortgage Corporation (Freddie Mac), and the Federal National Mortgage Association (Fannie Mae). These MBSs are called *agency pass-throughs,* and the payments of interest and principal are considered secure. But the cash flow on these instruments may vary from month to month, depending on the actual prepayment rate of the underlying mortgages. Some private institutions also package various types of mortgages known as *private-label* MBSs.

The market does not call for a rating for agency pass-through securities, because an agency can provide two types of guarantees. The first type of guarantee requires the timely payment of both interest and principal, referred to as a *fully modified pass-through.* The second type of guarantee, in addition to the timely payment of interest, requires that the scheduled principal repayment be made no later than a specified date. Agency pass-throughs of this type are called *modified pass-throughs.*

These mortgage securities are traded in terms of their assumed average life rather than their maturity. The average life is the average amount of time that will elapse from the date of purchase until principal is repaid based on an assumed prepayment projection. In addition, the MBS market differs from other fixed-income markets in several ways. In the MBS market, a pool prefix and a pool number identify pass-throughs. The prefix indicates the type of pass-through, and the pool number gives information on the specific mortgage collateral and the issuer. A TBA trade does not specify the pool information upfront. The option of what pools to deliver is left to the sellers, as long as they satisfy the Bond Market Association's guidelines for standards of delivery and settlement for MBSs. The TBA trades give yet another advantage to the seller. The Bond Market Association *delivery variance* permits an under- or overdelivery tolerance of 0.01 percent on the TBA trades of Fannie Mae, Freddie Mac, and Ginnie Mae pass-through securities.

Prepayment

Homeowners have the option to pay off the outstanding mortgages. The difficulty in valuing mortgage pass-throughs results from the uncertainty about when the borrower will exercise this option. Projecting the cash flows from a pass-through requires making assumptions about future prepayments. The most widely used prepayment assumption is the prepayment speed assumption (PSA) developed by the Bond Market Association. The PSA assumes that the prepayment for new mortgage loans begins at 0.2 percent per annum in the first month and increases by 0.2 percent per annum each month as the mortgages age, eventually reaching a constant rate of 6 percent at thirty months.

Both projected and historical prepayment rates are quoted as a percentage of the PSA. For example, a 50 percent PSA means the prepayment rate is 50 percent of the PSA benchmark, and a 200 percent PSA indicates twice the benchmark prepayment speed. Figure 11-2 shows the annual prepayment rates for 50, 100, and 200 percent PSAs.

The prepayment rate can be converted to a concept called the *single monthly mortality* (SMM) rate to estimate the amount of prepayment in the upcoming month, using the conversion formula:

$$\text{For months } 1 \le t \le 30, \text{ SMM} = 1 - \{1 - 0.02\% \times t\}^{1/12}$$

$$\text{For months } t > 30, \text{ SMM} = 1 - \{1 - 6\%\}^{1/12} = 0.00514$$

Table 11-2 shows the SMM for months one to thirty based on 100 percent PSA.

Therefore, a prepayment rate of 6 percent can be converted to a SMM of 0.514 percent. A 0.514 percent SMM means that approximately 0.514 percent of the remaining mortgage balance, less the scheduled principal payment for the month, will prepay this month.

Valuation of MBS is critically dependent upon prepayment forecasts, which in turn are determined by the path of interest rates. The procedure used in most valuation modeling of MBS first specifies the interest rate process, which is used in Monte Carlo simulation procedures to simulate interest rate paths. The cash flows each month along each path are projected based on the empirical model of prepayment behavior. The total cash flows along each path are discounted at the appropriate spot rates. This process is repeated for numerous paths, and for each path the present value is determined. The average present value on all interest rate paths is the theoretical value. If the aver-

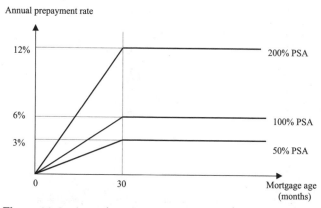

Figure 11-2. Annual prepayment rates and prepayment speed assumption benchmark.

Table 11-2. Single monthly mortality rate and prepayment speed assumption benchmark.

Month	100% PSA prepayment per annum (%)	Single monthly mortality rate (%)
1	0.2	0.01668
2	0.4	0.03340
3	0.6	0.05014
4	0.8	0.06691
5	1.0	0.08372
6	1.2	0.10055
7	1.4	0.11742
8	1.6	0.13432
9	1.8	0.15125
10	2.0	0.16821
11	2.2	0.18521
12	2.4	0.20223
13	2.6	0.21929
14	2.8	0.23638
15	3.0	0.25351
16	3.2	0.27066
17	3.4	0.28785
18	3.6	0.30507
19	3.8	0.32232
20	4.0	0.33961
21	4.2	0.35692
22	4.4	0.37428
23	4.6	0.39166
24	4.8	0.40908
25	5.0	0.42653
26	5.2	0.44402
27	5.4	0.46154
28	5.6	0.47909
29	5.8	0.49668
30	6.0	0.51430

age present value is greater than the market price, the security is underpriced. On the other hand, the MBS is overpriced if the average present value is lower than the market price. When the market price equals the average present value, the security is fairly priced.

Collateralized Mortgage Obligations

Investors found the prepayment risk of the pass-through MBSs undesirable, and thus growth in this market slowed. To deal with this problem, Wall Street devised the *collateralized mortgage obligation* to alter the prepayment risk of MBSs. A CMO does not eliminate the prepayment concern, but instead, it transfers this risk among different tranches. This broadens the appeal of the security to various traditional fixed-income investors.

A CMO is a security backed by a pool of mortgages or mortgage pass-throughs, and its structure redistributes the cash flows from the pool of collateral over a series of classes (called *tranches*). All tranches have different maturity dates, cash flow features, and risk exposure. Typically, CMO issuers first pay the interest to the bondholders in each tranche. The principal payments from the underlying collateral are used to retire the classes of bonds on a priority basis. The final tranche of a CMO is often called the accrual bond or the Z-bond. Holders of these securities do not receive cash until all earlier tranches are paid in full. This type of CMO is known as sequential pay CMO.

After the introduction of sequential pay CMOs, the planned amortization class (PAC) and targeted amortization class (TAC) have also emerged. A PAC structure separates the collateral's principal into PAC bonds and the companion bonds. The amortization schedule for the PAC bonds remains fixed within a certain range of prepayment speeds. The companion bonds absorb prepayment risk for the PAC bonds. The structure leads to stable average lives for the PAC bonds. The companion bonds, on the other hand, have more volatile lives than otherwise similar sequential bonds. Similar to a PAC structure, a TAC is scheduled to receive a specified monthly prepayment. Any excess prepayment is distributed to non-TAC classes. When prepayments are not sufficient to support the TAC classes with the scheduled principal repayment, TAC's average maturity lengthens.

Stripped Mortgage-backed Securities

Stripped mortgage-backed securities are pass-throughs that divide the cash flow from the underlying collateral on a pro rata basis across the security holders. For example, the cash flow on an 8 percent pass-through security could be redistributed to create one new security with 9 percent coupon (called premium strip) and another with a 7 percent coupon (called discount strip).

Securities also may be partially stripped so each class receives some interest and some principal. When securities are completely stripped, all the interest is allocated to one class of security, known as *interest only* (IO), and the entire principal to another, called *principal only* (PO). The PO security trades at a discount. The yield an investor will realize depends on the prepayment behavior. The faster the prepayment, the higher the yield. When mortgage rates decline, prepayments will speed up, accelerating payments to the PO investors. The unanticipated larger amount of cash flow will now be discounted at a lower interest rate. The result is that the price of a PO rises with a declining mortgage rate. When the mortgage rate rises, prepayments will slow down, resulting in a lower cash flow. Coupled with a higher discount rate, the price of a PO falls with rising mortgage rates.

On the other hand, IO holders receive only interest on the amount of principal outstanding. If the mortgage rate declines, prepayments speed up. The smaller amount of principal outstanding results in a decline of income for IO investors. Although the cash flow will be discounted at a lower rate, the net effect is typically a lower price for the IO. On a reverse interest rate trend, the expected cash flow improves but the cash flow is discounted at a higher rate. The net effect may be either a rise or a fall in IO value, depending on the magnitude of the change.

Callable Pass-throughs

A recent development in the MBS market is the callable pass-through, which is created by separating a mortgage pass-through into a callable class and a call class. The callable class investors will receive all of the principal and interest from the underlying mortgage loans. In contrast, the call class holders have the right to call the underlying pass-through at a stated price (usually par plus accrued interest) from the callable class holders after a specified period of time has passed.

The callable class holder is long a bond and is short a call option. But rather than just being short a series of call options to a number of mortgage borrowers who may or may not exercise the option to pay off mortgages early, the callable class is also short one call option to the call class investor. The call class investor will call the underlying pass-through from the callable class holder in a much more efficient way than the mortgage borrowers. Hence, the callable class holder will have a lower return relative to the pass-through investors if interest rates decline.

Asset-Backed Instruments

This market refers to asset-backed securities (ABS) as securities backed by nonmortgage assets such as installment loans, leases, receivables, home equity loans, tax liens, revolving credit, commercial loans, and high-yield bonds. In 1992, the SEC amended its rules to permit shelf registration and public sale of investment-grade ABSs. In 1994, Congress adopted amendments to the Secondary Mortgage Market Enhancement Act of 1984 to provide an exemption from state securities laws for highly rated securities backed by certain financial assets similar to the exemption already enjoyed by MBSs. Finally, in August 1996, Congress approved legislation to allow the creation of *financial asset securitization trusts* (FASITs). Similar to real estate mortgage investment conduits, FASITs also permit greater flexibility—such as allowing the replacement of prepaid loans after the initial sale of the security; the pooling of mixed asset types such as residential and commercial mortgage loans along with credit card receivables, auto loans, and equipment loans; and the inclusion of construction loans. With the adoption of the FASIT, many of the benefits of REMIC treatment have been extended to nonmortgage asset securitization.

Credit Card Receivables

The market for securities backed by credit card receivables has grown significantly, from $147.9 billion in 1995 to more than $300 billion in 1999. This growth is attributable to the widespread use of credit cards by consumers, along with greater acceptance of cards by merchants and service providers.

The use of securitization as a financing tool for card issuers has increased in volume and importance. Securitization frees up capital on a bank's balance sheet. In recent years, it has been the primary funding source for specialized credit card banks. These banks have benefited from funding at a lower rate and from low capital charges.

Credit card securitizations use a master trust structure under which the seller can sell multiple securities from the same trust, all of which share the credit risks as well as cash flow from one large pool of credit card receivables. For example, an issuer could transfer the receivables from one million credit card accounts to a trust, then issue multiple securities in various denominations and sizes. When more financing is needed, the issuer transfers more accounts to the same trust. It can then issue more securities. The master trust structure benefits the issuer, since the cost and effort involved with issuing a new series from a master trust is lower than creating a new trust for every issue.

Trust assets that have not been allocated to any series of securities are known as the seller's interest. The size of the seller's interest is equal to the difference between the total principal receivable balance of the trust portfolio and the principal balance of all outstanding securities issued through the trust. Seller's interest fluctuates as the amount in the trust portfolio increases or decreases. The seller's interest serves two key purposes. First, this ownership interest acts as a buffer in instances when account payments exceed account purchases. Second, it absorbs reductions in the receivable balance due to receivable dilution or readjustment of noncomplying receivables.

The typical trust setup has three different cash flow periods: revolving, controlled amortization or controlled accumulation, and early amortization. During the revolving period, monthly principal collections are allocated between the seller and the investor interest on a pro rata basis. The investor's portion of principal collections is then reinvested in new receivables. During this period, principal cannot be used to pay down the investor interest unless the actual credit enhancement exceeds the required enhancement.

At the end of the revolving period, the controlled amortization (or accumulation) period begins. Ordinarily, the controlled accumulation or controlled amortization period starts one year before the expected payment date. In the case of the controlled amortization period, principal collections are not reinvested but are paid to investors in twelve equal controlled amortization payments. If principal collections exceed the controlled amount, the excess will be reinvested in new receivables or paid to the seller. If the issue is structured with a controlled accumulation period, a principal funding account is established. The controlled payments are deposited in the account every month until the expected maturity date. At the end of the accumulation period, investors will be repaid in a single payment.

Early amortization is triggered by severe asset deterioration, problems with the seller or servicer, or certain legal troubles. Once triggered, the deal automatically enters an early amortization period and repays investors immediately. This protects investors from a long exposure to a deteriorating transaction.

Common forms of credit enhancement in credit card securitization are excess spread, cash collateral account, collateral invested account, and subordination. The yield on credit cards is relatively high and is usually enough to cover the interest payment to investors in addition to servicing fees and any losses during the month. The remaining yield is called excess spread. Available excess spread may be shared with other series, used to pay fees to credit enhancers, deposited into a spread account for the benefit of the investors, or released to the seller.

A cash collateral account is a segregated trust account, funded at the outset of the deal by a third-party bank, that can be drawn on to cover shortfalls in interest, principal, or servicing expense for a particular series if the excess spread is reduced to zero. Cash in the account is invested in high-quality, short-term securities. Draws on the cash collateral account may be reimbursed from future excess spread.

The collateral invested account is an uncertificated ownership interest in the trust, subordinate in payment rights to all investor certificates. It serves the same purpose as the cash collateral account, making up for the deficit if the excess spread balance is reduced to zero. If the collateral invested account is drawn on, it can be reimbursed from future excess spread.

Another common form of enhancement is the senior/subordinate structure that has two types of investor ownership in the trust: senior participation in the form of class A certificates or subordinate participation in the form of class B certificates. Class B will absorb losses allocated to class A that are not already covered by other forms of credit enhancements discussed above. Draws on the subordinate certificates may be reimbursed from future excess spread. Principal collections will be allocated to the subordinate investors only after the senior certificates are repaid in full.

Automobile Loan Receivables

Automobile loan securitization has been a vital part of total ABS volume. Strong vehicle sales, attractive funding rates, and investor demand for short-term, highly rated securities have driven the outstanding volume from $44.6 billion in 1995 to $83 billion in the third quarter of 1999. The vast majority of loans in auto securitizations originate with the loan application sent to the finance company by a dealer. A very small portion of auto loan securitizations contain loans directly originated by the issuer. The quality of auto loans depends on vehicle age, down payment, advance rate, depreciation, term distribution of loans, and geographic diversification.[1]

The two main structures in auto loan securitization are grantor trust and owner trust. Grantor trusts require principal distributions on underlying securities to be made on a pro rata basis. Hence, the senior and subordinate classes in a grantor trust normally will have the same average life. However, in an owner trust, cash flows can be allocated in any manner stipulated by the deal documents.

The primary forms of credit enhancement are reserve accounts, overcollateralization, subordination, excess spread, and bond insurance. Most auto loan securitizations use reserve or spread accounts, which are funded with an initial deposit and trap excess spread up to a required amount. Subordination and overcollateralization are similar because both represent a seller's interest in the underlying receivables. If collections are insufficient to make scheduled payments, funds otherwise payable to the seller or to junior bondholders will be used to pay senior bondholders. Pure overcollateralization consists of an ownership interest in the receivables retained by the seller and does not have a coupon interest associated with it. Subordinate tranches generally have coupon expenses and therefore will result in less cash for senior bonds than pure overcollateralization.

Student Loans

Student loan securitizations are backed by three primary sources: the Federal Family Education Loan Program (FFELP), the Federal Direct Student Loan Program (FDSLP), and alternative loans. Under the FFELP, loans are funded by private lending institutions and insured by the federal government. FDSLP, on the other hand, funds student loans by the federal government. Alternative loan programs refer to loans funded by private lending institutions with or without an insurance guarantee from a private institution.

FFELP is the largest of the three programs. Under this program, private institutions fund loans to borrowers, regardless of their ability or willingness to repay the loans.[2] The loans are insured by private guarantee agencies up to the federal default reimbursement limit, currently at 98 percent. Loans disbursed prior to October 1, 1993, are guaranteed at 100 percent. If default occurs, the guarantee agency reimburses the defaulted loans to the lending institutions but will receive reimbursement from the Department of Education.

Under the FDSLP, the U.S. government funds student loans directly to eligible students. The purpose of this program was to make federal government student loan lending more cost efficient as a result of direct government involvement. But the program has not been as successful as anticipated. In addition, the majority of schools that have participated in the FDSLP are trade schools, whose graduates historically have the highest default rate of all school types.

The third type of program involves education loans that are funded by private institutions without any federal government involvement. These loans may or may not be insured by private third parties. If insured, the insurer is responsible for the defaulted loans. The largest private guarantor is the Education Resources Institute.

A widely used vehicle for issuing student loan ABS is the owner trust—a structure that permits principal collections to be used to pay interest on the bonds, providing the needed liquidity in the early years of a student loan transaction. This structure was first used in 1993 by Society National Bank (renamed Key Bank U.S.A.) in a $200 million transaction with a three-tranche sequential pay structure.

In a senior/subordinated structure, the underlying loans support both the senior and subordinated bonds. Additionally, reallocation of subordinated cash flow also supports the senior bonds. As a result, issuers have been able to achieve a higher rating on the senior tranches, resulting in lower overall funding costs. Payments of principal can be either pro rata or sequential pay. In pro rata structures, principal on the subordinated tranche is payable before the senior tranche is paid in full, if funds are available. In a sequential pay structure, no principal is payable to the subordinated tranche until the senior tranche has been retired.

Student loan ABSs are generally structured with reserve accounts because liquidity is needed to make interest payments on the bonds before receiving reimbursement of defaulted claims. The reserve account contains liquid collateral and earns an interest rate generated by an investment in highly rated securities. The reserve account may be funded out of proceeds of the bond issuance.

Tax Lien

Municipalities are taking advantage of the ABS market to securitize municipal assets for sale to ABS investors. Tax liens are the most prominent of these assets and continue to grow. A tax lien is a lien placed by a municipality on real property for nonpayment of taxes. Many states have already implemented a statutory procedure that allows municipalities to sell the accrued taxes, plus interest and penalties, annually in a public auction. Tax certificates representing a first priority lien position against a property for the amount of unpaid taxes are awarded at auction. There is a statutory holding period during which the property owner may extinguish the lien by paying the outstanding taxes plus penalties and interest. If the property owner pays the amount owed in full, the tax certificate holder is made whole by the county. However, if the property owner fails to pay by the end of the holding period, the tax certificate holder can file for a tax deed or follow alternative procedures necessary to obtain title to the property.

Many tax lien securitizations are structured around a Delaware business trust, established for the sole purpose of acquiring title to the tax liens from the originator or municipality and issuing the bonds. The structure is designed, in part, to obtain a higher rating for the bonds than would be possible were the originator or the municipality itself to act as issuer. Although the originator or municipality has beneficial ownership of the trust property, legal title to the liens and other collateral rest with the trust. The transfer of the collateral to the trust is treated as a true sale.

Credit enhancement has primarily been in the form of overcollateralization. Transactions also have included rated subordinate tranches, cash accounts to fund servicer working capital requirements, and liquidity reserves to cover bond interest in case of a shortfall in collections.

Tobacco Settlements

In November 1994, Mississippi filed the first state lawsuit against the tobacco industry. Many states have since initiated similar legal actions. When the news media published a series of stories that probed how much the tobacco industry officials knew of the dangers of smoking and withheld from the public, antismoking sentiment quickly spread throughout the country. The Senate Commerce Committee came close to brokering a $500 billion settlement, but negotiations fell apart in April 1998 after RJR Nabisco balked.

The tobacco companies began to negotiate with individual states. As Florida, Minnesota, Mississippi, and Texas reached settlements of $40 billion, the attorneys general of several key states tried to salvage some sort of master agreement. Eventually, the other 46 states agreed to drop pending lawsuits in return for payments of $206 billion. The total settlement came to $246 billion, to be paid over the next twenty-five years. Moreover, the payments could go on indefinitely. As long as participating manufacturers sell cigarettes, payments continue.

Many states are looking to monetize their settlements. Some states and municipalities favor securitization because of concern about the lengthy payout schedule of the settlement and the business risks still facing the tobacco industry. It is better to transfer that risk to bondholders. Proponents of securitization argue that it is a way to diversify the tobacco settlement windfall. In November 1999, New York City and Nassau County (New York) were the first to issue $709 million and $300 million, respectively, of the so-called tobacco bonds backed by their share of the master settlement. To issue the bonds, New York City created a stand-alone, bankruptcy-remote entity. The new bonds are secured by payments from the four tobacco companies and are not considered city debt. The city avoided state debt constraints and shielded itself from responsibility for the debt should the cigarette manufacturers' payments stop or significantly decrease. Because the proceeds will be used for capital spending, the bonds are tax exempt.

Such tobacco bonds are more complex than typical asset-backed securities. Tobacco bonds combine the elements of corporate, asset-backed, and municipal securities. The payments are tied to cigarette sales (corporate), issuers are borrowing based on an anticipated stream of money from the settlements (asset-backed), and municipalities are issuing them (municipal).

Collaterialzed Bond/Loan Obligations

The collateralized bond obligation (CBO) and the collateralized loan obligation (CLO) markets emerged in the late 1980s with the repackaging of high-yield, speculative-grade bonds or loans into highly rated paper. CBOs are bonds collateralized by a portfolio of high-yield bonds. CLOs are backed by portfolios of syndicated high-yield or investment-grade loans. In both cases, cash flows from the underlying financial instruments are used to pay off investors in rated securities.

Market Value versus Cash Flow Structure CBO

Capitalizing on the arbitrage opportunities that exist between high-yield bonds and the lower-cost funds of highly rated debt is the primary motivation behind a market value CBO. The transaction is generally structured with multiple classes of rated debt and a layer of unrated equity and invests in a pool of investments that is diverse in obligator, industry, and asset class. In order to gauge the performance of the transaction, the asset manager will mark to market the value of each investment on a regular basis, usually weekly or biweekly. Furthermore, the CBO is limited to the amount of debt that can be outstanding as a percentage of the current market value of assets. This limitation is based on the price volatility and liquidity of the assets in the pool. If the value declines below the acceptable levels, the asset manager must take corrective actions. If the value remains at acceptable levels, the assets will be liquidated and the proceeds paid to investors.

Cash flow CBOs, on the other hand, are based on a pool of assets with predictable cash flows. The ongoing market price of collateral assets is not important in a cash flow deal. Instead, it is the ability of each asset to pay scheduled principal and interest that makes these deals successful.

Bank Collateralized Loan Obligations

A collateralized loan obligation is a security backed by loans. Nonbank participants issuing CLOs are often motivated by spread arbitrage derived from an asset mix of high-yield and distressed loans. In bank CLOs, the motivation is to reduce capital requirements and fund low-yielding assets. The underlying collateral is composed mostly of investment-grade and some noninvestment-grade corporate loans. There are generally several tranches of rated securities, as well as an unrated equity tranche retained by the issuing bank. The subordinated tranche or the equity absorbs the first losses from default. Hence, the most senior tranche holds the least credit risk and receives a higher rating than the subordinated tranches.

Master Trust

A *master trust* structure allows the issuer to sell multiple series from the same trust. Each series shares the credit risk and cash flow from one large pool of assets. The structure is attractive to issuers because it is more efficient and cheaper to issue an additional series out of a master trust than it is to create a new one. Investors benefit as well. Securities issued out of a master trust are backed by one large, diverse pool of assets containing a mix of seasoned and newly originated loans. Each series issued from a master trust represents an undivided interest in the trust's receivables. Another feature of a master trust is the *seller's interest* (called equity), an interest in the trust assets that has not been allocated to any series. The seller's interest is equal to the amount of receivables in the trust that are not matched with corresponding certificated liabilities. For example, assume a master trust contains $200 million of receivables and it has issued one series that has a certificate balance of $194 million. The seller's interest is the difference between the receivables and the certificate interest in the master trust. In this example, the seller's interest would be $6 million.

Master trust series have three main periods: revolving period, controlled amortization or accumulation period, and early amortization period. During the revolving period, investors receive interest only each month. Principal collections are paid back to the seller to acquire new assets. The seller's interest is reduced by the amount of the principal collections paid back to it and it is increased by any additional loans that are conveyed to the trust.

The revolving period is typically followed by a period in which principal is returned to investors, referred to as the controlled amortization period. During this period, investors receive a partial amortization payment each month until the bonds are retired at the end of the specified maturity. In contrast, during a controlled accumulation period, principal is not used to amortize investor certificates. Rather, it is kept in a trust account until its balance equals the face value of the rated certificates. At the expected final payment date, the funds in the account are paid in a lump sum to investors.

The final period common to all master trust structures is the early amortization period. Certain events will prematurely amortize the bonds. These events can occur at any time during the revolving, controlled amortization, or controlled accumulation period and include the dollar amount of credit enhancement falling short of the required level, the seller's interest falling below the required level, or the insolvency of the seller.

Credit Enhancement

The most common form of credit enhancement is subordination. In the multitranche or senior/subordinated CBO/CLO, the subordinated tranches support the senior tranches. Holders of the senior debt tranches have priority of payment over the holders of any junior debt tranche. Therefore, junior debt tranches are rated lower than the senior debt. However, the junior debt carries a higher interest rate. If overcollateralization is the only credit enhancement in a senior/subordinated structure, the overcollateralization amount is set at the estimated level of credit losses that the structure is expected to withstand without causing a loss to the holders of the rated senior debt. For example, suppose a collateral pool with a total par value of $200 million supports a cash flow transaction involving the issuance of $160 million of rated senior debt. This "80/20" structure is comprised of 80 percent senior debt and 20 percent unrated supporting debt or equity. The level of overcollateralization is 125 percent, which equals the ratio of assets to the amount of senior debt. If the subordinated debt was issued in the amount of $14 million and equity in the amount of $6 million, overcollateralization for the $14 million junior class would be provided by the equity investment.

Cash collateral or reserve accounts are another form of credit enhancement. Cash reserves are often used in the initial phase of a cash flow transaction. Cash proceeds from the sale of CBO/CLO securities can be used to purchase the underlying collateral or to fund reserve accounts.

Excess spread is generated when the interest earned on the assets is higher than the interest rate paid on the rated CBO/CLO securities. Excess spread can be used to purchase additional assets, build reserves against future credit losses and liquidity risks, or it can be passed along to the senior debt investors. Another method of credit enhancement involves insuring the rated securities with a financial insurance policy. The insurance transfers the credit risks associated with the underlying assets from the holders of the rated securities to the insurance company.

Asset-Backed Commercial Paper

Asset-backed commercial paper (ABCP) programs provide a valuable, flexible alternative for companies seeking short-term financing and have become a significant segment of the commercial paper market. An ABCP conduit is a bankruptcy-remote special purpose company that raises funds by issuing commercial paper to purchase trade receivables or term assets from one or more sellers. Many ABCP programs are established by commercial banks or finance companies to provide trade receivables financing for their customers.

Other ABCP programs are established as a means of financing credit card portfolios or other types of receivables.

The ABCP market has become a significant segment of the capital markets, growing from just $50 billion in outstanding volume in 1991 to more than $500 billion at the end of 1999. The growth has been fueled by the continued expansion of existing programs, the entrance of new programs into the market, and the proliferation of new asset types.

Fully versus Partially Supported

ABCP conduits are generally categorized by their level of program-wide credit enhancement, which determines whether a conduit is fully or partially supported. A fully supported ABCP program uses one single external support facility, generally provided by a highly rated bank or group of banks, to provide 100 percent coverage against credit and liquidity risk. The credit support often takes the form of a letter of credit or an irrevocable revolving commitment to either purchase assets from the issuer or to make loans to the issuer. The credit enhancer will absorb any credit losses on the assets. The main risk to investors in a fully supported program is that the rating of the support provider may be downgraded, resulting in a lower credit of the ABCP.

The rise of bank risk-based capital standards has imposed significant costs on support providers in fully supported programs. Risk-based capital standards require banks to maintain capital for the entire face amount of ABCP outstanding under certain ABCP programs because the support has been viewed as a direct credit substitute and not merely as a loan commitment. Hence, partially supported programs are created to reduce capital requirements.

A partially supported ABCP program typically has two supporting facilities. The credit enhancement facility is intended to cover losses on the receivables, up to a specified amount (usually 10 or 15 percent of the total amount of ABCP outstanding). The credit enhancement facility provides only partial coverage against losses. The liquidity facility primarily covers liquidity risk.

Single-seller versus Multiseller

ABCP programs can also be categorized as either single-seller programs or multiseller programs. A single-seller program is a bankruptcy-remote special purpose company that issues ABCP to fund the assets of a single originator or seller. Multiseller conduits combine the assets of several unrelated sellers into one diverse portfolio of assets supporting the commercial paper issuance.

Credit Enhancement

There are generally two levels of credit protection in ABCP conduits: pool-specific and program-wide enhancement. Pool-specific support protects investors against losses, dilution, yield risk, obligator default, and servicing risks associated with an individual transaction. The many forms of pool-specific protection include overcollateralization, recourse to the seller, third-party support, or excess spread. Pool-specific credit enhancement covers defaults on a specific seller's receivables and cannot be used to fund losses in any other pools.

Program-wide credit enhancement is a fungible layer of credit protection provided by a third party. It can be drawn upon when a transaction's pool-specific credit enhancement has been exhausted and may be in the form of an irrevocable loan facility, a letter of credit, or a surety bond from a monoline insurer. The rating of the third-party credit enhancer must be at least as high as that of the commercial paper. Program-wide enhancement provides the program sponsor with more flexibility in the application of its credit and investment policies and enhances its ability to meet the unique needs of its clients.

Liquidity Support

An integral part of every ABCP program, liquidity support is often in the form of either a loan agreement or an asset purchase agreement. Under an asset purchase agreement, the liquidity provider agrees to purchase nondefaulted assets when liquidity is needed. Under a loan agreement, the liquidity provider agrees to lend funds to the conduit. While credit enhancement covers asset defaults and dilution, liquidity providers commit to making funds available to the conduit for reasons other than credit deterioration of the portfolio assets to ensure timely payment to investors. Such noncredit events include market disruption, an issuer's inability to roll the CP, or asset-liability mismatches.

Summary

The asset-backed securities market benefits both issuers and investors. For issuers, securitization is an efficient way of financing operations at a lower cost and is a flexible tool in managing the balance sheet. For investors, securitized assets provide a broad selection of fixed-income alternatives previously unavailable. Because of its many advantages, the market for ABS has grown to trillions of dollars.

The two key features of securitization are cash flow and credit risk. In terms of cash flows, transactions can be structured as pass-throughs or multiple classes. Securitized instruments expose investors to credit risk, and all asset-backed securities are credit enhanced to provide investors greater protection against losses. The amount and type of credit enhancement depend on the historical loss experience of similar loans and the rating sought by the issuer.

Assets that have been successfully packaged and sold in the ABS market include mortgage loans, credit card receivables, auto loans, student loans, trade receivables, tax liens, sports facility revenues, tobacco settlement payments, commercial loans, and high-yield bonds. The technique also has been used successfully in asset-backed commercial paper, providing a valuable, flexible alternative for companies seeking short-term financing.

Selected Bibliography

Border, S., and A. Sarker. "Securitizing Property Catastrophe Risk." *Current Issues in Economics and Finance* 2:9 (August 1996), Federal Reserve Bank of New York.

Britt, P. "Asset Securitization." *America's Community Banker* 5:4 (April 1996): 10–14.

Fabozzi, F. J. *Handbook of Mortgage-Backed Securities.* Chicago: Probus Publishing, 1995.

Grant Thornton LLP. "Tax Provisions in August 1996 Laws: Provisions Affecting Financial Services Business." Minneapolis: Grant Thornton, 1997.

Henderson, J. *Asset Securitization: Current Techniques and Emerging Market Applications.* London: Euromoney Publications, 1997.

Hu, J. C. *Basics of Mortgage-Backed Securities.* New York: McGraw-Hill, 1997.

Kendall, L. T., and M. J. Fishman, eds. *A Primer on Securitization.* Cambridge, Mass.: MIT Press, 1996.

Lockwood, L. J. "Wealth Effects of Asset Securitization." *Journal of Banking and Finance* 20:1 (January 1996): 151–164.

Milbank, Tweed, Hadley & McCloy. "Capital Markets Updates: 1997—The Year of the FASIT?" New York: MTHM, 1997.

Nirenberg, D.Z., C. J. Burke, and S. L. Kopp. "FASITs—The Small Business Act's New Securitization Vehicle." *Journal of Taxation* 85:5 (November 1996): 1–11.

Rosenthal, J. A., and J. M. Ocampo. *Securitization of Credit: Inside the New Technology of Finance.* New York: John Wiley, 1988.

Notes

1. Advance rate is defined as the loan balance as a percentage of the manufacturer's suggested price.

2. The PLUS program requires some credit evaluation, but it comprises a relatively minor portion of the FFELP.

12

Mutual Funds

Once an investment policy statement has been developed for an investor, the question becomes how to implement the policy. Several approaches can be taken. First, investors can implement the strategy directly by purchasing securities that will meet their needs. Investors can "go it alone" by researching the investments by themselves, or they can work closely with an investment advisor to select the appropriate securities.

Another approach investors can use is to build a portfolio indirectly through the use of investment company products such as mutual funds and closed-end funds. In many cases, the investment strategy will be implemented through a combination of direct investment in securities and investment in mutual funds. One major advantage of mutual funds and closed-end funds is that they allow investors with limited resources the opportunity to build a core portfolio of investments. This chapter discusses the use of mutual funds to implement an investment strategy. Chapter 13 discusses the use of closed-end funds in the investment process.

The Mutual Fund Business

The first open-end mutual fund in the United States, the Massachusetts Investors Trust, started in 1924. This revolutionized the mutual fund industry with a continuous offering of shares as well as shares that could be sold back to the fund at anytime.

The 1929 stock market crash and the Great Depression prompted Congress to enact laws to regulate securities and financial markets, including mutual funds. The Securities Act of 1933 required for the first time a prospectus describing the fund. The Securities Exchange Act of 1934 made mutual fund distributions subject to SEC regulation. Two other important laws relating to mutual fund and investor protection were adopted in 1940. The Investment Company Act requires that a mutual fund prices its assets based on the market value every day, prohibits transactions between a fund and its manager(s), limits leverage, and requires the board to include a minimum of 40 percent of independent directors. The Investment Advisors Act requires the registration of all investment advisers to mutual funds.

Mutual fund investing began to grow in popularity in the 1940s and 1950s, and explosive growth occurred in the 1980s. In 1960, there were 160 funds and $17 billion in assets. Ten years later, there were 361 funds with total assets of $47.6 billion. By 1980, the number of funds had reached 564, and total assets under management crossed over the $100 billion mark to $134.8 billion. Another milestone was reached in 1990, when the 3,105 funds managed more than $1 trillion of assets. By the end of 1996, total industry assets increased to $3.5 trillion. Total net assets increased by about $1 trillion in 1997. The total amount of money invested in mutual funds increased to more than $6.8 trillion by early 2000.

The growth of the mutual fund industry is in part due to the introduction of new products and services. Innovations in investment and retirement vehicles also have swept the industry:

- 1971—The first money market mutual funds were established.
- 1974—ERISA was enacted and IRAs were created.
- 1976—The first tax-exempt municipal bond funds were offered.
- 1978—The 401(k) retirement plan was created.

The enormous growth and diversity of the mutual fund industry have led to the development of new fund categories or investment objectives. Today's mutual fund menu ranges from aggressive growth to global bond to niche funds that specialize in one segment of the securities markets.

Furthermore, in recent years the U.S. economy expanded at a healthy pace, job growth was modestly strong, inflation remained low, and corporate earnings advanced further. As a result, the interest rate environment has been favorable and stock prices have continued to increase.

International Dimension

An increasing proportion of U.S. mutual fund assets is being invested overseas. U.S. investors have increased holdings of international and global equity and bond funds. Mutual funds are also growing in many other parts of the world. Merrill Lynch's purchase of Mercury Asset Management signifies the importance of the global asset management markets by giving them access to the asset management business in the United Kingdom and Europe. Worldwide assets in mutual funds grew from $2.853 trillion at the end of 1991 to $7.651 trillion by September 30, 1998. During this same time period, the number of open-end investment companies increased from 12,586 to 31,570.

The growth in mutual fund assets worldwide can be attributed to several factors. First, the securities markets of many developed countries have benefited from favorable economic conditions in recent years. At the same time, emerging markets have prospered because of new investment opportunities arising from financial reforms, privatization, and rapid economic growth. Second, mutual fund investing is popular because it provides a way of achieving the goals of a comfortable retirement and improved living standards. Third, many countries face the prospect of aging populations and the pressure to reduce deficits, so they are encouraging private savings such as defined-contribution retirement plans. Finally, the continued growth of the middle class worldwide is expected to lead to greater global expansion of mutual fund investing.

Organization of a Fund

Mutual fund operations must comply with many federal laws and regulations. The SEC under the Investment Company Act of 1940 (ICA) and the Investment Advisers Act of 1940 (IAA) regulates the mutual fund industry. Fund companies offering shares to the public must register them pursuant to the Securities Act of 1933 and provide notice filings to states in which they intend to offer their shares. Securities firms selling funds to the public are subject to the regulation as broker-dealers under the Securities Exchange Act of 1934. Plus, the Internal Revenue Code of 1986 grants pass-through tax treatment to mutual funds, but only if they follow certain operational requirements.

Mutual funds have several unique features. First, almost all mutual funds are externally managed, and all activities are carried out by third parties such as investment managers, broker-dealers, and banks. Second, mutual funds continuously offer new shares to the public, except when the funds are closed to new investments. Mutual funds also stand ready to redeem outstanding shares upon request at the net asset value. Third, the government imposes strict requirements on the structure and operations of investment companies and imposes special responsibilities on their independent directors.

Setting up a mutual fund operation is a costly process. Legal fees generally run to $100,000 or more for preparing the federal registration statement, contracts, and corporate documents. Printing and other expenses also can add significantly to the cost. In addition, the ICA requires that a new fund must have assets of at least $100,000 before distributing shares to the public. The adviser or sponsor typically contributes this initial capital. In addition to the expenses of establishing a mutual fund, the ongoing operation is also costly. There are expenses for management, transfer agents, custodians, accounting, and other business activities. To be viable, a fund needs to reach $50 to $100 million in assets within a relatively short time after start up.

Mutual Fund Structure

The structure of a typical mutual fund includes directors/trustees, an investment adviser, an administrator, a principal underwriter, a custodian, a transfer agent, and shareholders. The directors or trustees[1] of an investment company must perform their responsibilities with the care expected of a "prudent person." They are expected to evaluate the performance of the investment adviser, principal underwriter, and other parties that provide services to the fund. The ICA requires that at least 40 percent of the fund's board of directors be "independent" directors who serve as watchdogs for shareholder interests and provide a check and balance on the adviser and other persons affiliated with the fund. Investment advisory and distribution contracts must be approved by a majority of a fund's independent directors.

The investment adviser is responsible for making portfolio selections in accordance with the objectives and policies set forth in the mutual fund's prospectus. The adviser carries out these responsibilities pursuant to a written contract with the fund. Most advisory contracts provide for an annual fee based on a percentage of the fund's average net assets during the year (generally between 0.5 percent and 1.5 percent but much lower for index funds).[2] The adviser owes the fund a fiduciary duty under the IAA. An administrator is the adviser or an affiliated entity that provides administrative services, including assuring compliance with applicable regulation. Fund administrators typically pay for office space, equipment, personnel, and accounting services. Other administrative responsibilities might include filing SEC, tax, and shareholder reports.

Mutual funds generally distribute their shares through principal underwriters or direct marketing.[3] The SEC under the 1934 Act regulates principal underwriters as broker-dealers. Most principal underwriters are also members of the National Association of Securities Dealers (NASD) and therefore are subject to its rules governing mutual fund sales practices.

Most funds use bank custodians. The SEC requires mutual fund custodians to protect the funds by segregating their portfolio securities from the rest of the bank's assets. Fund transfer agents maintain records of shareholder accounts. Transfer agents typically serve as dividend disbursing agents as well. They prepare and mail to shareholders periodic account statements, tax information, and other shareholder notices. Some transfer agents also prepare and mail statements confirming shareholder transactions and maintain customer service departments to respond to shareholder inquiries.

Mutual fund shareholders are entitled to redeem shares based on the net asset value on the request date. Shareholders also have certain voting rights. Although most mutual funds no longer have annual shareholder meetings, certain changes do require shareholder approval, including changes in the investment advisory contract, investment objectives, or policies deemed fundamental.

The SEC advertising rules permit only two types of advertisements: *tombstone advertisements* that contain limited information about the fund and the *omitting prospectus*, which may contain more information such as fund performance. However, an advertisement cannot include an account application or invite prospective investors to send money. The advertisement can only invite investors to request the full statutory prospectus. Also, the NASD requires mutual fund distributors and dealers to submit all advertising and sales literature for staff review. Once cleared by the NASD, the SEC does not require additional filings.

Types of Funds

Mutual funds can be classified in a number of different ways depending on how the fund is managed and what types of securities the fund purchases. One basic distinction between funds is whether they are actively or passively managed. An actively managed fund attempts to add value by pursuing a strategy of actively selecting securities in an attempt to beat the fund's benchmark. A passively managed fund, often referred to as an index fund, simply tries to match the performance of some index such as the S&P 500 or the Russell 2000. Passive funds have advantages over actively managed funds: because they incur relatively low expenses and because of their low portfolio turnover rate, they tend to be tax efficient.

Aggressive Growth Funds

Funds can also be classified based on the types of strategies they follow. Aggressive growth funds are highly speculative because they pursue a strategy of purchasing the stocks of companies that have the greatest chance for capital appreciation. These types of companies tend to be small, unproven companies that have the potential to become the next Microsoft or Cisco Systems but who face great risk in the marketplace. In many instances, these companies have little or no earnings and perhaps no viable product. The chances for success of these companies is relatively small; however, those that do succeed are likely to see their stock price rise many times.

Growth Funds

Growth funds seek capital appreciation through investment in well-established large- or midcap companies with above-average growth potential. Growth funds are less risky than aggressive growth funds because the majority of the fund's holdings are in established companies that already have earnings and a viable product. The goal for the manager of a growth fund is to find companies whose earnings growth will exceed that expected by the market. These funds still face significant risk because earnings growth may not beat the expectations of the market.

Equity Income Funds

Equity income funds invest in stocks with high dividend yields. Equity income funds tend to emphasize the preservation of capital and tend to be much less risky than either growth or aggressive growth funds. Equity income funds tend to hold mature, blue-chip companies that pay reasonable dividends as well as utilities and other high-yielding stocks.

Growth and Income Funds

Growth and income funds seek to balance current income and long-term capital gains. Growth and income funds tend to use high-yielding stocks to generate the income component of the fund's returns, although they may opt to hold some bonds to enhance current income. These funds also tend to favor high quality blue-chip stocks. The income component and the more conservative nature of these funds make them much less risky than growth or aggressive growth funds.

Balanced Funds

Balanced funds hold a balanced portfolio of stocks and bonds in an attempt to generate both current income and long-term capital gains. Unlike growth and income funds, balanced funds use bonds to generate the current income component of their returns. Balanced funds generally set a range for their stock/bond-asset mix. For example, a fund may hold between 25 and 50 percent of its assets in bonds. One advantage of balanced funds is the discipline imposed on the fund's managers. Because the fund must rebalance the portfolio to maintain the stock/bond mix, the manager is required to sell stocks when prices are high and use the proceeds to purchase bonds. Similarly, when the market falls, the manager is forced to purchase stocks when prices are low. Balanced funds tend to have lower risk than all equity funds.

Bond Funds

Bonds represent debt obligations of companies and state, local, federal, and foreign governments. These obligations consist of interest payments made by the issuer to the bondholder and a promise to return the principal when the bond matures. Because the payments from the issuer to the bondholder represent a legal obligation, bond funds tend to be conservative.[4] Each type of bond has different interest rate risks, tax consequences, and cash flow characteristics.

Bond funds are classified by the types of bonds they purchase and the average maturity or duration of the bonds held in the portfolio. Some of the bond funds available to investors are:

- *Government bond funds*—invest in U.S. Treasury and agency securities.
- *Mortgaged-backed bond funds*—invest in various types of mortgage-backed securities such as GNMA issues.
- *High-grade bond funds*—(sometimes known as investment-grade bond funds) invest in highly rated corporate bonds.
- *High-yield corporate bond funds*—(sometimes known as junk bond funds) invest in less creditworthy bonds for the higher yields they offer.
- *Municipal bond funds*—invest in tax-exempt state and local bonds. Municipal bonds are exempt from federal tax and from state tax in the issuing state. Single-state funds tend to be advantageous for residents of that state because interest is also exempt from state income tax. Multistate funds are exempt from federal income tax; however, bondholders may be subject to state and local income tax on any interest from the bonds.

An investor should consider several issues when deciding on the purchase of a bond mutual fund. First, when purchasing a bond fund, the maturity of the bond fund does not decrease over time as is the case with the direct purchase of a bond. Therefore, an investor who purchases a bond fund with average maturity of seven to ten years will not see the maturity diminish with the passage of time. A bond investor also should consider the expenses of the fund. In the case of stocks, an argument can be made that additional research expenses allow the manager to improve performance. However, when considering a government bond fund, the homogeneity of the assets don't allow even the most brilliant fund manager to add much value. In addition, the lower historical returns of bonds relative to stocks make expenses much more important to the investor's realized return.

Index Funds

Index funds attempt to match the performance of some index like the S&P 500, Russell 2000, or Wilshire 5000. The appeal of index funds is their low cost, tax efficiency, and the fact that most actively managed funds fail to beat the market index on a consistent basis. There are several ways that a fund can construct a portfolio to match the performance of its index. The first method—a *full replication* strategy—is simply to purchase all the securities held in the portfolio in the same proportions as they are held in the index. A second approach—*sampling*—attempts to match the performance of the index without purchasing all the securities in the index. For example, a statistical sampling technique may be used to purchase 300 of the stocks in the S&P 500 index. The sampling approach may choose to hold all the industries in the index in their same proportions but not all the stocks. A third approach—*enhanced indexing*—uses an approach similar to the sampling approach except the portfolio is tilted to reflect the most promising stocks in the industry in an attempt to beat the index by a small percentage each year.[5]

Sector Funds

Sector funds focus on companies in specific sectors of the economy. They allow investors to invest in a specific area of the economy such as health care or the Internet without having to search out individual stocks. For example, sector funds exist for technology, utilities, transportation, the Internet, health care, and precious metals. In general, these funds have a goal of capital appreciation. Because the portfolio is concentrated in a specific sector of the economy, these funds tend to be highly risky.

International Funds

International funds invest in the securities of non-U.S. stocks and thus allow investors to participate in the success or failure of non-U.S. companies. There are numerous categories of international funds. Some funds can invest anywhere in the world, whereas other funds limit their investments to a particular country or region. Other funds may invest in less-developed or emerging markets. Funds also can use an approach of indexing to some international benchmark or build a portfolio based on individual security selection.

One argument for international investing that is gaining popular acceptance is that investing abroad can reduce the overall risk of an investor's portfolio. The diversification benefit results from the lower degree of correlation between international stocks and U.S. equities. The lower the correlation between assets, the greater the benefits of diversification.

Global Funds

Global funds are similar to international funds except they allow fund managers to purchase U.S. securities as well. This gives fund managers more leeway in determining which securities to add to the portfolio. One drawback to global funds is that the portfolio may become more heavily weighted toward U.S. stocks than the investor desires.

Money Market Funds

Money market funds invest in short-term debt obligations of various borrowers such as the U.S. Treasury, state governments, or corporations. The short-term nature of the fund's assets makes money market funds suitable for meeting investors' short-term savings needs. Money market funds are classified in a number of ways.

- Government securities money market funds—These types of funds invest in obligations of the U.S. Treasury or government agencies and are virtually default free.

- Tax-exempt money market funds—These funds invest in short-term tax-exempt municipal securities.

- General-purpose money market funds—These funds invest in a variety of short-term instruments, from Treasury bills to commercial paper to certificates of deposit.

Mutual Fund Fees

Mutual fund shareholders should be concerned with two types of costs. First, the cost of buying shares in the fund or the costs imposed on the shareholder for redeeming shares can differ significantly from fund to fund. Some funds charge a fee or commission known as a load to buy shares in the fund. In this case, the offering price or price paid for a share will exceed the fund's net asset value. These types of funds are referred to as *load funds*. The purpose of the load is to pay a commission to the financial planner or broker selling the fund. A second type of fund allows investors to purchase shares directly from the investment company at a price equal to the fund's net asset value. These types of funds are referred to as *no-load funds*.

The difference in the cost between load and no-load funds can be significant, as some funds charge loads as high as 8.5 percent of net asset value. Sometimes a fund may charge a fee to redeem shares, known as a *back-end load*. In many cases, the back-end loads start at high levels and then decline over a period of time. The purpose of a back-end load is to discourage investors from switching out of funds, a practice that can be expensive for the funds.

How much the load of a fund impacts the returns to shareholders depends on how long the fund is held. Because the load is a fixed percentage of the net asset value and is only paid when shares are purchased, the impact diminishes with time. Funds held for short periods of time will be affected more by the load than funds held for long periods of time. Table 12-1 provides an example of how the impact of loads diminishes over time. It is assumed that the investor begins with an initial investment of $1,000 and that the fund grows at a compound rate of 10 percent per year.

From Table 12-1, it can be seen that the greatest impact on the returns occurs for short holding periods. For example, for a fund charging a 1 percent load fee, the lost rate of return for the first year is 110 basis points.[6] However, if the investor holds the same fund for twenty years, the impact of the load is only 6 basis points per year. The impact is even more obvious for the fund charging a load fee of 8.5 percent. For a one-year holding period, the fund loses 935 basis points; however, when the holding period is extended to twenty years, the fund loses only 49 basis points per year.

The second type of cost that shareholders bear is the cost of operating the fund. The fund's expenses are determined by the fee paid to the managers of the fund and the other expenses incurred in running the fund. The costs of running the fund differ depending on the type of fund being managed. For example, an emerging markets fund is likely to experience greater expenses

Table 12-1. Effect of load fees on holding period returns.

		Annualized holding period returns (%)				
Load (%)	Shares purchased	1 year	3 years	5 years	10 years	20 years
0.0	100.0	10.00	10.00	10.00	10.00	10.00
1.0	99.0	8.90	9.63	9.78	9.89	9.94
3.0	97.0	6.70	8.89	9.33	9.67	9.83
5.0	95.0	4.50	8.14	8.88	9.44	9.72
8.5	91.5	0.65	6.79	8.06	9.03	9.51

Table 12-2. Holding period accumulation values.

Expense ratio (%)	Net return (%)	Holding period accumulation values				
		1 year	3 years	5 years	10 years	20 years
0.2	9.8	$1,098	$1,324	$1,596	$2,547	$6,487
0.5	9.5	$1,095	$1,313	$1,574	$2,478	$6,142
1.0	9.0	$1,090	$1,295	$1,539	$2,367	$5,604
1.5	8.5	$1,085	$1,277	$1,504	$2,261	$5,112
2.0	8.0	$1,080	$1,260	$1,469	$2,159	$4,661

than a large-cap U.S. fund due to the greater transactions costs in many developing overseas markets. The manager's investment philosophy also plays an important part in determining the expenses of the fund. For example, a manager who believes in a buy-and-hold strategy will have lower transactions costs than a manager who is constantly turning over the portfolio.

As we saw in Table 12-1, the impact of load fees on an investor's returns diminishes over time because the load fee is incurred when the shareholder purchases shares. However, because expenses are incurred each year, the higher the expense ratio of the fund, the greater the impact on the investor's accumulation values as time passes. Table 12-2 shows the accumulation values for funds with different expense ratios for a $1,000 initial investment.

From Table 12-2, we can see that the difference between the low-cost fund (0.2 percent) and the high-cost fund (2 percent) grows significantly over time. For a one-year holding period, the difference is only $18, but for a 20-year holding period, the difference is more than $1,800.

A final fee that a fund can charge is known as a 12b-1 fee, named after the 1980 SEC rule that allows it. The rule allows funds to deduct as much as 0.75 percent of average net assets per year to cover the distribution costs of the fund. These costs include advertising, commissions paid to brokers, and general marketing expenses and are charged on an annual basis. This means that 12b-1 fees have the same detrimental compounding effect as the fund's expenses.

Buying and Selling Mutual Funds

Investors who are interested in purchasing shares in a mutual fund have several alternatives. First, many investment companies allow investors to purchase shares directly on either a no-load or low-load basis. A prospectus and

application can be obtained directly from the fund, and investors can purchase shares by completing the application and remitting funds either
through check, wire transfer, or transfer from another fund. Most funds have
minimum initial investment amounts; however, some funds waive the initial
minimum for investors who agree to invest a regular amount (usually $50 or
$100) through direct transfer from their bank accounts, sometimes referred
to as *automatic investment plans.*

A second method for purchasing shares in a mutual fund is through a
broker or financial planner affiliated with the fund. Mutual funds of the
major brokerage houses are sold through their own brokers and other brokers.

A third method for purchasing mutual fund shares is through a *financial
supermarket* such as Charles Schwab. These discount brokers sell a range of
no-load mutual funds. One advantage of dealing with a financial supermarket rather than purchasing directly from the fund is that the investor receives
a consolidated statement and can execute transfers from one family of funds
to another with relative ease.

Technology and Mutual Funds

Technological changes have allowed mutual funds to offer a number of new
services. Many funds now offer prospective investors the opportunity to
download prospectuses and applications directly from the Internet. The technology also has allowed shareholders the opportunity to check account balances and transfer money from one fund to another directly from the fund's
Web site. Internet technology also enables mutual funds to deliver online
education to shareholders and prospective shareholders. Many funds offer
online surveys that allow the investors to determine appropriate investment
strategies and asset allocation.

Pension Plans

Institutional investors[7] have increasingly turned to mutual funds as investment options. As a result, even though individuals continue to control the
majority of mutual fund assets, the mutual fund industry is seeing a shift in
business toward an increasingly institutional customer base. Over the past
several years, institutional assets have accounted for an increasing share of
total mutual fund assets.

The mutual fund assets held by IRAs and employer-sponsored pension
plans have increased significantly. Several factors have contributed to the
growth in the retirement holdings of mutual funds. First, the overall size of

the employer-sponsored pension market had expanded to $6.6 trillion at the end of 1996, from about $1.1 trillion in 1981. Second, defined-contribution plans have become increasingly popular. At the end of 1996, the defined-contribution market was $1.8 trillion, of which $577 billion was held in mutual funds. Mutual funds are attractive to employees because they offer professional money management, investment diversification, liquidity, and price transparency. Employers favor mutual fund assets because they partially relieve them from having to serve as investment adviser and they provide record keeping functions as well. The third factor contributing to the growth of mutual funds in pension planning is the IRA market, which had grown to $1.3 trillion by the end of 1996. Although new contributions to IRAs have been slow since the passage of the Tax Reform Act of 1986, the Taxpayer Relief Act of 1997 is expected to provide a boost. Qualified investors can invest as much as $2,000 annually to a Roth IRA and watch the sum grow tax free.

Tax Issues

How a mutual fund is managed can determine the shareholder's tax liability. For pension funds and other tax-exempt institutions, the tax efficiency of the fund is of no consequence. However, for individuals, the tax efficiency of the fund determines both the investor's tax liability and the investor's after-tax return. The factors that affect a fund's tax efficiency include:

- The fund's portfolio turnover. In general, the higher the turnover, the greater the tax liability.

- The composition of the fund's securities. Funds with high-yielding stocks will have higher tax liabilities on the dividends than funds that purchase low-yielding stocks.

- The tax management strategies of the fund.

Fund Distributions

Investors who buy shares of a fund at the end of the year should determine when the fund will distribute dividends and capital gains to fundholders. Shareholders of funds are subject to dividend and capital gains distributions even if they have the distribution rolled into additional shares. Investors who purchases shares at the wrong time will be taxed on dividends or capital gains they never receive. This occurs because a fund's net asset value reflects the price of the securities it holds and any undistributed dividends and capital

Table 12-3. Cost and tax consequences for fund purchase.

Date of purchase	Price paid per share	Dividends received	Pretax net cost	Tax liability
December 9	$10	$2	$8	$2,000[a]
December 10	$ 8	$0	$0	$ 0

[a] $2 per share distribution × 1,000 shares.

gains. When investors purchase shares of a fund but do not receive the dividends or capital gains, they pay a lower price per share.[8]

To illustrate this point, consider the following example. Suppose an investor wishes to purchase 1,000 shares of a mutual fund currently selling for $10 per share on December 9. The fund will distribute $2 per share in dividends, with an ex-dividend date of December 10. Therefore, the $10 price per share can be broken into two parts: the $2 distribution of dividends and a value for the fund's net assets of $8. Assuming that the value of the fund's securities does not change between December 9 and 10, an investor who would not be entitled to the dividend would pay $2 less for a share of the fund.[9] Table 12-3 presents a comparison of the differences in costs and tax liabilities for purchasing on December 9 and 10.

From Table 12-3, we can see that shareholders pay the same pretax cost whether they purchase shares on December 9 or 10. However, if the shares are purchased on December 9, the shareholder pays $10 and receives a $2 dividend distribution. These distributions are taxable and, in this example, leave the shareholder with a $2,000 tax liability that would not have been incurred if the fund had been purchased one day later.

Regulation of Mutual Funds

The investment management industry is highly regulated. Federal securities laws that govern the industry include the Investment Company Act of 1940 (ICA), the Investment Advisers Act of 1940 (IAA), the Securities Act of 1933, and the Securities Exchange Act of 1934. In addition, other regulations include the Internal Revenue Code of 1986, state notice filing requirements, and antifraud statues.

Investment Company Act of 1940

Mutual funds are a class of investment companies defined in the ICA as "management companies," which are subclassified as either diversified or nondiversified. A diversified company has at least 75 percent of its total assets in cash and cash items, government securities, securities of other investment companies, and other securities. The investment in each security is limited to an amount not greater in value than 5 percent of the fund's assets and not more than 10 percent of the outstanding voting securities of each issuer. The ICA also regulates the ability of mutual funds to employ certain investment techniques such as repurchase agreements, futures, options, and swaps. Under the ICA, certain fund policies may not be changed without shareholder approval. The act also imposes specific prohibitions against certain transactions between a fund and its principal underwriter, investment adviser, or other affiliated persons. As such, a mutual fund's principal underwriter or an affiliated person may not knowingly sell to or purchase from the fund any security or other property, nor may they borrow any money or other property from the fund.

The ICA requires all funds to safeguard their assets by placing them in the hands of a custodian and by providing fidelity bonding of officers and employees of the fund. The act also requires daily valuation of the securities held in a mutual fund portfolio. The ICA requires all mutual funds to maintain detailed books and records regarding the securities owned by the fund and the fund's outstanding shares, file semiannual reports with the SEC, and send such reports to shareholders. Independent accountants must certify the financial statements in a fund's annual report.

Mutual funds are subclassified as closed-end and open-end investment companies. Open-end funds redeem shares at any time upon shareholder request. The funds are required to pay redeeming shareholders at net asset value within seven days of receiving such request. Closed-end funds, in contrast, do not redeem their shares. Shares of closed-end funds are typically listed and traded on stock exchanges.

Another important regulatory issue is ICA's prohibition of interdealing by investment banking houses. Under the ICA, underwriters are prohibited from feeding affiliated funds during a public offering in which they participate, subject to special exemptions. The purpose of this prohibition is to prevent underwriters from dumping to their kindred funds any unmarketable securities they have underwritten. The exemptions cover municipal bond issues and public registered stock issues, where a fund group can purchase up to 4 percent of such securities underwritten by its Wall Street parent. The explosive growth of mutual funds has made investment companies significant purchasers in syndicated offerings. This growth has put pressure on the old regulation, so in 1996, the SEC proposed rule changes to lift the cap to 10 percent of a domestic issue or a foreign security in an acceptable market abroad. Wall Street firms are lobbying to remove the cap limitation and widen the exemptions to include Rule 144A private placements.

Investment Advisers Act of 1940

The IAA regulates the activities of investment advisers, including advisers to investment companies and private money managers. The IAA regulation covers any person, absent exclusion or an exemption, engaging in the business of providing advice or issuing reports about securities to clients for compensation. Excluded from the definition of investment adviser are:

- U.S. banks and bank holding companies
- Instrumentalities of the United States or any state
- Government securities advisers
- Publishers of newspapers and magazines of general and regular circulation
- Lawyers, accountants, teachers, and engineers, provided that the advice is solely incidental

Under the Investment Advisers Supervision Coordination Act of 1997 (IASCA), an investment adviser must register with the SEC if it:

- Has more than $25 million in client assets under management, or
- Advises registered investment companies, or
- Is not regulated or required to be regulated by the state in which it maintains its principal office, or
- Is exempted from the prohibition of registration by the SEC.

Any investment adviser who advises a registered investment company is required to register with the SEC. The same requirement applies for advisers who perform contractual subadvisory services to a registered investment company. Investment advisers who do not advise a registered investment company may rely on existing exemption such as federal de minimis exemption from SEC registration. Such exemption applies to investment advisers who had fewer than fifteen clients during the past twelve months, do not hold themselves out to the public as investment advisers, and do not advise any registered investment company. The IASCA defines the term "assets under management" to include only securities portfolios for which an investment adviser provides continuous and regular supervisory or management services. Because the assets under management for some advisers might fluctuate above and below $25 million, causing needless SEC and state registrations and withdraws, the SEC has raised the threshold for mandatory SEC registration to $30 million. When assets under management dip below $25 million, withdrawal from SEC registration is required.

Investment advisers who are not regulated or required to be regulated by the state in which they have their principal office must register with the SEC, even if they do not have $25 million under management. The SEC retains the regulatory responsibility with respect to small advisory firms only if their principal office is in a state that has not enacted an investment adviser statute or the adviser is a foreign adviser doing business in the United States.

Pursuant to ERISA Section 3(38)(B), an investment manager must be registered with the SEC as an investment adviser. So advisers who would no longer be eligible for continued registration with the SEC would become ineligible to act as investment managers under ERISA after the National Securities Markets Improvement Act of 1996. To address this concern, Congress, on October 30, 1997, amended ERISA to permit non–SEC registered investment advisers to act as fiduciaries under ERISA.

The IAA also establishes requirements governing the operation of a registered adviser and the relationship between the adviser and its clients. The most important requirements include record keeping, brochure rule, advisory contracts and performance fees, conflicts and antifraud provisions, and duty to supervise.

If an investment adviser is not registered under the IAA because it has less than $25 million in assets under management and does not advise a registered investment company, then it may be required to register under state law. State-registered investment advisers whose assets under management grow to $30 million are required to register with the SEC. All states have the authority to enforce actions against SEC-registered investment advisers and associated persons under their antifraud laws. States also retain the authority to receive copies of documents filed with the SEC for notice purposes or to impose fees on investment advisers.

Generally, a state is free to regulate any investment adviser who is not SEC-registered and has either a place of business in the state or clients who are residents of the state. States may not, however, require registration of an investment adviser who does not have a place of business in the state and who had fewer than six resident clients during the preceding twelve months (called national de minimis exemption).

The Securities Act of 1933

The 1933 act requires that all prospective investors receive a current prospectus describing the fund and that the fund provide, upon request, a statement of additional information.

Mutual funds are subject to special SEC registration rules because they continuously offer new shares to the public. In order to facilitate the continuous offering of shares, the Securities Act of 1933 permits a mutual fund to maintain an "evergreen" prospectus (that is, updated at regular intervals and whenever material changes occur) and register an indefinite number of shares. After the end of each fiscal year, mutual funds pay a registration fee to the SEC based on the shares actually sold. Mutual funds are permitted to net redemption against sales when calculating their SEC registration fees.

The Securities Exchange Act of 1934

The 1934 act regulates broker-dealers, including principal underwriters and others who sell mutual fund shares, and requires their registration with the SEC. The 1934 act requires broker-dealers to meet financial responsibility requirements, maintain extensive books and records reflecting their own financial position and customer transactions, segregate customer securities in custodial accounts, and file detailed annual financial reports with the SEC and their industry self-regulatory organization. In addition, all sales and research personnel must demonstrate their qualifications by passing an examination administered by the NASD. A mutual fund's principal underwriter is required to have a registered principal, who must take special qualification examinations administered by the NASD.

Internal Revenue Code of 1986 and State Laws

The Internal Revenue Code of 1986 provides mutual fund entity-level tax exemption if the fund (1) satisfies various tests, such as those relating to asset diversification and sources of income, for qualification as a regulated investment company (RIC) and (2) meets certain income distribution requirements. One important consequence of the RIC status is that a mutual fund is relieved of entity-level tax to the extent that it distributes substantially all of its income to its shareholders. Mutual fund shareholders report on their tax returns the dividends received from the fund.

Another important consequence of the RIC status is that the "character" of the mutual fund's income often flows through to its shareholders. The types of income that retain their character when flowed through a mutual fund include long-term capital gains (paid out as a capital gain dividend) and municipal bond income exempt from federal taxes (the exempt-interest dividend). In addition, all local governments recognize that the character of federal obligation interest, which is exempt from state and local taxation, can flow through a mutual fund to its shareholders.

State Laws

State registration of mutual fund shares is not required. A state in which a fund intends to sell its shares, however, may require a notice filing. In addition, mutual funds must pay a fee to each state in which they intend to offer their shares and comply with any state antifraud provisions. Once the notice filing requirements are satisfied, a mutual fund may sell its shares in a state.

Most states have adopted securities laws that require the registration of broker-dealers who offer securities in those states. In addition, investment advisers to mutual funds may be required to make a notice filing and pay a fee in states in which they do business.

Summary

Mutual funds provide investors with an important tool for financial planning, allowing those with limited wealth the opportunity to obtain a diversified, professionally managed portfolio. Mutual funds also have become an important part in the retirement process, making up a large percentage of IRA, 401(k), and other retirement plans.

Selected Bibliography

Bogle, J. C. *Common Sense on Mutual Funds: New Imperatives for the Intelligent Investor.* New York: John Wiley, 1999.

Gitman, L. J., and M. D. Joehnk. *Fundamentals of Investing,* 7th ed. Reading, Mass.: Addison-Wesley, 1999.

Liaw, K. T. *The Business of Investment Banking.* New York: John Wiley, 1999.

Reilly, F. K. and E. A. Norton. *Investments,* 5th ed. Fort Worth, Tex.: Dryden Press, 1999.

Notes

1. A board of directors governs a mutual fund when the fund is established as a corporation. A board of trustees governs the fund when it is established as a business trust.

2.   The expense ratio for an index fund can be less than 0.2 percent.

3.   For example, in 1994, through sales force the mutual fund industry sold $854 billion, and direct marketing took in $471 billion. In 1995, sales force contributed $820 billion in new investments, and direct marketing was responsible for $571 billion new cash flow.

4.   The two exceptions are funds that invest in emerging market debt and funds that seek out the bonds of distressed companies.

5.   Technically, enhanced indexing doesn't represent the passive investment strategy associated with indexing.

6.   The 110-basis-point loss is calculated as the 100-basis-point cost of the load plus the ten basis points that the portfolio loses by having one less share appreciating at 10 percent.

7.   Institutional investors include retirement plan sponsors, foundations, nonprofit organizations, personal trusts and estates, and corporations.

8.   This date is known as the *ex-dividend date* and is four business days before the date of record. On the ex-dividend date, the seller of the stock is entitled to receive the dividend or capital gain.

9.   Technically, the fund's price falls by less than the amount of the distribution due to tax consequences.

13

Closed-End Investment Companies

Closed-end funds provide investment professionals the opportunity to offer clients an investment vehicle that many new investors may be unaware of. Closed-end funds are financial intermediaries that purchase a pool of securities and sell shares to the public. Like open-end investment companies, or mutual funds, discussed in Chapter 12, closed-end funds provide investors with professional management and diversification. However, a closed-end investment company differs from its open-end counterpart because it issues a fixed number of shares to the public. These shares are then purchased in much the same way that the stocks of a public company are traded. If shareholders wish to liquidate their holdings in the fund, they do not redeem those shares from the fund, but rather must find someone willing to purchase those shares. Likewise, an investor who is interested in purchasing shares in the fund must find someone who owns shares and is willing to sell them.

Like mutual funds, closed-end funds come in many types with a wide range of objectives. There are *general equity funds, specialized equity funds, country funds, regional funds, preferred stock funds,* and funds that invest in a range of fixed-income investments. Two special types of funds, a *real estate investment trust* (REIT) and a holding company depositary receipts (HOLDRs), while technically not closed-end funds, are very similar in nature and will also be discussed in this chapter.

Organization of Closed-End Funds

Closed-end funds are organized like other incorporated public companies with a board of directors elected by shareholders. Like their mutual fund counterparts, the closed-end fund board selects an investment advisor to handle the investment research and portfolio management responsibilities for the fund.

Comparing Closed-End and Open-End Mutual Funds

There are a number of advantages to using closed-end investment companies and open-end mutual funds as investment vehicles.

- *Professional management*—Investors who use either of these investment vehicles gain the advantage of professional management, which includes research on the securities in the portfolio and a constant monitoring of the assets in the portfolio.

- *Diversification*—By purchasing shares in either a closed-end fund or a mutual fund, investors receive the advantages of having a broadly diversified portfolio. This is especially important for small investors whose resources may be insufficient to adequately diversify their portfolios.

- *Economies of scale*—Both closed-end funds and mutual funds are able to transact at much lower costs than a small individual investor. In addition to reducing transactions costs, the costs of record keeping are much lower for funds than for individuals.

There are a number of differences between closed-end funds and their open-end mutual fund counterparts. The first difference is the number of shares outstanding. In an open-end fund, the company increases the number of shares in the fund when there is a net inflow of cash and reduces the number of shares when there is a net outflow of cash. This can lead to a number of issues that the fund manager must address. First, a mutual fund must keep a certain amount of the portfolio in cash in order to provide for possible redemptions from the fund. In a rising stock market, this can lead to a drag on the fund's performance. If the manager does not hold a sufficient amount of the fund's portfolio in the form of cash, then he or she may need to sell off some of the securities in the portfolio in order to meet the redemptions. Selling off some of the fund's portfolio can lead to greater transactions costs, increased tax liabilities for fundholders, and opportunity costs should those securities rise in value in the future.

A large inflow of funds can also lead to problems. Large inflows of cash force managers to either purchase securities that they feel are only marginally desirable in order to keep the fund fully invested or hold large amounts of cash until suitable investments can be found. In addition, as the size of the fund grows, it may become more difficult for the manager to find enough quality investments to improve the performance of the fund. This can be especially true when the fund invests in smaller companies or in a particular sector of the economy.

Closed-end funds do not suffer from these problems because a fixed number of shares are issued and the fund does not redeem shares from shareholders. This means that the fund manager does not have to hold excess cash in order to meet possible share redemptions, nor does the manager need to reinvest large sums of cash coming into the fund. The fund manager therefore is able to manage the portfolio without regard to possible cash inflows or outflows. Table 13-1 provides a comparison of open-end and closed-end funds.

One important difference that is discussed in more detail in the next section is the fact that closed-end funds can sell for prices that differ significantly from the value of the fund's net assets or net asset value (NAV).[1] This means that an investor could pay, for example, $.80 or $1.25 for $1 of the fund's net assets. This discount or premium from the NAV can have important consequences for the fund's yield and return. In addition, changes in the discount or premium of a fund from its NAV offer investors a number of possible trading strategies.

Another major difference between open- and closed-end funds is that closed-end funds can leverage their holdings through the use of either debt or preferred stock.

The leverage of a closed-end fund can have value to an investor. Unlike other forms of investment leverage, such as purchasing securities on margin, the investor does not directly incur the costs of the leverage. In the case of a leveraged closed-end fund, the costs are born by the fund. This increased leverage magnifies the investor's gains or losses. In addition, when investors purchase shares of the fund at a discount, they also receive a leverage effect, as the net assets that they control are greater than the price paid for the fund.

Table 13-1. Comparison of open-end and closed-end funds.

	Open-end fund	Closed-end fund
Number of shares	Variable	Fixed
Price	Based on net asset value	Can sell for a discount or premium to net asset value depending on supply and demand for fund
Shares redeemed by fund	Yes	No
Traded on exchange or over-the-counter	No	Yes
Liquidity	High	Depends on supply and demand for fund shares

Listing and Trading of Closed-End Funds

Closed-end funds are listed on organized exchanges or the over-the-counter market. The trading of closed-end funds parallels the trading of the equities of public companies. Unlike mutual funds, which continually issue or redeem shares, closed-end funds have a fixed number of shares. In order to purchase shares in a closed-end fund, an investor contacts a broker who seeks out an investor who owns the shares and is willing to sell them.

From Figure 13-1, we can see that the mutual fund issues additional shares when an investor wishes to purchase shares in the fund. In the diagram, the investor and the mutual fund deal directly, with no broker. There are funds that are sold only through brokers; however, in both cases, the number of shares of the mutual fund will increase when an investor wishes to purchase. In the case of the closed-end fund, the fund is not involved at all when an investor wishes to purchase shares. Funds are simply transferred from one investor to another.

The price paid for the shares can differ significantly from the net assets of the fund. If there is great demand for the fund, then the fund will sell for a premium. If demand for the fund is weak, then the fund may sell at a discount to its net asset value.

Another advantage of closed-end funds is the ability of the investor to specify the transaction price through the use of limit orders or stop loss orders. Mutual funds, on the other hand, handle transactions at the NAV at the close of business. By specifying the buy or sell price, an investor may be better able to manage potential movements in the price of the fund. For example, the use of a stop loss order may allow an investor to limit his or her downside risk.

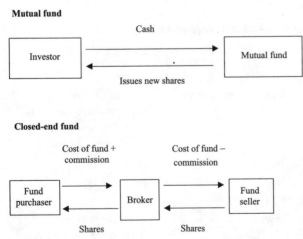

Figure 13-1. Closed-end versus mutual fund purchase.

Likewise, the use of a buy limit order may allow the investor to purchase shares at a target price without constantly monitoring the price of the fund. In addition, investors have the opportunity to engage in short sales of closed-end funds, a transaction that is unavailable for mutual fund shares. Short selling closed-end funds not only allows investors to profit from declines in the value of the fund, but also opens up a range of hedging and arbitrage opportunities. Some of these strategies are discussed later in the chapter.

Discount or Premium

An important issue to consider when purchasing a closed-end fund is the discount or premium at which the fund shares trade. Because closed-end funds issue a fixed number of shares and are traded in the same manner as public companies, they can sell for prices that differ significantly from what the fund's assets are actually worth (NAV). When the cost of the shares trades at a price above its NAV, the fund is selling at a premium. Likewise, when the cost of the shares trades at a price below its NAV, the fund is said to be selling at a discount. The percentage discount or premium for the fund can be computed as

$$Premium/Discount = \frac{(Market\ Price\ - NAV)}{NAV}$$

When the result of the above equation is positive, the fund trades at a premium, and when the result is negative, the fund trades at a discount.

Closed-end funds sell for values that differ from their NAV for a number of reasons:[2]

- Demand for the fund—Some funds trade at a premium because there is a strong demand for the fund. For example, some country funds may trade at premiums because a large number of people wish to invest in that country and a closed-end fund may be the only alternative.

- Ignorance—Many closed-end funds trade at a discount because of the limited amount of knowledge that the general public has about such funds. Most individuals have heard of mutual funds, but many people are unaware of closed-end funds as an investment alternative.

- Tax liability—Some funds trade at a discount because the fund has large unrealized capital gains that may have significant tax consequences to investors in the future.

- Performance—Funds that consistently outperform indexes are likely to sell at a premium, whereas funds that consistently underperform are likely to sell at a discount.

- News—Economic, social, or political news about a country will determine how much investors are willing to pay for shares of a fund.

- Market sentiment—When investors are particularly bullish about a country or region, they may be willing to pay a premium to purchase shares in a closed-end fund.

- Excess supply—The introduction of new funds with similar investment strategies or investing in similar markets may increase the discount of these closed-end funds.

- Conversion to an open-end fund—When a fund sells at a significant discount to its NAV, takeover rumors may exist or the fund may choose to become open-ended, thus eliminating the discount.

- Lack of sponsorship—Funds may sell at a discount because most brokerage firms tend to avoid recommending closed-end funds in favor of investments that generate higher sales commissions.

When funds sell at prices that differ from their NAV, the return received by shareholders will differ from the performance of the fund. The difference is determined by changes in the discount or premium relative to the NAV. If a shareholder purchases shares in the fund at a discount and sees the discount diminish, the shareholder's return will exceed the performance of the fund. Likewise, if the investor purchases the fund at a premium and sees the premium increase, the shareholder's returns will exceed the return of the fund. Therefore, a diminishing discount or increasing premium will enhance an investor's return, and an increasing discount or decreasing premium will reduce an investor's return.

Types of Closed-End Funds

Like their mutual fund counterparts, closed-end funds come in a variety of types with a number of investment objectives. The most common type of closed-end funds are bond funds. Table 13-2 provides data on the closed-end funds available. The largest category based on net assets is national municipal funds. Single state municipal funds comprise the greatest number of funds.

Bond Funds

Bond funds are by far the largest segment of the closed-end fund market. Bond funds selling at a discount to their NAV provide investors with an opportunity to enhance their yield. For example, suppose a bond fund has a

Table 13-2. Industry statistics.

Statistic	Value
Total number of closed-end funds (U.S. exchanges only)	530
Total Assets[a]	$123,370.37

[a] *Net assets, expressed in millions of dollars, and exclude leveraged capital (preferred stock, debt, etc.) which totals about $28 billion.*

Assets by Classification

Category	Abbreviation	Funds	Assets[a]
Corporate—High yield	CHY	33	$7,351.89
Corporate—Investment grade	CIG	4	$643.78
Emerging market equity	EME	6	$821.26
Emerging market income	EMI	7	$1,355.65
Equity income	EQI	8	$1,085.56
General Bond—Investment grade	BDI	12	$1,593.24
General mortgage	MTG	26	$9,025.49
Global equity	GLE	7	$562.75
Global income	GLI	30	$8,803.12
Government bond	GOV	8	$2,463.79
Growth and income	GCI	26	$11,549.06
Growth—domestic	GRD	23	$6,779.38
Loan participation	LPF	4	$3,015.69
Multi-Sector bond	MLT	13	$5,031.71
Municipal—high yield	MHY	5	$1,218.53
Municipal—national	MNL	96	$31,292.02
Municipal—single state	MSS	123	$13,936.36
Non-U.S. equity	FOR	82	$11,562.27
Sector—energy/natural resources	ENR	2	$474.82
Sector—financial services	FIN	4	$1,363.07
Sector—health/biotechnology	HLT	3	$844.27
Sector—precious metals	GPM	3	$376.99
Sector—utilities	UTL	3	$2,219.65

Source: Closed-end Fund Association Web site (www.cefa.com).

NAV of $10 but is currently selling for $8. If the fund pays $.50 in interest each year, then the yield as a percentage of NAV would be 5 percent ($.50/$10). However, because the investor paid only $8 for each share, the yield is 6.25 percent ($.50/$8). The advantage of purchasing this closed-end fund for $8 is that the investor receives $10 in net assets. The investor may benefit further from purchasing this fund if the discount narrows during the holding period.

Country Funds

Country funds have become an important type of closed-end fund because they give investors an opportunity to invest in places that may not be available to individual investors or may be too expensive or complicated for individual investors. For example, some foreign countries prohibit investments by individual investors; thus, a closed-end country fund represents a way for an investor to participate in the success or failure of that country's economy. Even when a country allows individual investment, individuals may have difficulty evaluating appropriate investments in foreign lands.

Real Estate Investment Trusts

Real estate investment trusts (REITs) are another financial vehicle that small investors may have little or no knowledge of. This investment vehicle provides investors with limited resources the opportunity to participate in real estate investments. Real estate can be an important component of a well-diversified portfolio and offers investors a hedge against inflation.

REITs are a type of closed-end investment company that invests in various types of real estate and mortgages. REITs were first established by the Real Estate Investment Trust Act of 1960, which governs the rules for selecting investments and distributing income. REITs are required to pay out 95 percent of their income in the form of dividends, keep 75 percent of their assets in real estate investments, and earn at least 75 percent of their income from real estate. REITs must have at least 100 shareholders, and less than 50 percent of the outstanding shares must be concentrated in the hands of five or fewer shareholders. Finally, each of the investments must be held for a minimum of four years. REITs, like other closed-end investment companies, trade on organized exchanges, such as the NYSE and the AMEX, or the over-the-counter market.

Like mutual funds, each type of REIT has certain investment objectives. REITs are generally classified into three categories:

- *Equity REITs*—invest in properties such as office buildings, shopping centers, apartments, and hotels.

- *Mortgage REITs*—invest in construction and mortgage loans to real estate investors.

- *Hybrid REITs*—invest in both properties and mortgages.

Table 13-3 presents data on the annual market capitalizations for the three categories of REITs from 1971 to 1999.

Real estate investment trusts are unique from other types of closed-end investment companies because the assets held by REITs are not constantly traded, and, therefore, data can be difficult to obtain and analyze. Rather than look at actual transaction data, which are available for stocks, bonds, and many derivative securities, REIT data often use appraisal data or use the income generated from the properties. Table 13-4 presents some of the common sources of data used for measuring REIT performance.

REITs can be a valuable tool for rounding out an investor's portfolio. First, real estate tends to be a good hedge against inflation. Many individuals may recall the high rates of inflation during the 1970s were accompanied by skyrocketing real estate prices. Second, REITs give investors the opportunity to invest in high-yielding securities that still offer some opportunities for growth. Finally, real estate offers investors the opportunity to diversify their investment portfolios. The diversification benefit results from the low degree of correlation between REITs and U.S. stocks.

HOLDRs

Holding company depositary receipts or *HOLDRs* are a new, quasi-type of closed-end fund. Technically, the HOLDRs represent trusts that are to be dissolved in forty years. However, because they issue a fixed number of shares and trade on the American Stock Exchange, they are very similar to closed-end funds. The HOLDRs hold an unmanaged basket of stocks and trade like individual stocks. There are a number of advantages of this new type of fund. First, the costs of running the fund are low because there is no active management of the portfolio. Second, an investor can place limit orders to buy or sell at specific prices. Finally, there are some unique tax benefits to these funds.

HOLDRs were created by Merrill Lynch but are traded by all brokerage firms. HOLDRs are similar to closed-end funds or index shares, known as SPDRs. In the case of HOLDRs, trades must be made in round lots of 100 shares. The composition of the fund never changes unless there is a merger, in

Table 13-3. Annual market capitalization.

Equity market capitilization outstanding
(in millions of dollars at year end)

End of year	Composite		Equity		Mortgage		Hybrid	
	Number of REITs	Market capitalization	Number of REITs	Market capitalization	Number of REITs	Market capitalization	Number of REITs	Market capitalization
1971	34	1,494.3	12	332.0	12	570.8	10	591.6
1972	46	1,880.9	17	377.3	18	774.7	11	728.9
1973	53	1,393.5	20	336.0	22	517.3	11	540.2
1974	53	712.4	19	241.9	22	238.8	12	231.7
1975	46	899.7	12	275.7	22	312.0	12	312.0
1976	62	1,308.0	27	409.6	22	415.6	13	482.8
1977	69	1,528.1	32	538.1	19	398.3	18	591.6
1978	71	1,412.4	33	575.7	19	340.3	19	496.4
1979	71	1,754.0	32	743.6	19	377.1	20	633.3
1980	75	2,298.6	35	942.2	21	509.5	19	846.8
1981	76	2,438.9	36	977.5	21	541.3	19	920.1
1982	66	3,298.6	30	1,071.4	20	1,133.4	16	1,093.8
1983	59	4,257.2	26	1,468.6	19	1,460.0	14	1,328.7

1984	59	5,085.3	25	1,794.5	20	1,801.3	14	1,489.4
1985	82	7,674.0	37	3,270.3	32	3,162.4	13	1,241.2
1986	96	9,923.6	45	4,336.1	35	3,625.8	16	1,961.7
1987	110	9,702.4	53	4,758.5	38	3,161.4	19	1,782.4
1988	117	11,435.2	56	6,141.7	40	3,620.8	21	1,672.6
1989	120	11,662.2	56	6,769.6	43	3,536.3	21	1,356.3
1990	119	8,737.1	58	5,551.6	43	2,549.2	18	636.3
1991	138	12,968.2	86	8,785.5	28	2,586.3	24	1,596.4
1992	142	15,912.0	89	11,171.1	30	2,772.8	23	1,968.1
1993	189	32,158.7	135	26,081.9	32	3,398.5	22	2,678.2
1994	226	44,306.0	175	38,812.0	29	2,502.7	22	2,991.3
1995	219	57,541.3	178	49,913.0	24	3,395.4	17	4,232.9
1996	199	88,776.3	166	78,302.0	20	4,778.6	13	5,695.8
1997	211	140,533.8	176	127,825.3	26	7,370.3	9	5,338.2
1998	210	138,301.4	173	126,904.5	28	6,480.7	9	4,916.2
1999	203	124,261.9	167	118,232.7	26	4,441.7	10	1,587.5

Note: Market capitalization equals price of shares multiplied by the number of shares outstanding.

Table 13-4. REIT investment performance measures.

Real estate-equity returns	Description of data
NAREIT—equity REIT share price index and dividend series	Monthly index computed based on share prices of REITs that own and manage real estate assets. Security prices used in the index are obtained from the NYSE, the AMEX, and the NASDAQ. Dividend data are collected by NAREIT. Properties owned may be levered or unlevered. Index values are available from 1972 to the present.
NAREIT—mortgage REIT share price index and dividend series	Monthly index computed on share price data of REITs that make primarily commercial real estate loans (construction, development and permanent) although some make or purchase residential loans (both multifamily and single family). Prices obtained from the NYSE, the AMEX, and the NASDAQ. Dividend data are collected by NAREIT. Monthly index values are available from 1972 to the present.
NAREIT—hybrid REIT index	Monthly index compiled by NAREIT from share prices and dividends for REITs that (1) own properties and (2) make mortgage loans. Sources of data are the same as for equity and mortgage REITs. Index values available from 1972 to present.
NCREIF Property Index—National Council of Real Estate Investment Fiduciaries	Data are contributed by members of NCREIF, based on 1,500 to 2,000 properties owned by pension fund plan sponsors through investment managers. An index is calculated quarterly and data consist of (1) net operating income and (2) beginning and end of quarter appraisal values for all properties. Actual sale prices are used as available. Quarterly index values are available from 1978 to the present.

Source: Adapted from W. B. Brueggerman, and J.D. Fisher, eds. *Real Estate Finance and Investments,* 10th ed. (New York: McGraw-Hill), exhibit 21-1, 684.

which case the new company could stay in the portfolio or could be dropped. If a company is sold, it is not supposed to be replaced.

Closed-End Fund Indexes

Indexes provide a useful benchmark for determining the overall direction of various subsets of the market. Indexes allow investors to gauge the overall movement of a class of investments by looking at a single number. The most widely watched closed-end fund index is the Herzfeld Closed-End Fund Average (HCEFA).

Created on December 31, 1987, by Thomas J. Herzfeld Advisors, Inc., the HCEFA consists of sixteen closed-end funds. Funds included in the average are weighted approximately equally, and the average was pegged at the average of the Dow Jones Industrial Average, which stood at 1938.38. The average can be found in *Barron's*.

Herzfeld has also created an average of single country closed-end funds. The average began on December 31, 1989, with twenty funds, with five additional funds being added to reflect global economic changes.

Expenses and Unique Risk Factors

Closed-end funds have a big cost advantage over their open-end fund counterparts because they do not need to deal with cash inflows or redemptions. This means that the fund does not need to hold excessive amounts of cash to fund redemptions, which can lead to a significant drag on performance during rising markets. In addition, fund managers can maintain more stable portfolios because they will not need to sell assets to fund redemptions. This can reduce both transactions costs and realized capital gains.

The major risk that closed-end fund investors face when compared to an open-end mutual fund is the change in the discount or premium. If the fund's discount widens or the premium shrinks, investors will see their return reduced. Another factor that can affect an investor's return is a rights offering in which the fund issues additional shares to shareholders, usually at a discount. The additional shares can have the effect of diluting earnings and perhaps increasing the discount to NAV.

A final consideration for shareholders is the amount of unrealized capital gains of the fund. If the fund is converted to an open-end fund, some of the gains may need to be realized as the fund raises cash to cover possible redemptions. These realized gains could have significant tax consequences for shareholders.

Trading Strategies

A number of strategies can be used to enhance one's opportunity for succeeding in closed-end fund investing. Generally, these strategies deal with hedging or arbitraging against a fund's discount.[3] Other opportunities occur when an open-ending, takeovers, or reorganizations of closed-end funds occur. The general approach to successfully profiting in closed-end funds is to purchase funds at large discounts and sell them once the discount has narrowed. A simple method for doing this is to track a fund's discount from its NAV over some specific time period, determine a rule of buying when the discount is at its largest average discount, and sell when the fund's discount narrows to its smallest average discount. By purchasing when the discount is excessive and selling when the discount narrows, the investor will realize enhanced returns over the fund's total return on a NAV basis.

Some of the specific closed-end fund investing techniques outlined by Herzfeld are:

1. Buying a closed-end fund selling at an excessive discount and simultaneously shorting another closed-end fund that is priced at a premium. In a falling market, the fund selling at a premium is likely to see a greater price decrease than the fund selling at a discount. In this case, the investor realizes a profit from the short sale that more than offsets the losses from the closed-end fund that was purchased.

2. An alternative to strategy one would be to buy the closed-end fund selling at an excessive discount and simultaneously short an equivalent amount of stocks in the same fund's portfolio.

3. Buying a closed-end bond fund at an excessive discount and simultaneously short U.S. Treasury bond futures or a combination of Treasury and corporate bonds. If the bond market rallies, the discount on the bond fund narrows and should become more profitable than the loss on the short position.

4. Buy a closed-end fund that is to become open-ended and is selling at a discount, and sell short the stocks in the fund's portfolio. As the fund approaches the date when it will become open-ended, the discount will narrow.

5. The Herzfeld Hedge—Buy a closed-end fund at an excessive discount and sell naked call options against the fund's portfolio positions. If the market declines, the stock will exert pressure on the premium of the option. This is likely to lead to a greater gain on the short option position than the loss on the long fund position. If the market rises, in-the-money options will

tend to lose their premiums and not rise as fast as their underlying stocks. In addition, as time passes, the option loses value.[4]

6. The Reverse Herzfeld Hedge—Sell short a closed-end fund selling at a premium and write naked put options against the fund's portfolio positions.

Rights Offerings

Rights offerings present another trading opportunity. A rights offering gives existing shareholders the opportunity to purchase additional shares that the fund is issuing. The purpose of a rights offering is to give existing shareholders an opportunity to maintain their percentage stake in the fund. Rights offerings also can be a less expensive way for funds to raise money. The major advantage to shareholders is that investors get to purchase shares at a substantial discount. Although this may seem like a good deal for shareholders, rights offerings can lead to a dilution in NAV, a fall in share price, and a widening of the discount to NAV.

Open Ending

One situation that offers investors an opportunity to reap additional profits is the open-ending of a closed-end fund. In an open-ending, the closed-end fund converts to an open-end mutual fund, one that now stands ready to redeem shares from shareholders. Open-ending through a takeover or reorganization may occur because shareholders or management become unhappy with the fund's excessive and persistent discount to NAV. Open-ending the fund allows investors to realize a gain as the discount disappears. By definition, an open-end fund must trade at its NAV.

The likelihood of open-ending depends on a number of factors.[5] First, the size of the discount from NAV will be important in determining whether shareholders will attempt to force management into open-ending the fund. Large and persistent discounts from the fund's NAV may encourage shareholders or an outsider to force management to open-end the fund. A second factor that must be considered is the liquidity of the assets held by the fund. If the fund holds illiquid, privately placed securities, then the probability of open-ending diminishes. Illiquid securities make it difficult for the fund to sell securities in order to meet shareholder redemptions. Finally, provisions in the fund's charter as well as state regulations can make it more difficult for certain funds to be converted to an open-end fund. Many of the charter provisions are similar to antitakeover provisions used by other types of corporations. Some of these provisions include super majority voting and poison pills.

Summary

Closed-end investment companies offer both small and large investors many of the same investment opportunities as mutual funds plus a number of advantages. The advantages include the use of limit orders and short sale opportunities. In addition, a number of trading strategies unique to closed-end funds give investors expanded profit opportunities. Finally, a specific type of closed-end investment company—REITs—allow small investors to add real estate investments to their portfolios, a strategy that can improve diversification and serve as a hedge against inflation.

Selected Bibliography

Block, R. L. *Investing in REITs.* Princeton, N.J.: Bloomberg Press, 1998.

Brueggerman, W. B., and J. D. Fisher, eds. *Real Estate Finance and Investments,* 10th ed. New York: McGraw-Hill, 1997.

Fredman, A. J. "What You Need to Know About Investing in Closed-End Funds." *AAII Journal* (January 2000): 2–8.

Gitman, L. J., and M. D. Joehnk. *Fundamentals of Investing,* 7th ed. Reading, Mass.: Addison-Wesley, 1999.

Herzfeld, T. J. *The Encyclopedia of Closed-End Funds,* 1997/1998 ed. Miami: Thomas J. Herzfeld Advisors, Inc., 1997.

Notes

1. NAV = total net assets ÷ total number of shares.
2. Information on closed-end funds can be found at the Internet Closed-End Fund Investor: www.icefi.com.
3. For a detailed discussion, see chapters 9 and 10 of *The Encyclopedia of Closed-End Funds.*
4. The loss in an option's value as time passes is referred to as time decay.
5. A complete discussion of the point system used by Thomas J. Herzfeld Advisors, Inc. can be found in T. J. Herzfeld, *The Encyclopedia of Closed-End Funds.* (Miami: Thomas J. Herzfeld Advisors, 1997/1998 edition).

14

Futures

The futures market offers investment professionals a number of investment opportunities, from reducing or eliminating risk to speculating on price movements in the spot or cash market to adjusting the composition of a portfolio.

Types of Futures Contracts

Futures or forward contracts represent agreements to take or make delivery of some commodity at a later date. The difference between forward and futures contracts is that futures are standardized so that size, delivery procedures, expiration dates, and other terms are the same for all contracts. This standardization allows futures to be traded on exchanges, which provides liquidity to market participants. Forward contracts, on the other hand, represent privately negotiated contracts between two parties. This allows the contract to be tailored to meet the needs of both parties. Forward contracts have several disadvantages compared to futures contracts. First, forward contracts lack liquidity, which can make it difficult to establish a position or close out a position, should the need arise. Second, there is always *counterparty risk*—the risk that one party will default.

Futures have a number of useful applications. First, they can be used to hedge risk in the spot or cash market. By taking a position opposite to that position held in the spot market, it is possible to reduce or even eliminate risk. Second, because futures are essentially costless, they can be used to speculate on the future price of a commodity. Third, because the futures contract is based on delivery of some asset or commodity in the spot market, there should be a relationship between the two prices. If these prices get out of line, an opportunity to arbitrage the difference between the two prices will exist. When the spot and futures contracts are based on some stock market index, we refer to this opportunity as index arbitrage. Fourth, futures contracts can be used to minimize the cash drag a portfolio experiences by holding excess cash. Finally, futures can be used to adjust the risk of a portfolio.

Specification of the Futures Contract

Because a futures contract calls for delivery of some commodity, contracts are very specific regarding the quality and grade of the commodity to be delivered. For example, the random length lumber futures contract, which trades on the Chicago Mercantile Exchange, requires that the lumber be grade stamped construction and standard, standard and better, or #1 or #2 two-by-fours of random lengths from eight feet to twenty feet. In addition, the delivery location is also specified. In many instances, there are several alternative delivery locations. When alternative delivery locations are used, the price received by seller of the futures contract may be adjusted depending on the location chosen.

Reading Newspaper Quotes

The *Wall Street Journal* and other business periodicals provide price quotations daily on the various futures contracts. Quotes are provided for each commodity and are grouped together by commodity group. Table 14-1 presents the futures quote for oats for February 15, 2000.

The first row of the table lists the commodity, the exchange the commodity is traded on, the size of a contract, and how prices are quoted. For example, the oats contract trades on the Chicago Board of Trade (CBOT), has a standard contract size of 5,000 bushels and is quoted in cents per bushel. For each contract, the following information is also provided:

- *Open*—opening price for the day.
- *High*—the highest price the contract traded for during the day.
- *Low*—the lowest price the contract traded for during the day.

Table 14-1. Futures quote for oats, February 15, 2000.

OATS (CBT) 5,000 bu.; cents perbu.

	Open	High	Low	Settle	Change	Lifetime High	Lifetime Low	Open Interest
Mar	109 1/2	110 1/4	109 1/4	109 1/4	+ 1/4	135	107	4,336
May	116 1/4	117	115 1/2	116	+ 1/2	133	112 1/4	5,551
July	115 1/4	115 3/4	114 3/4	114 3/4	+ 1/2	124 1/4	110 1/2	4,384
Sept	119	119	119	119	+ 1	130	115 3/4	877
Dec	126 1/4	126 1/2	126 1/2	126 1/2	+ 1	135	123	2,391

- *Settle*—the settlement price, which is the price used to calculate the daily gains and losses for the day. It is usually the average of the last few prices traded at the end of the day.

- *Change*—the change in the settlement price from the previous day.

- *Lifetime high and low*—the highest and lowest futures price achieved in trading over the contract's lifetime.

- *Open interest*—the number of contracts outstanding. It is the number of positions that have not been closed out. Because of the difficulty in determining open interest, the information is one trading day older than the other information provided in the quotes.

Basis

Basis is an important concept in understanding the pricing and risk of using futures contracts. Basis is the current cash or spot market price of the commodity minus the price of the futures contract on that commodity.

$$\text{Basis} = \text{Current Cash Price} - \text{Futures Price}$$

The basis can be either positive or negative. When the basis is positive, prices in the cash market are higher than the futures prices. When the basis is negative, prices in the cash market are lower than the futures prices. During the life of a futures contract, the basis will change. As the contract gets closer to expiration, the basis becomes smaller. At expiration, the basis of a contract will be zero because the futures price at expiration must equal the spot or cash market price.

Although the basis of a contract will equal zero at expiration, it can fluctuate during the life of the contract. The basis of a contract can widen or narrow, thus affecting the effectiveness of a hedge. This type of risk is referred to as *basis risk*.

Futures Pricing

The value of a futures contract is determined by the underlying commodity and the principle of arbitrage. Arbitrage occurs when it is possible for investors to earn a guaranteed profit without using any of their own money. This opportunity arises when the relationship between cash and futures prices gets out of line. In principle, the value of a futures contract should be equal to the current cash market price plus any cost of carrying the commodity. These costs include interest, storage, and insurance costs. When the prices of the two markets get out of line, arbitrageurs will drive the prices back to their equilibrium state by purchasing in the market where the price is too low and simultaneously selling in the market where the price is too high. For example, suppose the price of gold in the spot market is $300 per ounce. If the interest rate is 5 percent per year, then the futures price for a contract that expires in one year should be $315 ($300 × 1.05). If the futures price is less than $315—for example, $310—then the futures price is too low relative to the cash market price. To earn an arbitrage profit, an investor would buy the futures contract at $310 and sell short gold in the spot market for $300. The money from the short sale would be invested at the 5 percent interest rate. At the end of the period, the investor will have $315 in the bank but will need only $310 to settle the futures contract. The gold will then be used to close out the short position. In this case, the investor will earn a guaranteed $5 without investing any money. This is an arbitrage profit. A similar result will occur if the futures price is too high relative to the cash market price.

Listing of Futures Contracts

Four basic categories of futures contracts can be traded. The underlying asset or commodity can be a physical commodity, a foreign currency, an interest-earning asset, or an index.

The exchanges determine what contracts to offer based on the likely demand. Whenever a commodity is sufficiently active in the cash market and it is determined that enough individuals or institutions could benefit from a futures contract in that commodity, an exchange may decide to introduce a new contract.

Regulations

Regulation of the futures markets is designed to create fair and efficient pricing, trading integrity, and financial soundness. The Commodity Futures Trading Commission (CFTC)—the federal regulatory agency that oversees trading in commodities futures—has a number of specific powers. First it has approval of new contracts. To receive approval, the contract must show that it contains a useful economic purpose such as making hedging possible. The CFTC also regulates trading rules including daily permitted maximum price fluctuations, minimum price fluctuation limits, and certain features of the delivery process. In order to prevent speculators from having undue influence on the market, exchanges also impose limits on the size of a position that can be taken by an individual or institution. For example, the random length lumber contract traded on the Chicago Mercantile Exchange imposes a position limit of 1,000 contracts, with no more than 300 in any one delivery month. These limits are waived for bona fide hedgers.

In addition to the CFTC, regulation also takes place at the broker level, by futures exchanges and clearinghouses, and by the National Futures Association (NFA). Brokers, because of their close relationships with customers, may be able to identify violations of position limits. Brokers are responsible for knowing the customer's positions and intentions and to ensure that the customer does not place the system in jeopardy. Futures exchanges and clearinghouses are required to control the conduct of exchange and clearing members. Finally, the NFA screens applicants for registration and reviews personal background information before allowing individuals to register as futures professionals.

Trading Futures Contracts

The standardization of futures contracts makes it possible for them to be traded on the open market. Unlike forward contracts, which are negotiated in the over-the-counter market, futures can be purchased and sold on exchanges such as the Chicago Board of Trade and the Chicago Mercantile Exchange.

According to federal law, and the rules of the exchange, trading can take place only during trading hours in a designated trading location known as the *pit.* The pit is an actual physical location where futures contracts trade by a system of *open outcry,* in which traders make their offer to buy or sell available to all other traders in the pit. Traders also use a system of hand signals to express their desire to buy or sell.[1] However, all offers to buy or sell must be made through open outcry.

A market participant can either buy or sell a futures contract. When the contract is purchased, the purchaser agrees to take delivery of the commodity at the agreed-upon price. The purchase of a futures contract is referred to as a *long futures position,* and it will be profitable if the price of the commodity rises. When the futures contract is sold, the seller agrees to make delivery of the commodity at the agreed-upon price. The sale of a futures contract is referred to as a *short futures position,* and it will be profitable when the price of the commodity falls.

The Chicago Board of Trade (CBOT) offers a system of "electronic open outcry,"[2] a paperless trading floor environment that allows firms to manage customer business from both off-floor and on-floor locations. The system begins with an electronic order ticket that allows new information such as price and the opposing broker to be added to the ticket. This ticket is routed directly to the floor of the exchange from a customer using an Internet connection, from an off-floor futures commission merchant (FCM) member firm staffperson using an order entry/management system, or from FCM trading floor staff using an order entry device to enter orders or to confirm flashed/headset-entered orders. In 1999, more than 2.1 million orders were electronically received by CBOT floor brokers.

Clearing and Settlement

In order to smooth trading and settlement, each futures exchange uses a clearinghouse. The clearinghouse guarantees both sides of the transaction by acting as a middleman between trades. Therefore, all buy orders are essentially purchased from the clearinghouse, and all sell orders are essentially sold to the clearinghouse.

Margin Requirements and Daily Settlement

Although futures contracts are essentially costless, a good-faith deposit known as *margin* is required. Margin requirements vary from contract to contract and may vary by broker. Margin can be posted in cash, a bank letter of credit, or in a short-term U.S. Treasury security.

There are three types of margin that traders must be concerned with. *Initial margin* is the amount a trader must deposit before trading any contracts. In many cases, the initial margin is 5 percent or less of the underlying commodity's value. Although 5 percent seems rather small, a system of *daily settlement* or *marking-to-market* is used, which means that traders are required to realize any losses in cash on the day they occur. When the equity in a trader's account falls below the *maintenance margin* level, the trader receives a *margin call*, which requires additional funds to be placed into the account. The amount that needs to be deposited is known as *variation margin* and must be sufficient to raise the account balance to the initial margin level. Example 14-1 presents an illustration of the marking-to-market procedure.

Closing a Position

A trader can close out a futures position via four methods: delivery, cash settlement, offset, and an exchange of physicals. Many futures contracts call for the *delivery* of some commodity, which entails completion of the futures contract by the physical delivery of the specified commodity. In recent years, the exchanges have introduced contracts that allow for *cash settlement*, whereby traders make payments to settle any differences in losses or gains. In general,

Example 14.1. Marking-to-market.

Suppose on Wednesday, September 1, 1999, an investor wishes to buy one December 1999 gold futures contract on the New York Commodity Exchange (COMEX). The contract is for 100 ounces of gold. Let's assume that the current price of gold is $300 per ounce and that the initial margin requirement is $2,000. Also, let's assume that the maintenance margin is $1,500. Finally, assume that the investor closes out his or her position on Wednesday, September 8, 1999.

Date	Settlement price	Daily gain (loss)	Other entries	Account balance	Explanation
September 1	$399	(100)	+2,000	$1,900	Initial margin of $2,000, but price fell by $1 so the investor loses $100.
September 2	$401	200		$2,100	Price rises by $2 so investor makes $200.
September 3	$394	(700)		$1,400	Price falls by $7 and investor loses $700.
September 6	$397	300	+600	$2,300	$600 deposited to meet margin call because balance fell below $1,500 maintenance margin level. Price rose $3 and investor made $300.
September 7	$395	(200)		$2,100	Price falls by $2 and investor loses $200.
September 8	$396	100	(2,200)	$ 0	Sold contract for $396 and received $2,200

physical delivery and cash settlement are rarely used to close out a futures position.

The most common method for closing out a futures position is *offset* or a *reversing trade*. In offset, traders simply engage in the opposite position they hold, thus creating a net position of zero. For example, a trader who owns one September wheat contract can close the position by selling one September wheat contract. Example 14-2 illustrates how a trade is reversed.

The final method traders can use to close an account is through an exchange for physicals. In an exchange for physicals, two traders agree to a simultaneous exchange of a cash commodity and futures contracts based on that cash commodity. Example 14-3 illustrates exchange for physicals.

Example 14-2. Reversing trade.

Suppose on October 1, investor A sells one December corn contract at 213 cents per bushel. By selling the contract, investor A is obliged to deliver 5,000 bushels of corn to the clearinghouse in December and will receive 213 cents per bushel. If investor A does not wish to deliver the corn and would like close out the position on October 15, he or she can close out the position by purchasing a December corn contract. This is a reversing trade and is illustrated in the table below.

Date	Investor A's initial position	Investor B
October 1	Sells one December corn contract for 213 cents per bushel.	Buys one December corn contract for 213 cents per bushel.
	Investor A's reversing trade	**Investor C**
October 15	Buys one December corn contract for 205 cents per bushel.	Sells one December corn contract for 205 cents per bushel.

Notice that investor A may close out his or her position by buying a contract from a different investor than the one who bought the original contract. After the reversing trade, investor A's net position is zero.

Example 14-3. Exchange-for-physicals.

Let's consider investors A and B from Example 14-2. Investor A has sold a corn futures contract and wishes to deliver the corn. Investor B has purchased a corn futures contract and wishes to take delivery of the corn. The transaction can take place as an exchange-of-physicals and is presented in the table below.

Investor A	Investor B
Short one corn futures. Owns the corn and wishes to sell.	Long one corn futures. Wants to acquire the actual corn.
Agrees with investor B to sell the corn and cancel the corn futures. Delivers the corn and receives payment from investor B.	Agrees with investor A to buy the corn and cancel the corn futures. Receives the corn and pays investor A.
Reports the exchange-for-physicals to the exchange. The exchange adjusts the books to show investor A is out of the market.	Reports the exchange-for-physicals to the exchange. The exchange adjusts the books to show investor B is out of the market.

Delivery

Although most futures contracts are closed out, the party with the short position may choose to deliver the commodity. If this is the case, this investor must have his or her broker issue a *notice of intention to deliver* to the exchange clearinghouse. The notice will specify how many contracts will be delivered, where delivery will be made, and what grade will be delivered in the case of commodities. The exchange will then use some predetermined method for selecting the long futures party to receive delivery. If the notices are transferable, the long party has a period of time, such as half an hour, to find another long party that is willing to take delivery. When a party takes delivery, the proverbial delivery of hog bellies on the long party's front lawn does not occur. Rather, the long party receives a warehouse receipt in return for payment. The party taking delivery is then responsible for all warehousing costs. For parties that maintain a position in the futures contract, there are three important days they must consider:

■ First notice day—the first day that a notice of intention to make delivery can be submitted to the exchange.

■ Last notice day—similarly, the last day to notify the exchange about the intention to make delivery.

■ Last trading day—is usually a few days before the last notice day.

Parties that are long a futures contract and do not wish to take delivery should close out their positions prior to the first notice day.

Accounting and Taxation

Accounting and tax treatment of futures contracts can be quite complicated, and a complete discussion is beyond the scope of this book. However, FASB Statement No. 80, Accounting for Futures Contracts, established accounting standards in the United States for all futures contracts other than foreign currency futures, which are covered by FASB Statement No. 52, Foreign Currency Translation. Both statements require that changes in market value be recognized when they occur unless the contract position qualifies as a hedge. When the position is not used as a hedge, gains or losses will be recognized in the year they occurred, even if the contract has not been closed out. For example, if an investor takes a speculative position in September 2000 for a March 2001 contract and closes out the position in March 2000, any gains or losses at the end of December 2000 will be recognized and reported on the investor's 2000 taxes. The remaining gains or losses from December 2000 to

March 2001 will be recognized on the 2001 tax return. However, if the same investor uses this same contract as a hedge, all gains or losses would be recognized in March 2001 and reported on the 2001 tax return.

Hedging, Speculation, and Arbitrage

Three types of positions can be taken in futures contracts: hedging, speculation, and arbitrage. Hedgers are concerned with reducing or eliminating risk. Speculators are interested in profiting from movements in the price of the futures contract. Finally, arbitrageurs attempt to profit from price discrepancies in the cash and futures markets.

Hedging

Hedging entails the reduction of risk by taking an opposite position in the futures market from the trader's cash market position. For example, a farmer who owns wheat (long) would like to protect himself from a decline in the price of wheat. By taking a short position in wheat futures, the farmer can reduce the risk associated with a fall in the price of wheat. If the price of wheat falls, the farmer will sell his wheat for less in the cash market but will profit from the wheat futures position. Similarly, a bread manufacturer would like to be protected from an increase in the price of wheat. To protect itself from rising wheat prices, the manufacturer would buy wheat futures. If the price of wheat rises, the value of the futures contract will also rise, thus leading to a gain on the futures position. This gain will offset some or all of the additional cost of purchasing the wheat.

Hedge Ratio

Because futures contracts are standardized in terms of size, it is necessary to determine the number of contracts needed to hedge a position in the spot market, or the *hedge ratio*. Several types of hedge ratios can be produced depending on the type of risk that the hedger is concerned with. However, the following factors are usually important determinants of the hedge ratio:

1. Size of the spot or cash market position.

2. Size of the futures contract.

3. Sensitivity of spot price and futures price relative to some external factor such as changes in the interest rate.

The first two factors are quite obvious. The larger the size of the spot market position relative to the size of the futures contract, the greater the number of contracts necessary to hedge the risk. The third factor adjusts the number of contracts for the different sensitivities of spot prices and futures prices. For example, suppose an investor wishes to hedge the purchase of 180-day T-bills with a 90-day T-bill futures contract. Because of the difference in maturities (duration), the price of 180-day T-bills is twice as sensitive to a change in interest rates as the futures contract. In this case, approximately twice as many futures contracts must be used to hedge the risk. As another example, suppose a portfolio manager wishes to hedge the adverse effect of a stock market correction. The manager can hedge by using an S&P 500 stock index futures contract. However, if the volatility of the portfolio is different from the S&P 500 index, then the number of contracts used for the hedge must be adjusted. If the portfolio is more volatile than the S&P 500 index, then the number of contracts used to hedge the risk will need to be adjusted upward. If the portfolio is less volatile than the S&P 500 index, then the number of contracts used to hedge the risk will need to be adjusted downward.

Rolling the Hedge Forward

When an individual or institution wishes to hedge for an extended period of time, a contract of sufficient duration may not exist. In this case, the hedger can use a series of futures contracts to hedge the risk, a strategy known as *rolling the hedge forward*. For example, an energy supplier concerned about an increase in the price of oil, to hedge the risk, would take a long position in the futures contract. If the firm is unable to find a contract of sufficient duration, it can roll the hedge forward by purchasing a futures contract at time t. In the next period, time $t+1$, the first contract would be closed out, and a long position in a contract expiring at a later date would be purchased. The firm would continue this procedure for the entire hedge period.

Cross-hedging

Despite the many traded futures contracts, there are numerous commodities and financial assets that an individual or institution may wish to hedge for which no futures contract exists. In this case, a *cross-hedge* can be constructed by using a traded futures contract that is highly correlated with the cash market commodity. For example, if a company wishes to hedge a commercial paper issue, it can use another short-term interest rate contract such as a Treasury bill or Eurodollar futures contract to hedge the risk.

Speculation

Speculators differ from hedgers because they attempt to earn profits by assuming the risks of holding only the futures contract. Speculators profit when prices move in the direction they predicted. Futures can be an extremely useful tool for speculation because of the low costs (only a small margin requirement) and the ease of entering and exiting the market. For example, speculators profit from a long position in a futures contract if prices rise, and they profit from a short position if prices fall. Speculators are an important part of the system because they often assume the other half of the transaction needed by hedgers.

Speculators fall into one of three categories based on the length of time they hold their position. *Scalpers* have the shortest time horizon over which they are planning to hold the futures contracts. Generally, scalpers try to get a feel for the trading among other market participants and may hold their positions for a few seconds or a few minutes. Scalpers can be useful to the market because their constant trading provides liquidity to the market. *Day traders* take a much longer view of the market than scalpers and try to profit from price movements that take place over the course of a trading day. Generally, day traders get their name because they do not hold their positions overnight. *Position traders* have the longest time horizon of the three, holding their positions for weeks or even months. Two types of position traders include those who hold spread positions and those who hold outright positions. Of the two, spread position traders are the more risk averse because they hold positions in two or more contracts. An intracommodity spread involves using two or more contract maturities for the same underlying commodity. The spread is created by purchasing one contract and selling another. A trader that uses an outright position uses only one futures contract and makes a bet on the price direction of that contract. If the trader is correct, then she will profit from such a position. However, if she is wrong, losses can be significant because there is no other offsetting position.

Arbitrage

The final type of player in the futures market is the arbitrageur. Arbitrageurs attempt to profit by finding mispricings between the cash and futures markets. If the futures price is too high relative to the cash market price, then arbitrageurs will sell futures and buy in the cash market. If the futures price is too low relative to the cash market price, arbitrageurs will buy the futures and sell in the cash market.

A popular arbitrage strategy—index arbitrage—compares the futures price of some stock market index, such as the S&P 500, with the cash market value of the index. In many instances, the arbitrageur uses only a subset of the index to arbitrage the trade. For example, a computer model may find that comparing the pricing of 300 of the stocks in the index with the S&P 500 stock index futures contract is sufficient to determine price discrepancies. By trading only 300 stocks, the arbitrageur reduces transactions costs and speeds the transactions process.

Applications of Futures Contracts

Futures have a number of interesting applications beyond hedging, speculation, and arbitrage. For portfolio managers, most of these strategies entail using futures contracts to adjust the stock/cash mix of the portfolio. This allows managers to adjust the risk of the portfolio, exploit movements in the market, and even adjust the average size of the assets held in the portfolio.

Dynamic Asset Allocation (Portfolio Insurance)

Dynamic asset allocation or portfolio insurance is a technique that seeks to limit the downside risk of a portfolio while still maintaining its upside potential. In essence, portfolio insurance seeks to create a *synthetic call option* by using futures contracts to adjust the stock and cash mix of the portfolio.

Portfolio insurance was the brainchild of Hayne Leland, a professor at the University of California.[3] He wondered whether the financial community would be interested in a product that would protect a portfolio on the downside, but still allow the portfolio to benefit should the market rise. Leland realized that the insurance represented an option, and, because he was not an expert in option theory, he enlisted the help of his colleague, Mark Rubinstein. Together, they found a way to replicate the option payoff strategy by adjusting the composition of a portfolio's stock and cash mix.[4]

Portfolio insurance involves setting a floor below which the value of assets should not fall. When the total value of assets is very close to this floor, the portfolio may consist entirely of cash. As stock prices rise and the value of the portfolio moves away from the floor value, the percentage of the portfolio devoted to stocks is increased. By adjusting this stock/cash mix, Leland and Rubinstein found that they were able to create a payoff that was similar to a call option.

One problem with portfolio insurance is that it requires a continual adjustment of the stock/cash mix. Selling stocks to raise cash is an expensive and time-consuming task. In addition, most fund managers dislike the idea of deciding which stocks to sell. However, the advent of stock index futures became the solution to the problem. Shorting futures provides the equivalent of selling stocks, whereas buying futures provides the equivalent of buying stocks. The liquidity of the futures market enables investors to quickly adjust the stock/cash mix of the portfolio while incurring only minimal transactions costs.

Using Futures to Reduce Cash Drag

In a rising market, any assets held in the form of cash will reduce the performance of a fund. This reduction in performance, referred to as *cash drag*, can occur because of a large inflow of money that the manager has not had a chance to invest or because a manager cannot find any suitable stocks to purchase. How significant is cash drag? If the market is returning 15 percent on equity and returns on money market instruments are 6 percent, then a modest 5 percent cash holding will reduce returns by 9% × 0.05 or 45 basis points of underperformance.

Money managers can reduce cash drag by using index futures to increase the fund's equity exposure. The use of index futures, such as the S&P 500 futures contract, offers a number of benefits. First, unlike the selection of individual stocks, futures contracts can be purchased quickly because no stock selection needs to be made. Second, futures are inexpensive because only a small margin requirement is required. Third, positions can be unwound rapidly if the manager finds suitable securities to add to the portfolio. Through the use of futures, a money manager can quickly invest new inflows of money into the fund until suitable securities can be determined. Equity exposure is increased by purchasing stock index futures.

Using Futures to Adjust the Risk of a Portfolio

An interesting application of stock index futures is that they can be used to adjust the risk of a portfolio. A fund manager who believes that the market will rise may wish to increase the systematic risk of the portfolio by either using any cash holdings to purchase additional equities or changing the composition of the portfolio to hold more risky stocks. Similarly, a fund manager who expects the market to fall would decrease the systematic risk of the portfolio by either selling stocks and holding a greater proportion of the fund in cash or changing the composition of the portfolio to hold less risky stocks.

One problem with purchasing or selling securities to adjust the risk of a portfolio is that a decision needs to be made regarding which securities to sell or purchase. This can be a time-consuming task and can be costly in terms of transactions costs. In addition, increasing portfolio turnover can increase the fund's realized capital gains, which can have significant tax consequences for shareholders of the fund. A simpler approach is simply to use stock index futures to adjust the systematic risk.[5] By purchasing stock index futures, fund managers can increase the risk of the portfolio, and selling stock index futures can reduce the systematic risk. This method can be implemented quickly and without changing the overall composition of the portfolio.

Transporting Alphas

Alpha refers to a manager's ability to earn an excess return on a risk-adjusted basis, which is sometimes known as security selection.[6] One problem with security selection is that it may impact a portfolio's desired asset allocation. For example, if a pension fund manager prefers to be invested in large-cap stocks but finds an exceptional small-cap manager, how can the fund maintain a large-cap allocation while taking advantage of the small-cap manager's positive alpha? The pension fund manager can purchase the fund of the small-cap manager and simultaneously take a short position in the Russell 2000 Index, which is an index of small-cap stocks.[7] By using the futures, the portfolio has maintained a neutral position in small-cap stocks, while still benefiting from the small-cap manager's ability to select superior stocks.

Adjusting the Capitalization of the Portfolio

Futures can be used to adjust the portfolio toward a different market capitalization without the expense of buying and selling the securities in the portfolio. Suppose a fund manager runs a large-cap equity fund, but believes that midcap stocks will outperform large-cap stocks over the next six months. The manager can tilt the portfolio toward a smaller market capitalization by purchasing S&P MidCap 400 index futures and selling S&P 500 index futures. This is equivalent to selling large-cap stocks and using the proceeds to purchase midcap stocks. Similarly, a manager could shift a midcap fund toward larger-cap stocks by selling the S&P MidCap 400 index futures and purchasing the S&P 500 index futures.

Using Futures to Defer Taxes

Futures contracts can be used to cash out a position in the cash market while not actually realizing any capital gains, an approach that allows investors to defer possible capital gains taxes. For example, suppose an investor has a stock portfolio with significant capital gains and plans to liquidate the portfolio in order to finance a new business venture. This investor is concerned that the market is too high and that a correction may take place before she begins her new business. If it is currently November 2000 and the funds for the new business are not needed until February 2001, selling the stocks today will force the investor to realize the capital gains and pay taxes in April 2001. If she can defer the sale of the stocks until 2001, she will not have to pay the capital gains tax until April 2002. By selling a futures contract, the investor essentially cashes out her stock position without realizing the capital gains, which allows the capital gains tax to be deferred for an additional year.

Using Globex to Predict the NYSE Opening

The Globex is an electronic market that opens thirty minutes after the 4:15 P.M. close of the Chicago Mercantile Exchange and remains open until fifteen minutes prior to the opening of the New York Stock Exchange. Many market watchers use the Globex S&P futures to predict the opening of the S&P 500 index. If the Globex futures are trading above the fair market value of the S&P 500's previous day close, then the market is likely to open strong. If the Globex futures are trading below the previous day's fair market value, then the market is likely to open weak.

Adjusting Treasury Bill Maturities

Futures contracts on T-bills can be used to adjust the maturity of T-bills. An investor who wishes to shorten the maturity of a 180-day T-bill to 90 days can sell a T-bill futures contract that expires in 90 days. This will force the investor to deliver the T-bills when the contract expires, thus shortening the maturity to 90 days. Likewise, an investor can lengthen the maturity of a T-bill by entering into a contract to purchase T-bill futures that expire when the T-bill matures. In this case, the investor rolls over the T-bill investment into another T-bill upon maturity of the first bill. This rollover, in essence, extends the maturity of the T-bill.

Summary

Futures markets serve an important function to society and can be a useful tool for investment professionals. Futures contracts allow individuals and institutions that have positions in the cash market to hedge those risks from adverse price fluctuations. Farmers, corporations, and investors can use futures to reduce or eliminate risks without liquidating their cash market positions. Futures also allow portfolio managers to adjust the risks and asset allocation of a portfolio.

Selected Bibliography

Hill, J. M. and R. K. Cheong. "Minimizing Cash Drag with S&P 500 Index Tools." *Equity Derivatives Research*. New York: Goldman Sachs, 1996.

Kolb, R. W. *Futures, Options and Swaps*. Blackwood, N.J. Blackwell Publishers, 1997.

Luskin, D. L. *Portfolio Insurance: A Guide to Dynamic Hedging*. New York: John Wiley, 1988.

Notes

1. A primer on hand signals can be found on the CME Web site at http://www.cme.com/educational/hand1.htm.
2. For more information, see the CBOT Web site, www.cbot.com
3. H. E. Leland and M. Rubinstein, "The Evolution of Portfolio Insurance." In *Portfolio Insurance: A Guide to Dynamic Hedging*, ed D. L. Luskin. (New York: John Wiley, 1988), chap. 1.
4. H. E. Leland and M. Rubinstein, "Replicating Options with Positions in Stocks and Cash," *Financial Analysts Journal* 37 (July/August 1981), 63–72.
5. The total risk of an asset is composed of diversifiable (nonsystematic) risk and nondiversifiable (systematic) risk. Systematic risk for a stock or portfolio is given by the stock or portfolio's beta.
6. A complete discussion of alpha can be found in Chapter 17.
7. B. I. Jacob and K. N. Levy, "Alpha Transport with Derivatives," *Journal of Portfolio Management* 26 (May 1999), 55–60.

15

Options

Options represent a class of securities sometimes referred to as *derivative securities* because their value is derived from some other security. An option gives the holder the right but not the obligation to buy an asset in the case of a call option or sell in the case of a put option at a prespecified price during a specific time period. The price at which the security is bought or sold is known as the *exercise* or *strike price*. Because the option does not obligate the holder to transact, it provides unique payoff possibilities. When used in different combinations, options allow the creation of almost any contingent payoff imaginable. There are two fundamental types of options: the *American option* and the *European option*. An American option allows the holder to exercise the option any time up to expiration. A European option allows the holder to exercise only at expiration.

Listing of Options Contracts

The listing of options on the exchanges is determined by the exchanges and *not* by the company whose underlying stock makes up the option. In the past, companies have taken legal action to attempt to keep options on their stock from being listed on an exchange. Listing requirements may include the number of periods a firm needs to post positive earnings, the current price of the stock, and the market value of the firm. In addition to listing requirements, exchanges also maintain slightly less stringent requirements to maintain listing. Table 15-1 presents the major option exchanges.

One of the key factors that an exchange uses to determine whether a firm's stock should be listed is the demand for the options. Exchanges seek listings that will generate sufficient volume and profitability.

Reading Option Quotations

Quotes for stock options can be found in the *Wall Street Journal* and various other papers. Table 15-2 presents stock option quotations from February 17, 2000, for Amazon.com.

Table 15-1. Principal option exchanges in the United States.

Exchange	Securities Traded
Chicago Board Options Exchange (CBOE)	Options on individual stocks, options on stock indexes, options on Treasury securities
Philadelphia Stock Exchange (PHLX)	Stocks, futures, and options on individual stocks, currencies, stock indexes
American Stock Exchange (AMEX)	Stocks, options on individual stocks, options on stock indexes
Pacific Stock Exchange (PSE)	Options on individual stocks and a stock index
New York Stock Exchange (NYSE)	Stocks and options on individual stocks and a stock index
Chicago Board of Trade (CBOT)	Futures, options on futures for agricultural goods, precious metals, stock indexes, and debt instruments
Chicago Mercantile Exchange (CME)	Futures, options on futures for agricultural goods, stock indexes, debt instruments, and currencies
Coffee, Sugar and Cocoa Exchange (CSCE)	Futures and options on agricultural futures
Kansas City Board of Trade (KCBT)	Futures and options on agricultural futures
MidAmerica Commodity Exchange (MIDAM)	Futures and options for agricultural goods and precious metals
Minneapolis Grain Exchange (MGE)	Futures and options on agricultural futures
New York Cotton Exchange (NYCE)	Futures and options on agricultural, currency, and debt instrument futures
New York Futures Exchange (NYFE)	Futures and options on stock indexes
New York Mercantile Exchange (NYME)	Futures and options on energy futures

Source: Adapted from Kolb, 319.

■ The first row of the first column shows the ticker symbol for the company's stock. The remaining rows in the first column list the close price for the stock from the previous day. Because the close price for the stock is the same for all options listed, the price is the same in each row.

■ The second column shows the exercise prices for the different options.

Table 15-2. Option quotations for Amazon.com on February 17, 2000.

Options	Strike	Expires	Call Volume	Call Last	Put Volume	Put Last
AMZN	70	Feb	171	$5\,1/2$	1455	$3/4$
$74\,7/16$	70	Mar	67	$9\,7/8$	483	$4\,5/8$
$74\,7/16$	75	Feb	628	$2\,5/16$	1094	$2\,1/2$
$74\,7/16$	75	Mar	350	$7\,1/8$	165	7
$74\,7/16$	80	Feb	684	$3/4$	388	$5\,7/8$
$74\,7/16$	80	Mar	349	$5\,1/4$	72	10
$74\,7/16$	85	Feb	490	$1/4$	61	10
$74\,7/16$	90	Feb	297	$1/8$	130	$15\,1/2$
$74\,7/16$	100	Feb	464	$1/16$	22	$25\,7/8$

Source: Wall Street Journal, February 17, 2000.

- The third column displays the expiration months for the different options.
- The fourth column shows the volume for the call option given in the appropriate row.
- The fifth column shows the price or premium for the given call option.
- The sixth and seventh columns display the volume and premium for the given put options.

Regulations

Regulation of the options markets is meant to ensure a fair and orderly marketplace. Like other securities, the Chicago Board Options Exchange (CBOE) and the Options Clearing Corporation (OCC) are under the jurisdiction of the SEC and are obliged to follow federal securities laws and regulations.

One of the major issues in regulating the options markets is the protection of investors.[1] The Options Clearing Corporation is supported by a three-tier safeguard system. First, the OCC sets stringent standards regarding the qualifications for membership. The second line of defense against defaults by clearing members is member margin deposits. The final line of defense is member contributions to the clearing fund.

Two additional types of regulation of options markets are *position limits* and *exercise limits*. Position limits limit the number of contracts an investor can hold. Exercise limits determine the number of contracts that can be exercised by any individual or group of individuals in any five consecutive business days. Limits for equity options are determined by the volume and number of shares outstanding of the underlying equity issue. The position limits are also determined by the position taken by the trader. A trader who holds options for hedging purposes is allowed to hold more contracts than a trader who holds options for speculative purposes.

Furthermore, under Regulation T and NYSE rules, a firm cannot lend money on an option position because, when the option expires, the loan will be unsecured. Therefore, options must be paid in full. Option margin, therefore, exists to protect the firm from possible risks that the investor will not be able to meet an obligation under the terms of the option. Unlike positions in stocks or bonds, options represent an intent to buy or sell rather than actual ownership. Therefore, depending on the circumstances, margin requirements may or may not be necessary. Option margin represents protection to the firm. If there is no risk to the firm, then there is no need for margin. For example, an investor who buys a call option has the right, but not an obligation, to purchase shares of the asset at the exercise price. This right does not pose any risk to the firm; therefore, no margin is required. However, an investor who writes a call option must deliver shares of stock at the exercise price at the discretion of the option holder. Because this position does present a risk to the firm that the writer may not be able to deliver, margin is required.

Trading Options

There are three types of traders on the floor of an exchange:

- Market makers—typically own or lease a seat on the options exchange and trade for their own accounts. Market makers have an obligation to make a market for the option by standing ready to buy and sell options.

- Floor brokers—execute the order on the floor of the exchange. Their job is to ensure the best price and execute the trade rapidly. Floor brokers typically represent brokerage houses and usually work for a salary or receive commissions.

- Order book officials—employees of the exchange who can also trade, but not for their own accounts. Order book officials facilitate the flow of orders and disclose the best limit orders awaiting execution.

Types of Orders

Positions can be either buy or sell orders and can be used to open a position or close a position. Thus, there are four possible categories of transactions:

1. Open a position with a purchase

2. Open a position with a sale

3. Close a position with a purchase

4. Close a position with a sale

In an opening position transaction, investors buy option contracts that were not written previously. This transaction increases the number of options outstanding, which is referred to as *open interest*. In the case of a closing position transaction, investors take a position opposite to the one they hold. An investor who has written the option will buy an identical option. An investor who has purchased an option will sell or write an identical option. A closing position transaction has the effect of canceling the investor's position and thus reduces open interest.

Once investors decide what position in an option to take, they can place either a *market order* or a *limit order*. A market order instructs the broker to execute the trade immediately at the best available price. A limit order instructs the broker to fill the order only if it can be transacted at a specified price or better.

An Example of the Trading Process

To illustrate the trading process, let's assume that an investor wishes to purchase ten call options on Microsoft stock. First, the investor decides on the exercise price, the expiration date, and possibly the maximum price he or she is willing to pay. The investor might instruct his or her broker to purchase ten MSFT/SEP/95 calls at an opening transaction of $8^1/_2$ or better to be *good-until-cancelled*. The limit order of $8^1/_2$ and the good-until-cancelled is just one of a number of different orders that the investor could use. The investor could have instructed the broker to buy at the market and not specify the limit price of $8^1/_2$. In addition, the investor could have specified for how long the limit order was in effect. For example, a *day order* would be cancelled at the end of the day if the limit price was not reached.

Options Clearing Corporation

Playing a central role in the success of the option exchanges, the clearing-house is a financial institution associated with the option exchange that guarantees the integrity of all trades. That is, market participants need not worry about being paired off with a counterparty that might default on the other end of the transaction. This greatly reduces the costs of transacting for buyers and sellers of options, because they do not need to evaluate the creditworthiness of the counterparty.

The clearinghouse, the *Options Clearing Corporation*, first attempts to match all trades at the end of the day. For each transaction such as a buy, there should be a matching sell order. The clearinghouse tries to match the paperwork from both sides of the transactions. If the two records agree, the trade is said to be a *matched trade*. The process of matching trades and tracking payments is called *clearing*. If the records of the two sides do not agree, the trade is said to be an *outtrade*, and the two sides and the exchange work to resolve the discrepancy.

Basic Options Strategies

There are four basic strategies available to options traders:

1. Buy a call option
2. Sell a call option
3. Buy a put option
4. Sell a put option

By combining these four basic positions with each other or with the purchase or sale of the underlying security, traders can create almost any conceivable payoff strategy. Aside from the four basic strategies listed above, investors can also take a long position (buy) in the stock or take a short position (sell) in the stock. Figure 15-1 illustrates the payoff for buying the stock.

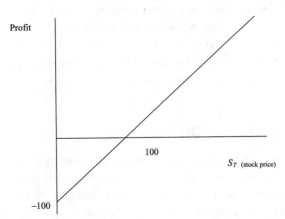

Figure 15-1. Payoff diagram for a long stock position.

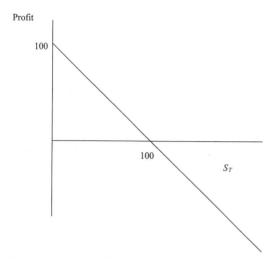

Figure 15-2. Payoff diagram for a short stock position.

In Figure 15-1, we can see that purchasing the security has unlimited possible profits, because there is no upper limit on the price of the stock. Losses are limited to the price paid for the stock because the stock's price cannot fall below zero.

Figure 15-2 illustrates the payoff to selling the stock short. Here, we see the mirror image of purchasing the stock. In this case, there are unlimited possible losses. As the stock price rises, the short seller is forced to buy back the stock at a price higher than the stock's selling price. Profit potential is limited to the stock's selling price because the price of the stock cannot fall below zero.

Buying a Call Option

Buying a call option gives holders the right, but not the obligation to purchase the security at the exercise price during the specified time period. Because call holders are not obligated to purchase the underlying security if the transaction would be detrimental, the most the holder can lose is the premium paid for the option. In this case, the only two stock prices of interest are the stock's price above the exercise price, in which case the call option is *in-the-money*, and the stock's price less than or equal to the exercise price, in which case the call option is *out-of-the-money*. When the call option is in-the-money, the intrinsic value of the call is the difference between the stock's price and the exercise price. When the call is out-of-the-money, the call has no intrinsic value.

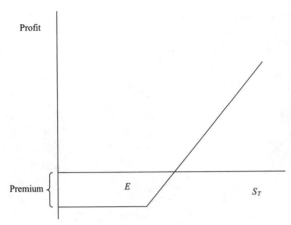

Figure 15-3. Payoff diagram for a long call.

The payoff picture for a call buyer can be seen in Figure 15-3. An individual purchases a call option because he or she believes that the price of the underlying asset will rise. As the price of the stock rises above the exercise price, the investor will profit. For every dollar that the price of the stock rises above the exercise price, the call buyer earns $1.

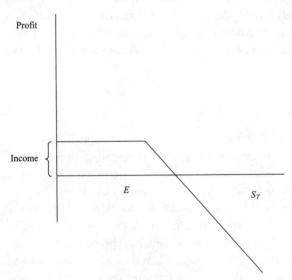

Figure 15-4. Payoff diagram for a short call.

Selling a Call Option

When selling a call option, sellers give the option holder the right to buy the stock at the exercise price during the specified time period. This means that the seller or writer of the call is obligated to deliver shares should the buyer of the option choose to exercise this right. Investors sell call options because they believe that the price of the stock will not rise prior to expiration. In this case, the seller will not have to deliver the shares of stock but will receive the option premium from the buyer. Figure 15-4 illustrates the payoff for a call seller.

Figure 15-4 illustrates the payoff picture for writing a call option. Notice that this transaction is the mirror image of buying a call option. For every dollar that the price of the stock rises above the exercise price, the call writer loses $1. Options are sometimes referred to as a *zero sum game* because the gains of the winner are exactly equal to the losses of the loser.

Buying a Put Option

Buying a put option gives buyers the right but not the obligation to sell the underlying asset at the exercise price during the specified time period. Put option purchases are used when you believe the price of the underlying asset will fall. If the price does fall, you can sell the asset at the higher exercise price, thus profiting from the option purchase. Put buying is similar to short selling an asset except the most the buyer can lose is the put premium. Also, because the holder pays a premium to own the option, profits differ from a short sale by the amount of the premium. Figure 15-5 illustrates the payoff for the purchase of a put option.

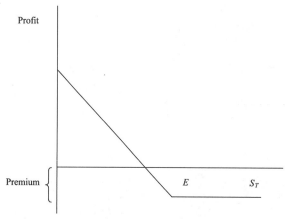

Figure 15-5. Payoff diagram for a long put.

Again, the profits from the option are tied to the price of the stock relative to the exercise price of the option. For the put buyer, profits are earned as the price of the stock falls. For every dollar the stock price falls below the exercise price, the put buyer earns $1.

Selling a Put Option

Sellers of put options receive premiums from put buyers for giving the put buyers the right to sell the stock to them at the exercise price. Investors sell a put option when they believe that the price of the stock will remain above the exercise price. If they are correct, they will receive the premium and will not have to deliver shares of the stock. A put option can also be sold in an effort to purchase the stock at a price lower than the current market price. If the price falls, put holders may exercise their option, which means that they will have to buy shares of the stock at the exercise price. Figure 15-6 illustrates the payoff for the sale of a put option.

As is the case with call options, the profits from selling or writing a put are the opposite of buying a put. Therefore, for every dollar that the stock's price falls below the exercise price, the put writer loses $1.

By combining put and call options with different exercise prices and with different positions in the underlying asset, it is possible to create almost any possible payoff diagram imaginable.

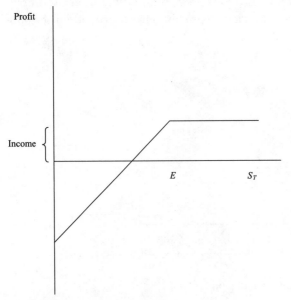

Figure 15-6. Payoff diagram for a short put.

Synthetic Put and Call Options

One interesting use of options is to combine the purchase or short sale of a stock to create an option-like payoff. Because this strategy does not entail a position in the option that is being replicated, these strategies are referred to as *synthetic options*. For example, by combining a long position in a stock with the purchase of a put option, a synthetic call option can be created. The purchase of the put option limits the downside loss of the long stock position, because, for every dollar the price of the stock falls below the exercise price, $1 is earned from the put option. If the stock price rises, the put option will expire worthless and the loss will be the premium paid for the option. Therefore, a payoff picture that is identical to a call option has been created, without the use of a call option. This strategy can be an excellent way for an investor to protect the value of a stock or a portfolio in the short run, while still retaining the opportunity to profit if prices rise.

A synthetic put option can be created by combining a short sale with the purchase of a call option. In this case, the call option limits the losses if the price of the stock should rise to the premium of the option. These strategies can be useful for creating an option-like payoff when a suitable option does not exist. For example, call options are more common than put options. An investor who cannot find a suitable put option may be able to create a synthetic put option by short selling the stock and purchasing an appropriate call option.

Trading Straddles and Strangles

A number of interesting payoff strategies can be created using options.[2] When investors believe that a security will make a big move in price but aren't sure in which direction the price will move, they can use options to create a position that will make money whether the price rises or falls. One such strategy is known as buying a *straddle*. An investor buys a straddle by purchasing both a put and a call option on the same stock with the same exercise price and expiration date. The cost of the straddle is the sum of the put and call premiums. Figure 15-7 shows the payoffs from the straddle.

In the case of a straddle, the investor earns $1 for every dollar the price of the stock moves above or below the exercise price. The strategy will just break even when the price of the stock moves enough to cover the cost of the premiums. Example 15-1 provides an example of the use of a straddle.

The straddle can be modified to reflect the investor's prediction of the likelihood of upward or downward moves in the price of the stock. For example, an investor who believes that the stock is more likely to rise in value than fall

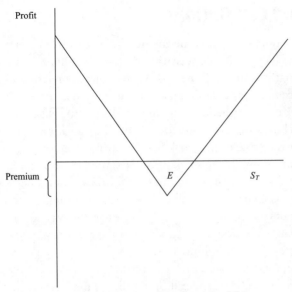

Figure 15-7. Payoff diagram for a long straddle.

can employ a strategy known as a *strap,* in which two call options are purchased for every one put option. Figure 15-8 presents the payoff for the strap.

Likewise, an investor who believes a downward movement in the stock's price is more likely than an upward movement can use a *strip,* which entails purchasing two puts for every call option purchased. Figure 15-9 presents the payoff for the strip.

The difference between the strap and the strip is shown in Figures 15-8 and 15-9. In the strap, two calls were purchased, and the payoff line for prices above the exercise price is twice as steep as the payoff line for prices below the exercise price. That is, the investor earns $2 for every dollar the price rises above the exercise price and $1 for every dollar the price falls below the exercise price. For the strip, the purchase of two puts for every one call makes the payoff line for prices below the exercise price twice as steep. In the case of a strip, the investor earns $2 for every dollar the price falls below the exercise price and earns $1 for every dollar that the price rises above the exercise price.

A similar strategy to a straddle is the use of a *strangle.* A strangle differs from a straddle because the exercise price of the put and the call are not the same. By using out-of-the-money puts and calls, the cost of the strangle is reduced. The shortcoming of this strategy is that the price needs to make a bigger move in either direction in order for the strangle to be in-the-money.

Figure 15-10 illustrates how the exercise prices for the strangle are split. From the figure, we can see that the stock price needs to move more, either higher or lower for the strategy to be profitable.

Example 15-1. Buying a straddle.

The stock of Orange Computers is currently selling for $51. The prices for call and put options expiring in three months are quoted as follows:

Exercise price = $50, call premium = $3
Exercise price = $50, put premium = $2

An investor believes that the price of Orange Computers will either rise or fall significantly based on the success of its new computer, the Navel. The investor can use a straddle to take advantage of this opportunity.

The payoffs from the strategy are:

Stock price range	Profit from call	Profit from put	Total profit
$S_T \leq \$50$	$-\$3$	$(\$50 - S_T) - \$2$	$(\$50 - S_T) - \$5$
$S_T > \$50$	$(S_T - \$50) - \$3$	$-\$2$	$(S_T - \$50) - \$5$

This straddle strategy will pay off if the stock's price is well below the exercise price, in which case we use the put option and discard the call option. When the stock's price is well above the exercise price, we can use the call option and discard the put option.

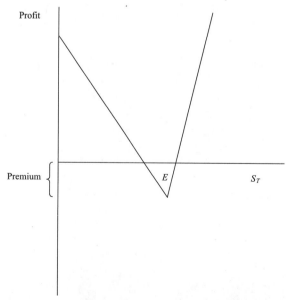

Figure 15-8. Payoff diagram for a long strap.

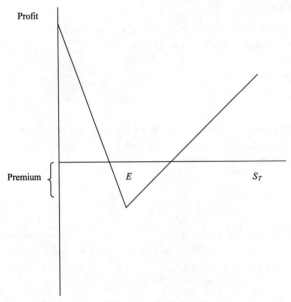

Figure 15-9. Payoff diagram for a long strip.

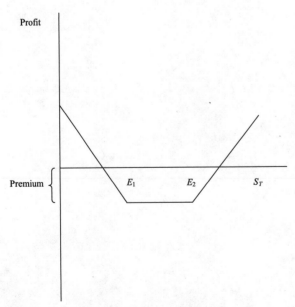

Figure 15-10. Payoff diagram for a long strangle.

Trading Spreads and Ratios
Spreads

A *spread* is created by purchasing and/or selling two or more options. The two most popular spread strategies are the *bull spread* and the *bear spread*. A bull spread takes advantage of a stock price that is expected to rise modestly. One method for creating a bull spread is to simply purchase a call option and sell a second call option with a higher exercise price.[3] Because the proceeds from the sale of the second call offset some of the cost of the strategy, a bull spread can be an inexpensive strategy to implement.

Notice from Figure 15-11 that there is a limit on both the profits and losses from this strategy. Example 15-2 illustrates how a bull spread is constructed with call options.

A bear spread is used to take advantage of a stock price that is expected to decline modestly. One method for creating a bear spread is to buy a put option and sell a second put with a lower exercise price. Again, because one option is being sold, the strategy can be relatively inexpensive. Figure 15-12 shows the details of a bear spread.

A third type of trading spread that can be created is a *butterfly spread*. An investor who is long a butterfly spread is expecting that the price of the stock will not move much prior to the expiration of the option. A butterfly spread can be created by combining a bull spread and a bear spread.

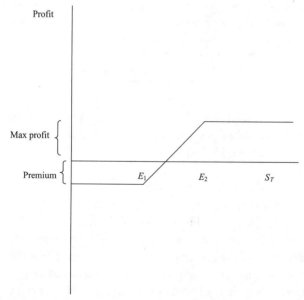

Figure 15-11. Payoff diagram for a long bull spread.

Example 15-2. Bull spread with call options.

The stock of Orange Computers is currently selling for $51. The prices for call options expiring in three months are quoted as follows:

Exercise price = $50, call premium = $3
Exercise price = $55, call premium = $1

An investor believes that the price of Orange Computers will rise from its current price of $51 to about $55. The investor can use a bull spread to profit from this prediction.

The payoffs from the strategy are:

Stock price range	Profit from long call	Profit from short call	Total profit
$S_T \leq \$50$	$-\$3$	$\$1$	$-\$2$
$\$50 < S_T < \$55$	$(S_T - \$50) - \$3$	$\$1$	$(S_T - \$50) - \$2$
$S_T > \$55$	$(S_T - \$50) - \$3$	$(\$55 - S_T) + \$1$	$\$55 - \$50 - \$2 = \$3$

This profit table differs from the payoff table because it includes the cost of the options and because the actual exercise prices are substituted for E_1 and E_2.

When the stock price is below $50, neither call option is in-the-money and the payoff is the cost of the bull spread, which is the amount paid for the call with the $50 exercise price less the amount received for the call with the exercise price of $55. When the stock price is between $50 and $55, the long call is in-the-money, and the short call is out-of-the-money. In this range, the profits are the difference between the stock price and the long call's exercise price ($50) less the cost of the strategy ($2). When the stock price is above $55, both calls are in-the-money, and the total profit is $3.

The payoff for a butterfly spread results in small losses if the price of the stock moves significantly and small gains if the price of the stock hovers around the exercise price. Example 15-3 illustrates how a butterfly spread is created using call options.

The bull, bear, and butterfly spreads use options that expire on the same date. However, a *calendar spread* or *time spread* option combination uses options with different expiration dates. The spread will have a horizon that terminates when the near-term option expires. By using different expiration dates, investors can speculate on future stock prices and take advantage of different sensitivities of the options. One such sensitivity—referred to as *time decay*—is how the option's value changes as the option moves toward expiration. Because different options have different time decay characteristics, it is

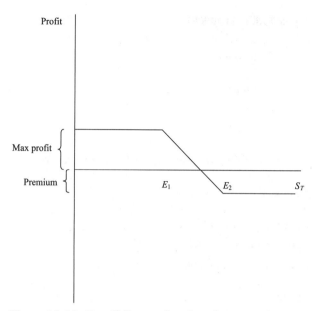

Figure 15-12. Payoff diagram for a long bear spread.

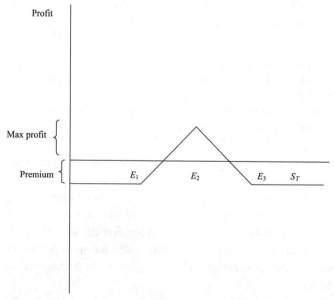

Figure 15-13. Payoff diagram for a long butterfly spread.

Example 15-3. Butterfly spread with call options.

The stock of Orange Computers is currently selling for $54. The prices for call options expiring in three months are quoted as follows:

Exercise price = $50, call premium = $6
Exercise price = $55, call premium = $3
Exercise price = $60, call premium = $1

An investor believes that the price of Orange Computers will not move much in the next three months. The investor can use a butterfly spread to profit from this prediction. The investor creates the butterfly spread by:

1. Buying one call with an exercise price of $50.
2. Selling two calls with an exercise price of $55.
3. Buying one call with an exercise price of $60.

The payoffs from the strategy are:

Stock price range	Profits from first long call	Profits from short calls	Profits from second long call	Total profits
$S_T < \$50$	$-\$6$	$\$6$	$-\$1$	$-\$1$
$\$50 < S_T$ $\$55$	$(S_T-\$50) -\$6$	$\$6$	$-\$1$	$(S_T-\$50) -\$1$
$\$55 < S_T < \$60$	$(S_T-\$50) -\$6$	$-2(S_T-\$55)+\$6$	$-\$1$	$(\$60-S_T) -\$1$
$S_T \geq \$60$	$(S_T-\$50) -\$6$	$-2(S_T-\$55)+\$6$	S_T-E_3	$-\$1$

When the stock's price is below $50, all three calls are out-of-the-money. When the stock's price is above $50 but below $55, profits will rise until they reach a maximum of $4. Once the stock price rises above $55, the butterfly spread loses a dollar for every dollar the stock price rises. Finally, once the stock price rises above $60, the second long call kicks in and profits remain constant.

---

possible to create profit opportunities by using options with different sensitivities.

In the previously discussed spreads, the strategy was created by spreading across exercise prices (as is the case in bull and bear spreads) or across time (in a calendar spread). In a *diagonal spread*, both the expiration date and the exercise prices are different. A number of different calendar spreads can be created. The profit patterns of these spreads are similar to the corresponding bull and bear spreads.

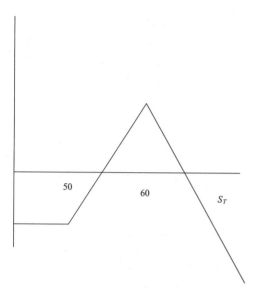

Figure 15-14. Call ratio spread.

Ratios

A *ratio* is a spread where there is not a one-to-one relationship between the option purchased and the option written. For example, a *call ratio spread* could be created by purchasing one call option with an exercise price of $50 and writing two call options with an exercise price of $60. Figure 15-14 illustrates the payoff for such a call ratio spread.

Summary of Trading Strategies

By combining put options, call options, and stocks, it is possible to create an instrument that will profit in almost any state. Table 15-3 summarizes the different possible payoff strategies.

From the table, we can see that it is possible to create instruments that profit in bullish, bearish, and neutral market conditions. In addition, it is possible to create instruments that profit when the market makes a big move in one direction, regardless of which direction it moves in.

Pricing Options

Option pricing models can be extremely complicated, yet the intuition that underlies these models is quite simple. Options, like futures contracts and other derivative securities, are priced using the principle of arbitrage. That is,

Table 15-3. Summary of payoff strategies.

Strategy	Market bias	Profit potential	Loss potential
Long stock	Bull	Unlimited	Limited
Short stock	Bear	Limited	Unlimited
Long call	Bull	Unlimited	Limited
Short call	Bear	Limited	Limited
Long put	Bear	Limited	Limited
Short put	Bull	Limited	Limited
Bull spread	Bull	Limited	Limited
Bear spread	Bear	Limited	Limited
Long butterfly	Neutral	Limited	Limited
Short butterfly	Mixed	Limited	Limited
Long straddle	Mixed	Unlimited	Limited
Short straddle	Mixed	Limited	Unlimited
Long strangle	Mixed	Unlimited	Limited
Short strangle	Neutral	Limited	Unlimited
Ratio call spread	Mixed	Limited	Unlimited
Ratio put spread	Mixed	Limited	Limited
Call ratio back spread	Mixed	Unlimited	Limited
Put ratio back spread	Mixed	Limited	Limited

identical things must have identical prices; otherwise, it would be possible to earn a riskless profit without using any money. The intuition behind option pricing lies in the fact that the value of a call option is perfectly correlated with the value of the stock. Therefore, by purchasing the stock and writing call options in the correct proportions, one can create a riskless portfolio. This riskless portfolio must earn the risk-free rate of interest, otherwise an arbitrage opportunity will exist. The number of call options to write for every share of stock purchased is known as the *hedge ratio*.[4]

In 1973, Fischer Black and Myron Scholes produced the first satisfactory option pricing model.[5] The Black/Scholes model says that a European call option's value depends on five factors:

1. The current price of the stock (S).

2. The exercise or strike price of the option (E).

3. The time until the option expires (T).

4. The volatility of the stock's returns (σ^2).

5. The risk-free rate of interest (r).

Table 15-4. Summary of effect of changing one variable on the price of an option.

Variable	Call	Put
Stock price	+	−
Exercise price	−	+
Time to expiration	+	+
Volatility	+	+
Risk-free interest rate	+	−

An interesting aspect of the Black/Scholes model is that only the volatility of the stock's returns needs to be estimated; the other four factors can be found simply by looking in the business section of the paper. Table 15-4 summarizes the effect of changes in these variables on the price of an option.

The pricing of a put option is found by applying the same concept of arbitrage. This relationship is known as *put-call parity*.[6] Intuitively, by purchasing a call option and writing a put option, it is possible to create a payoff that is identical to purchasing the stock and borrowing the present value of the exercise price.

Measuring Volatility

In order to use the Black/Scholes model, the stock's volatility must be estimated. Two methods for estimating the volatility are *historical volatility* and *implied volatility*. The historical approach uses historical data and assumes that past volatility is a good indicator of current volatility. In this case, historical return data are collected and the annualized variance is computed. The implied volatility approach assumes that the Black/Scholes model correctly prices options. Here, different volatilities are substituted into the formula until the Black/Scholes price equals the current market price for the option. Estimating the implied volatility for options with different exercise prices usually yields slightly different estimates, in which case an average of the estimates is usually used.

Using Options to Manage Investment Risks

One powerful use of options is in the management of investment risks. Put options are sometimes thought of as insurance contracts that can be used to reduce the loss associated with a fall in the price of a security. Not surprisingly, the cost of this "insurance policy" is the *premium* paid for the option. By purchasing put options, option holders guarantee the minimum price they receive for the asset. If the stock price rises, the put option expires worthless. However, if the stock price falls, the holder of the put option can sell the security at the exercise price.

Taxation of Options

Taxation of option transactions can be extremely complicated. In addition, tax laws have changed in the past and we can expect that they will change in the future. Here, we present some basics for the four basic option positions.

Long a Call

Whether profits or losses from a long call option position are treated as long-term or short-term capital gains depends on the length of the holding period. If the call is held for more than one year, gains are treated as long-term capital gains or losses. If the call is purchased and sold in one year or less, the gains or losses are considered short-term. If the call is exercised, the premium paid, the exercise price, the commissions for the purchase of the call, and the brokerage commission paid upon exercise are included in the basis of the stock. The holding period for the stock acquired from exercising the call begins on the day following the exercise of the call and does not include the holding period of the call.

Short a Call

When an investor writes or sells a call, the premium received is not treated as immediate income. Instead, the treatment of this income is not determined until the writer's obligation to deliver the underlying security expires or until the writer either sells the call or sells the underlying stock as a result of the assignment of the call. If the writer's obligation expires, the premium is always treated as a short-term gain, regardless of the length of time the call was outstanding.

Long a Put

When a put option is purchased and sold prior to expiration, the length of the holding period determines whether the gain or loss is considered short-term or long-term. If the put is exercised, the cost of the put and the commission on the sale of the stock reduce the realized gain of the underlying stock delivered.

Short a Put

When a put option is written, the premium of the put is not considered income until the put writer's obligation is terminated. Closing an uncovered put before assignment results in a short-term gain or loss, regardless of the length of time the put is outstanding. If the put expires, the writer realizes a short-term gain from the premium received. If the put is exercised against the writer, the strike price and commissions less the premium received become the basis of the stock acquired. The holding period for the stock begins on the day after the stock's purchase.

Tax Loss Harvesting

Options can be a useful tool for harvesting tax losses. In many instances, an investor may wish to sell a stock with a capital loss in order to offset a realized gain elsewhere in the portfolio. However, if an investor sells the stock and repurchases the security within thirty days, IRS Section 1091, the wash-sale rule, is triggered. Investors cannot use call options to avoid the wash-sale rule. However, a short put can be used to help harvest a tax loss without violating the wash-sale rule. The investor can sell a put and keep the money in a money market account for thirty-one days. If the price of the stock rises during this period, the premium from the put sale will offset some of the losses. If the price of the stock falls, the put will be in-the-money and the seller of the put will incur losses.

Converting Short-term Capital Gains

The difference in tax rates between short-term and long-term capital gains enables investors to reduce their tax liability by minimizing the recognition of short-term capital gains and trying to extend the time of realization of the gain so that it qualifies as a long-term gain. One method is to sell call options against the underlying stock rather than sell the stock itself. In order to benefit from this preferential treatment, investors must sell *qualified call options*, ones that are either at-the-money or out-of-the-money.

Summary

The unique payoff characteristics of options allow investors opportunities to create a limitless number of payoff strategies. Options can be used to participate in upward price movements of a stock or to take advantage of falling prices. These strategies can be inexpensive to implement in the short run using options. Options can also be used to hedge risks. Spreads can be used to inexpensively benefit from small movements in the underlying asset.

One limitation of options is their short-term nature. Investors often fail to realize that most options expire worthless and that maintaining a certain position requires buying a new option and paying the premium, a potentially costly endeavor over the longer run.

Selected Bibliography

Cox, J. C., and M. Rubinstein. *Options Markets.* Englewood Cliffs, N.J.: Prentice-Hall, 1985.

Hill, J. M. "Equity Derivative Strategies." In *Investment Counseling for Private Clients.* Association for Investment Management Research, 1999.

Kolb, R. W. *Futures, Options and Swaps.* Blackwood, N.J.: Blackwell Publishers, 1997.

Notes

1. See Chicago Board Options Exchange, "Investor Protection," www.cboe.com/exchange/clearing.htm.

2. For additional strategies, see Chicago Mercantile Exchange, "21 Proven Strategies for E-mini S&P 500 Options."

3. Although there are numerous methods for creating many of these spreads, for brevity we only present one.

4. F. Black and M. Scholes. "The Pricing of Options and Corporate Liabilities," *Journal of Political Economy* 81 (May/June 1973): 637–659.

5. The Black/Scholes Option Pricing Model is

$$C = SN(d_1) - Ee^{-rT} N(d_2)$$

where,

$$d_1 = \frac{\ln(S/E) + (r + .5\sigma^2)T}{\sigma\sqrt{T}}$$

$$d_2 = d_1 - \sigma\sqrt{T}$$

6. Put-call parity is given by the following equation:

$$P = C - S + Ee^{-rt}$$

16

Swaps and Other Derivatives

Derivatives encompass a whole class of securities that derive their value from some other security. Chapters 14 and 15 covered two of the most common exchange-traded derivatives: futures and options. *Swaps,* on the other hand, represent privately negotiated or over-the-counter securities. Swaps are contracts between two or more institutions known as *counterparties* in which an agreement is made to exchange cash flows in the future according to some prearranged formula. Although options and futures have a long history, swaps are a relatively new tool for investment management. The first currency swaps began in the late 1970s when currency traders developed swaps techniques to circumvent British control on the movement of foreign currency. The first interest rate swap occurred in 1981 and was an agreement between IBM and the World Bank.[1]

Trends and Regulatory Issues

Swaps are privately negotiated contracts sometimes referred to as over-the-counter derivatives. The swaps market has exhibited tremendous growth over the past two decades. In the late 1980s, the notional principal of outstanding swaps hovered around $1 trillion, by the mid 1990s, this number had grown to more than $10 trillion. By some estimates, the current level is about $30 trillion. Much of the growth is the by-product of volatility in the financial markets. Many of the swaps that have been created allow market participants to hedge volatility in the financial markets.

Although swaps share some of the same characteristics as exchange-traded derivatives, such as futures and options, there is one big difference. Because swaps are negotiated individually, the transactions are not guaranteed by an exchange clearinghouse. This can lead to default or *counterparty risk* that one counterparty will be unable to honor the obligation of the swap. One major advantage of swaps is the privacy it affords to the counterparties. By bypassing the floor of the exchange and negotiating contracts directly, parties can maintain a level of privacy that is not available when exchange-traded derivatives are used. Another advantage of swaps is that, unlike highly regulated

exchange-traded derivatives, swaps are subject to almost no government regulation.

Swaps as Forward Contracts

A simple way to view a swap is as a series of forward contracts in which two
parties agree to exchange some asset for a cash payment at some later date. If
the forward agreement is cash settled, then the contract consists of an
exchange of cash flows on the expiration date. This is a one-period swap
agreement. If the contract is for more than one period, as is the case in most
swaps agreements, then the swap consists of a series of forward contracts, with
each forward contract expiring on the date that cash flows are to be exchanged.

Interest Rate Swaps

The simplest swap is the plain vanilla interest rate swap, which is the exchange of a fixed interest rate for a floating interest rate. The swap is based on
an amount of principal that is not actually exchanged and is therefore referred
to as the *notional principal.* Figure 16-1 illustrates a plain vanilla interest rate
swap in which party A has a fixed-rate debt obligation, and party B has a
floating-rate debt obligation. In this example, party A wishes to convert this
obligation to a floating rate obligation, and party B wishes to convert to a
fixed rate obligation.

In Figure 16-1, party B pays party A a fixed rate of 12 percent and receives
a floating interest rate of LIBOR (London Interbank Offered Rate) +2 percent. By swapping the cash flows, the parties have created the type of debt
obligation they desire. Let's consider the cash flows from this transaction. In
this example (shown in Table 16-1), we assume that the swap agreement is for
three years and that the LIBOR rate used on the floating rate loan is the rate
at the beginning of the period. Therefore, on October 3, 2000, party A
receives $5.5 million ([9% + 2%]/2) of the $100 million notional principal
and pays $6 million. The net cash flow is therefore +$500,000 to party A. On
April 3, 2001, party A receives a greater cash flow because interest rates have

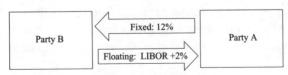

Figure 16-1. Plain vanilla interest rate swap.

Table 16-1. Interest rate swap cash flows.

Cash flows (in millions of dollars) to party A (the floating rate receiver) in a $100 million three-year interest rate swap when a fixed rate of 12 percent is paid and LIBOR + 2 percent is received.

Date	LIBOR rate (%)	Floating cash flow	Fixed cash paid	Net cash flow
April 3, 2000	9.00			
October 3, 2000	9.20	+5.5	−6.0	−0.50
April 3, 2001	9.60	+5.6	−6.0	−0.40
October 3, 2001	10.00	+5.8	−6.0	−0.20
April 3, 2002	10.20	+6.0	−6.0	0.00
October 3, 2002	10.40	+6.1	−6.0	+0.10
April 3, 2003	10.60	+6.2	−6.0	+0.20

risen. Notice that on April 3, 2002, no cash flow is exchanged because the amount received by party A is exactly equal to the amount paid.

In the above example, party A and party B negotiated the terms of the swap directly. However, in many cases, a *swap facilitator* or *swap bank* assists in the completion of the swap. A *swap broker* simply acts as a go-between, bringing the two counterparties together. *Swap dealers* transact for their own accounts to help complete the transaction. Figure 16-2 illustrates a swap transaction when a financial institution is used to facilitate the swap.

In Figure 16-2, party A can borrow short-term at LIBOR, and party B can borrow at a fixed rate of 4.5 percent. However, party A would like a fixed-rate loan, and party B would like a floating-rate loan tied to LIBOR. By entering into an interest rate swap, party A and party B can convert their loans as desired. In this case, the financial institution comes between party A and party B and keeps a quarter percent of the money on both sides of the cash flow for a total of half a percent.

In most instances, it is unlikely that two companies will wish to engage in opposite positions of the same swap at the same time. So typically large finan-

Figure 16-2. Interest rate swap when a financial institution is used.

cial institutions are prepared to enter into a swap agreement without having an offsetting counterparty. This is known as *warehousing* interest rate swaps.

Valuing an Interest Rate Swap

A plain vanilla interest rate swap can be viewed as an exchange of cash flows from two bonds. One bond represents a fixed-rate bond and the other represents a floating-rate note tied to LIBOR. Therefore, the value of the swaps agreement is simply the difference between the value of the two bonds. For the counterparty that is receiving the floating rate and paying the fixed rate, the value of the swap is

$$V_{swap} = B_{floating} - B_{fixed}$$

Likewise, the value to the counterparty receiving the fixed rate and paying the floating rate, the value would be the value of the fixed-rate bond less the value of the floating-rate bond. The value of the two bonds can be found by computing the present value of the cash flows.

Equity Swaps

An *equity swap* is an exchange of the cash flows (dividends plus capital gains) of some equity index for either a fixed or floating rate of interest. Equity swaps can be used to manage the risk of a portfolio in much the same way that futures contracts can be used to hedge or reduce the risk of a stock portfolio. For example, suppose a stock fund manager believes that the price of stocks will fall. The manager can enter into an equity swap where he pays the return on the S&P 500 index and receives the return, for example, on thirty-year Treasury bonds. If the market does fall in value, the manager may receive more from the equity swap than he pays, thus improving the return of the portfolio. By entering into an equity swap, the manager does not have to decide which stocks to sell, nor does he incur the tax liabilities from selling some of the stocks at a capital gain.

As another example, an equity swap can be used by an individual who has the majority of her wealth tied up in the stock of one company. In order to diversify her risk without selling the stock, she can enter into a swaps agreement to receive the return on the S&P 500 and to pay the return on her company's stock. This allows her to diversify her holdings from a single issue to a broad-based index like the S&P 500. This strategy does not come without risks, however. First, the counterparty that is to pay her the return on the S&P 500 could default, something known as counterparty risk. Second, the stock in her company could greatly outperform the S&P 500 index, thus necessitating a large payment to the counterparty.

Currency Swaps

A plain vanilla currency swap is more complicated than a plain vanilla interest rate swap because cash is actually exchanged. Therefore, unlike an interest rate swap with one cash flow, a currency swap has three sets of cash flows. The first cash flow entails an exchange of cash—for example, dollars for German marks. The second set of cash flows entails the exchange of periodic interest payments denominated in the appropriate currency. Finally, the principal that was exchanged in the first set of cash flows is exchanged. For example, suppose the spot exchange rate between German marks and U.S. dollars is two marks per dollar. If the interest rate is 8 percent in Germany and 10 percent in the United States, party X, who holds DM 20 million and would like to exchange them for dollars, could enter into a currency swap agreement with party Y. Figure 16-3 illustrates this plain vanilla currency swap.

Another difference between a currency swap and an interest rate swap is that there are four possible types of currency swaps based on the different pos-

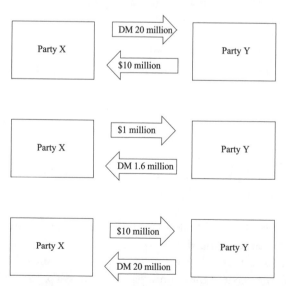

Figure 16-3. Plain vanilla currency swap.

sible interest rate combinations. If we assume that one of the interest rates is a U.S. dollar rate, then the possibilities are:

- Fixed U.S. rate for a fixed foreign rate
- Fixed U.S. rate for a floating foreign rate
- Floating U.S. rate for a fixed foreign rate
- Floating U.S. rate for a floating foreign rate

Notice in Figure 16-3 that there are three sets of cash flows in the currency swap. The two additional sets of cash flows are the exchange of principal at the beginning and end of the period. The annual interest payments in Figure 16-3 represent the amount of money in dollars (marks) times the U.S. (German) interest rate.

Valuing a Currency Swap

In the absence of default risk, a currency swap, like an interest rate swap, can be valued as a position in two bonds. In the case of a currency swap, the two bonds are bonds of two different countries. Like the interest rate swap, this swap is valued as the difference between the two bonds. However, because one bond is denominated in another currency, we need to use the spot exchange rate so that both bonds are denominated in the same currency. If one of the bonds is a U.S. bond, then the value of the swap to the receiver of U.S. dollars and a payer of foreign dollars will be

$$V_{swap} = B_{dollars} - S_0 B_{foreign}$$

where S_0 is the current spot exchange rate expressed as the number of dollars per unit of foreign currency.

Commodity Swaps

In a commodity swap, the counterparties make payments based on the price of a commodity. One party pays the fixed price of the commodity, and the other pays the floating price over the life or *tenor* of the swap. The first commodity swap was created by Chase Manhattan Bank in 1986. In most instances, the commodity is not exchanged. Commodity swaps are similar to hedging with futures contracts. However, swaps allow the terms of the contract to be tailored to meet the needs of the counterparties. Also, swaps can be structured for longer time periods—for example, five or seven years.

Credit Derivatives

Becoming increasingly popular, credit derivatives can help banks, financial companies, and investors manage the credit risk of their investment by insuring against adverse movements in the credit quality of the issuer. Credit derivatives can be used by financial institutions to adjust the risk profile of a loan portfolio. Credit derivatives might be applied by:

■ Commercial banks to change the risk profile of loan books

■ Investment banks to manage bond and derivatives portfolios

■ Manufacturers to manage the exposure to a single customer

■ Equity investors in project finance to deal with unacceptable sovereign risk

■ Institutional investors to enhance yield or to speculate

■ Employees to secure deferred remuneration

Four broad types of credit derivatives include credit default swaps, credit spread options, total return swaps, and credit-linked notes. The first credit derivative deal took place in 1993 when Bankers Trust and Credit Suisse Financial Products in Japan sold notes whose redemption value depended on specified default events. The market got off to a slow start because of many widely reported disasters in financial derivatives. But the market has approached a volume of some several hundred billion dollars and is rapidly expanding.

Credit Default Swaps

A credit default swap is a bilateral contract in which one counterparty pays a premium in return for a contingent payment triggered by the default of one or more third-party reference credits. The premium is typically expressed in basis points of the notional amount, while the contingent payment is determined by the decrease in the price of the security below par after the reference credit has defaulted. By using credit default swaps, a financial institution or other type of business can reduce the loss resulting from the default of a firm's customers.

For example, in June 1997, an international bank that already had a basket of twenty loans totaling more than $500 million to mostly investment-grade companies wanted to lend more money to the same companies.[2] J. P. Morgan sold the bank the right to require Morgan to pay off any of the loans if one of the borrowers goes bankrupt. Morgan can retain the default risks in its portfolio and collect the premium or sell them to institutional investors such as insurance companies, hedge funds, or other banks. Meanwhile, Morgan's client

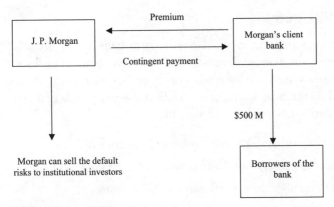

Figure 16-4. Credit default swap.

retains the actual loans and the customer relationship. The transaction can be depicted as shown in Figure 16-4.

This transaction is actually a put option on a portfolio of loans or bonds. The client bank receives a payoff if a borrower goes bankrupt—that is, it has the right to sell the default loans to Morgan at par. In a similar manner, bond investors can use this type of credit option to hedge against a decline in the price of a bond. As an example, an institutional investor with a portfolio of five-year Italian government bonds pays the counterparty a premium of, say, twenty basis points a year. The counterparty is obligated to make a payment if Italy defaults on its debt, in which case the contingent payment is par less the final price. Of course, the notional principal and maturity can be tailored to provide the exact amount and tenor of protection required.

Corporations and investors in projects stand to benefit as well. Take an engineering company, who may sell all of its heavy drilling equipment in the next several years to just a few customers. If one of the customers goes bust, the equipment will idle in inventory with no one else to sell to. To hedge against this risk, the engineering company can buy a credit swap on a notional principal that compensates for the loss of the sale. In project finance, an equity sponsor to a large project may want to hedge the portion of sovereign risk not guaranteed by an export credit agency-backed facility. It could enter into a credit default swap with a notional principal equal to the amount not covered by the sovereign guarantee.

Credit Spread Options

Credit spread options focus on the yield differential between credit-sensitive instruments and the reference security. Credit spread options are used by bond issuers to hedge against a rise in the average credit risk premium. As an illustration, suppose a Baa-rated company is planning to issue $50 million of two-year bonds in three months. The interest rate the company anticipates paying is the current spread of sixty-five basis points over the two-year Treasury notes. If there is an increase in the average risk premium for Baa companies before the bond's issuance, the interest payments will rise.

To hedge against the widening of the spread, the company could purchase a put option with a strike at the current level of spread. If the average risk premium rises above the strike rate in three months, the higher interest payments will be offset by gains from the option. Since the payment from the put option offsets the increased borrowing costs, purchasing the put option provides a hedge against increases in the credit premium. Alternatively, suppose that the credit risk premium falls. The put option has no payoff, but the company saves financing costs at the lower spread. Thus, purchasing the put option allows the corporate user to insure against increases in the credit risk premium while maintaining the benefits of lower funding costs if the spread declines.

Credit spread contracts also have been used successfully in emerging markets, where a credit spread is generally expressed as the yield spread of an emerging market instrument over the yield of a "risk-free" bond. Many structures are available that allow investors to bet on a specific credit spread or a basket of credit spreads. For example, when the sovereign Brazil 2027 global bond was offered at a spread of 525 basis points over the U.S. Treasury long bond, an institutional investor of Lehman Brothers' "locked in" a spread of 575 over the settlement in one year. The net settlement on the end date is determined by the credit spread of the Brazil 2027 bond at that time. In this trade, the notional size is $10,000 per basis point of spread tightening or widening. The investor will receive $10,000 at the end date for each basis point by which the Brazil credit spread is below 575 but will pay $10,000 for every basis point the spread is greater than 575.

Total Return Swaps

In a total return swap, the market risk of the underlying asset is stripped out and transferred without actually transferring the asset. For example, a bank originates a loan and then collects and passes along the loan payments (total returns) to the swap dealer. In return, the dealer pays the bank a floating rate of interest such as a spread over three-month LIBOR. Periodically, the swap is settled on the market value of the loan. Any positive change in value is paid by the bank to the swap dealer, the default risk holder. Conversely, the dealer pays any negative change to the bank. The effect of this swap for the bank is to trade the total return from its loan portfolio for a guaranteed return of a spread over three-month LIBOR. Because the swap dealer now guarantees the return, the bank has eliminated the credit risk on this loan.

Total return swaps offer two advantages. First, they allow banks to diversify loan credit risk while maintaining confidentiality of clients' financial records. Second, the administrative costs of the swap transaction are lower than for a loan sale.

Credit-Linked Notes

A credit-linked note is a structured note in which the bond has an embedded option that allows the issuer to reduce the note's payments if a key specified financial variable deteriorates. For example, an automobile financing company may use debt to fund a portfolio of auto loans. To reduce the credit risk, the company's credit-linked note promises to pay lenders higher coupon rates and the principal if the delinquency is below, say, 5 percent. However, if default exceeds 5 percent, investors accept a formula with potential loss of interest and principal. Some banks market a product known as *zero-one* structure. Instead of some coupon or principal loss, investors lose their entire principal if there is a higher default rate.

An automobile financing company would issue a credit-linked note because it provides a convenient mechanism to reduce the company's credit exposure. If default rates are high, the earnings are reduced, but the company pays a lower interest rate. Investors would consider buying such a security because they earn a higher expected rate of return than a comparable bond.

Caps, Floors, and Collars

A *cap* represents a call option on interest rates or asset prices that pays off if interest rates or the price of the asset rises above a certain level. Purchasing a cap on interest rates protects investors against rises in interest rates. For example, assume that bank A buys a 7 percent cap at time zero from bank B with a notional face value of $50 million. Bank A will pay bank B a premium in return for receiving compensation from bank B should interest rates rise above the 7 percent cap rate. Let's also assume that payments are to be made at the end of the first year, the second year, and the third year. The effect of this transaction is to cap bank A's floating-rate liabilities at a percent. Table 16-2 presents an example of the payoffs from bank B to bank A given different interest rates.

From Table 16-2, we see that at the end of year one and year three the cap rate of 9 percent is exceeded, and bank B is required to pay bank A the dif-

Table 16-2. Payments under the cap.

End of year	Cap rate (%)	Actual interest rate (%)	Interest differential (%)	Payment from bank B to bank A
1	9	11	2	$1 million
2	9	8	−1	0
3	9	12	3	$1.5 million
Total				$2.5 million

ference in the interest rates times the notional face value of $50 million. However, at the end of year two, the cap rate is not exceeded, and, therefore, bank B does not have to pay bank A.

A *floor* represents a put option on interest rates or asset prices that pays off if interest rates or the price of the asset falls below a certain level. By purchasing a floor on interest rates, an investor is protected from falling interest rates. For example, assume that bank C buys a 5 percent floor at time zero from bank D with a notional face value of $50 million. Bank C will pay bank D a premium in return for receiving compensation from bank D should interest rates fall below the 5 percent floor rate. Let's also assume that payments are to be made at the end of the first year, the second year, and the third year. Table 16-3 provides an example of the payoffs from the floor.

From Table 16-3, we can see that at the end of year one the interest rate is not below the floor, so no payment is made. However, at the end of years two and three, the interest rate is below the floor, and a payment is made from bank D to bank C.

A *collar* is created by taking a simultaneous position in a cap and a floor. In this case, the investor receives a payoff if interest rates rise excessively or if interest rates fall excessively. For example, suppose bank E buys a cap with an interest rate of 8 percent and a floor with an interest rate of 4 percent. Bank E receives payments if interest rates rise above 8 percent or fall below 4 percent. Table 16-4 illustrates the payoff for different interest rates.

Table 16-3. Payments under the floor.

End of year	Floor rate (%)	Actual interest rate (%)	Interest differential (%)	Payment from bank D to bank C
1	5	6	−1	$0
2	5	3	2	$1 million
3	5	2	3	$1.5 million
Total				$2.5 million

Table 16-4. Payments under the collar.

End of year	Floor rate (%)	Cap rate (%)	Actual interest rate (%)	Interest differential (%)	Payment to bank E
1	4	8	10	1	$1 million
2	4	8	2	2	$1 million
3	4	8	6	0	$0
Total					$2 million

By using a collar, bank E protects itself from increased interest rate volatility; that is, the collar ensures that the interest rate will lie between 4 and 8 percent.

Applications of Swaps and Other Derivatives

Swaps and the other derivatives discussed in this chapter have a number of interesting applications in the management of risk for nonfinancial institutions, financial institutions, and individuals. They can be used to manage risk or create a number of synthetic securities.

Asset and Liability Management

Banks and other financial institutions can use swaps to manage their assets and liabilities. For example, banks finance many long-term assets such as loans using short-term deposits. This mismatching of the time horizons or durations of assets and liabilities can lead to interest rate risk. In this case, a rise in interest rates will lead to an increase in the cost of the bank's funds, while there will be little or no change in the return on assets. By using an interest rate swap, the bank can enter into an agreement to receive a floating rate of interest while paying a fixed rate. If interest rates rise, the bank will receive a higher interest rate. The use of an interest rate swap essentially allows the bank to exchange its floating-rate liabilities for a fixed-rate liability that better matches its assets.

Synthetic Securities

A synthetic security is created by combining securities to create a payoff that is identical to another type of security. By using swaps in conjunction with different types of debt, it is possible to alter the payoff of the original type of debt. A firm could combine a floating-rate loan with an interest rate swap to create a synthetic fixed-rate debt by entering into a pay fixed receive floating swap. Similarly, a firm could create a synthetic floating-rate debt obligation from a fixed-rate obligation by entering into a pay floating receive fixed interest rate swap. Firms also can use a swap to create synthetic callable debt from a noncallable debt issue or create synthetic noncallable debt from a callable debt obligation by entering into an interest rate swap.[3] Investors also can apply the same techniques in order to convert a fixed-rate investment to a floating-rate investment and vice versa.

Equity Risk Management

As mentioned previously, portfolio managers who believe that stock prices will fall might enter into an equity swap in which they receive the return on some asset such as Treasury bonds and pay the return on some index like the S&P 500.

An equity swap can also be used to diversify an individual investor's portfolio. For example, an investor who has a large proportion of wealth tied up in the stock of the company he or she works for may wish to diversify the portfolio. One method for diversifying would be to sell the stock in the company and diversify into other stocks or mutual funds. However, selling the stock may be undesirable for a number of reasons. First, the sale of the stock may trigger capital gains taxes. Second, a high-level executive may not wish to sell the company's stock because the market may view such a move negatively. By entering into an equity swap in which the investor pays the return on the company's stock and receives, for example, the return on the S&P 500 index, the investor is, in effect, diversifying from a holding of one stock to a broadly diversified stock index. The advantage of this transaction is that it allows the individual to receive the benefits of diversification without selling stock in the company.

Collars also are commonly used by individuals who have a great deal of wealth tied up in one stock. For example, Time Warner Vice Chairman Ted Turner has used a collar to hedge the risk of a price decrease in the value of Time Warner stock. Collars can be created by purchasing a call option with an exercise price equal to the floor and selling a put option with an exercise price equal to the cap. By selecting the appropriate put and call combination, the collar can be created at no initial cost because the cost of the call option is offset by the amount received from writing the put option. This strategy is known as a *zero cost collar*. As is the case with most hedging strategies, the hedger gives up potential returns for a guaranteed minimum price. Should the price of the stock move outside the cap range, the hedger must give up gains because the stock must be sold at a below-market price. Most zero cost collars are conducted through a financial institution because of the complexity in pricing out such a strategy. However, the strategy also could be created using exchange-traded options.

Adjusting the Fund's Capitalization

Because swaps can be viewed as a series of forward rate agreements, any strategy that uses forward or future contracts can also be constructed using swaps. Chapter 14 discussed how large-cap fund managers could adjust the capitalization of stocks in a portfolio by selling S&P 500 futures and purchasing a contract on S&P Midcap 400 futures. This same strategy also could be created by entering into a swap agreement to receive the return on the S&P Midcap 400 index and pay the return on the S&P 500 index.

Transporting Alphas

Alpha measures a fund manager's ability to earn an excess return on a risk-adjusted basis.[4] Swaps can be a useful tool for adjusting the allocation of a portfolio while still benefiting from the manager's ability to earn excessive returns. For example, suppose a fund follows a successful strategy of small stock selection—that is, the fund has a positive alpha. However, suppose the plan sponsor would like the fund manager to follow a large-cap investing strategy. Rather than have the fund manager abandon the successful small-cap strategy, the fund can engage in an equity swap in which it pays the return on some small-cap index and receives the return on some large-cap index. In this way, the returns reflect large-cap stocks, but the fund still retains the manager's positive alpha.

Summary

This chapter discusses a number of powerful tools that can be used to manage risk and transform the payoffs of different types of assets and liabilities. Swaps represent a class of over-the-counter securities that allow institutions to hedge a number of different types of risk. By entering into a swaps agreement, a company or individual can adjust the cash flow of its portfolio to better meet its needs. In addition, swaps can be used to increase diversification without selling a current holding of securities or to transform fixed-rate loans into floating-rate loans. Because swaps are negotiated between two counterparties, any possible payoff that meets the needs of the counterparties can be created. This flexibility makes them more valuable than standardized, exchange-traded securities such as futures contracts.

Other types of derivative securities such as floors, caps, and collars also can be used to hedge interest rate risks or to lock in the price of a stock.

Selected Bibliography

Hull, J. C. *An Introduction to Futures and Options Markets.* New York: Prentice-Hall, 1998.

Kolb, R. W. *Futures, Options and Swaps.* Blackwood, N.J.: Blackwell Publishers, 1997.

Saunders, A. *Financial Institutions Management: A Modern Perspective.* Chicago: Irwin, 1997.

Notes

1. Kolb, R. W. *Futures, Options and Swaps.* (Blackwood, N.J.: Blackwell Publishers, 1997).

2. As reported in "Dizzying New Ways to Dice Up Debt," *Business Week*, July 21, 1997, 102–103.

3. A complete discussion of synthetic securities can be found in Kolb.

4. See Chapter 17 for more on performance measurement.

17

Benchmarks and Portfolio Performance Evaluations

Determining the performance of a portfolio is an important part of the investment business. Attracting and keeping investors is highly dependent on the performance of a fund or a portfolio manager. In addition, compensation in the money management industry is largely based on the performance of a fund relative to some predefined benchmark. This chapter describes some of the properties of good benchmarks and how to evaluate the performance of a fund.

Return Calculations

In order to evaluate investment performance, we need to calculate the return on the investment or portfolio. The return of a security has two components: the change in price (capital gains) and any income distributions paid by the security. The formula for the total return of an asset is

$$R_t = \frac{[MV_t - MV_{t-1}] + D_{t-1}}{MV_{t-1}}$$

where

R_t = *total* return between time $t - 1$ and t

MV_t = market value of the asset at the end of period

MV_{t-1} = market value of the asset at the beginning of peric

D_{t-1} = *accrued* income between time $t - 1$ and t

In the above equation, the difference between the market value of the asset from the beginning of the period to the end of the period represents the capital gains component of the return. The income component is represented by the dividend income, D_{t-1}.

The rate of return of an investment may be computed in several ways.

■ Dollar-weighted or internal rate of return—looks at the interest rate that makes the present value of the cash flows equal to the original cost of the investment. One problem with this method is that it includes cash inflows and outflows, which are largely beyond the control of the fund manager.

■ Time-weighted returns or geometric returns—have been the industry standard since 1966 because they do not depend on the timing of cash flows. In addition, time weighting considers the compounding of returns. The time-weighted returns are calculated as follows:

$$R = [(1 + R_1)(1 + R_2)...(1 + R_T)]^{1/T}$$

■ *Arithmetic returns*—are simply the arithmetic average of the returns over the compounding interval. This method does not account for the compounding of interest and can be computed as:

$$\text{Return} = \frac{\sum_{t=1}^{T} R_t}{T}$$

In cases where an asset's returns fluctuate, the arithmetic return will be higher than the geometric return. As a general rule, the time-weighted or geometric returns should be used with historical data because the compounding of returns is assumed, and the arithmetic returns should be used for forecasting.

Indexes and Averages

Market indexes and averages can play an important role in analyzing the performance of the stock market and as a benchmark for comparison. The Dow Jones Industrial Average, the S&P 500, the NASDAQ Composite, the Russell 2000, and the Wilshire 5000 are all commonly reported indexes. In many instances, these indexes are used as performance benchmarks for portfolio managers. Each index has a different characteristic that affects their usefulness as a benchmark. Understanding how an index is constructed is important to understanding why the value of an index changed. In addition, understanding how indexes are constructed can be useful in determining how to construct an appropriate benchmark for evaluation.

Construction of the Index

Construction of an index begins with a determination of what the index should represent. Some indexes represent small companies, others represent large companies, still others attempt to represent the entire stock market. Once the goal of the index has been determined, the universe of securities that are eligible for inclusion can be determined. The final two issues are which securities to include in the index and how to weight each security in the index.

The three methods for weighting an index are price weighting, market value weighting, and equal weighting. The method of weighting that is used will have a great impact on how the value of the index changes over time. In a price-weighted index, securities with the highest price will be given the greatest weight in the index. Therefore, a $5 movement in a stock priced at $200 per share will impact the index more than a $5 movement in a stock priced at $50. The Dow Jones Industrial Average represents a price-weighted index. A market value weighting gives greater weight to securities with greater market capitalizations. Therefore, the price movement of a company that has a $100 billion market capitalization will have a greater impact on the index than a stock with only a $2 billion market capitalization. The S&P 500 index is a market value–weighted index. Finally, if equal weighting is used, a $1 change in the price of a security impacts the index the same as a $1 change in the price of any other security.

Domestic Stock Indexes

The most popular stock market index is the *Dow Jones Industrial Average* (DJIA), a price-weighted index consisting of thirty large industrial stocks. The composition of the DJIA changes from time-to-time to reflect changes in the economy and the relative importance of industries or changes in the dominant companies within each industry. The most recent change occurred on November 1, 1999, when Home Depot, Inc., Intel Corp., Microsoft Corp., and SBC Communications, Inc., were added to the average to reflect the importance of technology and changes in the retail sector of the economy. Although the DJIA is the most widely reported index of the market, it is rarely used as a performance benchmark because of its narrow composition and its price weighting.

The *NASDAQ Composite* is a market value–weighted index of stocks that trade in the over-the-counter market. In the past, the NASDAQ consisted of smaller companies that did not qualify for listing on the New York Stock Exchange. However, many large technology companies (Microsoft, Dell Computers, and Intel Corp.) that were originally listed on the NASDAQ have chosen to remain even though they could opt for listing on the NYSE. In recent years, the growth of these tech giants has made the NASDAQ an index of technology performance.

The *S&P 500 Index* is a market value–weighted index of NYSE, AMEX, and NASDAQ stocks. It consists of 400 industrial companies, twenty transportations, forty utilities, and forty financials. Because its construction is much broader than the DJIA, the S&P 500 is widely used as a performance benchmark for large-cap stocks. Many mutual funds report the performance of the S&P 500 in their quarterly reports to provide investors with a benchmark for comparison

The Wilshire 5000 is a market value–weighted index that consists of stocks on the NYSE, AMEX, and over-the-counter markets. Although the index began with 5,000 stocks, it currently consists of more than 7,000 stocks. The Wilshire 5000 is generally considered the index for the entire stock market.

The Frank Russell Company of Tacoma, Washington, produces three widely cited indexes. The best known of these is the Russell 2000, which is a market value–weighted index of small company stocks. The Russell 2000 is widely used as the benchmark for small-cap stocks. The Russell 1000 index is a market value–weighted index of the 1000 largest stocks, and the Russell 3000 index consists of stocks in both indexes.

Foreign Stock Indexes

A number of foreign indexes also are watched by market participants. The *Nikkei Stock Average Index* is a price-weighted index of 225 stocks on the Tokyo Stock Exchange. The Nikkei is used much like the DJIA in the United States to provide a gauge of the performance of Japanese stocks.

The Financial Times Stock Exchange 100 or *FTSE 100* (pronounced footsie 100) is a market value–weighted index of the 100 largest stocks that trade on the London Stock Exchange.

The Hang Seng Index is a widely followed index of Hong Kong's stock market. The index currently consists of thirty-three constituent stocks that are representative of the market. These stocks represent approximately 70 percent of the total stock market capitalization of the Stock Exchange of Hong Kong, Limited.

The most widely followed international index by pension funds and other institutional investors is the Morgan Stanley Capital International Europe, Australia, Far East Index (EAFE). The index covers more than 2,000 companies in twenty-one countries.

Bond Market Indexes

Like stock market indexes, a number of bond market indexes track various segments of the bond market. The Lehman Brothers Aggregate, the Merrill

Lynch Composite, and the Salomon Brothers Composite are indexes of U.S. investment-grade bonds. All three indexes are market value–weighted and contain over 5,000 issues. The indexes include government, corporate, mortgage-backed, and asset-backed bonds.

Performance Composites

When examining the performance of portfolios under a manager it is necessary to separate the portfolios by investment objective. For example, it would be inappropriate to cluster together a portfolio that consists of long-term government bonds with a small capitalization equity portfolio. In 1993, the Association for Investment Management Research (AIMR) introduced the first industry-wide performance presentation standards to allow for greater comparability, accuracy, and fairness in the presentation of performance presentations. The standards were set up to deal with several practices that hindered comparability of performance, including the following:

- Representative accounts—managers often chose to present only the returns of their best performing accounts.

- Survivorship bias—managers presented return performance that excluded accounts whose poor performance led to termination.

- Portability of investment results—managers presented performance that was not the record of the firm, but rather the manager's record from a previous employer.

- Varying time periods—managers presented performance for a selected time period during which the fund produced outstanding returns.

One of the most important concepts of the AIMR Performance Presentation Standards (PPS) is the definition of a composite—a collection of portfolios that represents a similar strategy or investment objective.

Some of the principal requirements of the AIMR PPS are presented in Table 17-1.

Benchmark Construction

In order to compare a portfolio's performance to a benchmark, an appropriate benchmark must be constructed. Many funds use the Standard and Poor's 500 Index as their performance benchmark, but in many cases it may be an unsuitable benchmark. Benchmarks need to be constructed that are appro-

Table 17-1. Highlights of AIMR Performance Presentation Standards.

To be considered in compliance with the AIMR PPS, the presentations must incorporate:

- Presentation of a least a ten-year performance record (or since the inception of the firm if less than ten years).
- Presentation of annual returns for all years.
- All fee-paying accounts under management must be included in one composite.
- Use of time-weighted rates of return, with valuation on at least a quarterly basis and geometric linking of wealth relatives.
- Only actual portfolios under management to be included in calculations. No simulated or model portfolios.
- Measures of risk within a composite must be included (internal risk).
- Market value–weighting of performance composites of individual accounts.

Mandatory disclosures

- The number of portfolios and amount of assets included in each composite, and the percentage of the firm's total assets that each composite represents.
- Whether performance results are calculated gross or net of investment management fees, the manager's fee schedule, and, for net results, the average weighted management fee.
- If the full performance record is not in compliance, the noncompliance periods and a description of how noncompliance periods are out of compliance.
- The existence of a minimum asset size below which portfolios are excluded from a composite.

Source: AIMR Performance Presentation Standards, (Charlottesville, VA.: AIMR, 1993).

priate for each type of manager or type of fund. This type of comparison is similar to comparing athletes of different eras or different ages. For example, when golf phenom, Tiger Woods was ten years old, he stood head and shoulders above other ten-year-olds and perhaps even twelve- or thirteen-year-olds. However, if someone would have compared a young Tiger to professionals on the PGA Tour, certainly he would have underperformed at that benchmark. Similarly, fund managers who invested in high technology and Internet stocks greatly outperformed managers that invested in financial stocks in 1998 and 1999. Does this indicate that these high tech managers were superior, or could their performance be attributed to running a fund that was in the right place at the right time?

Several characteristics necessary for any useful benchmark are:[1]

- Unambiguous—The names and weights of securities comprising the benchmark are clearly delineated.

- Investable—The option is available to forego active management and simply hold the benchmark.

- Measurable—It is possible to readily calculate the benchmark's own return on a reasonably frequent basis.

- Reflective of current investment opinions—The manager has current investment knowledge of the securities that make up the benchmark.

- Specified in advance—The benchmark is constructed prior to the start of an evaluation period.

These factors ensure that the portfolio is compared to a suitable benchmark and that the investor could actually consider the benchmark as an investment alternative. Many benchmarks may seem reasonable at first glance; however, if the investment is not available to the client, then the performance of the benchmark cannot be translated into actual gains. For example, some managers compare their performance to the median fund manager—an inappropriate approach because the median manager cannot be determined before the performance evaluation period and is therefore not investable. In addition, the median manager may have a unique investment style that is difficult to replicate and therefore inappropriate as a benchmark for comparison.

One method that has been proposed for examining a manager's performance is to decompose it into three components:[2]

- The return due to the market index

- The return due to a manager's style, which is defined to be the difference between the market index and the manager's benchmark

- The return due to active management

This approach recognizes that a manager may select securities not only through active management but also in a style that differs from the market index. When evaluating a manager, it is necessary to construct benchmarks that recognize this difference in style. For example, comparing a growth manager to an index fund such as the S&P 500 would ignore the manager's style because the index consists of both a value and a growth component. In addition, the S&P 500 consists of large-cap stocks, which also may be inappropriate as a benchmark.

Recognizing an investment manager's style is important in determining how much of a manager's performance is due to active management and how much is due to style. For example, fund managers who followed an Asian international investment style greatly underperformed the S&P 500 index in 1998. This weak performance was due to the currency crisis in southern Asia and not to the managers' abilities. All fund managers investing in this region performed poorly. The real issue here is how a manager's performance compared to funds that also invested in Asia. Good managers would have outperformed their benchmark even if they underperformed the S&P 500. Likewise, many of these Asian fund managers greatly outperformed the S&P 500 index in 1999, as many of the Asian markets rebounded from 1998. Were these same fund managers now geniuses, or simply fortunate to be in the right place at the right time? Once again, a top manager would have outperformed an appropriate benchmark for Asian funds.

Sharpe's Style Analysis

Nobel prize winner William F. Sharpe developed a method for separating a manager's returns into a style component and a security selection component.[3] Sharpe uses a multifactor model, where the factors are the returns to different types of investments such as small capitalization stocks and bonds. The R^2 from the regression measures the style component of the return, and one minus the R^2 measures the security selection component.

Sharpe's style analysis is especially useful for determining who gets credit for the performance record. For example, if a pension fund requests that a manager follow a large capitalization growth strategy, the manager should not get credit for the part of this performance that is due to the large capitalization growth strategy, but rather should get credit for the selection of outstanding growth stocks only. In addition, style analysis can be useful in determining whether managers are following the strategy they have been employed to use.

Performance, Costs, and Taxes

When evaluating the performance of a manager or a fund, costs and taxes should be taken into consideration. A fund manager may underperform an index such as the S&P 500; however, the return of the S&P 500 is stated without regard to transactions costs, making the return on the index unattainable. In addition, the different investment strategies employed by a manager will lead to different tax consequences for the investor. A fund with a high turnover rate may experience a significant amount of capital gains taxes that will reduce the fund's after-tax return. Therefore, a fund that has a high turnover rate may not outperform a fund that is more tax efficient, even though it outperforms the fund on a pretax basis. Active fund managers can also reduce the tax liability using a number of strategies, including harvesting losses to offset gains, selling securities with the highest cost basis first, and using derivative securities such as futures contracts to postpone the realization of capital gains.

In a study covering the period 1982–1991, it was found that, of 72 large equity mutual funds, fifteen beat the results of a hypothetical "closed-end index 500" on a pretax basis.[4] However, when taxes were included, only five funds beat the hypothetical index.

Risk-Adjusted Performance Measures

In order to compare different funds or portfolios, it is necessary to consider both the risk and return. Funds can outperform other funds or their benchmark for several reasons. First, a fund manager may have superior skill at selecting securities, which is sometimes referred to as security selection. Second, a manager may be able to predict overall movements in the market and may be able to time when, and in what market, funds should be invested, which is known as market timing. Both of these are skills for which the manger should be rewarded. However, a third way that a manager can outperform others is to take on additional risks. In this case, the issue is how to deal with funds that have different levels of risk. A common method for making these comparisons is to use risk-adjusted performance measures, which use one of two approaches:

- They look at the return for a given level of risk or the return per unit of risk.

- They adjust the portfolios to have the same level of risk as some predefined benchmark.

In the first case, a fund is ranked based on how well a manager generates return for the amount of risk that the fund takes. In the second case, all portfolios are adjusted to have the same level of risk, and the ranking is then determined based on which funds have the highest return.

A Brief Review of Capital Market Theory

Evaluating the performance of a portfolio requires a benchmark for comparison. All of the measures of portfolio performance discussed in this section use models of the capital markets to rank securities. Both the *capital market line* and the *security market line* or *capital asset pricing model* have been widely used in a number of aspects of financial theory, including portfolio evaluation.

The capital market line shows the risk and return tradeoff for different combinations of a riskless asset and a portfolio consisting of all risky assets held in their market value proportions. This portfolio, which is referred to as the *market portfolio,* is theoretical and impossible to define. In order to deal with this problem, most academics and analysts use a market index such as the S&P 500 as a proxy for the true market portfolio. The equation for the capital market line is

$$\overline{R}_p = R_f + \left[\frac{\overline{R}_m - R_f}{\sigma_m} \right] \sigma_p$$

The above model says that the expected return of a portfolio depends on the return that would be earned if no risk were taken, plus a premium for the risk of the portfolio. The measure of risk used in this model is the standard deviation, which is a measure of the total risk of the portfolio. In this model, the best or optimal portfolio is the market portfolio M. All investors will, therefore, choose some combination of portfolio M and a riskless asset such as Treasury bills. Investors adjust their degree of risk by adjusting their asset allocation. Conservative investors will hold a high percentage of their wealth in the form of Treasury bills, with little or no allocation to portfolio M. More aggressive investors may choose to leverage their portfolios by borrowing so that they can invest more than 100 percent of their wealth in risky portfolio M. Figure 17-1 presents a graph of the capital market line.

A second model that is based on the capital market line is the capital asset pricing model (CAPM) or its graphic depiction, which is known as the security market line (SML). The CAPM relates the expected return of an individual asset with its nondiversifiable risk or beta.[5] The logic behind using nondiversifiable risk rather than total risk is that investors should not be rewarded for taking on risks that they can diversify away. The equation for the CAPM is

$$\overline{R}_i = R_f + \beta_i \left[\overline{R}_m - R_f \right]$$

The CAPM says that the expected return on some asset i depends on the risk-free rate and an additional premium based on the amount of nondiversifiable risk of the security times the market risk premium. Figure 17-2 presents a graph of the security market line.

Notice that the difference between the capital market line and the security market line is the measure of risk that is used as the independent variable. In the CML, it is the standard deviation or total level of risk. In the SML, it is the asset's systematic or nondiversifiable level of risk as measured by beta.

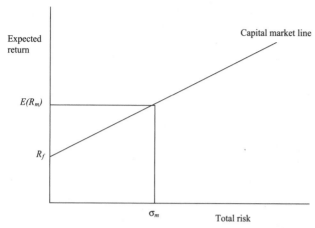

Figure 17-1. Capital market line.

The equation for the capital market line and the equation for the capital asset pricing model both represent equations for a straight line. Measures of portfolio performance often look at where a portfolio plots relative to the line (see Figure 17-3). In both cases, portfolios that plot above the line indicate a superior performance, whereas portfolios that plot below the line indicate inferior performance.

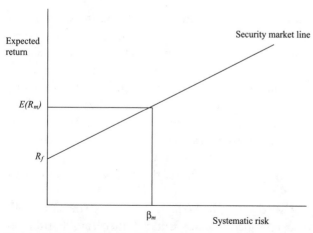

Figure 17-2. Security market line.

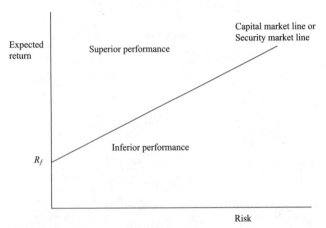

Figure 17-3. Market lines and performance evaluation.

Sharpe Ratio

The Sharpe ratio looks at the excess return per unit of total risk.

$$S_p = \frac{R_p - R_f}{\sigma_p}$$

where

R_p = return of the portfolio

R_f = risk free interest rate

σ_p = standard deviation of the portfolio

The Sharpe ratio measures the excess return that the portfolio earns over the risk-free interest rate per unit of total risk or standard deviation and therefore examines the risk premium relative to the capital market line. The Sharpe ratio assumes that the investor holds only two assets, the risk-free asset and some risky portfolio. Geometrically, the Sharpe ratio measures the slope of a line from the risk-free asset to the risky portfolio being analyzed. The steeper the slope, the greater the risk-adjusted performance. Like the CML, investors need not invest 100 percent of their wealth in the portfolio, but can choose a lower level of by investing some of their wealth in the risk-free asset. Figure 17-4 presents a graph of the Sharpe ratio for portfolios A and B and the market portfolio.

In Figure 17-4, we can see that portfolio A has a steeper slope than the CML and therefore exhibits superior performance. On the other hand, portfolio B has a slope flatter than the CML and thus exhibits inferior performance.

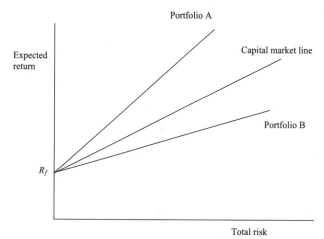

Total risk

Figure 17-4. Graphical depiction of the Sharpe ratio.

Treynor Measure

The Treynor measure is similar to the Sharpe ratio except it uses systematic risk or beta as its measure of risk.

$$T_p = \frac{R_p - R_f}{\beta_p}$$

where

R_p = return of the portfolio

R_f = risk free interest rate

β_p = systematic risk of the portfolio

The Treynor ratio measures the risk premium per unit of systematic risk and therefore examines the excess return of the portfolio relative to the security market line. Like the Sharpe ratio, the Treynor measure looks at the slope of a line running from the risk-free asset to the portfolio being analyzed. Figure 17-5 presents a graphical depiction of the Treynor measure.

From Figure 17-5, we can see that portfolio A exhibits superior performance because it plots above the SML. Likewise, portfolio B exhibits inferior performance because its slope is flatter than the SML.

The Treynor measure and the Sharpe measure may provide different rankings because of different levels of diversification in the portfolios being compared. If all portfolios are perfectly diversified, then both measures will yield the same result. Consider the following example. Portfolio A has an expected return of 15 percent, a standard deviation of 1, and a beta of 1.5. Portfolio B has an expected return of 15 percent, a standard deviation of 2, and a beta of

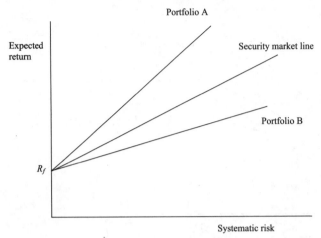

Figure 17-5. Graphical depiction of the Treynor measure.

1.2. Further, let's assume that the risk-free interest rate is 5 percent. Using this information, we can compute the following Sharpe and Treynor measures:

$$S_A = \frac{15\% - 5\%}{1\%} = 10$$

$$S_B = \frac{15\% - 5\%}{2\%} = 5$$

$$T_A = \frac{15\% - 5\%}{1.5} = 6.67$$

$$T_B = \frac{15\% - 5\%}{1.2} = 8.33$$

In this example, portfolio A is ranked higher than portfolio B when the Sharpe ratio is used. However, the rankings are reversed when the Treynor measure is used. The difference is due to the different levels of diversification of the two portfolios. Portfolio A is better diversified and hence has a lower level of total risk than portfolio B. Which measure we use depends on the role the fund plays in the entire portfolio. If the fund makes up the entire portfolio, then the level of total risk is most important and the Sharpe ratio is preferred. If the fund is only a small part of a much larger portfolio, as might be the case in a pension fund, the amount of risk that the fund brings to the entire portfolio is most relevant. In this case, it is the systematic risk that is of concern and so the Treynor measure should be used.

Jensen's Alpha

Jensen's alpha compares the return earned by the portfolio to what the capital asset pricing model predicts the portfolio should return for its given level of risk. A positive alpha signifies that the manager is adding value to the portfolio.

$$\alpha_p = R_p - [R_f + B_p(R_m - R_f)]$$

Figure 17-6 presents a plot of Jensen's alpha for portfolio A and portfolio B. Portfolio A lies above the SML and therefore has a positive alpha, indicating that the manager has provided superior performance. On the other hand, portfolio B lies below the SML and therefore has a negative alpha. The manager of portfolio B has produced a portfolio return that is lower than it should be for the level of risk taken by the portfolio.

Jensen's alpha indicates the excess return for a given level of systematic risk. Geometrically, it is the vertical distance that a portfolio's return lies above the security market line.

The Modiglianis' M^2

M^2 is a method for ranking portfolios developed by analyst Leah Modigliani and her grandfather, Nobel prize winner, Franco Modigliani. The M^2 adjusts the portfolio so it has the same total risk as the benchmark S&P 500 index. The total risk is adjusted by creating a portfolio that consists of the fund and a position in Treasury bills. Portfolios with total risk that is less than the index are leveraged up by borrowing at the risk-free rate to buy more of the port-

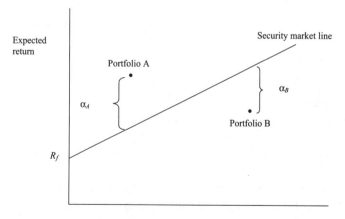

Figure 17-6. Graphical depiction of Jensen's alpha.

folio. Funds with total risk that is greater than the index have their systematic risk reduced by creating a portfolio that consists of the fund and Treasury bills. For example, a fund with a total risk twice that of the index will have half of its assets placed in Treasury bills. The returns on these risk-adjusted portfolios are then computed and a ranking is constructed. Because the rankings are based on the total risk of the portfolio, M^2 will give the same rankings as the Sharpe ratio. Table 17-2 summarizes the four types of performance measures.

Market Timing versus Security Selection

Managers can add value through the methods of *market timing* or *security selection*. In market timing, managers attempt to determine the overall direction of the market and adjust the portfolio allocation to take advantage of their forecasts. If the market is expected to rise, managers will increase the portfolio's stock exposure or they will increase the systematic risk of the fund. If the market is expected to fall, managers will reduce the fund's equity exposure and hope to buy shares when the market is at or near the bottom. Portfolios can be adjusted by purchasing and selling stocks or through the use of futures contracts.

Security selection, on the other hand, does not depend on the overall direction of the market. In this case, managers simply purchase the best securities for the portfolio. The effects of security selection and market timing can be separated by considering the allocation of the portfolio (market timing) and the return generated by the portfolio (security selection) relative to some index.

Return market timing =
(Portfolio weight × Index return) – (Index weight × Index return).

Return security selection =
(Index weight × Portfolio return) – (Index weight × Index return).

In the above equations, we can see that the difference between security selection and market timing is determined by the first term. For market timing, we're interested in how managers adjust the weights of the portfolio to earn an abnormal return. A good market timer will be able to outperform the market even if the fund only generates the same returns for each asset class as the index. Why? Because the manager successfully adjusts the allocation to stocks during bull market periods, while shifting into safer assets such as bonds and cash during bear market periods. Managers who rely on security selection to outperform the market will generate abnormal returns by selecting the outstanding securities within each asset class. They will be able to out-

Table 17-2. Summary of performance measures.

Performance measure	Risk adjustment	Interpretation	Use
Sharpe ratio	Portfolio standard deviation	Measures the excess return per unit of total risk. Measures both risk-adjusted return and the degree of diversification of the portfolio. It is the slope of a line from the risk-free rate to the portfolio being analyzed.	Use when the portfolio makes up a high percentage of the investable funds.
Treynor measure	Portfolio beta	Measures the excess return per unit of systematic or nondiversifiable risk It is the slope of the line running from the risk-free rate to the portfolio being analyzed.	Use when the portfolio is a part of a number of portfolios.
Jensen's alpha	Portfolio beta	Measures the excess return for a given level of systematic risk. It is the vertical distance between the portfolio's returns and the security market line.	Use on any portfolio.
M^2	Risk adjustment consists of leveraging or unleveraging the portfolio to have the same total risk as the benchmark portfolio.	Determines how well the portfolio performs relative to the benchmark, when both have the same degree of total risk. Gives the same ranking as the Sharpe ratio.	Use when the portfolio makes up a high percentage of the investable funds.

perform the market even when the index weights for each asset class are used. In both instances, the returns generated by a passive strategy of index weights and index returns are subtracted from the fund's returns in order to determine the excess return over the passive indexing strategy.

After-Tax Performance Evaluation

The models previously discussed evaluate portfolios on a pretax basis. This method of performance evaluation may be valid for institutional investors, who do not have to deal with taxes, but is inappropriate for individual investors. Although it may seem appropriate to evaluate funds and managers on a pretax basis because of the multitude of different tax situations for each investor, some recognition of taxes needs to be made in order to evaluate the performance of funds and managers for individual investors.

Taxes are important to consider because fund A may have a higher pretax return than fund B; however, fund B's after-tax return may be greater than fund A's. In this case, fund A would be considered superior using most performance evaluation measures when, in fact, the investor would be better off with fund B.

The *tax efficiency* of a fund is determined by several factors. First, portfolio turnover plays a large role in determining the amount of realized capital gains that the fund will need to distribute to shareholders. In addition, funds with high turnover rates may realize short-term gains, which historically have been taxed at higher rates than long-term capital gains. However, investment advisers need to be careful when examining the turnover of a portfolio. A fund with a high turnover rate may be able to limit the amount of taxable gains if portfolio losses are used to offset gains in the portfolio.

The second factor that affects the amount of tax a portfolio faces is the composition of the fund's returns. Portfolios that derive a large portion of their gains from dividends rather than capital gains will incur greater tax liabilities for investors. Ideally, a fund would not only generate returns using capital gains, but would strive to have those capital gains remain unrealized in order to postpone the tax liability.

The third factor affecting a portfolio's taxes is the amount of cash inflows versus the amount of withdrawals. Portfolios with large outflows relative to inflows may force portfolio managers to realize capital gains in order to satisfy the redemptions. In this case, some consideration needs to be given for the lack of control the fund manager has over the fund's cash flows. In some instances, cash outflows may result from the poor performance of the fund relative to its peer group. However, in many cases poor performance may simply occur because the fund invests in an out-of-favor market or country. For example, during the latter part of 1998, many funds that invested in Asia saw a large amount of cash outflows due to an economic and financial crisis in that part of the world that caused all funds invested there to perform poorly. The cash outflows caused many of these funds to realize capital gains in order to meet share redemptions. The poor performance and the subsequent redemptions had little to do with fund managers' competence, but rather were the unfortunate result of the economic crisis. In this case, tax liabilities of the fund should not be held against the fund manager.

A final consideration regarding the tax efficiency of a fund results from the manager's ability and awareness in implementing a tax efficient strategy. A fund manager who considers taxes to be important may use tax-efficient strategies such as selling the highest cost basis securities first or using derivative securities to postpone capital gains. A fund also may impose restrictions on shareholders who engage in excessive transactions (for example, redemption fees) in order to reduce the transactions costs and tax consequences to other shareholders.

One method for evaluating the after-tax performance of a portfolio is to use the AIMR Performance Presentation Standards algorithm. According to this algorithm, managers are to use the maximum federal tax rate for each type of client. This can be a problem because different clients face different tax rates even if their incomes are similar. For example, one client may have capital loss carryforwards from unsuccessful investments that will effectively lower this individual's tax rate. In addition, the AIMR PPS informs managers that they are to ignore state and local taxes—a problem in high tax states such as California, where the maximum income tax rate is 11 percent. Another problem that arises from measuring after-tax performance is how to deal with unrealized capital gains. The AIMR PPS recommend ignoring future taxes; however, ignoring the gain overstates the after-tax performance of a portfolio with large unrealized gains relative to a fund with few unrealized gains. The only time ignoring unrealized capital gains is appropriate is when the portfolio is likely to be held until the death of the owner. In this instance, the securities benefit from a stepped up cost basis at the death of the owner, and all capital gains are forgiven.

One method for dealing with unrealized capital gains is to use an *accrual equivalent* capital gains tax rate.[6] This method finds the tax rate that would give the client the same portfolio value at the end of the holding period whether the gains are realized each year or at the end of the entire holding period. For example, suppose an investor invests $1,000 in an asset today and will withdraw the money in twenty years. If the investor does not withdraw any money until the end of the twenty-year holding period, the after-tax value of the portfolio at the end of twenty years assuming a 12 percent return each year would be

$$(1 - 0.20) [\$1,000(1 + 0.12)^{20} - \$1,000] + \$1,000 = \$7,917.03$$

To compute the accrual equivalent rate, we need to find out the return that needs to be earned on an after-tax basis for twenty years so that we have $7,917.03 in the account. That is, we solve the following equation:

$$\$1,000(1 + r)^{20} = \$7,917.03$$

Solving gives us $r = 10.9$ percent. The accrual tax equivalent is the percentage difference between the amount earned before taxes and 10.9 percent.

$$\text{Accrual equivalent tax } = \frac{12\% - 10.9\%}{12\%} = .0917 \text{ or } 9.17\%$$

So the accrual equivalent tax rate is 9.17 percent, which is much lower than the current 20 percent rate on capital gains. The low rate reflects the long holding period before capital gains are realized.

Summary

Determining the performance of a fund or a fund manager is an important part of the investment management process. The major issues in performance evaluation are what to measure and how to construct appropriate benchmarks for comparison. Generally, portfolios are evaluated on a risk-adjusted basis to account for the risk that the manager assumes. In determining the risk-adjusted return, the evaluator needs to determine the appropriate type of risk to consider. Should the total risk of the portfolio be considered, or should only the nondiversifiable or systematic risk of the portfolio be considered?

Another important issue discussed in this chapter was the determination of an appropriate benchmark. In general, funds should construct benchmarks that are appropriate for the style and size of the fund being evaluated. In addition, the benchmark should not be just a hypothetical construct but should represent an actual investment alternative.

The final consideration that should be given when evaluating performance is the client's tax liability. Because of different tax circumstances, the best portfolio for each investor will differ.

Selected Bibliography

Bailey, J. V. "Are Manager Universes Acceptable Performance Benchmarks?" *Journal of Portfolio Management* 18:3 (Spring 1992): 9–13.

Bailey, J. V. "Evaluating Benchmark Quality." *Financial Analysts Journal* 48 (May/June 1992): 33–39.

Bailey, J. V., T. M. Richards, and D. E. Tierney. "Benchmark Portfolios and the Manager/Plan Sponsor Relationship." In *Current Topics in Investment Management.* New York: Harper Collins, 1990.

Dietz, P. O., H. R. Fogler, and D. J. Hardy. "The Challenge of Analyzing Bond Portfolio Returns." *Journal of Portfolio Management* (Spring 1980), pp. 53-58.

Jacob, N. L. "Evaluating Investment Performance." In *Investment Management,* eds. P. L. Bernstein and A. Damodaran. New York: John Wiley, 1998, 329–371.

Jeffrey, R. H., and R. D. Arnott. "Is Your Alpha Big Enough to Cover Its Taxes?" *Journal of Portfolio Management* 19 (Spring 1993): 15–25.

Poterba, J. M. "After-Tax Performance Evaluation." In *Investment Counseling for Private Clients.* Charlottesville, Va.: Association for Investment Management Research, 1999.

Reilly, F. K., and K. C. Brown. *Investment Analysis and Portfolio Management.* New York: Dryden Press, 1997.

Sharpe, W. F. "Asset Allocation: Management Style and Performance Measurement." *Journal of Portfolio Management* 18:2 (Winter 1992): 7–19.

Stokes, J. "AIMR's Performance Presentation Standards." *Journal of Performance Measurement* (Winter 1997/1998): 18–24.

Notes

1. J. V. Bailey, T. M. Richards, and D. E. Tierney. "Benchmark Portfolios and the Manager/Plan Sponsor Relationship." In *Current Topics in Investment Management* (New York: Harper Collins, 1990).

2. See Bailey, Richards, and Tierney.

3. W. F. Sharpe, "Asset Allocation: Management Style and Performance Measurement," *Journal of Portfolio Management* 18:2 (Winter 1992): 7–19.

4. R. H. Jeffrey and R. D. Arnott, "Is Your Alpha Big Enough to Cover Its Taxes?" *Journal of Portfolio Management* 19 (Spring 1993): 15–25.

5. Beta measures the volatility of a security relative to some market index. A beta greater than one indicates greater return volatility than the market. A beta less than one indicates that the security is less volatile than the market index.

6. J. M. Poterba, "After-Tax Performance Evaluation." In *Investment Counseling for Private Clients* (Charlottesville, Va.: Association for Investment Management Research, 1999).

Glossary

Active management Investment strategy where the manager attempts to outperform the market actively trading securities in the portfolio.

Aftermarket The public market for a security after the initial public offering.

American depositary receipt (ADR) A registered certificate issued by an American depositary evidencing ownership of a particular foreign issuer.

Asset securitization The process of packaging illiquid individual loans and debt instruments into liquid securities.

At-the-money A case where the exercise price of the option and the price of the underlying security are equal.

Automatic investment plan A plan offered by many mutual funds that allows shareholders to have a certain amount of money automatically invested in the mutual fund. Funds are usually withdrawn directly from the investor's bank account.

Back-end load The charge when mutual fund shares are redeemed. Also called the redemption fee.

Basis The difference between the cash market price and the futures price of a commodity.

Basis point One one-hundredth of 1 percent.

Basis risk The risk in hedging that results from a change in the difference between the cash market price and the futures price (basis) of a commodity.

Bear spread A trading position using options that is used when the investor is mildly bearish.

Benchmark portfolio A portfolio that is established to allow for comparison of fund performance. The benchmark portfolio should have similar risk and style characteristics as the portfolios that are compared to it.

Best efforts An underwriting arrangement in which underwriters agree to use only their best efforts to sell the shares on the issuer's behalf.

Bid-ask spread The difference between the price at which the dealer is willing to buy a security (bid price) and the price at which the dealer is willing to sell the security (ask price). This spread is the dealer's profit.

Black/Scholes option pricing model Option pricing model derived from arbitrage conditions that says that a European call option's value is dependent on the current stock price, the exercise price, the time until the option expires, the volatility of the stock's returns, and the risk-free interest rate.

Brokers Serve as liaisons who buy and sell securities for customers.

Bull spread A trading position using options that is used when the investor is mildly bullish.

Calendar spread A spread that uses options with different expiration dates but the same underlying stock.

Call market A market where trading for a security takes place only at specified times.

Call option An option that allows the holder to purchase shares of the asset at the exercise price.

Cap Represents a call option on interest rates or asset prices that pays off if interest rates or the price of the asset rises above a certain level.

Capital asset pricing model An equilibrium model that bases the expected return on an asset by its systematic (nondiversifiable) risk.

Capital market line Graph that shows the risk-return tradeoff for a portfolio consisting of a riskless asset and the market portfolio. Graphically, it is the line tangent to the efficient frontier.

Clearing The processing of a trade and the establishment of what the parties to the trade owe each other.

Clearinghouse A financial institution at the futures and options exchanges that mediates between buyers and sellers and guarantees both ends of the transaction.

Closed-end fund An investment company that issues only a limited number of shares, which it does not redeem. Shares are traded like shares of a stock in the securities markets.

Collar A hedging strategy that is created by taking a simultaneous position in a cap and a floor.

Collateralized mortgage obligation (CMO) A mortgage-backed security that has separate tranches with a range of maturities backed by one or more pools of mortgages or pass-throughs.

Commodity Futures Trading Commission The federal agency that governs futures trading.

Commodity swap An agreement where the counterparties make payments based on the price of a commodity.

Continuous market A market where stocks are priced and traded continuously.

Correlation A measure of the degree of association between two variables that is normalized to lie between -1 and $+1$.

Counterparty risk Risk that the other party in the transaction will not honor the terms of the contract.

Covariance Measures the degree of association between two variables.

Credit default swap A synthetic instrument in which one counterparty pays a premium in return for a contingent payment triggered by the default of the reference credits.

Cross-hedge A hedge that uses a futures contract on an asset that is highly correlated with the spot asset.

Crossing system Allows institutions to trade portfolios of stocks with each other.

Counterparty risk The risk in an over-the-counter transaction that the other party defaults on the obligation.

Currency swap An agreement in which the two counterparties agree to exchange certain amounts of currencies on scheduled dates.

Day trader A speculator in the securities market that holds a position in a contract for a period longer than a scalper, but not usually overnight.

Defined benefit pension plan A pension plan where the company agrees to pay employees certain benefits, which are usually based on age, years of service, and average salary upon retirement.

Defined contribution plan A pension plan where the employer makes certain contributions to the employee's account, but makes no guarantee of the benefit upon retirement. Pension benefits will depend on the amount contributed and the rate of return earned.

Derivative security A class of security that "derives" its value from some other asset. Includes futures, options, and swaps.

DK Don't know, indicating one party lacks knowledge of a trade or receives conflicting instructions from a counterparty.

Dollar-weighted return Is the interest rate that makes the present value of the cash flows equal to the initial cost of the security. Also known as the internal rate of return.

Due diligence Obligation of the underwriter to investigate and assure that there are no misstatements or omissions in the registration statement.

Dynamic asset allocation An asset allocation strategy that continually monitors and adjusts the composition of the portfolio.

Effective date Date when an offering is declared effective by the SEC. The issue can now be sold to the public.

Efficient frontier A curve that is constructed by finding all the efficient portfolios in risk-return space.

Efficient portfolio A portfolio that has the highest expected return for a given level of risk.

Emerging market The securities markets of developing countries.

Enhanced indexing A portfolio management approach whereby managers attempt to beat the index by adjusting the holdings of the index to reflect their forecasts.

Equity swap An agreement in which one counterparty agrees to pay the return on some equity instrument such as the S&P 500 in return for some other payment.

ERISA The Employee Retirement Income Security Act of 1974 that regulates pension plans.

Exchange for physicals A method for closing out a futures position whereby two traders agree to a simultaneous exchange of a cash commodity and futures contracts based on that cash commodity.

Exercise price The transaction price specified in an option contract. Also known as the strike price.

Fallen angel A bond rated investment grade at issue but downgraded to junk status because of a deterioration in the issuer's financial position.

Fedwire A Federal Reserve communications and settlement system that enables financial institutions to transfer funds and book-entry securities.

Filing date The day the underwriter turns in the registration statement with the SEC.

Firm commitment A type of underwriting agreement in which investment bankers risk their own capital by purchasing a whole block of new securities from the issuer and then reselling them to the public.

First notice day The first day that sellers of a futures contract can notify the exchange that they plan to deliver the commodity.

Floor Represents a put option on interest rates or asset prices that pays off if interest rates or the price of the asset falls below a certain level.

Forward contract A privately negotiated contract in which one party agrees to deliver some commodity at a specified delivery date in exchange for a specified payment at the delivery date with a second party.

Fourth market Term for the direct trading of stocks between buyer and seller without the use of a broker.

Front-end load A fee charged by the mutual fund when shares of the fund are purchased.

Fundamental analysis An investment approach that looks at the economic and business fundamentals of a firm in order to determine its valuation.

Futures contract A highly standardized marketable contract that calls for the exchange of a particular commodity or security at a specified delivery date in exchange for a specified payment at the delivery date.

Glass-Steagall Act The 1933 act that separates commercial and investment banking activities.

Global depositary receipt (GDR) The underlying shares are held with a local custodian, and the depositary issues certificates to foreign markets.

Globex An after-hours electronic trading market for futures contracts.

Green shoe option An option allowing investment bankers to purchase up to a specified number of additional shares from the issuer in the event they sell more than agreed upon in the underwriting agreement. Also called overallotment option.

Gross spread The difference between the price offered to the public and the price the underwriter pays to the issuer.

Hedge A strategy that involves using derivative securities to reduce or eliminate the risk exposure of an underlying asset.

Hedge ratio The number of futures or options contracts that must be used to offset the price volatility of an underlying commodity.

Impact cost The additional costs that result from rising prices as an investor purchases a large amount of a security.

Implementation shortfall The difference between the returns earned on a "paper portfolio" and the actual gains attained in the market.

Indenture A bond contract that sets forth the legal obligations of the issuer and names a trustee representing the interests of the bondholders.

Index arbitrage A trade that takes place when prices in the cash and futures markets differ sufficiently to allow a trader to earn a risk-free profit.

Initial margin Amount that an investor must put up in cash to purchase a security on credit.

Initial public offering (IPO) A company's first equity issue in the public market.

Instinet An interactive system that allows for buyers and sellers to search for the other half of the transaction and negotiate and execute a trade directly.

Interest rate swap A contract between two parties in which each party agrees to make a series of interest payments to the other on scheduled dates.

In-the-money An option that has a positive intrinsic value.

Investment Advisers Act The 1940 act requires registration of investment advisers and compliance with statutory standards.

Investment Company Act The 1940 act governs the activities of investment companies.

Investment policy statement Document that outlines the objectives and constraints of an investor.

Jensen's alpha A measure of a portfolio's risk-adjusted performance that looks at the vertical distance between the portfolio's return and the return predicted by the capital asset pricing model.

Junk bonds High-yield debt instruments with credit ratings below investment grade.

Last notice day The last day that sellers of a futures contract can notify the exchange that they plan to deliver the commodity.

LIBOR London Interbank Offered Rate. It is the rate on dollar-denominated deposits traded between banks in London.

Limit order An order that instructs the broker to fill the order only if it can be transacted at a specified price or better.

Load fund A mutual fund that charges a fee (load) to buy into the fund.

M^2 A measure used to adjust the risk of a portfolio by leveraging the portfolio up or down until it has the same total risk as the market index. Rankings will be identical to those using the Sharpe ratio.

Maintenance margin Level of equity at which an investor will receive a margin call.

Margin account An account in which a firm lends money to a customer to purchase or sell short securities.

Market maker Individual or institution that holds an inventory of securities and ensures that a buyer exists for sellers and a seller exists for buyers.

Market order An order that instructs the broker to fill the order immediately at the best possible price.

Market timing Investment strategy in which the investor attempts to outperform the market by either moving into or out of stocks or by adjusting the risk of the portfolio to reflect the future outlook of stocks.

Marking-to-market The settlement process used to adjust the margin account of a futures contract for daily changes in the price of the contract.

Mortgage pass-through Securities backed by pools of mortgage obligations in which payments of the underlying mortgages are passed on to the security holders.

Mutual fund An investment company that pools together money from investors and invests the proceeds according to the objectives of the fund. Sometimes referred to as open-end funds because the fund continues to issue shares as cash flows in and stands ready to redeem shares at the net asset value.

Net asset value (NAV) The net assets of the mutual fund divided by the number of shares outstanding.

No-load fund A mutual fund that sells shares at the net asset value.

Notional principal Amount of principal that is the basis of a swap agreement. This amount is not actually exchanged and is therefore referred to as notional.

Offset A method for closing out a futures position by entering into the opposite transaction. Also known as a reversing trade.

Open-end fund An investment company that continually issues new shares to the public and redeems them on demand. Also, the formal name for a mutual fund.

Open ending The process by which a closed-end fund converts to an open-end fund.

Open interest The number of futures or options contracts that have not been closed out.

Opportunity cost The cost of not executing the trade.

Out-of-the-money An option that has no intrinsic value.

Passive management Investment strategy where the manager does not attempt to outperform the market and simply holds all securities in some index. Also known as indexing.

Portfolio insurance A strategy that attempts to create a call option payoff by adjusting the stock/cash mix of a portfolio.

Position trader A speculator in the futures market that holds a position for an extended period of time, often days or even months.

Preliminary prospectus The preliminary prospectus is filed with the SEC and is provided by underwriters to prospective purchasers. It does not disclose the offering price, underwriting spread, or net proceeds. Sometimes known as a red herring.

Prepayment The option that homeowners have of paying off the outstanding principal on their mortgage early.

Private placement The sale of new securities to a few qualified investors instead of through a public offering. Privately placed securities do not have to be registered with the SEC.

Prospectus The first part of the registration statement that contains detailed information on the issue and on the issuer's condition and prospects.

Put-call parity Arbitrage relationship that says that a portfolio that consists of a long call and a short put should equal the value of the stock less the present value of the exercise price. Can be used to price any of the four components based on the other three.

Put option An option that allows the holder to sell shares of the asset at the exercise price.

Qualified institutional buyer An institution that has at least $100 million of securities under investment. For registered dealers, the requirements are $10 million.

Quiet period The period that begins with the signing of the letter of intent and ends twenty-five days after the effective date if the security is listed on an exchange or quoted on NASDAQ. During this period, the company is subject to SEC guidelines on publication of information outside the prospectus.

Ratio spread A type of spread where the ratio is not one-to-one. For example, a call ratio spread could consist of purchasing one call and writing two calls.

REIT Real estate investment trust. A fund that pools the money of numerous investors and uses the proceeds to purchase real estate or mortgages.

Relative valuation Investment approach that compares the relative value of a firm with another firm or the industry average.

Repurchase agreement In a typical repurchase agreement transaction, a dealer puts up liquid securities as collateral against a cash loan while agreeing to repurchase the same securities at a higher price that reflects the financing costs at a future date.

Restricted security Security purchased in a private placement directly from an issuer that is subject to a one-year holding period restriction.

Rights offering An offering of securities whereby current shareholders are given the first opportunity to purchase additional shares of the security, usually at a discount.

Risk arbitrage A strategy in the merger and acquisition market where the target stock is purchased while the acquiring company's stock is sold short.

Rule 80A Circuit breaker that restricts index arbitrage trading when a collar of 2 percent around the closing value of the DJIA is exceeded.

Rule 80B Circuit breaker that imposes trading halts based on 10, 20, and 30 percent declines in the DJIA.

Russell 2000 A market value weighted index of 2000 small company stocks compiled by the Frank Russell Company.

S&P 500 A market value weighted index of 500 large company stocks compiled by Standard and Poor's.

Samurai bond Yen denominated bonds issued in the Japanese market.

Scalpers A speculator in the futures market who holds a position for a very short time period, often only a few minutes.

Securities Act This 1933 act requires registration of a new security issue unless an exemption is available, also known as "truth in securities" law.

Securities Exchange Act This 1934 act requires timely and accurate disclosure of material information and prohibits sales practice abuses and insider trading.

Security market line A plot of the expected return for assets against their systematic risk. Graphical depiction of the capital asset pricing model.

Sharpe ratio A relative measure of a portfolio's ratio of return to total risk.

Shelf registration An issuer files a single registration document indicating that it intends to sell a certain amount of securities at one or more times within the next two years. Also known as Rule 415.

Short sale The sale of a security that is not owned by the seller in the expectation of falling price or as part of an arbitrage.

Soft dollars Costs charged by brokers that exceed the pure transaction cost of executing the trade.

Specialist A member of certain SEC-regulated exchanges who serves as a market maker and is there to ensure that there is a fair and orderly market.

Standard deviation The square root of the variance.

Straddle A trading strategy using options that attempts to benefit from large price moves in the underlying asset. Constructed by simultaneously purchasing both a put and a call option with the same exercise price and expiration date.

Strangle A trading strategy similar to a straddle except the exercise prices of the put and call are not the same. Both exercise prices are chosen so the options are out-of-the-money.

Strap A trading strategy similar to a straddle except two call options are purchased for every put option. This strategy is used when the trader believes the stock is more likely to rise in value.

Strategic asset allocation Long-term asset allocation decision.

Strike price See exercise price.

Strip A trading strategy similar to a straddle except two put options are purchased for every call option. This strategy is used when the trader believes the stock is more likely to fall in value.

Swap A derivative security in which two parties agree to exchange cash flows based on some notional amount.

Systematic risk Risk that cannot be diversified away. Usually measured by an asset's beta. Sometimes referred to as market risk or nondiversifiable risk.

Tactical asset allocation Short-term deviations from the policy asset allocation that attempt to profit from the mispricing of securities or alternative forecasts for the economy.

Technical analysis Investment strategy that attempts to identify trends in price and volume data in order to determine when to purchase and sell an asset.

Third market Refers to the trading of a stock that is listed on an exchange and traded in the over-the-counter market.

Time-weighted rate of return Is the geometric average of the holding period returns.

Timing cost The cost of not executing an entire order at the same time.

Tombstone A boxed-in ad that appears in financial sections of newspapers or magazines and announces a new security issue.

Treynor measure A relative measure of a portfolio's ratio of return to systematic risk.

Upstairs block market Place off the floor of the exchange where institutional investors trade large blocks of stocks.

Variance A measure of the spread of a distribution around the mean or average value. Often used in finance to measure risk.

Variation margin Amount the investor must place in the account to bring the equity back to the initial margin requirement.

Wash-sale rule IRS rule that disallows the recognition of losses from the sale of a security if a "substantially identical" security is purchased thirty days before or after the sale.

Wilshire 5000 A market value weighted index of stocks on the NYSE, AMEX, and NASDAQ. Consists of over 7,000 stocks and is generally used as an index for the entire stock market.

Index

About the Authors

K. Thomas Liaw is a professor of finance and the chairman of the department of economics and finance at The Peter J. Tobin College of Business, St. John's University. He has a consulting practice and is invited to speak on various subjects of investment banking and capital markets at business conferences and corporate training programs regularly. Professor Liaw has published in the areas of investment banking, Treasury coupon rolls, repurchase agreements, and mergers and acquisitions. His principal areas of teaching and research include capital markets, trading, and investment banking. His most recent book publication is *The Business of Investment Banking* (John Wiley & Sons, 1999). He has also co-edited several books on emerging markets. Professor Liaw holds his Ph.D. from Northwestern University.

Ronald L. Moy is an associate professor of finance at The Peter J. Tobin College of Business, St. John's University. He has taught courses in investments and financial markets for more than a decade. He has published in a number of areas in finance, including insurance, mutual fund costs and performance, and asset pricing. He has written several educational supplements in the areas of portfolio management, financial management and business statistics. His professional interests include investment strategies, portfolio management and Internet commerce. He is a Chartered Financial Analyst. Professor Moy holds his Ph.D. from Rutgers University.